Advanced Praise for
Federal Prison Handbook

Christopher Zoukis never ceases to amaze me. His talent for and generosity in sharing his knowledge and experience of the ins and outs of life in federal prison with current inmates, future inmates, and their families and even lawyers is a testament to his desire to make a positive difference. This book, written in a straightforward style, is a true resource for anyone involved with the prison system. **– Alan Ellis, preeminent federal criminal defense attorney, past President of the ACLU of Central Pennsylvania, past President of the National Association of Criminal Defense Lawyers, Fellow of the American Board of Criminal Lawyers, and author of the renowned *Federal Prison Guidebook.***

This unique book is actually three books in one. First, it's an encyclopedia of everything that a prisoner's family needs to know about doing whatever can possibly be done to help a loved one get through the prison experience. Second, it's a no-holds-barred, how-to guide for a first-time inmate that explains in the plainest of terms what a prisoner must do -- and, just as importantly, what not to do -- to survive from the first chilling trip on the inmate bus through the many long days and nights ahead in the jungle. Third, for a battle-tested lawyer like myself with 45 years of criminal litigation behind me, it is the go-to reference book for answering all those "good questions" the incarcerated client asks but which the attorney doesn't know the answer to because they never teach you in law school what everyday life in prison is really like. Family member, first-time inmate or experienced criminal litigator, this is a book you want in your library. **– Kent A. Russell, J.D., expert attorney specializing in habeas corpus and author of the *California Habeas Handbook.***

The *Federal Prison Handbook* is an excellent resource for individuals currently incarcerated or facing incarceration in a federal prison. **– Brandon Sample, J.D., federal-prisoner-turned-attorney, author of *The Habeas Citebook: Ineffective Assistance of Counsel*, and Executive Director of Prisology.**

The *Federal Prison Handbook*, which is far more than one of the many ubiquitous prison "survival guides" available, provides a wealth of useful information and solid advice for those entering the federal prison system as well as those already serving time in BOP facilities. Writing from his own personal experiences, the author has amassed a treasure trove of penal acumen and knowledge. Rather than learn from your own mistakes -- which can be dangerous or even fatal behind bars -- this title is well worth purchasing and reading cover-to-cover, even if you're not facing hard time. – **Alex Friedmann, Managing Editor of *Prison Legal News*, Associate Director of the Human Rights Defense Center, and President of the anti-private prison Private Corrections Institute.**

The *Federal Prison Handbook* is one of my go to guides for matters related to the federal prison system. It is an invaluable resource for attorneys like myself, prisoners, and their families. – **Jeremy Gordon, J.D., federal criminal defense and appellate attorney with national practice, former state prosecutor, and General Counsel of Prisology.**

This is the most informative, concise prison handbook that we've ever seen; and we've seen them all. The *Federal Prison Handbook* is an absolute must for lawyers, paralegals, professors, counselors, librarians, prison officials, Members of Congress and, of course, federal inmates and their families, friends and associates (past, present and future). We at FedCURE are overwhelmingly impressed. Hats off to Christopher and Middle Street Publishing for this valuable resource. What a fantastic way to spend your time while incarcerated. We predict hundreds of thousands of folks will benefit from the *Federal Prison Handbook*. – **Mark A. Varca, J.D., Chairman of FedCURE.**

A highly informative and comprehensive overview of the Federal prison system that will prove most valuable to anyone seeking to understand its hidden inner workings. – **David Skarbek, King's College London professor and author of *The Social Order of the Underworld: How Prison Gangs Govern the American Penal System.***

Christopher Zoukis has a wealth of experience from which to draw. We worked together on a case and I was always impressed at how thorough and inquisitive he was. His commitment to helping prisoners knows no bounds. The *Federal Prison Handbook* will help answer basic questions that do not get addressed or discussed by anyone else, but is handled here. – **Steven Rosenfield, prisoner civil rights attorney for 40 years, Co-Founder of the Virginia Association of Criminal Defense Lawyers, Past President of the Charlottesville-Albemarle Bar Association and Past President of the Board of Virginians for Alternatives to the Death Penalty.**

I have never been inclined to recommend prison guide books, but Chris really nails this one. I've worked with federal inmates for over 30 years, both as a career Federal Bureau of Prisons employee and in private practice, and I can honestly say that the *Federal Prison Handbook* is a must-read. Chris covers all the bases and provides extensive details on the nuances of federal prison culture. – **Jack Donson, nationally awarded retiree of the Federal Bureau of Prisons, Director of Case Management & Programs of FedCURE, Chair of the American Bar Association's standing sub-committee on Federal Bureau of Prisons policy, and Marywood University adjunct professor of criminal justice.**

Christopher Zoukis has once again provided an invaluable resource for incarcerated men and women. His newest book, the *Federal Prison Handbook*, also includes tools and information for friends and families of prisoners, students, attorneys, criminal justice professionals, and anyone who wants to understand what a person goes through who needs to survive and maybe even thrive while incarcerated. From entry into prison, to prisoner economy, to tips about race and culture behind bars, Zoukis writes a book that is both engaging and highly practical, filled with invaluable experience and research. – **Jean Trounstine, professor, prison activist and author, whose most recent book is *Boy With A Knife: A Story of Murder, Remorse, and a Prisoner's Fight for Justice.***

Tips and "cautionary tales" garnered from years of experience by author Christopher Zoukis, incarcerated in the Bureau of Prisons for 10 years, make the carefully researched *Federal Prison Handbook* a one-of-a-kind resource for men (their loved ones and others) entering and surviving the Federal prison system. What makes Zoukis' book especially valuable is how it details the mountain of rules, policies, and regulations combined with the insider's view of how to navigate life in the Federal prison system. – **Lois Ahrens, Director of The Real Cost of Prisons Project and a founding member of The National Council of Incarcerated and Formerly Incarcerated Women and Girls.**

Christopher Zoukis' new book, *Federal Prison Handbook*, must have been an enormous undertaking. It is an exhaustive attempt to explain the federal prison system, both from an official viewpoint and from a prisoner's viewpoint. I know that Christopher is a very thorough person because I've read his other books on education in prison and our local volunteer who visits him reports that he is a highly motivated person who has a desire for learning more and enjoys interacting with people. I recommend this book to learn more about the federal prison system. – **Eric Corson, Executive Director of Prisoner Visitation and Support, a nationwide visitation program for federal and military prisoners.**

An essential guide to surviving a world of ever-present danger -- down to the minutest detail. Has the most scope in the prison genre. – **Shaun Atwood, author of *Hard Time, Prison Time, Pablo Escobar* and *American Made*.**

Prison education expert Christopher Zoukis provides a comprehensive guide to all aspects of federal prison -- from the dreaded intake, to details of daily living, to preparation for release. The *Federal Prison Handbook* is a must-have for anyone preparing to serve a term of federal incarceration. – **Terri LeClercq, Ph.D., University of Texas, School of Law retired professor and author of *Prison Grievances*.**

While not a panacea for the systemic ills of the criminal justice system, Christopher Zoukis' *Federal Prison Handbook* provides an "insiders" informed and well researched view of what life is like for the incarcerated. This book is a must read for anyone engaging at any level of law enforcement, criminal justice, and prison reform. I will certainly be using it in my Juvenile Justice: Dismantling the School-to-Prison Pipeline course next semester. – **Ade Ofunniyin, Ph.D., College of Charleston professor.**

Federal Prison Handbook

BOOKS BY CHRISTOPHER ZOUKIS

Federal Prison Handbook: The Definitive Guide to Surviving the Federal Bureau of Prisons

College for Convicts: The Case for Higher Education in American Prisons (McFarland & Co., 2014)

Prison Education Guide (Prison Legal News Publishing, 2016)

Federal Prison Handbook

The Definitive Guide to Surviving the Federal Bureau of Prisons

Christopher Zoukis

Middle Street Publishing

Charleston, South Carolina

Published in the United States by Middle Street Publishing.

Middle Street Publishing is a South Carolina not-for-profit dedicated to social justice, prison education and prison reform. MSP operates PrisonEducation.com, ChristopherZoukis.com and PrisonerResource.com.

Middle Street Publishing
Info@PrisonerResource.com

ISBN: 978-0-6927997-3-4 (pbk)
ISBN: 978-0-9913302-2-5 (ebk)
ISBN 10: 0692799737

Library of Congress Control Number: 2016918406
Middle Street Publishing, Sullivans Island, SOUTH CAROLINA

Legal Notice to Readers

This publication is designed to provide accurate and authoritative information in regard to the subject matter covered. It is based upon sources believed to be accurate and reliable and is intended to be current as of the time it was written. It is sold with the understanding that the publisher, author and distributor(s) are not engaged in rendering legal, accounting or other professional services. If legal advice or expert assistance is required, the services of a competent professional person should be sought. This publication is not a substitute for legal advice from a licensed attorney.

To confirm that the information contained herein has not been affected or changed by recent developments, traditional legal research techniques should be used, including checking original and primary sources, along with local court rules where appropriate.

The publisher, author and distributor(s) make no representations concerning the contents of this publication and disclaim any warranties of merchantability or fitness for a particular purpose.

The publisher, author and distributor(s) do not support or advocate the violation of any criminal law or Federal Bureau of Prisons rule or regulation.

Printed in the United States of America

Dedication

Sangye Rinchen
November 24, 1963 to June 12, 2016

To my dear friend and law partner Sangye Rinchen. It was a long and eventful ride. It's strange how the world puts people together. I don't think that a more unlikely combination could be thought up. Together we took the prison reform and prison litigation worlds by storm. I am sad that you're gone, but I am happy that we were able to get you home before you passed. Thank you for your loyalty, support and guiding hand. You helped to put me on a better, more successful path. For that, and for all that is to come, I am forever grateful.

Ashley Jean Arnold
June 29, 1982 to February 24, 2015

To my dear friend and colleague Ashley Jean Arnold, who took her life at Federal Correctional Institution Petersburg on a Tuesday afternoon. While we fought the Federal Bureau of Prisons for years in a vigorous attempt to force them to treat your gender dysphoria, it was all too little, too late. I will never forget how they led you to your death, Ashley, and I will not stop fighting until justice is served. You prove that prisoners' rights advocates truly are engaged in work that is a matter of life and death.

Table of Contents

Acknowledgements

First and foremost, I'd like to thank Mom and Dad for their impassioned support during these challenging years. They have stood by me while I've answered the call of prison education and prisoners' rights advocacy. Their support has been both emotional and financial. This text could not have been completed without their integral support.

A huge debt of gratitude is owed to my editors Laine Cunningham and Barbara Carole. Both were instrumental in researching, editing, and finding a home for this work. Life simply wouldn't be what it is without them.

My thanks to Sangye Rinchen, Darrell Hoover, Rex Powell, and Lewis Patt, Jr., who critiqued this work and helped turn it into what it is today. May you continue to find my faults and help me grow through them for years to come.

Thanks to Kamea Zelisco and Susan Mate at MKT Communications, Rachel Friedman at EMSI Public Relations, and Kris Black at Black & Hue for their terrific assistance with everything technological, online, and book marketing-related. Kamea, Susan, Rachel, and Kris, together we are making a real difference.

Last but certainly not least, my writing endeavors wouldn't be possible without the competent legal teams at The Law Offices of Alan Ellis, The Jeffrey E. Fogel Law Office, and Rosenfield & Wayland. Attorneys Alan Ellis and Todd Bussert led the team that defended me when I was locked in solitary confinement on disciplinary charges fabricated in response to my prison education advocacy and writing efforts. While Jeff Fogel and Steven Rosenfield weren't around for the first batch of retaliatory incident reports, they valiantly defended me against the second wave designed to censor my writing and advocacy efforts. All fought hard so that I am now able to write again.

Introduction

The Need for This Book

Incarceration is a growing trend in American society. In the last four decades, American prison populations have increased by over 700 percent.[1] This equates to nearly 1 in 100 American adults behind bars.[2] One in 35 American adults are under some form of judicial supervision (prison, probation, and parole)[3] at an absurd cost of $74 billion annually … a number that exceeds the gross domestic product of over 130 nations.[4]

Clearly the American criminal justice system has gone awry. My own research, presented in *College for Convicts: The Case for Higher Education in American Prisons* (McFarland and Company, 2014), shows 1.7 million current prisoners, 2.3 million confined in prisons and jails, and 5.6 million under some form of judicial supervision. For nearly 1 out of every 100 Americans, incarceration will be a fact at some point in their lives.[5] While more than 95 percent of prisoners will one day be released (around 650,000 each year), the majority will return to custody – they will recidivate – within five years of release.[6]

Federal sentencing data is just as alarming. In 2013, only around 3 percent of cases went to trial. Some (8 percent) were dismissed but the vast majority were resolved through plea bargains. Sentencing guidelines and mandatory minimums mean that defendants who plead out received significantly lower sentences than those who went to trial.[7] Once sentenced, inmates are housed in one of the Federal Bureau of Prisons' 125 stand-alone facilities, in a private contract facility, or in a satellite prison camp. In 2014, federal prisons were on average 30 percent over capacity; individual facilities could be more than 50 percent over capacity.[8]

With such large numbers of American citizens incarcerated, the need for this text becomes evident. If you don't know someone ensnared by the American criminal justice system, someone you know surely does. Someone connected to you or to a close friend probably needs this book.

Who Goes to Prison?

No one type of person goes to prison. As I look around the dayroom of my medium-security federal prison, I see whites, blacks, Hispanics, Native Americans, and others. I see bank robbers, child pornographers, drug dealers, embezzlers and forgers, and those convicted of conspiracies of many different flavors. I see young men in their late teens and old men in their late sixties. I see Protestants, Buddhists, Catholics, Muslims, Wiccans, and more. I see men who were leaders of business and finance, and I see those who didn't even have a cardboard box to call home.

American corrections – incarceration in particular – touches every facet of our society. No one is immune to the criminal justice system, yet virtually everyone on their way to prison lacks accurate information about what to expect.

This text seeks to remedy that. It provides information those new to the Federal Bureau of Prisons need to make their stay a safe, somewhat manageable one. More than that, the text provides expert, researched advice, analysis, and information about all facets of prison life.

How Can This Book Help New Arrivals and Old Hats?

This guide to surviving federal prison seeks to be a resource for new arrivals and to assist those who have already served significant time. As such, it is comprehensive, structured, and thoroughly researched.

Those of us who have served significant time understand what prison life is like. We have adapted to a world of confinement and near-constant conflict. This text provides new arrivals with an understanding of this and all other components of prison life. While others have attempted to do so with their own texts, none have succeeded.

This handbook breaks new ground with its well-organized review of relevant policies, regulations, and case law. While prisoners can tell you what is wrong with the system, they generally have no idea where their rights end and the rights of the prison administration begin. This text remedies that unfair situation. We hope this will make all the difference for any period of incarceration.

The comprehensive, researched, and useful nature of this book are revealed through examples of what this text does for the various groups in prison and those soon to arrive. For the first-time prisoner, this text:

- Explains what it is like to walk into a prison housing unit and greet one's cellmates for the first time ... and describes what to do if everything goes wrong.
- Discusses how to communicate with the outside world through the inmate telephone, TRULINCS computers, and postal correspondence.
- Explores what the commissary sells, the process of purchasing items, and how to safeguard them.
- Suggests what to do if a fight seems imminent, and explains how to protect oneself if it occurs.
- Describes how to protect oneself from scams and other schemes.
- Details how to locate a safe table in the chow hall, and notes what makes it safe.
- Advises what to do if you are sexually harassed or assaulted, and illustrates the avenues for reporting the abuse.
- Explains how the underground economy works and how to safely participate, including how to select, interact with, and pay a "store man."
- Notes the various methods for having funds deposited on a commissary account via postal money orders, Western Union, or MoneyGram.
- Points out the various players in the prison administration hierarchy, what they do, and when it is appropriate to speak with them.

For those who have served significant time in prison, the text:

- Provides detailed instructions on the disciplinary process, how case law, federal regulations, and prison policies impact the process, and how to defend against an incident report throughout the issuing and investigating stages and on appeal.

- Details the regulations, policies, and procedures of the Special Housing Unit along with privileges afforded to those locked in the SHU and how to enforce them if they are denied.
- Explains the process of minimizing risks when locating a tattoo artist, obtaining the required equipment, and keeping oneself healthy and disease-free.
- Suggests what to do if caught drinking or using drugs, and how to appeal an adverse disciplinary finding.
- Illustrates the rights of incarcerated writers and those who would like to advocate from prison.
- Lists various work assignments commonly available and the hidden benefits of each, including the benefits of access and skills offered on the black market.
- Provides detailed information on the Federal Bureau of Prisons' health services offerings, policies, and procedures, and what to do if medical or dental care is denied or not in line with community treatment standards.
- Presents available education services inside prison and via correspondence, including a list of top vocational, college, and legal programs in which prisoners can enroll.
- Explains how the Inmate Financial Responsibility Program (IFRP) works and how disagreeable contracts can be fought.
- Provides guidance on how to navigate gang and convict cultures, including how to remain independent of gang affiliation.

Who Else Can Benefit from Reading This Book?

While a book about surviving federal prison is naturally of use to current and soon-to-be federal prisoners, several other distinct groups will find this text useful:

Families and friends of the incarcerated. Prison is a vastly different world with a culture that is completely alien to those who have never experienced it.

This book will help those who know prisoners better understand what their loved ones and friends are going through on the inside. It will add context to phone calls, letters, emails, and visits, and provide a sense of comfort through understanding.

Attorneys, prison consultants, and other legal professionals. As surprising as it might seem, many criminal defense attorneys know little about prisons. Their work tends to end after sentencing or, if it continues, is of a post-conviction variety. They don't understand what their clients will go through or are going through. This text helps legal professionals understand prison life and, perhaps more importantly, allows them to insert themselves into the mix when their incarcerated clients need them most.

Academics, sociologists, and criminal justice students. Prisons are known by many, yet understood by few. Individuals in academia study corrections as if it is a social mechanism. But prison is also an unfortunate way of life and a state of being. This text will help these groups understand the personal impact of corrections, recognize the ways correctional officials interact with prisoners, and inject a strong dose of truth into academia's sanitized and well-scrubbed view of American corrections.

Corrections professionals. This text can help corrections professionals understand incarceration from the other side of confinement. By hearing the narratives told by those who have served time, prison officials can improve their practices for the betterment of all.

This Book's Unique Perspective

This book and its author are different than many other prison survival guides and their authors. Most prison how-to books are written by one of three groups:

- Criminologists with little or no hands-on, in-prison experience;
- Former inmates who have spent very little time in prison, usually at the lowest security levels; or
- Hardened criminals whose advice is not realistic or is only useful to similar individuals.

Unlike these typical groups, I am a college-educated federal prisoner who has served significant time at the medium security level in the Federal Bureau of Prisons, and at the medium and low security levels in the North Carolina Department of Corrections. While my experience has helped create this work, it is not solely based upon my life behind bars.

Instead, I approached this text as I did *College for Convicts*. Extensive research was undertaken through in-depth interviews with individuals who have been incarcerated for decades. Much of this text was reviewed and critiqued by those individuals. In addition, I have engaged in a critical literature review of close to twenty texts on surviving prison, nearly the entire range currently available. This book therefore exceeds the scope and usefulness of leading texts in the field.

The Author

As the author of a book on surviving prison, it is prudent to trust me as your guide through this unfortunate and life-altering experience. In order for you to trust me, you need to know who I am.

I am a thirty-year-old federal prisoner who has been incarcerated since I committed a crime as a high school senior. I like to think of myself as both a student and a scholar of prison life, particularly in educational matters.

In that respect, my time in prison has been eventful. I published *College for Convicts* along with the *Prison Education Guide* (Prison Legal News Publishing, 2016). I founded the *Education Behind Bars Newsletter*, *PrisonEducation.com*, *PrisonerResource.com*, and *ChristopherZoukis.com* with the help of my outside supporters, contributed many articles to *The Huffington Post*, *Prison Legal News*, and the *New York Daily News*, taught writing classes to my fellow prisoners, won two PEN American Center writing awards, and earned a Bachelors of Arts in Interdisciplinary Studies (Business/Law) via correspondence … all since coming to prison in 2006. I am now a graduate student at Adams State University, where I am pursuing a Masters in Business Administration.

I believe my experiences as a prison education and prisoners' rights activist, a consultant to several prison consulting firms, and a contributing writer to *Prison Legal News*, the *New York Daily News*, and *The Huffington Post* position me to speak with authority and integrity on prison matters. In fact, *Yahoo Finance*, the *Wall Street Journal's Market Watch*, *Truth Out*, and dozens of other major media outlets have interviewed me concerning Federal Bureau of Prisons operations and my experiences as an incarcerated writer. I've even spent long stretches in "the hole" as a direct consequence of speaking up on education in prison.

My experience has been diverse, and includes surviving a "gladiator school" type of youth detention center in the North Carolina Department of Corrections. I have earned numerous academic, vocational, legal, and religious credentials despite the hardships inherent in growing up in prison and correspondence study. I have persevered in the face of administrative and cultural admonishment.

I haven't said it or heard it; I've *done* it. And that is why you should trust me as your guide.

Notes

1. "The Price of Prisons: What Incarceraton Costs Taxpayers." The Vera Institute of Justice. January 2012. Retrieved from http://www.vera.org/sites/default/files/resources/downloads/price-of-prisons-updated-version-021914.pdf.
2. Travis, Jeremy, Western, Bruce, and Redburn, Steve, Editors; Committee on Causes and Consequences of High Rates of Incarceration; Committee on Law and Justice; Division of Behavioral and Social Sciences and Education, *The Growth of Incarceration in the United States: Exploring Causes and Consequences.* National Research Council. National Academies Press (NAP), 2014.
3. "The Prison Crisis." American Civil Liberties Union. Retrieved from https://www.aclu.org/prison-crisis.
4. Kincade, Brian. "The Economics of the American Prison System." Smart Asset. March 23, 2016. Retrieved from https://smartasset.com/insights/the-economics-of-the-american-prison-system.

5. "Prison Population Statistics." Crime Museum. Retrieved from http://www.crimemuseum.org/crime-library/prison-population-statistics.
6. James, Nathan. "Offender Reentry: Correctional Statistics, Reintegration into the Community, and Recidivism." Congressional Research Service, January 12, 2015. Retrieved from https://fas.org/sgp/crs/misc/RL34287.pdf.
7. Rakoff, Jed. "Why Innocent People Plead Guilty." *The New York Review of Books,* November 20, 2014.
8. "Federal Prison System." U.S. Government Accountability Office. Retrieved from http://www.gao.gov/key_issues/federal_prison_system/issue_summary.

Part I – Overview

One

An Overview of the FBOP

The Federal Bureau of Prisons

The Federal Bureau of Prisons (FBOP) is the federal government's prison system. The system is comprised of 125 total federal institutions, 68 satellite prison camps, and contracts with 13 private facilities housing 195,947 sentenced inmates, detainees, and persons under community confinement (e.g., halfway houses).

The federal facilities are divided amongst six geographic regions, each of which is governed by a regional office headed by a regional director. The six regions include the Mid-Atlantic Region (MXR), North Central Region (NCR), Northeast Region (NER), South Central Region (SCR), Southeast Region (SER), and Western Region (WXR). Each office is overseen by the FBOP's Central Office in Washington, DC. Each of the 125 federal prisons has its own institutional makeup, policies, procedures, and general mode of operation.

History of the FBOP

The history of the Federal Bureau of Prisons started before the agency ever existed. The federal court system was created in 1789. For most of the next century, federal prisoners were housed in local or state facilities. By the late 1890s, seven prisons had been established to house federal prisoners.[1]

The official start of the FBOP is credited to the so-called Three Prisons Act of 1891. This identified for Congress three sites for the federal government's first penitentiaries. Congress was very slow in the development of these three facilities. Between the passing of the Three Prisons Act and breaking ground for the United States Penitentiary Leavenworth, six years had passed. In total, it took twenty-five years for USP Leavenworth to be constructed. The penitentiary was constructed by inmates who lived in an adjacent old military fort.[2]

Following the construction of USP Leavenworth, USP Atlanta (GA) was opened in 1902 and USP McNeil Island (WA) was opened in 1909. USP McNeil Island had previously been a territorial jail built in 1875. The first federal prison for women, Federal Prison Camp Alderson, opened in 1928. The infamous Alcatraz prison in San Francisco Bay was opened in 1934.[3]

The Federal Bureau of Prisons was formally established by Congress in 1930. The goal of the prison system was, according to the FBOP, "[to] provide more progressive and humane care for Federal inmates, to professionalize the prison service, and to ensure consistent and centralized administration of the 11 Federal prisons in operation at the time."[4]

By the end of 1930, the FBOP operated fourteen institutions that housed more than 13,000 federal inmates. Ten years later, the FBOP had expanded to twenty-four institutions that housed more than 24,360 federal inmates. According to the Bureau, "[e]xcept for a few fluctuations, the number of inmates did not change significantly between 1940 and 1980 (when the population was 24,252)."[5]

Although the number of federal inmates did not increase, the number of institutions nearly doubled from 24 to 44 by 1980. From 1980 to 1989, the FBOP experienced significant inmate population growth, from 24,000 to approximately 58,000 federal prisoners. Between 1987 and 1992 alone, the Bureau opened twenty new federal prisons. Through the 1990s the inmate population doubled again, reaching 136,000 by the end of 1999. Much of this growth was "[due to] efforts to combat illegal drugs, weapons, and immigration [violations]."[6]

From the 1990s to the present, the FBOP's population has grown to a total of 195,947 men and women, as of May 2016. During fiscal year 2012, the Bureau had an operating budget of approximately $6.6 billion, second only to the Federal Bureau of Investigation's $8 billion. While the Bureau has continued to add bed-space by building new facilities and revamping old ones at significant expense, its prisons now hover at about 140 percent of designed capacity.

This overcrowding was deemed a hazard to staff, inmates, and the public in a recent Government Accountability Office report called *Bureau of Prisons: Growing Inmate Crowding Negatively Affects Inmates, Staff, and Infrastructure.* The house is becoming more expensive, more crowded, and is crumbling, yet no solutions or plans are currently being implemented to find a path out of the overburdened reality.

Security Levels

The Federal Bureau of Prisons houses its prison population at institutions with five different security levels: Minimum, Low, Medium, High, and Administrative.[7] These prisons differ based on the populations they house, the format of inmate housing, security components of the prison and perimeter (e.g., external patrols, towers, security barriers, detection devices, etc.), and staff-to-inmate ratios. Essentially, the lower the risk of the population, the lower the security level; the higher the risk, the higher the security level.

Minimum Security

Many minimum security federal prisons are also called Federal Prison Camps (FPCs). "[T]hese facilities feature dormitory housing, limited or no perimeter fencing, and a relatively low staff-to-inmate ratio. Some are located next to military bases, making it possible for inmates to help serve the labor needs of the base. Many FBOP facilities have a small, minimum security camp adjacent to the main facility. These satellite prison camps provide inmate labor to the main institution and to off-site work programs."[8]

Federal Prison Camps are the lowest security custodial prisons in the FBOP. They tend to house very low-level, nonviolent offenders (around 17 percent of the federal prison population). Camp inmates do not have a significant history of violence, escape, or institutional disciplinary violations, and are usually relatively close to release. Only individuals with less than ten years remaining on their sentence are housed there. Sex offenders and other high-risk inmates are not eligible for camp placement.

Former Wall Street lawyer Matthew Kluger, who was transferred to Morgantown, West Virginia after the time remaining on his sentence dropped below ten years, noted the difference. "Here no one is big and tough," he said. "This is like Camp Cupcake. These are people who have no interest in losing their ability to be in a place that looks this nice and that has no fence. So even people who are not good people tend to behave themselves here. I've seen a couple of fights, but they're more like middle school fights" with a few lazy swings and very little blood.[9]

Kluger also made an interesting note about the staff. Other facilities, he felt, were staffed by individuals who had taken their shot at the FBI or other governmental agencies. When they didn't make the cut, they took the second-best choice at a prison. In the camp, however, the staff were nearly all from the local area. The camp jobs were very good compared to other choices, so the staff had a very different attitude.[10]

Only the most trusted inmates are housed in FPCs because the camps aren't fenced. The freedom of movement is significant, so access to the library, email, sports facilities like the track, the basketball court, and the gym, along with the cafeteria is much easier. Inmates exercise much greater control over their own movements. Visitation is also much easier as inmates are rarely subjected to a visual search after meeting with friends or family. Visitors also have a much easier time signing in and out during their trips.[11]

Also at the lowest level of security are community confinement centers (CCCs). These facilities house inmates close to release, generally with less than a year remaining, in a halfway house environment. Because these facilities serve a special mission, inmates from all security levels might be placed there. CCC inmates might also include those sentenced to community confinement by the federal courts.[12]

Community Confinement Centers also include restitution centers, community treatment centers, mental health facilities, alcohol or drug rehabilitation centers, or other types of specialized facilities. They may help inmates with employment searches, vocational training, educational programs, and other approved programs they can pursue during their nonresidential hours.[13]

Low Security

Low-security federal prisons, also known as Federal Correctional Institutions (FCIs), "[f]eature double-fenced perimeters with electronic detection systems, mostly dormitory or cubicle housing, and a staff-to-inmate ratio that is somewhat higher than that of [FPCs]."[14]

These prisons hold the greatest percentage of federal prisoners, around 38 percent. They are relatively easy and see minimal problems with gangs and violence. Absent an order from the regional director, for a prisoner to be housed in a low-security federal prison, they must have less than twenty years remaining on their sentence. Those who are caught fighting, drinking, using drugs, or committing other serious infractions are generally sent to medium-security federal prisons.

A chief disadvantage of being a low-security inmate is a lack of bed space. With only forty-five institutions serving a huge population, inmates designated to or transferred to a low-security facility might wait several months for placement. The tradeoff for the relatively relaxed atmosphere is the likelihood of being assigned to dormitory style housing where privacy is at a minimum due to communal bathrooms and shower facilities.

Medium Security

According to the FBOP, medium-security federal prisons "[h]ave strengthened perimeters (double-fenced with electronic detection systems), mostly cell-type housing, a higher staff-to-inmate ratio than low security FCIs, and greater internal controls."[15]

Medium-security federal facilities hold around 29 percent of the inmate population. Mediums, unlike lows, vary significantly in terms of prison culture. Some mediums are exceptionally easy and laid-back. Others are hard yards where gangs are visible and violence is occasional or even regular.

For a prisoner to be housed in a medium, they must have less than thirty years remaining on their sentence. Occasionally lifers are assigned to a medium due to waivers by the regional director. A history of violence, escape, in-prison alcohol and substance abuse, and a lengthy disciplinary record will not preclude a prisoner from placement in a medium-security federal prison.

Most of these facilities are very crowded with two- or three-man cells supplemented by six-, ten-, or twelve-bed rooms, sometimes converted from day rooms or TV viewing areas. When President Obama visited a medium-security federal prison in El Reno, Oklahoma – the first time a sitting president visited a federal prison.[16] – he noted, "This is an outstanding institution within the system and yet they've got enormous overcrowding issues." His visit was intended to draw attention to the dire need for criminal justice reform.[17]

At many mediums, prisoners convicted of sex offenses (and others who are deemed unsavory) might have difficulty remaining in general population. The FBOP does have several medium security facilities where such offenses are not as problematic due to onsite Sex Offender Management Programs along with residential and non-residential sex offender treatment programs. See Chapter 12 for more information on sex offender programs.

High Security

High-security federal prisons are called United States Penitentiaries, or USPs, and "[h]ave highly secured perimeters featuring walls or reinforced fences, multiple- and single-occupant cell housing, the highest staff-to-inmate ratio, and close control of inmate movement."[18]

High-security federal prisons house the least number of federal prisoners, around 12 percent. USPs are some of the most violent and inhumane prisons in the world. Violence, drug use, and abuse – both at the hands of prison guards and fellow prisoners – is virtually systematic. Prisoners don't have fist fights; they stab one another with shanks, and gangs effectively run the compounds. Only the most hardened and brazen survive. Inmates with a history of cooperation with the government or sex offenses are usually unable to remain in general population. If they attempt to do so, they are often maimed or killed.

USPs are infused with tension, especially racial animus and geographically oriented turf disputes. While the Bureau does its best to play down the violence in USPs, several correctional officers have been murdered by inmates in recent years. Dozens of prisoners have been killed in the last decade.

Over a dozen USPs exist, but placement is less dependent on an inmate's state or region of origin and more on each institution's needs (i.e., racial breakdown, gang issues, etc.). As such, inmates beginning their sentence at the high security level are likely to be housed far from home.

Michael Santos, who spent time in more than a dozen federal facilities during his twenty-five year sentence, was determined to better himself during his incarceration. But, he notes, "High-security penitentiaries are not quite the same as universities. On more than one occasion, I had to walk through puddles of blood. I had to stay focused through lockdowns, mass violence, and the deafening noise of hatred." But he worked toward his goals and found success.[19]

Administrative Facilities

According to the FBOP, administrative facilities "[h]ave special missions, such as detaining pre-trial offenders; treating inmates with serious or chronic medical problems; or containing extremely dangerous, violent, or escape-prone inmates. They include Metropolitan Correctional Centers (MCCs), Metropolitan Detention Centers (MDCs), Federal Detention Centers (FDCs), Federal Medical Centers (FMCs), the Medical Center for Federal Prisoners (MCFP), the Federal Transfer Center (FTC), and the Administrative-Maximum USP (ADX)."[20]

In the ADX, the "Alcatraz of the Rockies," the inmates are those who are considered to have "absolutely no concern for human life," according to former FBOP director Norman Carlson. This is the highest-security prison in the U.S., and it was designed to be escape-proof.

The ADX holds 500 prisoners in eight units. Inmates include Ted Kaczynski, Atlanta Olympics bomber Eric Rudolph, 9/11 conspirator Zacarias Moussaoui, Oklahoma City bomber Terry Nichols, and a host of others who are locked into their cells most of the day. Prisoners who were originally assigned to other facilities but who became serious behavioral or flight risks are also at the ADX.[21]

A 2014 Amnesty International Report counts over forty states with supermax facilities housing at least 25,000 inmates.[22] ADX, the only federally operated supermax, locks down its inmates for twenty-two to twenty-four hours a day. Individuals can go several days without speaking to anyone. Most cells have compound doors consisting of an inner and outer door, which enhances the sense of isolation.

Some cells do have radios and black-and-white televisions. The shows consist of religious, educational, and general interest programs. Inmates at some point might be able to work at a prison job like cleaning showers. Otherwise inmates must be escorted by guards, and wear leg irons, handcuffs, and waist chains whenever they are moved. Recreation, which lasts one hour, takes place in an outdoor pen slightly larger than the cell. Only the sky is visible.[23]

Since the different administrative facilities hold such diverse missions, they cannot be designated as easy, hard, or indifferent. Depending on the mission of the institution, the institutional culture may vary.

Population Characteristics: Inmates and Staff

The following inmate and staff population characteristics present a snapshot of the federal prison population and staff makeup. They demonstrate the breadth of persons incarcerated in and employed by the FBOP and the substantial diversity. All figures are accurate as of May 20, 2016.

Inmate Population

Total Population:	195,947
Total Sentenced Population in FBOP-managed Institutions:	159,498

Inmates in privately managed secure facilities, including inmates housed with a state or local government that has an Intergovernmental Agency Agreement (IGA) with the FBOP, number 22,694.

Inmates in other contract facilities, including those housed in community corrections centers, home confinement, jail/short-term detention, contract juveniles, and long-term boarders, number 13,755.

Inmate Breakdown

By Security Level[24]

Minimum	32,756	(16.7%)
Low	74,660	(38.2%)
Medium	58,344	(29.8%)
High	23,083	(11.8%)
Unclassified inmates	6,832	(3.5%)

By Gender[25]

Male	182,642	(93.3%)
Female	13,033	(6.7%)

By Race[26]

White (including Hispanic prisoners)	115,177	(58.9%)
Black	73,644	(37.6%)
Native American	3,954	(2.0%)
Asian	2,900	(1.5%)

By Ethnicity[27]

Hispanic	66,185	(33.8%)
Non-Hispanic	129,490	(66.2%)
Average Inmate Age[28]	39	

By Citizenship[29]

United States	151,722	(77.5%)

Mexico	29,776	(15.2%)
Columbia	1,753	(0.9%)
Cuba	1,233	(0.6%)
Dominican Republic	1,737	(0.9%)
Other/Unknown	9,454	(4.8%)

By Sentence Imposed[30]

Less than 1 year	441	(2.3%)
1 to 3 years	21,316	(11.6%)
3 to 5 years	24,125	(13.1%)
5 to 10 years	46,236	(25.1%)
10 to 15 years	37,597	(20.4%)
15 to 20 years:	20,644	(11.2%)
Greater than 20 years	23,347	(12.7%)
Life	294	(2.9%)
Death	56	(0.0%)

By Type of Offense[31]

Drug Offenses	85,419	(46.4%)
Weapons, Explosives, Arson	31,098	(16.9%)
Immigration	16,961	(9.2%)
Robbery	6,989	(3.8%)
Burglary, Larceny, Property Offenses	8,012	(4.4%)
Extortion, Fraud, Bribery	12,055	(6.5%)
Homicide, Aggravated Assault, & Kidnapping Offenses	5,586	(3.0%)
Miscellaneous	1,488	(0.8%)
Sex Offenses	14,592	(7.9%)
Banking & Insurance, Counterfeiting, Embezzlement	644	(0.3%)
Courts or Correction	841	(0.4%)
Continuing Criminal Enterprise	428	(0.2%)
National Security	75	(0.0%)

Staff Breakdown

By Race/Ethnicity[32]

White (non-Hispanic)	26,273	(63.3%)
African-American	8,846	(21.3%)
Hispanic	4,888	(11.8%)
Asian	934	(2.3%)
Native American	544	(1.3%)
Other	8	(0.0%)

By Gender[33]

Male	30,170	(72.7%)
Female	11,323	(27.3%)

Notes

1. Mary Bosworth, *The U.S. Federal Prison System*, (Thousand Oaks, CA: Sage, 2002), 4.
2. *Id.*
3. *Id.*
4. *About the Federal Bureau of Prisons*, U.S. Department of Justice, Federal Bureau of Prisons, at 2. Retrieved from www.BOP.gov.
5. *Id.* at 3.
6. *Id.*
7. Program Statement P5100.08, Inmate Security Designation and Custody Classification.
8. *State of the Bureau 2010*, U.S. Department of Justice, Federal Bureau of Prisons, at 2 (Washington, D.C. 2010).
9. Roberts, Daniel, "Life Behind Bars: Matthew Kluger Reveals All." *Fortune*. July 7, 2014.
10. *Id.*

11. "A Few Notes About Federal Prison Camps." Prison Justice for America. Retrieved from http://prison-justice.org/news-editorials/172-a-few-notes-about-federal-prison-camps.
12. Program Statement 7300.09, Community Corrections Manual.
13. "Community Confinement Law & Legal Definition." USLegal.com. Retrieved from http://definitions.uslegal.com/c/community-confinement/.
14. *State of the Bureau,* supra, at 2.
15. *State of the Bureau,* supra.
16. Finnegan, Conor, "How President Obama Wants to Change the Way Americans Go to Prison." July 16, 2015. ABC News. Retrieved from http://abcnews.go.com/Politics/president-obama-change-americans-prison/story?id=32477995.
17. Finnegan, Conor, "What President Obama Saw When He Visited a Federal Prison." ABC News. July 16, 2015. Retrieved from http://abcnews.go.com/Politics/president-obama-visited-federal-prison/story?id=32495425.
18. *State of the Bureau,* supra, at 2.
19. Santos, Michael, "How I Got Through 25 Years in Federal Prison." *Business Insider.* September 7, 2013. Retrieved from http://www.businessinsider.com/how-to-survive-federal-prison-2013-9.
20. *State of the Bureau,* supra, at 2.
21. Binelli, Mark, "This Place is Not Designed for Humanity." *New York Times,* March 29, 2015.
22. "Entombed: Isolation in the US Federal Prison System." Amnesty International. Retrieved from http://www.amnestyusa.org/research/reports/entombed-isolation-in-the-us-federal-prison-system?page=show.
23. Sanchez, Ray and Field, Alexandra, "What's Life Like in Supermax Prison?" CNN. June 25, 2015. Retrieved from http://www.cnn.com/2015/06/25/us/dzhokhar-tsarnaev-supermax-prison/.
24. "Prison Security Levels." U.S. Department of Justice, Federal Bureau of Prisons. May 20, 2016. Retrieved from www.bop.gov/about/statistics/statistics_inmate_sec_levels.jsp.
25. "Inmate Gender." U.S. Department of Justice, Federal Bureau of Prisons. May 20, 2016. Retrieved from www.bop.gov/about/statistics/statistics_inmate_gender.jsp.

26. "Inmate Race." U.S. Department of Justice, Federal Bureau of Prisons. May 20, 2016. Retrieved from www.bop.gov/about/statistics/statistics_inmate_race.jsp.
27. "Inmate Ethnicity." U.S. Department of Justice, Federal Bureau of Prisons. May 20, 2016. Retrieved from www.bop.gov/about/statistics/statistics_inmate_ethnicity.jsp.
28. "Inmate Age." U.S. Department of Justice, Federal Bureau of Prisons. May 20, 2016. Retrieved from www.bop.gov/about/statistics/statistics_inmate_age.jsp.
29. "Inmate Citizenship." U.S. Department of Justice, Federal Bureau of Prisons. May 20, 2016. Retrieved from www.bop.gov/about/statistics/statistics_inmate_citizenship.jsp.
30. "Sentences Imposed." U.S. Department of Justice, Federal Bureau of Prisons. May 20, 2016. Retrieved from www.bop.gov/about/statistics/statistics_inmate_sentences.jsp.
31. "Offenses." U.S. Department of Justice, Federal Bureau of Prisons. May 20, 2016. Retrieved from www.bop.gov/about/statistics/statistics_inmate_offenses.jsp.
32. "Staff Ethnicity/Race." U.S. Department of Justice, Federal Bureau of Prisons. May 20, 2016. Retrieved from www.bop.gov/about/statistics/statistics_staff_ethnicity_race.jsp.
33. "Staff Gender." U.S. Department of Justice, Federal Bureau of Prisons. May 20, 2016. Retrieved from www.bop.gov/about/statistics/statistics_staff_gender.jsp.

Two

Staff and Other Personnel

Through job assignments, educational classes, leisure activities, and other daily events, inmates come into contact with many of the prison staff. In the enclosed world of prison, it helps to get oriented on who rules that world and how the administration is structured. The following descriptions are laid out from the top down.

Wardens and Executives

In all FBOP facilities, the *Warden* is top dog, the chief executive officer.[1] Wardens report to the respective Regional Directors, who report to the Director of the Federal Bureau of Prisons, and generally remain only a few years at a particular institution. In recent years, the Bureau has added the post of Complex Warden to oversee the growing number of multi-security-level complexes such as Federal Correctional Complex Petersburg, which encompasses medium-, low-, and camp-level federal prisons.

Wardens, having worked their way through the ranks, supervise as many as 5,000 inmates and hundreds of employees. They wield wide discretion in their decisions, which can range from whether to authorize lethal force to the items sold in the commissary.

Most inmates never interact with wardens or others on the executive staff. For those that need to, most Wardens follow the FBOP tradition of "standing mainline" during the noon meal. Heads of the various departments make themselves available in or directly outside the chow hall so they can be approached directly.

The Warden is the final arbiter of all matters resolvable at the institutional level. As in any organization, the management style of different chief executives will vary. Some will answer emails from inmates directly; some will talk to inmates on the recreation yard; and some will rarely be seen. On the whole, most will direct your complaints or questions to a staff member lower on the chain of command.

Directly below the Warden are the *Associate Wardens* (AWs). There may be several AWs in any given institution, each one of which supervises a specific operational area. For example, the supervisor of prison industries, a.k.a. UNICOR, is an AW. They are typically available at mainline several times a week.

Some prison facilities also have an administrative assistant to the Warden. These individuals are generally more accessible than either the Warden or the AWs.

Correctional Services

The *Captain* supervises all correctional officers at FBOP facilities and is responsible for matters relating to the safety and security of inmates and staff.[2] Captains are usually at the same level as the AWs, and their directives and decisions are given equal weight. Wardens often defer to their judgment on correctional questions because the Captain is considered the expert in safety and security. Generally, inmates have few reasons to interact with the Captain.

Reporting directly to the Captain are the *lieutenants* who handle day-to-day decision-making.[3] Several lieutenants work in each facility, including an Operations Lieutenant and an Activities Lieutenant. They also work in the

Special Investigative Supervisor (SIS) Department and in the Assignment Office where staffing issues are handled.

Lieutenants are usually the boots-on-the-ground decision-makers. They initiate emergency procedures, lockdowns, or use of force. Lieutenants can overrule the non-correctional staff in most matters that require an immediate decision, and at least one is present whenever an inmate leaves for a trip to a hospital or a transfer.

Lieutenants handle much of the investigation and initial processing of disciplinary matters. The decisions they make include whether to lock up an inmate in the Special Housing Unit ("the hole") pending further investigation.

TIP: Lieutenants are usually very busy because they deal with a wide variety of matters. Avoid unnecessary drama when interacting with them. They are empowered to send inmates to the Special Housing Unit, and might choose to do so rather than engage in unpleasant interactions.

The frontline troops are *Correctional Officers.* In the FBOP, these entry level employees are traditionally referred to as COs … not as guards or other, less respectful labels.

COs in some facilities deal with enormous stress and danger in their roles as keepers of the keys. At the United States Penitentiary level, many wear stab vests under their uniforms for protection from inmate assaults. They must ensure order and perform the perpetual locking and unlocking of cells and doors. They also handle inmate head counts, searches for contraband on inmates, in cells, and at other locations. They also write reports and issue disciplinary citations. The role of the CO can vary from supervising an inmate work crew to staffing guard towers. They are authorized to fire lethal weapons at inmates.[4] COs represent the largest number of Bureau staff within prison facilities.

The FBOP requires a periodic rotation of duties for many CO posts.[5] Nevertheless, many inmates develop relationships with COs, which can be good, bad, or indifferent. Prisons are like small towns, and sometimes how well an inmate gets along with the line COs will impact their quality of life. Most experienced convicts take the position that it never hurts to be polite to the COs. They often reciprocate in kind.

> *TIP: It is smart to be polite but it is not smart to regularly associate with the COs. A simple "thank you" is a good idea but a long conversation behind closed doors – or even with the door open – leads fellow prisoners to assume that the inmate is an informant.*

Unit Management

Each housing unit is managed by the Unit Team whose members are: the unit manager, case manager, and correctional counselor, plus the unit secretary and unit officer.

Inmates will see their unit team every six months. At these meetings, the case manager will discuss the inmate's Custody and Classification points, which determine the security level they are housed at. The correctional counselor will discuss cell sanitation, any educational or rehabilitation programs they want the inmate to engage in, and so forth.

The *Unit Manager* is responsible for a prisoner's classification status, housing, and other matters, and oversees the correctional counselors, case managers, and unit secretaries assigned to individual housing units. A unit manager might be responsible for as many as four housing units that hold 500 or more inmates.

This staff position chairs the Unit Disciplinary Committee (UDC) hearings, Unit Team classification meetings, and other committees. Many have authority on matters relating to the Inmate Financial Responsibility Program (IFRP).[6] Beyond their supervisory duties, unit managers act as intermediate arbiters of formal and informal inmate complaints before the complaints are heard by the warden or other executive staff.

Correctional Counselors interact with inmates daily. They wear the uniform of a correctional officer and perform some traditional CO functions. Counselors who run the housing units are responsible, among other duties, for:

- Assigning inmates to beds and facilitating these changes;
- Inmate orientation;
- Unit Team classification;
- Unit Disciplinary Committee;
- Supervising, hiring, and paying inmate workers;
- Facilitating inmate self-help groups such as AA, NA, Anger Management, etc.;
- Distribution of cell sanitation supplies and unit resources;
- Supervising inmates' special mail, legal visits, and telephone calls;
- Processing inmate requests via other departments; and
- Establishing and enforcing unit rules and regulations.[7]

TIP: An inmate's relationship with their counselor can have a significant impact on their life during incarceration. The Correctional Counselor can determine cell or dormitory or job assignments, how quickly a visitor clearance form is approved, and even how much toilet paper is issued to an individual.

Case Managers are primarily responsible for computing inmate custody levels and classification scoring.[8] While decisions regarding these matters are governed by national policy, case managers exercise considerable judgment. Much of the classification process is subjective, and a case manager's opinion can significantly influence an inmate's custody and classification scoring.

For example, categories such as "responsibility" and "family ties" are only marginally guided by policy. Case managers can add or subtract several points toward an inmate's custody and classification score, so their judgment can have significant sway.[9]

Case managers generally direct Custody and Classification proceedings and might serve on Unit Disciplinary Committee (UDC) hearings. They do not wear uniforms. While some inmates seem to manufacture reasons to speak to unit staff, most inmates find that their interactions with case managers will be limited to the required Unit Team meetings.

In every housing unit there is a *Unit Secretary* who handles administrative matters for the unit management team.[10] Secretaries are often the ones who handle distribution of legal and certified mail to inmates, among other things, and they can be good allies. This is often an entry level position for people seeking higher posts within the FBOP.

Medical, Dental, and Psychology Professionals

In all general-population FBOP institutions, medical staff are organized as a Health Service Unit (HSU). HSUs are headed by a clinical director (CD) – usually a physician who is an outside contractor – and a health service administrator (HSA) who is the chief administrator for most institutions' Health Services Units.[11] The CD and HSA report directly to the warden. The FBOP hires many of its medical employees from the U.S. Public Health Service.

Inmates deal with their medical needs through their interactions with staff nurses, emergency medical technicians (EMTs), physician's assistants (PAs), and mid-level practitioners (MLPs) who are typically graduate physician assistants working with a licensed physician. These staff members handle virtually all routine care, sick-call appointments, and initial consultations. Assigned MLPs act as gatekeepers and an inmate's primary point of contact with the medical department. They evaluate the seriousness of a condition when a triage form for medical care is submitted.

Should an inmate require more specialized care, a registered nurse (RN) or licensed physician might be consulted. More specialized care is sometimes provided by local contract professionals such as psychiatrists, orthopedic surgeons, dermatologists, optometrists, etc.

Most HSUs also employ additional medical staff such as pharmacists, lab technicians, and medical records technicians. A CO is often assigned to the area as well.

TIP: FBOP medical staff are usually overworked, and their power to resolve many cases is circumscribed by policies and regulations that limit their discretion. It is wise to maintain a patient attitude when dealing with HSU professionals. If they do not, inmates risk some very long wait periods for service and appointments.

Dentists in the FBOP system come, for the most part, from the Commissioned Corps of the U.S. Public Health Service; in fact, they wear the uniform. Each institution should have at least one dentist, a dental assistant, and one dental hygienist on staff.[12] At some facilities, an inmate dental technician program trains qualified inmates for work in a dental office.

Dental technicians in the FBOP provide routine care and maintenance services (i.e., cleanings, check-ups, etc.), and perform traditional dental procedures (e.g., fillings, extractions, etc.), while more advanced procedures, such as those requiring oral surgery, are performed by professionals off-site.

There will be several *staff psychologists* in most Bureau facilities. They perform initial evaluations of new inmates, provide referrals for drug treatment programs, and counsel inmates.[13] In some institutions, sex offender management and treatment programs are also generated through the psychology department.[14] Although psychologists do not prescribe or dispense medications, they can provide referrals to the medical department when psychotropic medications are necessary.[15]

All FBOP psychology professionals are required by federal law to report evidence of an inmate "presenting a serious danger of violence" to himself or others.[16] This mandate, within the unique setting of a prison, dictates the kind of interactions the psychology staff has with inmates.

Within the psychology department, drug treatment specialists conduct substance-abuse treatment programs including a Non-Residential Drug Abuse Program, Drug Education Class, and others.[17] These workers are not doctors but are college graduates. Also within the department is the psychology secretary, who holds an entry-level position.

Religious, Educational, Recreational, and Other Staffing Areas

Normally there will be at least one *chaplain* on staff in each facility. In some instances there are several, in addition to others who occasionally arrive from different religious groups.

Chaplains oversee the religious services of the institution, scheduling and operating worship services for various religious groups.[18] Many facilities also offer religious video viewing and other study opportunities. Chaplains might be responsible for death notifications and grief counseling for inmates who lose loved ones, or for information regarding the hospitalization of family members.

> *TIP: Inmates should tell family members and friends that if they wish to notify them when an emergency arises – a death or serious illness, etc. – they should telephone the prison and ask specifically for the chaplaincy staff. Moreover, when making these calls, they should be very firm about wanting to receive a return call from the inmate. If they don't receive a call within twenty-four hours, they should call again and repeat the request. Unfortunately, FBOP staff are notorious for neglecting to pass on urgent messages like these.*

Teachers are headed by the Supervisor of Education. Ideally employing several full-time teachers, the Education Department provides teaching and training to inmates.[19] Many of these employees are dedicated to helping inmates educate themselves but some are uninspired. They might merely supervise inmate tutor-assistants. Some inmates have an aversion to schoolwork of any kind, and in these cases the education staff must act as de facto COs who are required to write incident reports for missing or tardy prisoner-students.

The *supervisor of recreation* and *recreation specialists* traditionally wear less formal attire than the rest of the prison staff, and are often seen in shorts and sports shirts. They supervise various sports leagues, hobby craft, and art programs as well as other leisure activities.[20] Members of the recreation staff might also be the easiest for an inmate to approach among FBOP employees, given their close interaction with inmates in a casual setting.

Facilities, food service, and *trust fund staff* are other specialist positions that help operate the institution and supervise inmate workers. The Facilities Department (also called Construction Maintenance) employs master and journeyman plumbers, electricians, and other professionals who do specialized work and supervise inmate workers below them.[21]

In the food services group are *food service administrators*, *cook supervisors*, and others who organize the preparation of meals and supervise large numbers of inmate workers.[22] Because food is a favorite target for inmate theft – the sale of stolen food items is big business in every prison – the food services staff must often perform security and custody functions as part of their regular duties.

Trust fund staff includes *laundry* and *commissary specialists*, *business office personnel*, and others who manage inmates and handle commissary sales, purchasing, and other tasks.[23]

Depending on the nature of the particular facility where the inmate is incarcerated, they might also interact with the *safety department staff*, *warehouse personnel*, and other FBOP employees.

Notes

1. 28 C.F.R. § 500.1(a).
2. Program Statement 5500.13, Correctional Services Procedures Manual.
3. *Id.*
4. 28 C.F.R. § 552.21; Program Statement 5566.06, Use of Force and Application of Restraints.
5. Program Statement 5500.13, Correctional Services Procedures Manual at § 101(1).
6. Program Statement 5321.07, Unit Management Manual at § 8.
7. Program Statement P3932.09, Correctional Counselor Training and Reference Guide.
8. Program Statement P3932.08, Case Management Training and Reference Guide.
9. Program Statement P5100.08, Inmate Security Designation and Custody Classification.
10. Program Statement P3933.03, Unit Secretary Training and Reference Guide.
11. Program Statement 6010.05, Health Services Administration; Program Statement 6031.04, Patient Care.
12. Program Statement 6400.02, Dental Services.

13. Program Statement 5310.12, Psychology Services Manual.
14. *Id.* at § 5.2.
15. *Id.* at § 3.2(C).
16. *Id.* at § 2.3.
17. Program Statement P5330.11, Psychology Treatment Programs.
18. Program Statement P5360.09, Religious Beliefs and Practices; 28 C.F.R § 548.12.
19. Program Statement 5350.28, Literacy Program (GED Standard); Program Statement 5300.21, Education, Training and Leisure Time Program Standards; 28 C.F.R. §§ 544.81 - .83.
20. Program Statement P5370.11, Recreation Programs, Inmate.
21. Program Statement P4200.10, Facilities Operations Manual.
22. Program Statement 4700.06, Food Service Manual.
23. Program Statement 4500.11, Trust Fund/Deposit Fund Manual.

Part II – Arrival and Orientation

Three

Entering the Compound

One of the most difficult moments for the new prisoner is arriving at the prison. Many questions arise like, *Will I be safe? Where will I live? Will I get along with my cellmates? Who will I talk to?* and *Where do I go to if I need help?* Or, with a feeling of dread, the inmate might wonder, *Can I handle this?*

Kristin Davis, who journaled about her experiences in the FBOP, wrote about going "inside the wall."

"In prison speak, going 'inside the wall' is the lingo used by inmates when they refer to entering a real prison facility. It is not about the actual wall surrounding the prison, but more about the feelings this wall provokes. The wall represents a sense of finality and it also represents a place of danger and intense fear."[1]

The goal of this chapter is to explain the first day of incarceration and to help those affected understand what is about to happen, how to safely manage it, and how to deal with the stress and anxiety of the process.

On the Bus

Incarceration begins to become a reality while on the bus or van en route to the prison. At this point, the inmate realizes there is no turning back, no chance of an alternative to imprisonment. During transport, all new arrivals experience some level of anxiety. No one wants their concern to show but it is there, even for those who have already served a number of years and are experienced doing time.

I'll never forget the first time I approached prison from a transport bus. We were a group of thirty, of whom only a few had ever served time before. The energy was palpable; everyone was on edge. All of us were peering through the steel security grates on the bus windows at the approaching menace.

Newly committed inmates should try to exercise control over their reactions while in transport. Everyone is nervous, to be sure, but if an inmate asks fearful questions, they'll create the impression of being a weakling. The bus ride to prison is like the first day of school: first impressions are important because others are trying to decide who will be left alone and who will be targeted.

While on the bus, inmates try to find someone with whom they have something in common and get acquainted. It is best not to choose anyone who looks like they will be easily intimidated as a buddy. However, inmates should not chose someone who acts like a bully either. Associations in prison can either be a strength or a downfall. Inmates should choose people who look like they will add strength, not those who will attract bullies.

Everyone's goal, especially as a first-time offender, is obscurity. Prisoners want to project strength and an ability to take care of themselves but they do not want to attract attention or stand out. By remaining unremarkable, being friendly, and making an acquaintance or two, inmates will be better prepared to start their term of incarceration on a stronger footing. When problems present themselves, they will be able to effectively manage the issues.

As our bus pulled into the parking lot, we saw a massive structure made of concrete, steel, and spools and spools of fencing and razor wire. Two perimeter patrol vehicles pulled up with armed prison guards. We waited. The guards unlocked a fence and motioned the bus inside. The fence was locked behind us. A large steel door slid open, and our bus pulled into a huge, dimly-lit garage.

Our names were called one after another. As each name was called, the rest of us became even more anxious until our own name was called. Then anxiety became internal panic. Once off the bus, each of us was thrown up against a wall and forcefully pat searched. The air was knocked out of me as a hand bit into my stomach. We had to line up with the others who had just experienced the same sadistic ritual of dominance.

Receiving and Discharge

Upon arrival at a federal prison, the first area where every inmate is taken is Receiving and Discharge (R&D) where they are catalogued and inventoried.[2] Inmates are booked into the prison system and into their specific prison facility. This is similar to booking at a county jail.

We had to take off all our clothes and place them in the brown paper bags in front of us. Once everyone was naked, we waited for our names to be called again. The guards inventoried our property and sent us to be fitted for prison clothes. In groups of twos and threes, they searched us. Fingers were run through our hair and mouths, we squatted and coughed, and our bodies were thoroughly inspected. Finally we received our clothing.

With our clothes on, we were fingerprinted, photographed, and issued an inmate identification card. They then placed us in a holding cell where we again waited to be called. We were interviewed by various members of the prison staff, including members of the psychology department, health services, a special investigative supervisor (SIS) technician, a classification officer, and a Unit Team member.

These interviews help prison administrators determine where an inmate should be housed, and whether they will be placed in general population. Issues that can prevent an inmate from going into general population might include tuberculosis or other communicable diseases, acute medical or psychological concerns, or orders to keep certain inmates away from others for their protection or because of a violent history. At some rougher medium and high security prisons sex offenders are also restricted from going into general population.

At the end of this interrogation, the less fortunate were sent to the Special Housing Unit to await placement in the general population. Others were mercifully allowed to enter the prison compound at once.

TIP: During these interviews, inmates should hold their cards close. As with interrogation by law enforcement officials, prison staff members are not necessarily there to help new arrivals. Some of the questions will help administrators place new arrivals in an appropriate housing unit; others will evaluate the inmate's intelligence or academic level.

Inmates should only provide answers that can't harm them. If the interviewers inquire about gang affiliation or more sensitive matters, such as cooperating with the government prior to sentencing or cooperation with prison authorities, inmates should politely decline to answer or simply act dumb. They already know what they need to know. There is no need to put yourself in a corner from day one. Corrupt prison officials have been known to disclose this sort of information to other inmates.

As we exited R&D, each of us received a bedroll that consisted of two blankets, two sheets, a washcloth, pillowcase, and a few basic hygiene items. All our personal property was seized and inspected. Allowed items (prescription medications, glasses, etc.) were returned. As for the rest, we had to choose whether to mail the items home, donate them to a local church or Goodwill, or have them destroyed.

At this time, we were also given an inmate identification card that we had to carry at all times. Later, we would learn that we had to use the ID card in the dining room, commissary, and other areas of the prison.

All this took place in an open compound, which meant that maybe a hundred of our fellow prisoners walking about could stare and scope out the "new fish."

Entering the Housing Unit

I made my way to a cluster of housing units alone. No prison guard guided me except to say, "Go to that building and give the guard your bed book card." When I reached the intersection of two buildings that housed approximately a thousand inmates, I asked where Housing Unit F-North was. The guard pointed me in the right direction. After climbing the stairs to my housing unit,

I located another guard and presented my bed book card. She pointed me to my cell and said, "Unpack."

On the first day, an inmate might be walked to their housing unit by a guard or the R&D staff might simply point them in the right direction. Either way, the walk is nerve-wracking. Walking into the housing unit, the inmate will look like an obvious new arrival wearing slip-on blue "bus" shoes, a white t-shirt, and khaki-colored pants with an elastic waistband.

TIP: If an inmate has trouble locating their housing unit, they should find an officer and ask for assistance. While it might feel more comfortable asking an inmate, it's usually safer to ask a guard. Inmates have been known to play tricks on new arrivals.

As the new arrivals walk into their housing unit for the first time, they should locate the unit officer and hand over their bed book card (a black-and-white card with their photo, name, inmate number, and description). The unit officer will direct them to their assigned cell and, if there isn't a mattress on the empty bunk they are assigned, the officer will locate one for the inmate.

TIP: It is normal to feel uneasy when exposed to new situations and circumstances. When entering the housing unit and searching for the right cell, a new inmate should try to appear as relaxed as possible. The best persona new arrivals can project is that of an average guy who is at peace with the situation. It's fine to be a bit curious, but it's not fine to act like a tough or angry person. This may incite someone to test their true mettle.

Greeting Cellmates and Fellow Inmates

As I approached my cell, I looked through the window in the door. One of my cellmates was there. He was taller than six feet with long dreadlocks. I knocked and explained that I had been assigned to the cell. Mercifully he welcomed me and pointed to the top of a three-tiered bunk bed. That bunk was mine.

I opened my bedroll and found that I had not been given any hygienic items. I asked the guard for some but she said there weren't any and I should check back later. I did twice more but no supplies were available. My cellmate was kind enough to lend me a bar of soap, a radio, and some stamps for spending money. He also took the trouble to explain the lay of the land. I was fortunate to get a good cellmate. And I have endeavored to be one, too, ever since.

Kristin Davis, upon entering a federal women's prison, was fortunate because she was greeted by a mentor. "These mentors," she wrote, "are other inmates who are there to help you acclimate to your new environment. The mentors also give you a few toiletries to help you along until you can go to the commissary and buy things. These items are donations from other inmates."[3]

Prison cells are unlocked for most of the day in general population. In the morning, the unit officers unlock each cell. Cell doors are locked again for the 4:00 p.m. count. When the count clears, they are unlocked again until 9:00 p.m., when cell doors are locked until 5:30 a.m.

When the unit officer brings the new arrival to their cell, they should look through the window before opening the door and entering. If at least one of the current occupants is there, they should introduce themselves. If no occupant is present, they should place their property on the chair near the door and then ask around to find out who their cellmate is. Then they should locate that person or persons and let them know they are now rooming with them. Inmates should not start unpacking or unloading their property into a locker without first speaking with the cell's occupants. No one wants a stranger to barge into their home unannounced.

Once the inmate has located their cellmate(s), they should defer to them as much as possible. Give them a few hours to clear their things off the assigned bunk or locker if they are storing items in either place. Ask what time the cellmates prefer to go to sleep and get up, their bathroom protocol, and preferences on other day-to-day matters.

At the women's facility, Davis learned the etiquette demanded by her cellmates. When using the toilet, any noise caused by body functions should be covered by flushing. When any of the women have their periods and need to change their pads or tampons, their cellmates politely look away.[4] Courtesy can prevent many problems and add a small feeling of comfort to inmates' lives.

For me, as the days went by I became more comfortable in my surroundings. The fear of entering the recreation yard and the anxiety of finding a place to sit in the chow hall subsided when I found people I had known from county jail. I was lucky. I felt free to ask basic questions and they served as my guides to prison life. Generally speaking, they took good care of me.

Matthew Kluger, a former attorney serving at a federal camp, noted that the "social stuff is very complicated. You've got an incredibly diverse crowd. You've got everything from inner city drug dealers to – well, I live next door to a Harvard grad."[5] Being able to get along with a broad range of individuals and personalities will make an inmate's life a lot easier.

Bit by bit I integrated into the prison society. I began by walking around the recreation yard with the guys I knew from county. Then I signed up for an educational class. I even started brushing up on prison-related law in the law library. I bought some typing supplies and started taking on paid typing projects. Soon I was no longer a new fish but just another regular on the line.

At that point, my days revolved around a self-imposed schedule. I woke up around 6:00 a.m., went to chow, worked out on the recreation yard for an hour or so, showered, worked on school work or wrote articles, ate lunch, did more school work or writing, ate dinner, worked out again and possibly played in a sports league game, watched some TV, and went to bed. While a regimented schedule that revolved around meals and inmate counts was imposed, I was still able to carve out a personal schedule. This has served me well for many years.

Integrating into the strange and toxic world of prison is not easy. Some people are so intimidated they refuse to enter the compound, preferring to stay in protective custody for months or years. Others arrive with an open mind and a cautious eye for trouble. I was of the latter type, and it worked well for me.

Years passed and I made a number of friends. I joined a few sports leagues (Ultimate Frisbee and soccer), I found a better cell, made a few enemies, got into a few fights, but I survived. Most importantly, I found projects to take up my days. Time started to pass faster and faster, driving me toward my release.

Life in prison is not enjoyable – there are bad days and troublesome situations that must be navigated with care – but it is bearable. Even a term of incarceration can be a learning experience, a time of personal growth. And that's the best any prisoner can possibly hope for.

"What Are You In For?"

Prisoners spend too much time exploring who is an informant or an undesirable sort, but it is a fact of prison life. At some point, someone will ask what brought an inmate to prison. If they are in for something like conspiracy to manufacture or distribute illegal substances, fraud, identity theft, insider trading, or any other of the garden-variety charges, they don't have a lot to worry about. They can feel safe in stating it succinctly – without offering specifics or names, since there are so many informants around.

If, on the other hand, the inmate is in for a sex-related crime such as production or possession of child pornography, or sexual offenses committed within the armed forces or on Indian reservations, things can get dicey. Inmates generally have contempt for people who commit sexual offenses. Any inmate incarcerated for that type of a crime should try to deflect the question unless they are incarcerated at a Sex Offender Management Program facility.

Lying about it is not a good idea because charges can be verified. Federal prisoners, often with long sentences, have had a lot of time to figure things out and develop a network of contacts outside of prison. An experienced inmate can "run someone's ticket," or check out a new arrival's paperwork, including research on why the person is in prison and whether they informed on someone.

Former attorney Matthew Kluger does this even though he's incarcerated at a federal camp. He says it's because so few people tell the truth about themselves. He justifies the move because "you're putting a certain amount of faith in them in spending time with them and you want to know to what degree you're being misled. The white-collar guys are actually much worse about that .... All these scam artists making up all these stories, and working on their next scam along with it."[6]

Inmates who are asked questions should avoid responses like, "I refuse to answer that question!" or "Bad stuff!" It is much better to quip back with something like "What are *you* in for?" or "Why do you care?" or "What's it to you?" They might even question the other inmate's motives for asking. An inmate should never actually accuse someone of being an informant (that can bring about regrettable consequences) but hinting at it is not a bad defense technique. In any case, the best way out is to try to brush off the question and move on to something else.

An experienced convict can have someone outside the prison search out a new arrival online. They might try to intimidate the new inmate into presenting paperwork that has their charge information and reveals whether or not they cooperated with authorities or have other "undesirable" attributes. An inmate placed in such a position should do what they can to get away from the situation.

This can be as simple as stating, "Don't mess with me, and I won't mess with you," or "I'm not looking for problems, but if they're coming, I'm game." In other words, show enough assertiveness to indicate that it will be more trouble to obtain the information than it's worth. Obviously, none of these are great options for the inmate charged with a sex-related crime but circumstances dictate many of their choices.

Race and Culture: If it Didn't Matter Before, it Does Now

In some prisons, race and culture determine various facets of prison life. Typically in high-security United States Penitentiaries or tougher medium-security federal prisons, inmates of the same race or ethnic background only associate and cell with one another. This is unfortunate because it sets up an "us-versus-them" mentality that tends to more easily incite hostilities. In other prisons, ethnic or racial grouping is not a large concern. Generally speaking, the higher the security level, the more of an issue ethnicity becomes. It depends entirely on the local practices of the inmate population.

Former Wall Street attorney Matthew Kluger, who served time in FCI Butner before moving to a camp, said, "Race matters. Yeah. Race definitely matters. I would say in some prisons they're 50 years behind the times. Here we're only 10 or 12 years behind, or 20 years behind the times .... by and large, there's a lot of suspicion and wariness."[7]

If an inmate is located in a prison where people of racial and ethnic backgrounds tend to stick together, they should adhere to the local custom. This will protect them and allow for as smooth a ride as possible. An adverse cellmate will probably inform a new arrival about this almost immediately. If not, an inmate can approach someone who looks like them and ask.

If inmate-implemented segregation is in effect and an inmate has been assigned to a cell that does not comply with local custom, they can refuse to bunk in the cell and request a new assignment. They can initially present their request to the housing unit officer or, better yet, to their correctional counselor.

This applies even when an inmate is in transit. When Kluger was transferred to the federal camp, he was held at the FBOP central transit center in Oklahoma City. His roommate was black but they talked and Kluger began to settle in. Then a white inmate pulled him aside and showed him the table he should use. Ten minutes later, a guard moved Kluger to a different room because his "friends" said it was unacceptable to them for him to be housed with a black inmate.[8]

Should an inmate refuse to bunk in a particular cell because of these concerns, only two options are available to the housing unit officer or correctional counselor: 1) assign them to a different cell, or 2) place them in the Special Housing Unit (SHU) until the matter is resolved. In my opinion, it is preferable to go to the SHU and deal with a disciplinary infraction than to offend other inmates and have to deal with the repercussions.

Again, this issue is only systematic at the high security level and sometimes at the rougher medium-security federal prisons. On the other hand, if a white-collar offender is housed at a minimum-security camp or a low-security prison, segregationist policies and politics probably will not come into play.

Refusing a Cell Assignment

If the cell assignment just isn't working out – because of charges, paperwork, racial/cultural incompatibility, or other reasons – the inmate should go to their unit officer and request a different cell. The unit officer probably won't fulfill this request but they can provide a referral to the lieutenant on duty or the correctional counselor if that person is on shift.

If referred, explain the situation in very general terms (for example, simply stating it isn't going to work and that a move is needed). Occasionally this is sufficient. Some correctional counselors might not be responsive to such requests, though, because they relish their authority over their housing unit. They don't have to deal with the explosions that occur between cellmates.

TIP: If an inmate finds himself needing a different cell, they should never inform the prison administration of the specific issues or the individuals involved. Providing names or specific issues may lead to those people being interrogated. The inmate risks being branded as a snitch or an informant.

If the staff refuses to resolve the issue, as a last resort the inmate can refuse to lock into their cell at night. That will force the matter and guarantee that they are sent to the SHU. It is better to spend a few days, or even a week or two, in the hole if a peaceful resolution isn't possible amongst cellmates. An angry inmate will get support from his associates.

Based on my experience, it is better to draw the ire of the administration than to incur the hostility of fellow inmates. Administration officials do not usually assault prisoners. Other inmates might.

Prison Politics: Informants and Sex Offenders

Specific prison politics come into play in a United States Penitentiary and at rougher medium security federal prisons. Prison politics usually relate to charges that landed an inmate in prison, racial issues, or paperwork. Politics might also be influenced by age, race, religion, or the geographic region inmates come from. They can intensify in facilities that house the most violent offenders.

Even if everything else seems clear, inmates want to avoid looking like they might be an informant. That means being civil to guards but not engaging with them for any length of time. Former senator Jeff Smith said "you can't be one of those guys who talks politics with the COs and just have a normal relationship with them. You just can't be that guy. It's a death knell."[9]

If an inmate is confronted by fellow prisoners who either know or suspect that the inmate is a sex offender or informant and aren't willing to let it go, few good options exist. If the prison is a low-security facility, the inmate will probably be able to say, "Leave me alone." At worst, they will be avoided or ostracized and harassed a bit.

At the higher security level, there is a greater risk of a violent confrontation. A group could corner the inmate and demand they "check in," which means asking to be put into protective custody by being confined to the Special Housing Unit (SHU). For details on the SHU, see Chapter 21.

The newcomer suspected of being an informant or sex offender might be "smashed off the yard." This means they are assaulted in front of prison staff so that the staff understands that this individual will not be allowed to walk that particular yard. There are other terms for this type of treatment. Inmates beaten off the yard are sometimes subjected to a "boot party," where they are stomped by other inmates in front of the lieutenant's office or chow hall. In a "blanket party," a blanket is thrown over an inmate's head and a group collectively assaults the victim.

Although wanton violence is extreme, the fact that there are terms to describe different scenarios indicates how systematic and relatively accepted – by inmates and staff alike – this violence actually is. The attacked inmate has three options: he can "check in" to protective custody and live in the hole, he can duck his head and try to avoid the hostile inmates, or he can fight.

If there is no space in the general population, or if an inmate requests protective custody, they will be placed in the SHU, also known as the hole or solitary confinement. It is best to not succumb to fear by checking in. Inmates should push through the tough first few days and start the adjustment process in their new surroundings.

Sometimes the newcomer's hand is forced. If a group of assailants gangs up on them, they have made up their minds. An inmate targeted by fellow prisoners intent upon causing physical harm can attempt to push his way through the gathering and get away as quickly as possible. If this is not possible, he should try to strike the lead agitator first. That might dissuade the others. Even if that is not successful, at least the inmate will be known as someone who will stick up for themselves.

If only one or two hostile inmates confront the newcomer, they can try to talk their way out of the volatile situation. If violence becomes imminent, the attacked person must do everything in their power to win. Steel-toed boots, which are issued to all federal inmates, are a terrific weapon. Throwing an assailant into bolted-down tables, cinderblock walls, and even telephone structures can be effective.

In the world outside of prison, violence is rarely the answer. It is a crude method of solving problems or differences. But in prison violence often rules, and even inmates who are not prone to violence should understand its value. Protection is the name of the game. Sometimes self-protection involves harming others before they can harm you. Even a weak inmate can knee someone in the groin, slam their head into a table, and kick them in the face when they are down. It's not pretty. It's not advised. But it may be effective.

If a sex offender or an informant is sent to a particularly rough high- or medium-security prison, serious consideration should be given to the risks. At some prisons, the staff will not allow sex offenders or informants to live in general population for fear of violence. At others, the staff might warn the offender but leave the decision up to them.

Depending on the inmate's strength and tolerance for conflict, remaining in the hole could be the smartest move. Some refuse to submit to threats or violence. They would rather stick it out and fight. In the end, each prisoner must make the decision in this life-or-strife world.

TIP: USP Tucson is one exception to the general rule. This high-security federal prison has a Sex Offender Management Program (SOMP) designation. It houses a large proportion of sex offenders and creates an easier environment for sex offenders as well as informants. See Chapter 12 for more information.

"Home" for Now

Once the new arrival has settled in, it is time to acclimate to the new surroundings. Prison will never substitute for a home but for a time, it has to become a surrogate. It might not be fun, safe, enjoyable, or stress-free (as some prisoners' original homes were not) but it is manageable. It is possible to carve out a life.

The one thing Kristin Davis found most bothersome about the federal women's facility was the lack of privacy. "I cannot just extricate myself from a situation here when I'm irritated or want some peace and quiet," she wrote. "I am trapped inside my living unit except for when we have a 'movement' . . . . " Otherwise, "We cook, we shop, we work out, we go to school, we bake birthday cakes, and plan celebration parties. Life goes on . . . even if it's life inside a prison."[10]

Once the new arrival feels comfortable roaming their housing unit, they should visit the various departments to see what the prison facility offers in terms of recreation, growth, and a progressive life. Prison life doesn't have to be about wasting years in anger at the world or watching endless soap operas and mindless TV. Incarceration can be a time of transformation and growth. Inmates should find a way to ensure that their life – even behind bars – is as fulfilling and productive as possible.

Notes

1. Davis, Kristin, "I've Been Moved 'Inside the Wall' In Federal Prison." XOJane. May 1, 2015. Retrieved from http://www.xojane.com/issues/on-going-inside-the-wall-in-federal-prison.
2. Program Statement P5290.15, Intake Screening; Program Statement 5800.12, Receiving and Discharge Manual; 28 C.F.R. §§ 522.20 - .21.

3. Davis, Kristin, "I Am Now Property of the Federal Government, Inmate 69007-054." XOJane. Jan 21, 2015. Retrieved from http://www.xojane.com/it-happened-to-me/kristin-davis-prison-journal.
4. Davis, Kristin, "Prison Etiquette 101 -- The Art of the Flush." XOJane, Apr 17, 2015. Retrieved from http://www.xojane.com/it-happened-to-me/manhattan-madam-kristin-davis-prison-etiquette.
5. Roberts, Daniel, "LIFE BEHIND BARS: Matthew Kluger Reveals All." *Fortune.* July 7, 2014.
6. *Id.*
7. *Id.*
8. *Id.*
9. Zengerle, Jason, "What a Jail Sentence Taught One Politician About Prisons." *GQ.* November 12, 2015.
10. Davis, Kristin, "This Is Prison." XOJane. May 8, 2015. Retrieved from http://www.xojane.com/it-happened-to-me/kristin-davis-this-is-prison.

Four

Daily Necessities

In this chapter, the basic necessities of daily life available within the FBOP are covered. These include the different types of housing units; common areas found within the housing units and how they are used; food service provided by the Bureau; meals created with purchases from the commissary; religious dietary needs; and laundry services.

Housing Units

Housing units are where inmates spend the majority of their time. It is where they sleep, shower, socialize, use the phone, watch TV, utilize the TRULINCS computers (for MP3 purchases and email), cook personal food, and work on personal projects. As such, housing units are a central aspect of inmate living.

> *TIP: Most prisons are either all-cell or all-dorm. As such, inmates will probably not have a choice about the type of housing they are assigned. See below for information on how to move to a new cell.*

Types of Housing Units

Two basic types of housing units exist within the FBOP: individual cells and dormitories. Each type has its own advantages and disadvantages. Depending on the preference of the individual inmate, either form can be a blessing or a curse.

Cells

For most inmates, housing units comprised of individual cells are preferable. In a cell, inmates will typically find one or two bunk beds, a toilet, a sink, and lockers. Sometimes a desk will be present. Typically an individual cell will hold one to four inmates, although a cell holding eight to twelve is not unheard of. Most housing units contain a variety of cells that have different occupancy levels. As time goes on, each inmate can make their way to a different form they prefer. Generally this occurs through inmate attrition.

Individual cells have many advantages over dorm settings. For starters, they are much more secure (they have doors that lock at night), quieter (again, the doors), and they afford a level of privacy. For those who prefer to engage in school work, reading, or writing, cells significantly minimize distractions. They also provide a sense of security and allow inmates to feel as though their life is more stable since they have a place that is relatively private and safe. While a cell won't feel like home, it will provide more privacy than a dorm.

Problems with cells typically revolve around the occupants. Diverse personalities will clash at times. Since inmates are forced into such close quarters, even cellmates who are friends can encounter problems. As such, inmates who live in cells need to keep in mind that aggravations and annoyances work both ways. It is better to encourage a culture of openness and discussion rather than allowing aggravations to fester and explode. If an inmate has ongoing problems with their cellmate, they can always attempt to move to more preferable housing.

Dorms

For some inmates, especially very social ones, the dorm setting is the way to go. In some dorms, bunk beds are lined up in rows inside a large room. In others, low walled cubicles within the room contain sets of bunks. It is not uncommon for fifty to a hundred inmates or more to live in a single dorm. Each inmate will be assigned a specific bunk and will have a locker nearby. Everything else is communal. In one or more large bathroom areas, there will be showers, a line of toilets, and a number of sinks.

Dorms hold the advantage of being busy places. For individuals who prefer to be more social, dorms allow them to carry on conversations virtually twenty-four hours a day. They allow groups of friends or cliques to constantly associate and thus, individual personality conflicts are more easily avoided. Just because an inmate is assigned to a specific bunk within a dormitory doesn't mean they must associate with others assigned bunks in their vicinity. In fact, while inmates are often civil with those who live around them, they are not necessarily good friends and don't necessarily hang out with them.

The problem with dorms is that they are often noisy places where personal space and security are limited. In a dorm, an inmate's every move is seen by others. Every time an inmate opens his or her locker, several sets of eyes can see what is inside. If an inmate ever leaves their radio on their bed or their locker unlocked, fate is being tempted. And having to use the bathroom in a communal setting where privacy is severely limited can be problematic for some. These are the main reasons why many inmates prefer to live in a housing unit that consists of cells.

> *TIP: Inmates who live in a dorm setting should keep close track of their personal property. They should always lock their locker, never leave out their radio or MP3 player, and always be aware of their immediate surroundings. This is basic safety advice but it is especially pertinent in a dorm.*

Transferring Bunk Assignments

If an inmate finds a particular living situation unbearable or if a more preferable bunk assignment becomes available, they can request a transfer. The politically correct way is to first approach the inmate(s) currently occupying that cell or bunk. If the existing occupant(s) is amenable, the inmate should fill out a cop-out (an Inmate Request to Staff form) and present it to the counselor in charge. At some institutions it is customary to have the existing occupant(s) sign the cop-out to prove that they are open to the move. At others, this isn't done because it aggravates the counselor.

> *TIP: In some facilities, counselors will defer to inmate politics when making cell assignments and allow various group representatives (shot-callers) to dictate cell assignments. As such, newly arriving inmates should ascertain the local custom before requesting a cell change.*

Often, more preferable housing assignments are based on seniority. If an inmate has been around for a long time, they have a better chance of obtaining the desired housing. Other factors such as disciplinary history, rapport with the counselor, and current housing can also enter the equation. For example, it can be easier to move from less preferable housing to more preferable housing rather than between housing that is equally preferable.

> *TIP: Inmates should never submit a cop-out requesting to move into a cell or to a certain bunk without first speaking with the existing occupant(s). To not do so is to invite strife and will offend everyone involved. Inmates should always be courteous and safe by inquiring before making the request.*
>
> *Also note that at times a counselor might offer a particular bunk assignment for one reason or another. Prior to accepting such an offer, inmates should always inquire with the existing occupant(s). While the counselor might be the one to officially make the move, he or she is not the one who will dictate the inmate's quality of life.*

Living Area Sanitation

To be a good citizen of a particular cell or living area, inmates will be required to clean the area periodically. While much of this will depend upon the kind of housing and occupants involved, it is a required component of living in prison.

If the inmate is housed in a cell setting, they should plan on cleaning their cell at least once or twice a week. If they are housed in a dorm setting, they should clean their immediate bunk area with the same consistency.

Cellmates or bunkmates share the responsibility of cleaning their mutual living area. In most cells, each cellmate will select a specific day(s) of the week to clean. This way everyone is pitching in equally and is being a responsible steward of their area. Cleaning an inmate's housing area includes sweeping, mopping, scrubbing, and so on. Supplies are issued through a supply closet within the housing unit. To not clean is to invite strife from the other occupants as well as infection. Prisons tend to be fairly dirty places.

In many institutions, living areas are to be "inspection ready" (clean, with all personal items put away) between the hours of 7:30 a.m. and 4:00 p.m. Areas that are not ready invite a guard or counselor to issue an incident report or harass the occupants.

> *TIP: Whenever leaving the living area, clean up whatever is lying around. This means locking all personal property in a locker or placing it on a clothes hook. By doing so, many problems can be avoided. No one likes living with a slob. If an inmate doesn't clean their area to please the administration, they should do so for the sake of their cellmate or bunkmate.*

Common Areas

All housing units have common areas. These areas are typically in the central area of the housing unit or within rooms inside the unit. In many federal prisons, TVs, microwaves, telephones, ice machines, showers, computers, and more are located either in common areas or in alcoves branching off from them. Most of these aspects are discussed thoroughly in other sections of this text, but will be touched upon briefly here.

TV Rooms and Mounted TVs

TVs are located either in TV rooms or are mounted on support beams in the central common area. In both areas, programming is either selected by majority opinion or a programming committee. Seating is designated by claimed areas that are considered unmarked property by the inmates who claim them.

Look before acting. As long as a new inmate observes first and doesn't attempt to impose their will on others, problems will be avoided and TV watching can be enjoyable. If not, the new inmate should plan on making enemies at best and fighting at worst.

Microwaves, Ice Machines, and Hot Water Dispensers

When available, microwaves, ice machines, and hot water dispensers are typically located in an alcove of the housing unit. Microwaves come in both the commercial and household varieties. As with TV rooms, microwaves can pose challenges for the new inmate. Often, select inmates will take over the microwave areas to cook large quantities of food stolen from the kitchen. When this occurs, other inmates must wait in a long line for their own needs. Needless to say, this causes strife. Never cut in line, and avoid hogging microwaves.

Ice machines tend to be located near microwaves. These are of the commercial variety and will resemble hotel ice machines. In cold months, ice will be plentiful. In hot months, there could be long lines of personal coolers lined up waiting for ice. Regardless of the situation, it is always best to be courteous and wait one's turn. Not doing so will almost certainly cause a conflict.

Some FBOP institutions also provide inmates with access to hot water dispensers. These dispense either 190 degree or 205 degree hot water from a tap. While some institutions offer both microwaves and hot water dispensers, it is becoming increasingly common for microwaves to be replaced with hot water dispensers.

Telephones and Computers

Telephones and computers are also located inside the housing units. While computers tend to be housed in alcoves, telephones are more likely to be in standing units that resemble the circular, three-unit pay phones found in malls or airports.

The same principles apply to telephones and computers as apply to TVs, ice machines, and microwaves. As long as the inmate stands in line, is courteous of others and doesn't disturb anyone, problems shouldn't occur. Since the FBOP sets strict, computer-controlled limits on the number and duration of telephone calls and the duration of email sessions, problems with phone or computer hogging behaviors rarely occur.

Showers

FBOP showers come in two primary varieties: rooms and stalls. Shower rooms are rooms that contain numerous shower heads for multiple inmates to use at a time, similar to those found at a gym. In this setup, inmates should use the shower by themselves or at the same time as their associates. If that isn't possible or practical, it is not unusual for inmates of different races or groups to utilize the showers at the same time. This can become necessary especially when the local institution only allows inmates to shower during certain periods of time, such as 6:00 p.m. to 8:00 p.m.

Shower stalls are small enclosures with a single shower head and a door or curtain. Stalls provide a greater amount of privacy, and are the preferred type of shower among inmates.

Regardless of how the showers are set up, the concept is generally the same. The inmates stand in line waiting their turn, take a shower in groups, or shower with other members of their group standing guard. In particularly rough medium- and high-security federal prisons, it is typical for inmates to walk to the shower in their work boots. If they have to fight, they won't do so in their shower shoes. This is not the case in low-security prisons or prison camps, where inmates often shower by themselves.

TIP: While some inmates hang their towel on a shower stall to hold their place and then leave to engage in other activities, this is not a smart move. Often hostilities occur when an inmate has to wait for someone to come back to claim the shower they're holding down or when an inmate ignores the hold and takes a shower. Play it safe and act like a decent human being with shower protocols.

Food Service

As is the case with many aspects of prison life, much of the public's perception about the food is exaggerated. It is neither gourmet nor garbage. Within the FBOP, it is fair to say that the inmates' dining experience will not be as good as one in a restaurant but it won't be much worse than the food served in a hospital.

While there have been instances of unsanitary conditions or health scares associated with food service in various American prison systems, the FBOP generally works hard to ensure that the food it serves meets American Correctional Association (ACA) standards and basic government regulations. Strict policies are in place to ensure that basic sanitary rules are followed and, while sanitation from institution to institution might vary at times, reported instances of health problems resulting from sanitation failures are rare within the FBOP.

Likewise, the quality of the food that is served usually meets basic nutritional standards (at least on paper).[1] Today, the FBOP has a national menu that all institutions are required to follow unless given a waiver for unique local conditions such as transport facilities, hospitals, etc.

Simply put, the food at FBOP facilities is generally edible, safe, and reasonably palatable.

The Chow Hall/Dining Room

All general population facilities in the FBOP have a central dining room and kitchen area where meals are prepared and served. Typically, meals are served three times a day with enough space to serve roughly a quarter to half of the inmate population at once. Policy dictates that each inmate be given at least twenty minutes to eat.[2] Most facilities will serve the entire population within an hour or hour and a half, often cycling through the population by serving a few housing units at a time.

Configurations vary but FBOP "chow halls" usually have rows of tables that seat anywhere from four to twelve inmates. Two or more serving lines usually operate at once, cafeteria-style, on which inmates are served entrees and measured-serving foods like desserts. Most facilities also have central buffet-style food bars for self-service soups or condiments.

Generally, inmates are served food on large plastic trays that are turned in for washing at the end of the meal. Plastic utensils are issued, as are drinking cups for consuming milk, juices, or water served via commercial dispensing machines. Ice is usually available, and morning meals often include self-service coffee or tea.

All inmates are permitted to eat once per meal. Most facilities have installed ID card scanners to limit inmates in this regard. Some institutions serve most of the meal on the main cafeteria line; others put many items on the bar. Most inmates find that they have enough to eat at each meal.

As might be expected, prison chow halls are a social hub. Within the FBOP, the noon meal is used for "main line," during which staff members from most administrative areas will stand inside or directly outside the dining room to make themselves available for inquiries. This generally includes executive level staff: wardens, associate wardens, and captains. There is a lot of activity.

Inmates attending chow are expected to meet local rules as to attire. Virtually every FBOP facility requires full khaki uniforms (or summer uniforms in some cases) for the noon meal Monday through Friday. Breakfast and dinner are usually less restrictive, although full uniform requirements for breakfast are not unheard of.

Dining Hall Etiquette: The Politics of Seating

Who sits where in the chow hall is sometimes a political matter. At some facilities, inmates have developed a rigid, nonnegotiable policy that dictates where each inmate may sit, right down to a particular table or seat. Other institutions have only general divisions while some have none at all. In more rigid facilities, no amount of staff intervention can prevent the strict pecking order from being enforced. Inmates have been known to attack each other over seating, and some have been killed over who "owns" a particular table.

The most common division among inmates in the chow hall is along racial lines. Even in more relaxed facilities, inmates tend to sit among their own racial group with areas in between sometimes being more fluid. In some facilities, it is simply not possible for an inmate of one race to sit in the area claimed by another. Such an act is viewed as a direct challenge and can be met with force.

Beyond racial distinctions, in higher-level security facilities there is little room for encroachment between gangs or "cars," groups of inmates from a certain area (for example, "the Boston car"). Anyone with no affiliation is often left scrambling for a seat in the "lame" seating area. At lower-level facilities and many FCIs, this is not the case. Disputes take on a lower level of violence and are more high-school in nature.

The bottom line when it comes to seating in any prison is that one should always ask around before taking a seat to be as courteous as possible and to avoid conflict. It must be remembered that the chow hall is the social center of any prison, so it is wise to act accordingly.

Meal Rotations

Not everyone can eat at once. In the FBOP, most facilities allow inmates to eat on a unit-by-unit basis, with full-time facilities or UNICOR workers at the head of the line.

While some prisons simply rotate the order for eating, many facilities tie placement in the chow rotation to weekly or biweekly housing unit inspections. Usually a staff member from the safety department (or in some cases, executive staff) will make the rounds, inspecting cells and common areas for safety and sanitation compliance, and deducting points for violations. FBOP culture insists on cleanliness, right down to sanctioning inmates for having dust on a locker – or even trash in a trash can! When inspections are the basis for establishing meal rotations, pressure from staff to be first can be strong.

Besides eating earlier, other incentives are involved with scoring higher in the meal rotations. Most FBOP facilities keep inmates in the units until chow is called. Those waiting to go to programs, recreation, or other destinations prefer to be higher on the list. Placement on a lower meal rotation can mean the difference between being able to eat and get to the commissary or not.

Eating from the Locker

No matter whether the food offered in the chow hall is tasty, some inmates will always make it their habit to prepare their own meals from items purchased from the commissary … or, ironically, stolen from the chow hall.

Most facilities equip the housing units with microwaves or hot water taps to heat food. Meals cooked in the units can be as simple as heating up a single Ramen soup in a bowl to frying chicken or making pizzas from scratch. The resourcefulness some inmates exhibit can be astounding, but most prison fare leans toward rice and pasta with fish or vegetables in a casserole-type dish. While prison recipes are beyond the scope of this book, the internet is awash with prison cookbooks written by inmates. Some of them are quite good. Two of my favorite meals are pepperoni pizza bagels and chili mac. Both can be made from items sold in the commissary.

If an inmate decides to cook elaborate meals in the microwave, it pays in the long run to be courteous. They should let others jump in for a quick warm-up of a cup of coffee or a snack. Too often, would-be gourmets will hog a microwave for hours. Inmates should treat others the way they wish to be treated.

Religious Diets

If an inmate is a member of a religious group that has recognized prohibitions against eating certain foods or other dietary rules, the FBOP will usually make accommodations. While the extent of such treatment can vary from prison to prison and from group to group, national policies guide inmates and staff through the process.[3]

For example, the FBOP offers a Certified Food program in which participants in the Jewish and Muslim faith groups are served meals that meet Kosher and Halal standards. Usually these meals are offered as prepackaged foods in single servings.

According to policy, these meals are handled pursuant to religious requirements using separate serving utensils and disposable bowls, spoons, and the like. The consensus among participants known to the author is that these meals generally meet their requirements but tend to include a large percentage of cold items and are of a limited variety.

Participation in the Certified Food program is voluntary and is arranged through the Religious Services Department. Usually an inmate is required to be a registered member of that faith group, and can be asked to fill out a questionnaire as to his or her beliefs to demonstrate religious sincerity. An inmate can be suspended or removed from a religious dietary program by eating from the general population line or for purchasing noncompliant foods from the commissary.

For inmates who choose not to eat meat for religious reasons, the FBOP does not presently offer special fare. Instead, each meal has a "no flesh" option in which the main entree will be a non-animal product like peanut butter in place of the general population offering. Most legal challenges in this regard have been unsuccessful because such alternatives are offered. However, every inmate who asserts that his or her religious diet requires special handling can utilize the Administrative Remedy Program to indicate that need.

Laundry Service

Among the most basic necessities prisoners have is a right to clean clothing and bedding.

Issued Clothing, Bedding, and Footwear

Upon arriving at a FBOP facility, inmates will be issued basic clothing, bedding, and footwear. These items will be provided through the laundry facility shortly after arrival, typically on the first weekday morning. At most facilities, inmates are measured for sizes of shirts, pants, underwear, and boots. This information is placed in a file retained by the laundry staff. Although the exact quantities vary from one institution to another, a general list of what is usually issued includes:

- T-shirts (white or brown)
- Boxers (white or brown)
- Women's underwear
- Sports bras
- Socks
- Khaki pants
- Khaki shirts (long- and short-sleeved)
- Belt

- Winter jacket
- Composite-toed work boots
- Mesh laundry bags (with laundry number affixed)
- Towels and washcloths
- Sheets, blankets, and pillowcase[4]

Long underwear, summer jackets, and other regionally necessary items might also be issued.

Inmates are able to purchase additional clothing items from the commissary. Such items include baseball hats, winter hats, large towels, higher-quality washcloths, better socks, t-shirts and boxers, long underwear, gloves, scarves, tank tops, and sweat suits.

Laundry Exchanges

FBOP policy requires that all inmates be supplied with "properly fitted, climatically suitable, durable, and presentable" clothing.[5] Such as, most facilities offer clothing exchanges to inmates on an annual or more frequent basis. Institutions are given wide latitude; while most issue new items whenever possible, others resort to new clothing only when used items, including socks and underwear, are not available.

Washing Clothing and Bedding

In May 2011, many prisons within the Bureau issued a notice to the inmate population regarding Presidential Executive Order 13423, which mandated a 2 percent annual reduction in water consumption by all Federal agencies. As a result, many federal prisons have phased out the individual washers and dryers that were located in the housing units for personal use. In their place, high-capacity central washers and dryers are now located in the laundry facility and operated by inmate laundry workers. The inmate population uses these for all their laundry needs.

Because of the large numbers of inmates in most federal prisons, a staggered schedule addresses the laundry. A typical schedule format is based upon individually assigned laundry numbers as in the following example:

Monday and Thursday:	Laundry numbers 1-800
Tuesday and Friday:	Laundry numbers 801-2200

TIP: At most federal prisons, laundry is dropped off between 6:00 a.m. and 7:30 a.m. Typical pick-up times are 12:00 p.m. to 6:15 p.m. Most facilities require inmates to drop off and pick up their laundry at a central location, and some facilities require that inmates include their bedding. Some do weekly bedding exchanges. Generally inmates will be able to wash all of their clothes in one bag. Some facilities have a weight limit per wash while others issue two bags.

TIP: When an inmate drops off their bag, they should make sure that the bag is secure. This will ensure that their laundry bag doesn't come open in the wash. It will also help cut down on theft by the inmate laundry workers. In some facilities, if an inmate is caught washing their clothes inside their housing unit, the guard might take the clothing or issue an incident report.

Generally, the centralized laundry procedures run smoothly at most institutions. Incidents of unsanitary procedures leading to the spread of diseases – a common inmate rumor – are virtually unheard of.

Notes

1. Program Statement 4700.06, Food Service Manual.
2. *Id.* at Ch. 11, §18(h).
3. Program Statement P5360.09, Religious Beliefs and Practices; 28 C.F.R. § 548.20.
4. Program Statement 5580.08, Inmate Personal Property.
5. Program Statement 4500.11, Trust Fund/Deposit Fund Manual at § 13.2(b)(1).

Five

Admission and Orientation

Upon arrival at a federal prison, inmates will be assigned to what is generally called Admission & Orientation status (A&O). This essentially means the inmate will not be assigned to any work detail or education schedule until their initial rounds to the various departments are complete. Once this phase of the introduction to prison life is finished – which can take up to twenty-eight days – the inmate is officially part of the general population.

Since federal inmates must understand a significant number of smaller critical components, this section will provide a broad overview of the essentials. Many of these sections are covered in greater detail elsewhere.

A&O Meetings and Rounds

Upon admittance to a federal prison, inmates must be evaluated and informed of the rules, regulations, and programs. They will speak with various staff in different departments and are required to attend certain meetings and screenings.[1]

General A&O Meeting

Within the first month of placement in a federal prison, all inmates are required to attend a general A&O meeting. Often this is held in the chapel area. During this hours-long meeting, the heads of most of the departments will describe their operations. Topics such as unit teams, education, recreation, local rules and regulations, religious services, and national disciplinary policy and procedures will be discussed.

> *TIP: While new arrivals might wish to ask a number of questions at A&O, it is often best not to. Asking a lot of questions will lengthen the meeting and annoy fellow inmates. Instead they should ask a trusted associate or a staff member … after the meeting has concluded.*

Issued Clothing, Linens, and Footwear

Within a day or two of arrival, the inmate will receive institutional clothing, linens, and footwear. Often this is done on the first full morning of their stay. See Chapter 4 for more information on issued property.

Medical, Dental, and Psychology Interviews

Prior to being released from A&O status, all inmates are required to meet with a staff member from the health services unit, dental department, and psychology department. At Health Services, inmates will fill out a questionnaire concerning their medical history and any specific problem areas. They will receive a tuberculosis test, have their weight, height, eyes, hearing, and blood pressure checked, and go through a general physical.[2] This physical examination is to be completed within fourteen days of arrival.

> *TIP: This is one time to ask questions and seek answers. Gaining access to healthcare in the FBOP is difficult.*

At the dental department, the inmate will have an initial evaluation to determine trouble spots that will be detailed in their dental records.[3] The inmate will be required to submit a cop-out in order to have any problems addressed. Just because the dental department locates problems does not mean they will address those issues. The wait for routine care can be months or years long.

While at the psychology department, the inmate will fill out yet another questionnaire and will speak with a staff member about the prison and their mental health.[4] Specific program offerings might be suggested at this point.

Initial Program Review

While on A&O status, each inmate will have their initial program review.[5] The inmate will be asked a significant number of questions about all areas of their lives.

The goal is to create a program review document that will follow the inmate for the rest of their incarceration. The initial program review will also familiarize the inmate with their unit team and housing unit regulations, and allow the unit team to offer suggestions or direction. Subsequent program reviews occur every 90 to 180 days depending on the amount of time remaining on the inmate's sentence.

TIP: Since this initial program review will be the basis for a document about the inmate, it is important that they put their best foot forward. Questions about mental health, drug abuse, and criminality will be asked. While it is never a good idea to be untruthful about such issues, it is a good idea to present the most compelling case.

Typical Schedule

Even within a federal prison, inmates have a significant amount of freedom. These freedoms include, with the exception of a few mandatory activities, what to do all day long. The only real times an inmate is required to be at certain locations or engaged in certain activities are between 9:15 p.m. lockdown and 5:30 a.m. on weekdays when the doors are unlocked (6:30 a.m. on the weekends); during the 4:00 p.m. count; and during the times they are supposed to be at their work detail, educational assignment, or call-out.

Inmates at camps or low-security facilities will probably live in a dorm. As such, they will not be locked in at night. They will simply need to be in their living areas during the 9:30 p.m. count. Afterward they can go about their business inside their housing units.

Outside of these mandatory events, inmates are free to sleep (but not under their blankets after 7:40 a.m. on weekdays), eat, watch TV, listen to the radio or their MP3 player, be on the recreation yard, and so on. Much of this will be dictated by personal desires. Some spend hours every day working on personal projects or studying; others literally watch TV sixteen hours a day.

Typical weekday and weekend schedules are:

- **Weekday**

5:30 a.m.	Doors unlock
6:00 a.m. to 7:00 a.m.	Breakfast
7:40 a.m.	Work call
7:50 a.m.	Morning census
10:30 a.m.	Recall
11:00 a.m. to 12:00 p.m.	Lunch
12:40 p.m.	Work call
12:50 p.m.	Evening census
3:30 p.m.	Recall
4:00 p.m.	Count
5:00 p.m. to 6:00 p.m.	Dinner
8:30 p.m.	Recall
9:15 p.m.	Lockdown

- **Weekend**

6:30 a.m.	Doors unlock
7:00 a.m. to 8:00 a.m.	Breakfast
9:30 a.m.	Recall
10:00 a.m.	Count
11:00 a.m. to 12:00 p.m.	Lunch
3:30 p.m.	Recall
4:00 p.m.	Count

5:00 p.m. to 6:00 p.m.	Dinner
8:30 p.m.	Recall
9:30 p.m.	Lockdown

Inmate Identification Card

Upon arrival at a federal prison, every inmate will be issued an inmate identification card.[6] Much like a driver's license, the ID card lists the inmate's name, register number, date of birth, eye color, height, and includes a photo. This card must be in the inmate's possession at all times. To be caught without one is to invite an incident report.

ID cards are required when eating, going to any appointments, going to visitation, and when shopping in the commissary if the institution doesn't have retina or fingerprint scanners. If an inmate loses the ID card, they can go to Receiving & Discharge during open house hours to obtain a new one.

TIP: When seeking a replacement ID card, inmates should assert that the card was stolen rather than lost or misplaced. Then the $5 replacement cost will be waived.

Controlled Movement

All federal facilities with the exception of prison camps and some low-security institutions utilize controlled movements. This means that movement throughout the prison is regulated by specific time periods. Generally, all internal doors and gates will be locked unless a move (called an "activities move") is happening. Moves typically last ten minutes, occur on the hour, and are announced on the institutional public address system. If an inmate is caught in a walkway after a move has closed, they will be directed to immediately make their way to their destination.

TIP: An inmate housed at an institution that utilizes controlled movement needs to plan their activities around the moves. They will be confined to the location in which they are present once a move closes. While it might be a hassle to get used to, the system eventually becomes second nature.

Recalls

At various times during the day, recall is announced. All inmates not on certain work details must return to their housing units. Typically, recalls will be announced at 10:30 a.m., 3:30 p.m., and 8:30 p.m. on weekdays. Modified times will be set for weekends.

Recalls ensure that all of the institution's inmates are in their housing units for release to the dining hall, are ready to be locked in for the 4:00 p.m. count, or are ready to be locked in their cells for the evening lockdown. Recalls can also occur at other times due to emergencies and adverse weather.

Sometimes if an inmate is out of place and isn't reporting to staff when paged over the public address system, a recall will be announced. When this occurs, the same principles apply. Inmates must return to their housing units. Recalls override all other institutional functions.

TIP: When an inmate is the subject of a recall, he or she will likely receive an incident report for being out of bounds. The prisoner might be locked in the SHU as a punishment pending resolution of the incident report. As such, if an inmate hears their name being paged over the institution's public address system, they should immediately report to staff.

Recreation Moves

At many institutions, a recreation move is called before breakfast and dinner. This is a five-minute special activities move to allow inmates to go from their housing units to the Recreation Department. This allows inmates who waive their right to go to each meal to arrive early for recreation. Inmates who go out on the recreation move will usually be required to stay there until the chow hall is closed or an activities move is called.

Inmate Counts

Counts are a fact of life in every prison. They ensure that no one has escaped and confirm the relative well-being of the inmates. Being counted becomes second nature for anyone confined in a penal institution.[7]

Official Counts

During official counts, inmates are locked in their cells and are required to stand, have their cell light on, and be counted. In the case of dorm housing, inmates stand by their bunks until they are counted. In the FBOP, such counts occur at 4:00 p.m. and 9:30 p.m. on weekdays with an additional stand-up count at 10:00 a.m. on weekends. Other official counts occur at 12:00 a.m., 3:00 a.m., and 5:00 a.m. daily, during which inmates can continue sleeping.

The guards take counts very seriously. As such, it is not advisable to interfere. That is a good way to receive either an incident report or a quick trip to the SHU.

Census Counts

Census counts are initiated twice a day on weekdays to ensure that inmates are where they are supposed to be. Generally, after the 7:40 a.m. and 12:40 p.m. weekday work calls, inmates are required to go to their cells or assigned bunks and be counted by their unit officer. This is to ensure that all inmates who are supposed to be at work and school are in fact there. Typically this count takes only a few minutes and inmates aren't locked into their cells.

A modification of the census count is the lockdown census count. All inmates already in their housing units are locked into their cells and counted, those on the recreation yard are counted, and all compound orderlies are specifically counted. The apparent goal of this type of census is to catch inmates outside of the areas where they are required to be.

The difference between a census and a lockdown census is that inmates in all parts of the prison are to be counted. The count takes about an hour to clear. Inmates are to remain where they are when a lockdown census count is announced. These usually occur once a month.

Bed Book Counts

A modification of traditional counts are bed book counts. These are typically called when someone is missing or is thought to be missing. These counts can occur at any time of the day or night.

All inmates are recalled and then locked into their cells where they must stand with their lights on. They must place their ID cards in their cell window. Inmates will be required to state their name and recite their register number so that the guards can ensure all inmates are present and in the right bed or cell.

Fog Count/Adverse Weather

If the institution is experiencing fog or other adverse weather – regardless of the time of day – operations usually cease and a fog count is implemented. If an institution is experiencing fog before breakfast, inmates will typically first go to breakfast and then return to their housing units, sometimes in regimented fashion. Fog counts are much like lockdown census counts. Adverse weather counts must be performed every two hours, so in some locations inmates might spend a lot of time in the unit during certain seasons.

Call Outs/Change Sheets

Every afternoon or evening, each institution issues a call-out sheet and a change sheet.[8] This document lists all appointments and work assignments or education schedule changes for the following day. Inmates are required to check the call-out sheet daily to see if they are on it. Any inmate on the call-out sheet will be required to abide by the instruction to be present at an appointment, start a different work assignment, be in the Education Department at a certain time for classes, and so forth.

If an inmate forgets to check the call-out sheet or refuses to go to a call-out, they run the risk of being issued an incident report or being placed in the SHU. It is imperative to abide by the appointments listed on the call-out sheet.

TIP: New arrivals sometimes forget to check the call-out list. When this occurs, most likely the inmate's unit officer will be radioed to send the inmate to their call-out. If an inmate notices that they've missed a move and are supposed to be somewhere else, they should speak with their unit officer and attempt to get released from their housing unit so that they can go where they are supposed to be before the staff starts looking for them.

Searches

Inmates are subject to a pat search at any time, and typically pass through metal detectors on a daily basis. A "visual search," really a strip search, is also permitted in many situations.[9]

A strip search will be conducted after a visit at a low-, medium-, or high-security facility, upon entering the institution or SHU if there is reasonable suspicion that the inmate might be concealing contraband, to inspect an inmate for injuries, or to discover evidence of disciplinary violations.[10] Female inmates who are strip searched during their menstrual cycles will be required to remove the tampon or pad during the search.[11]

Cells and other areas are subject to search at any time, as is the inmate's personal property. Generally these searches are for some form of contraband like stolen kitchen food or unauthorized items. The general definition for contraband is "[a]ny item or thing not authorized or issued by the institution, received through approved channels, or purchased through the commissary."[12]

When "soft" contraband (nuisance contraband like cardboard) is found, the officer will generally just throw it away. When "hard" contraband is found (drugs, weapons, etc.), the contraband will be forwarded to the lieutenant's office for further proceedings.

New inmates should be aware that searches are a regular occurrence. It is common for an inmate to be pat searched on their way out of the chow hall, to have guards search through their bag(s) on the way to the Recreation Department, and for unit officers to search a few cells each shift. This is just the way of life inside prison.

TIP: Inmates should never put themselves in a position where an officer has the power to sanction them for what's in their property. By maintaining a personal rule never to store or possess hard contraband, life will be much more stress-free. Engaging in nefarious activities simply isn't worth the risks.

Alcohol Detection/Drug Surveillance

All federal prisons have alcohol- and drug-use detection programs. While these can take several forms, the basics are fairly standard. From time to time, inmates will be called to the prison's compound office or their housing unit's officer's station to be tested with a breathalyzer. More often than not, this will be random. Entire work details have also been known to be breathalyzed.[13]

Drug surveillance is a bit more involved since the inmate has to be taken into the visitation room's bathroom and observed urinating into a testing cup. As such, drug tests are performed less often and on a smaller sample of inmates.[14]

The FBOP routinely tests for most recreational drugs like marijuana, heroin, cocaine, benzodiazepines, etc. A positive test or a refusal to provide a sample is a Greatest Severity (a "100 series") disciplinary offense. Inmates are generally given two hours to provide a urine sample. If the inmate states that he or she is willing but is having trouble, a captain or lieutenant is empowered to extend the time.[15]

Those with a "shy bladder" can sometimes provide a sample without direct visual supervision. Staff are accorded great discretion in such matters, but inmates should expect to be required to provide a sample while being observed.[16] At most institutions, a refusal amounts to an automatic trip to the SHU to await disciplinary action. A disciplinary finding for a positive sample also results in twenty-four months of regular urinalysis and other sanctions.[17]

It is common knowledge within federal prisons that testing can either be random or based on suspicion. In the former, inmates can be in the wrong place at the wrong time or can be randomly assigned to a list. More often, inmates who are suspected of drinking or using drugs are added to a "hot list" of inmates to be tested regularly.

TIP: Many tests are the direct result of informant information. Those who partake in alcohol or drug use should expect trouble at some point.

Special Diets

Most federal prisons don't afford inmates the right to special nonmedical or nonreligious diets. Religious needs can warrant a special diet and, if an inmate requires a special medical-ordered diet, the dining hall will provide the diet. If not, inmates in general population will have the option of either regular fare or heart-healthy fare. A "no flesh" option is usually offered for vegetarian inmates.[18]

All religious and medically required diets must be approved by either Health Services or the Chapel. This issue is discussed in detail in other chapters (Chapter 4, Daily Necessities; Chapter 9, Health Services; and Chapter 19, Religious Services).

Open House

Many departments will hold what is called an Open House. Inmates in general population can go to the department during specified hours and speak to staff. They can have their questions answered and their grievances addressed.

The Education Department, Psychology Department, each housing unit's Unit Team, and others will have a set day of the week – and a specific time window – for Open House. Typically, these sessions will occur once or twice a week for around an hour each.

Sentence Computation

Sentence computations are handled by the Designation and Sentence Computation Center (DSCC) in Grand Prairie, Texas. The DSCC handles the following concerns: good conduct time, jail credit, parole eligibility (if applicable), full-term expiration dates, projected release dates, actual release dates, and periods of supervision.[19]

Inmates are free to ask their Unit Team about these matters. If a resolution is not possible through those discussions, inmates might pursue the matter through the Administrative Remedy Program.

Detainers

Detainers are essentially requests from judicial bodies to hold an inmate as a result of a warrant based on pending, overlapping, or consecutive charges. They can also be the result of unsatisfied previous or current sentences. If an inmate has a detainer, the inmate will not be released from custody at the end of their sentence. Instead, the inmate will be held in the local jail or detention facility pending resolution of the charges/sentences, or until the issuing body takes them into custody.

If an inmate has a detainer, they are advised to contact the Records Department and their Unit Team to see if the detainer can be resolved before expiration of their sentence. An inmate can also make a request under the Interstate Agreement on Detainers, 18 U.S.C. Appendix 2, which requires any law enforcement body to resolve the matter within 180 days. This can be done by retrieving the offender and bringing them to court or dismissing the charges. The Interstate Agreement only applies to felonies, not misdemeanor detainers or parole or probation violation hearings.

If a detainer is not resolved, the inmate will not be eligible for halfway house or some program placements.

Good Conduct Time

Inmates sentenced after the Comprehensive Crime Control Act went into effect on November 1, 1987 receive fifty-four days of good conduct time per year.[20] For every year of clear conduct, they will receive a fifty-four-day credit on their sentence. As long as a federal inmate doesn't lose any good conduct time, they will serve about 87 percent of their sentence.

The deduction is computed at the end of every satisfactory year served pursuant to 18 U.S.C. § 3624(b), a point that is confusing to many inmates.[21]

> *TIP: Section 3624(b) requires that only sentences of "more than one year" receive good conduct time. Anyone facing a one-year term would be well-served to request a sentence of one year and one day to be eligible. These sentences are relatively commonplace. See, e.g., United States v. Gjokaj,*

2013 U.S. Dist. LEXIS 76876 (E.D. Mich., 5/31/13)(one year and one day imposed for bank fraud)."

If an inmate is not making satisfactory progress toward earning their GED or is refusing to participate in GED programming, the inmate will only receive forty-two days of good conduct time per year.[22]

Additional good conduct time, up to twelve months, can be awarded for participating in the Residential Drug Abuse Program (RDAP), which is covered in a later chapter. Individuals who self-surrender, or turn themselves in to a specific facility, receive an additional one-day credit. Before being admitted, individuals facing incarceration can calculate their expected release date on Federal-Prison.org using their sentence calculator.[23] Because calculations can be complex, inmates might ask someone outside the prison to run the calculations for them.

Good conduct time can be forfeited because of disciplinary matters. If an inmate receives an incident report and is sent in front of the discipline hearing officer for adjudication, specified amounts of good conduct time can be taken away.[24] This is only for guilty findings.

The amount of good conduct time lost will depend on the severity of the disciplinary violation, the conduct surrounding it, and the discipline hearing officer's preferences. Note that the Unit Discipline Committee (UDC) can only recommend the loss of good conduct time to the discipline hearing officer. The UDC cannot actually impose the sanction.

Compassionate Release

In 2014, over 100 federal inmates were approved for compassionate release.[25] This special form of release allows individuals who are facing extraordinary or compelling events to be released early. Often this is offered only for chronically ill or terminally ill inmates.

FAMM, Families Against Mandatory Minimums, reviewed Program Statement 5050.49, Compassionate Release/Reduction in Sentence: Procedures for Implementation of 18 U.S.C. §§ 3582(c)(1)(A) and 4205(g), which sets out the grounds for this type of release. They note that the FBOP has been far too reticent in considering compassionate release along with "unconscionable delays" in processing requests. Many prisoners die awaiting a decision.[26]

Three main categories of compassionate release are available: medical, non-medical, and elderly. Medical allows for terminal and debilitating medical conditions. Non-medical allows for non-medical reasons such as the need to care for a child and the need to care for a spouse or registered domestic partner. The elderly category allows for individuals who are at least seventy to apply for release even if they are healthy. Inmates who are at least sixty-five can apply if they have medical conditions.

Inmates who feel any of these conditions apply can speak with the staff member in the central office who is assigned to maintaining the reduction in sentence (RIS) database. FedCURE, Citizens United for Rehabilitation of Errants, works to fast-track compassionate release for terminally ill inmates. They can be contacted at:

Federal CURE
PO Box 15667
Plantation, Florida 33318-5667
www.fedcure.org

Pardons and Clemency

The founding fathers of this nation felt that the power to pardon prisoners and grant them early release was an important part of the system of checks and balances. The ability to pardon is important because it assumes that politicians – and by logical extension, courts – are not perfect. When the records of the Obama and Bush administrations for sentence commutations came under fire, citizens discovered how little it is used. While a dozen commutations were offered during a recently studied period, well over 11,000 requests were rejected.

President Obama pardoned eight federal inmates in December 2013. All had been convicted of crack cocaine crimes. All were first-time nonviolent offenders sentenced under the tough on crime rules.

"If they had been sentenced under the current law," Obama said, "many of them would have already served their time and paid their debt to society. Instead because of a disparity in the law that is now recognized as unjust, they remain in prison, separated from their families and their communities, at a cost of millions of taxpayer dollars each year."[27]

This move lead up to the Clemency Project. This program was set up by the Obama administration, and attempts to identify nonviolent, low-level offenders. Inmates need to meet the following criteria in order to access the clemency project:

- Currently serving a federal sentence and, if convicted today, would likely receive a "substantially" lower sentence;
- Have served at least ten years of their sentence;
- Do not have a "significant" criminal history;
- Have demonstrated good conduct; and
- Have no history of violence prior to or during imprisonment.[28]

Inmates who feel they meet the criteria are invited to fill out a survey if they are interested in seeking a commutation. The survey includes a question that allows inmates to request an attorney's assistance free of charge. Even if an inmate is unsure they will meet the requirements, their survey will be reviewed by the project's attorneys to ensure they can move forward.

Inmates who previously applied for commutations should also fill out the survey because they might be eligible under the 2014 guidelines. Inmates can represent themselves if they wish.[29]

In March 2016, Obama commuted the sentences of 61 prisoners, 25 of which came through the Clemency Project. As of the date of this printing, 35,000 federal inmates have applied and requested legal assistance. The Project has submitted 586 petitions to the Office of the Pardon Attorney, and nearly 100 more are very near to being submitted. Nearly 4,000 attorneys have been recruited and trained for the initiative; together they have donated over 50,000 hours.[30]

Due to the short time remaining in the Obama administration, inmates who apply now will likely find that they are reviewed by the next president.

Because the outcome of elections can never be foretold, inmates might want to make their application for clemency directly to the Pardon Attorney. Pro bono assistance will still be available even if an inmate files a *pro se* petition. Contact:

Office of the Pardon Attorney
145 N Street NE
Room 5E.508
Washington, D.C. 20530
Email: USPardon.Attorney@usdoj.gov

Exoneration

Exoneration is the official release of responsibility for an action. In other words, it wipes away blame. Convicted individuals can be exonerated because convictions were based on false confessions, or when new technologies like DNA testing clear a person convicted when those technologies didn't exist at the time of conviction. Official misconduct like perjury, withholding of evidence, and coercive interrogation techniques can also lead to exoneration.

Since 2009, nearly two dozen law enforcement offices in eleven states and the District of Columbia have opened conviction-integrity units. These units examine old cases to determine if errors were made and, if so, begin the steps to correct those errors. In 2015, 149 individuals were exonerated of crimes ranging from burglary to capital murder. This is the highest in any single year in nearly three decades. Overall, 1,733 exonerations have occurred since 1989.[31]

The Innocence Project, an organization that has worked since 1992 to free wrongly accused individuals through DNA testing, has enabled more than 300 people to regain the freedom they deserve. That number includes twenty individuals who were on death row. They found that individuals served an average of fourteen years before being released through exoneration.[32] Contact information for the Innocence Project is available in Appendix IV.

Parole

The Comprehensive Crime Control Act provides good conduct time; however, it rescinded federal parole. All offenders sentenced after November 1, 1987 are not eligible for federal parole. Notwithstanding annual rumors, as of this date there are no plans to bring back federal parole.

Notes

1. Program Statement 5290.14, Admission and Orientation Program.
2. Program Statement 6031.04, Patient Care at § 18.
3. Program Statement P6400.02, Dental Services.
4. Program Statement 5310.12, Psychology Services Manual at Chapter 4, § 1.
5. Program Statement P5322.13, Inmate Classification and Program Review at § 8.
6. Program Statement 5800.18, Receiving and Discharge Manual at Chapter 2, § 220.
7. Program Statement 5500.13, Correctional Services Procedures Manual.
8. Program Statement 5500.13, Correctional Services Procedures Manual at Chapter 3, §§ 306-307.
9. Program Statement 5521.06, Searches of Housing Units, Inmates, and Inmate Work Areas at § 2; 28 C.F.R. § 552.11.
10. *Id.*
11. Davis, Kristin, "Prison Etiquette 101 -- The Art of the Flush." XOJane, Apr 17, 2015. Retrieved from http://www.xojane.com/it-happened-to-me/manhattan-madam-kristin-davis-prison-etiquette.
12. Program Statement 5580.08, Inmate Personal Property at § 4; 28 C.F.R. § 500.1(h).
13. Program Statement 6590.07, Alcohol Surveillance and Testing Program; 28 C.F.R. § 550.10.
14. Program Statement 6060.08, Urine Surveillance and Narcotic Identification; 28 C.F.R. § 550.30.
15. Program Statement 6060.08, Urine Surveillance and Narcotic Identification.
16. *Id.*
17. *Id.*

18. Program Statement 4700.06, Food Services Manual at § 4(2).
19. Program Statement P5100.08, Inmate Security Designation and Custody Classification.
20. Program Statement P5884.03, Good Conduct Time Under the Prison Litigation Reform Act; 28 C.F.R. § 523.20.
21. *Barber v. Thomas*, U.S. 130 S.Ct. 2499, 2508-09 (2010).
22. *Id.*
23. Sentence Calculator. Federal-Prison.org. Retrieved from http://federal-prison.org/sentence-calculator/.
24. Program Statement 5270.09, Inmate Discipline Program; 28 C.F.R. § 541.3.
25. Bedard, Rachael, "When Dying Alone in Prison is Too Harsh a Sentence." *The New York Times.* Dec 28, 2015.
26. "New Compassionate Release Rules: Breaking It Down." FAMM. Retrieved from http://famm.org/wp-content/uploads/2013/07/FAMM-explains-new-compassionate-release-rules-FINAL.pdf.
27. "The Return of Clemency." Jan 18, 2015. Retrieved from http://www.gorillaconvict.com/2015/01/return-clemency/.
28. "Announcing New Clemency Initiative, Deputy Attorney General James M. Cole Details Broad New Criteria for Applicants." Department of Justice Office of Public Affairs. April 23, 2014. Retrieved from https://www.justice.gov/opa/pr/announcing-new-clemency-initiative-deputy-attorney-general-james-m-cole-details-broad-new.
29. "Frequently Asked Questions About Clemency Project 2014." FAMM. August 29, 2014. Retrieved from http://famm.org/frequently-asked-questions-about-clemency-project-2014/.
30. "The Return of Clemency," supra.
31. Editorial Board, "Prisoners Exonerated, Prosecutors Exposed." *The New York Times.* Feb 12, 2016.
32. "Exonerate the Innocent." The Innocence Project. Retrieved from http://www.innocenceproject.org/exonerate/.

Part III – Prison Life

Six

Travel within the FBOP

Virtually every prisoner confined within the FBOP will travel from one institution to another, whether it be by prison bus, airplane, or other means. With more than 200 institutions, the Bureau processes hundreds of thousands of inmate movements every year. While prison travel is sometimes unpleasant, it is generally safe and humane.

Initial Designation and Classification

Most federal inmates enter the travel pipeline after they are sentenced in federal court. Still considered to be in the custody of the United States Marshals Service until arriving at a FBOP facility, newly committed inmates are assigned an initial designation based on a "custody and classification" score computed by the Marshals Service. The score is forwarded to the FBOP's Designation and Sentence Computation Center in Grand Prairie, Texas for assignment of the inmate to a particular prison.[1]

If the inmate is confined at a non-FBOP institution, i.e., a county jail or state prison, they will usually be delivered to the Marshals Service at a federal courthouse or at a rally point for inmate transfers. If an "airlift" for inmates is taking place, the rally point might be a local airport.

Once underway, most inmates will travel by bus, van, or airplane to a federal holding facility, of which there are many. Some are located at FBOP mainline institutions like USP Atlanta, or at Metropolitan Correction Centers or Detention Centers like MDC Brooklyn. The Bureau also operates a dedicated transit center in Oklahoma City, Oklahoma. From these sites, inmates will be transported to their designated facility.

Most inmates travel while handcuffed through a waist chain with ankle shackles. Those inmates assigned "maximum" custody often endure "black box" handcuffs, which utilize a metal or hard plastic cover between the handcuffs to make escape less likely. Because movement of the arms is greatly reduced, black box travel is less than appealing. Inmates at the lower end of the security spectrum enjoy reduced restraints, often just handcuffs.

> *TIP: Inmates should inhale and extend their stomach if waist chains are used. Speak up at the time handcuffs or shackles are applied if they feel too tight. It is rare for staff to adjust restraints once travel is underway. They will usually heed a politely offered complaint on this subject, so speak up!*

Riding the Bus

Most FBOP travel is conducted via a fleet of buses. These vehicles generally conform to a standard model, with seating for forty inmates on a Greyhound-like coach. Most buses have padded vinyl seats, and a toilet and water source are located in the rear.

Prisoners can usually select their own seats. The bus rides tend to be long, sometimes all-day affairs, due to frequent stopping and a general lack of urgency. A box lunch is sometimes served, typically a sandwich, crackers, and an apple, to be eaten on the road (while handcuffed).

Three staff members are usually on the bus: a lieutenant and two COs, one of whom rides in the back. All will be armed with live ammunition weapons and various nonlethal ones like CS gas, rubber bullets, etc. While staff generally do not enforce much discipline on bus trips, they do expect inmates to fully comply with all directives, especially when entering and exiting.

TIP: Should trouble arise on the bus, such as a fight or other nonmedical problem, inmates should calmly move away. Staff respond to such events with force and generally don't concern themselves with accuracy when spraying CS gas, other chemical agents, or when firing non-lethal projectiles.

One individual who experienced the bus transport process wrote about it for her prison journal. Kristin Davis' 350-mile journey took seven days of ten-hour bus rides during which she was handcuffed. She was not told where she was going or the date on which she would be leaving. She told her family she might be out of touch for a week or so and then started her journey.

The bus was split into two cages, one for men and the other for women. They were cuffed using black boxes. Her cuffs were on so tightly she could not lower her hands enough to rest them in her lap.[2]

When traveling via the FBOP bus fleet, be prepared for anything.

Air Travel

Air travel within the Bureau of Prisons is not accurately depicted in movies like *Con Air.* Traveling by prison plane is usually uneventful, relatively comfortable, and generally boring. For the most part, the FBOP uses its own fleet of DC-9s and other commercial passenger jets. Most are refurbished after service in the major airlines. They are relatively clean and, not incidentally, appear to be well-maintained. None are known to have crashed or to have been involved in a major safety-related incident.

The flights are supervised by a combination of FBOP staff, U.S. Marshals Service personnel, and employees of a private contractor called JPATS who dress in uniforms. A deputy U.S. Marshal is usually in charge of inmate matters on the flight, and at least one medical officer is always on board.

Getting on or off a FBOP flight is the most trying aspect of most flights. Inmates arrive on buses that wait on the tarmac, usually at a remote area of a commercial or military airport, sometimes for hours. At some point, individuals getting on or off a flight will be lined up in rows on the tarmac to be pat searched and to have their identities verified. Inmates can spend as much as an hour waiting to board, dressed only in a jumpsuit or pants and a tee-shirt regardless of the weather. Shivering in January snow while the parka-clad staff chat and smoke cigarettes is not an experience that is quickly forgotten.

During boarding, the staff herds each inmate to a particular seat. Once the flight is underway, a bathroom break is usually called and a parade of inmates ensues. A box lunch is served if a flight encompasses the midday period. Inmates remain handcuffed while eating.

Inmates are expected to comply with every directive issued by staff on the plane. Arguing over seat placement, food, bathroom use, or any other issue will bring a swift and sometimes brutal response. Inmates are sometimes tasered for refusing to sit down, and unruly passengers can find themselves duct-taped and gagged. Control of the airplane is deemed an absolute requirement.

Oklahoma City

Most FBOP flights end up at the Federal Transit Center in Oklahoma City, Oklahoma. Inmates will find themselves part of an assembly-line process that involves walking from the plane to a ramp where chains are removed. They then walk to a series of holding cells where they are processed for eventual placement upstairs in a cell. The procedure can take several hours and is exhausting even for the most experienced inmate. This process is repeated in reverse upon departure.

Fortunately, most inmates passing through "OK City" spend less than a month there. The stay is usually boring. Units are set up like a new county jail block complete with a rec deck for outside air. Several TVs are in each unit, as are telephones and computer stations for inmates already enrolled in the TRULINCS system.

Holding Facilities

For many inmates, the most arduous part of their prison experience can be transfers. Inmates traveling in the Southeast might find themselves stuck in the holding units at USP Atlanta. Weeks can be spent in decrepit cells with one hour of daily shower or recreation time Monday through Friday. Other facilities dump transit inmates in SHUs. Services and amenities are very limited, and inmates are expected to simply endure.

TIP: Newly committed inmates must keep in mind that their conduct in transit will follow them to their final destination whether it involves disciplinary proceedings or less formal issues such as disputes with other inmates. The best advice for anyone in transit is to speak sparingly and wisely, and to mind their own business.

Notes

1. Program Statement P5100.08, Inmate Security Designation and Custody Classification.
2. Davis, Kristin, "I Just Spent the Last 7 Days Being Handcuffed on 10-Hour Bus Rides." XOJane, Mar 9, 2015. Retrieved from http://www.xojane.com/issues/kristin-davis-ive-been-re-designated-and-moved-to-another-prison-facility.

Seven

Work Assignments

All able-bodied inmates are required to hold an institutional work assignment for the duration of their incarceration.[1] The range of work detail possibilities is as diverse as that of jobs in traditional cities. There are electricians, plumbers, janitors, clerks, garbage workers, food service workers, and more. It is a well-known secret that inmates keep the prisons functioning. Outside of security matters, they handle everything.

Plenty of options for work assignments are available. Some work details are challenging and time-consuming while others are easy and infrequent. For the most part, inmates can find a job that fits their personality, schedule, and workload desire. It is up to the inmate to put in the effort to obtain – and retain – their employment of choice.

Types of Employment

In the outside world, many jobs must be done to keep a city functioning. The same is true with federal prisons. The difference is that while both skilled and unskilled jobs are available, compensation for institutional employment is usually paltry. The Inmate Performance Pay section in this chapter details the FBOP pay scale.

When compensation is not of paramount concern – for example, those with external sources of income (e.g., from family or friends) – other factors drive employment decisions. Some inmates choose a job based on the number of hours required, the prestige of the position (such as the head of a particular work detail), or because they like the work. Others enjoy the specific advantages of the job, which can include access to tools, the ability to influence work assignments within a particular work detail, access to food or supplies that can be sold on the underground market, and many other reasons.

The following is a general list of work assignments and their advantages and disadvantages. It should be noted that within each work detail, numerous jobs are available under a structured stratification system. The longer an inmate is employed within a certain work detail, the more they earn and the more power they tend to hold ... if they choose to climb the ranks.

Facilities

The Facilities Department offers work details that handle institutional maintenance and construction needs.[2] Facilities encompasses the components detailed below.

Electrical Shop: This detail is responsible for all electrical repairs within the institution. This includes lighting, power outlets, computer wiring, and all other electrical needs. Working in the electrical shop provides inmates with access to tools that can be used to repair radios, headphones, MP3 players, and other electronic devices for other inmates.

HVAC Shop: This detail is responsible for all heating and cooling systems and refrigeration systems, including ice machines, within the institution.[3] Inmates who are assigned to this work detail have clout with fellow inmates and staff because cooling systems always break down. Anyone who can fix the problem is valued.

Plumbing Shop: This detail is responsible for the repair and installation of hot and cold water supplies and returns as well as sewage lines. They also fix broken sinks, toilets, and showers. Inmates in this work detail have some degree of clout because they can remove the toilet flush timers some facilities install to limit the number of flushes allowed in a five-minute period.

Paint Shop: This detail is responsible for all institutional painting needs including painting the interiors and exteriors of buildings. This detail is desired due to the diversity of work and work locations.

TIP: Inmates in the paint shop can often make additional money by painting the cells of their fellow inmates. There is always work for this crew.

Maintenance Shop: These workers are generally equipped for repairing anything that isn't covered by the other shops. This includes concrete, sheet rock, roofs, windows, furnishings, and various types of equipment.

TIP: Inmates in the Maintenance Shop have access to various tools that can be used to perform services for fellow inmates.

Landscaping: This detail is responsible for cutting grass, planting shrubbery, snow removal, and all other institutional lawn care needs. A big plus is that the work is always outside and not stressful.

Food Service

Work details in the kitchen and dining room include preparing food, serving food, and cleaning up after meals.[4] The positions listed below are available.

Cooks, Bakers, and Line Prep: These jobs consist of preparing, cooking, and baking food to be served to either inmates or guards (typically in different areas). Some inmates in these positions are required to have specialized cooking and baking skills or training. This is a valued detail held by few inmates because workers have access to a wide range of food that is regularly stolen and sold. Head cooks are paid well in the kitchen, and stolen food brings top dollar on the housing unit black market.

Food Servers: These workers serve food in the chow line or restock the salad bar area. While these jobs don't pay a lot, they do provide access to food items that might interest fellow inmates. A large component of this detail involves dealing with the inmate population on a regular basis, which might appeal to certain personalities. The job can also involve a lot of stress because inmates always want more food and staff keep a close watch on portions.

Dining Room Workers: These jobs consist of wiping tables, cleaning floors, and bringing cups and trays from the dish room to the serving line. While not strenuous, it is menial. On the plus side, these positions can sometimes be very social.

TIP: Workers in the dining room position can help cooks and servers move food to the units for sale on the black market.

Dish Room: This job consists of washing trays and cups. Some prisons have a separate pots and pans area and work detail. If they are combined, the scrubbing of pots and pans is included. While this work detail offers a slightly higher wage than basic kitchen service, it is a lot of work and doesn't have many fringe benefits.

Commissary

The sole position available in the commissary is that of clerk. Clerks fill orders placed by the prison population and restock sold items. These jobs are highly desirable. Commissary workers are usually paid on the higher UNICOR pay scale [see the UNICOR section below].[5] This position also affords some status because the clerk knows when the commissary will be restocked, when new items will arrive, and what the new items will be.

Compound

The compound is the central area that houses walkways leading to the dining hall, recreation yard, education department, and all other non-housing areas. The job, consisting primarily of trash pickup, includes clerks and orderlies.

Clerks: This is the top tier of compound employment. Two or three inmates handle pay sheets, safety notification sheets, sanitary equipment checkout, and ensure that the work detail performs smoothly.

TIP: All clerk positions can earn extra money by helping fellow inmates obtain desired employment within their purview.

Orderlies: This is the typical compound position. Compound orderlies pick up trash around the compound. Since so many individuals are assigned as compound workers, this is sometimes a "no-show position" [see the section entitled "No-Show Jobs"] because workers are rarely required to show up for work or are only required to sign in and leave. Usually only four or five inmates who are the all-day orderlies actually work and get paid well for it. The orderly is a special category of compound job that is requested, not assigned.

Some facilities might have a Pigeon Sanitation Crew, a group of compound workers whose sole job is to clean up the mess that pigeons, seagulls, and other birds make. These inmates scrub the concrete on the walkways with long brushes. This labor-intensive job pays well. Another high-paying specialty position is snow removal. Because this crew often goes to work in the early hours to prepare the compound for morning activities, they are also usually better compensated.

Psychology Department

The Psychology Department employs only a small number of inmate orderlies to handle janitorial duties, act as receptionists, and even lead a few of the self-help groups. This is a desired position because it is indoors and in a professional setting. Due to the sensitive nature of the post, inmates in these positions are usually rotated out to other employment every year or so.

Chapel

The chapel employs clerks and orderlies. Orderlies handle janitorial duties, oversee chapel activities, check out books, manage the video/DVD program, and set up various services. This is a great area to work for the inmate who wants to avoid troublesome people and follow a more spiritual path.

Trash and Recycling

The trash and recycling work detail traditionally employs around six inmates. These inmates pick up the trash and recycling waste from the various housing units and transport it to the central trash and recycling location. This is a somewhat desired work detail because it pays better than most entry-level positions and it does not require a huge time commitment.

Recreation Department

The Recreation Department includes the recreation yard, the indoor recreation area, and hobby craft areas. In these areas, inmates from the entire prison congregate, play sports, work out, and engage in hobby craft projects. The jobs listed here are available.

Clerks: Unlike other work details, the clerks are primarily focused on distributing and collecting recreational equipment or maintaining hobby craft programs. They also handle the paperwork generated through these programs. These positions are higher paid and come with substantial authority. As such, there are few clerks.

Instructors and Referees: The Recreation Department regularly sponsors team sports like Frisbee, basketball, football, soccer, volleyball, softball, kickball, and hockey leagues as well as personal enrichment classes like yoga, painting, leather craft, abs classes, weight-loss groups, etc. These activities are managed by instructors (as in the case of yoga) or referees (as in the case of Frisbee).[6] While some prisons might count them as institutional jobs, most consider them to be supplemental work. Regardless, it does pay, and it provides substantial influence within the particular class area or league. Pay for these positions can vary from institution to institution.

Orderlies: Most inmates in the Recreation Department work on this detail. Recreation orderlies pick up trash, sweep, mop, and do other janitorial jobs. A big plus is that the work won't be time-consuming. It allows the inmate to hang out on the recreation yard and not be stuck in a housing unit or office. Pay is usually negligible.

Housing Units

Each housing unit has a large crew of workers. Most are orderlies who handle janitorial work. They sweep and mop the floors, scrub the showers, clean the microwaves, take out the trash, handle recycling, and perform other in-unit work.

The exception to the orderly position is that of the clerk. Each unit will have two or three clerks who are essentially head orderlies. These inmates ensure that the other orderlies show up and do their jobs. They also handle pay, clerical duties, and coordinate with the Unit Team on matters such as broken TVs or microwaves. They also pass out toilet paper and other necessities. Clerks are responsible for cleaning the Unit Team offices.

> *TIP: Head orderlies are often viewed with suspicion as informants even if this is not always the case.*

Education Department

The Education Department often employs some of the most competent and educated inmates. These workers essentially operate the entire department from teaching to cleaning.[7] The positions available in the Education Department are detailed in this section.

Tutors: This detail consists of teaching fellow inmates how to read, write, and perform math, usually as part of the GED and English as a Second Language (ESL) programs. Inmate tutors work in classrooms under the supervision of a staff educator.

Typical Education Departments will employ six to eight staff educators and twelve to sixteen inmate tutors. The inmate tutors do the majority of the teaching in the GED and ESL classes. At some facilities, tutors don't get paid well. However, they are always afforded some status and sense of self-worth through their tireless effort to educate fellow prisoners. This job is a calling, not a pastime.

Adult Continuing Education (ACE) Instructors: This detail consists of teaching fellow inmates either academic or vocational skills but not basic GED or ESL. ACE instructors teach classes on specific subject areas like bookkeeping, writing and publishing, CDL, money management, etc. This is not a high-paying job, but it fits into the calling of teaching. Some prisons consider this position to be a work detail, while others see it as supplemental.

Orderlies: This detail can be divided into two groups: orderlies who sweep, mop, wax, and take out the trash; and those who issue books in the leisure/law libraries. The former is a less desirable category than the latter because those who work in the leisure library have some status. They are in charge of the books and DVD/VHS programs some facilities offer, as well as a number of other resources.

No-Show Jobs

Inmates are required to hold an institutional work assignment but they are not necessarily required to hold a strenuous or time-consuming one. With federal prisons as overcrowded as they are, administrations have had to find jobs for all inmates. Invariably, this leads to a number of "no-show" jobs.

In all federal prisons, one or more work details will employ many more inmates than necessary. These are all low-paying jobs (from around $0.12 to $6.00 per month) but they don't require much more than signing in and leaving, if even that.

While each federal prison will vary, the compound work detail is a typical no-show job. This requires perhaps five or ten inmates a day to complete, and is mostly picking up stray trash. Yet over 100 inmates are often assigned to the weekday and weekend work details. Many on the compound weekend a.m. or p.m. shifts never show up because they aren't required to.

By assigning extra inmates to certain work details, two purposes are fulfilled: one, on paper, inmates are no longer idle; and two, easy, no-show jobs are created to fulfill the desires of many incarcerated persons. With this kind of job, inmates with external sources of income can effectively not work if they don't want to.

Prison Employment as a Way of Life?

Inmates find a plethora of ways to make the time pass. Some play cards or watch sports, attend chapel services, or aggressively pursue a higher education. Others throw themselves into a demanding and time-consuming work detail. Regardless of the choice, engaging in different activities turns the mind away from their incarcerated status.

If an inmate desires to pass time through demanding institutional employment, he or she should select a trade that allows them to grow as a tradesman and move up the employment hierarchy. If an inmate only has a few years until release, they can perfect a trade that may be of use upon release. Inmates who are in for life or are effectively in for life can create their own pathway in prison and earn enough money to afford a few creature comforts.

Duty Restrictions

Inmates with verifiable medical conditions that preclude them from safely working may be excused from employment by medical staff.[8] This is done through a document called the Duty Limitation Form, which can only be issued by a Health Services staff member. It must be reviewed and reissued on a regular basis.

More often than not, the form will specify which kinds of work the inmate can or cannot perform. For example, it might restrict the inmate from the steel-toed work boots that must be worn on most work details. Or it could exclude jobs that require prolonged standing. Depending on the restriction, the inmate might be given light duty work status. A typical example of a "no-prolonged standing" and "no-work-boots" assignment is a spoon roller in food service, a job that involves rolling plastic sporks and napkins together for six to eight hours a day. Not a difficult job but it is incredibly boring.

Only rarely will Health Services release an inmate from all work details. If this is the case, the inmate won't be required to work … in fact, they will not be allowed to work. Typically, this level of restriction is approved for someone who is recovering from surgery, preparing for surgery, or is very ill (not from a simple cold or the flu).

Inmate Performance Pay

Work in prison is not like work in society in many ways. Some might be surprised to discover that there is no such thing as a minimum wage for prisoners. Instead, pay is dictated by FBOP policy and not by federal law.[9]

Pay inside a federal prison is based upon a stratified system of different pay grades. At the bottom is maintenance pay, which is $5.25 per month.[a]

---

[a] *Some prisoners may make as little as $0.12 per month. Above that are grades 4 through 1. Grade 4 pays $0.12 per hour and Grade 1 $0.40 per hour. Most work assignments will record the total weekly work hours as 40, yet in the majority of cases the inmate won't be working nearly that many.*

The compound pay scale is as follows:

Grade 1	$0.40/hour
Grade 2	$0.29/hour
Grade 3	$0.17/hour
Grade 4	$0.12/hour
Maintenance pay	$5.25/month

Most inmates typically make somewhere between $5.25 and $54.00 per month in a normal compound job. At times, a supervisor might provide an inmate with a bonus that can increase pay up to 50 percent.

While different work details will be rated at different pay grades, a specific method can be used to climb the pay-grade ladder. Inmates should show up to work on time, put in more work than expected, and ensure that the supervisor – or the head inmate over the work detail (the "number one") – knows of their work and dedication. As time goes by, inmates will climb the ladder. Keep in mind that this climbing could, and often does, take years.

UNICOR

The Federal Bureau of Prisons operates a government-owned corporation called Federal Prison Industries, Inc., that is also known by its trade name, UNICOR. The stated mission of UNICOR "is to provide work simulation programs and training opportunities for inmates confined in Federal correctional facilities."[10]

UNICOR factories provide work for inmates in a variety of forms. As of 2010, there were 94 UNICOR factories operating at 70 sites employing 15,907 inmates, a decrease from a high of 23,152 inmates in 2008. The decrease occurred because UNICOR "was substantially negatively affected by the slow economy, increased costs of raw materials and staff salaries, legislation and changing demand for specific war-related items by the military."[11]

UNICOR factories use inmate labor to produce everything from Kevlar military helmets to executive office furniture to sensitive electronics and prison uniforms. UNICOR inmates also perform data entry work such as inputting patent and trademark documents for the Patent Office.[12]

UNICOR jobs are in great demand at most institutions largely due to the higher pay scale. Whereas non-UNICOR inmates can be paid anywhere from $5.25 per month and up for full-time labor, UNICOR's pay scale starts at $0.23 per hour (Grade 5) and goes up each time an inmate is promoted: $0.46 (Grade 4), $0.69 (Grade 3), $0.92 (Grade 2), and $1.15 (Grade 1).[13] Some factories operate on a piecework rate, as well.[14]

UNICOR inmates also receive holiday pay, overtime rates, and "longevity service credit," which can significantly increase their pay. Some inmates even draw "premium pay," which adds more.[15] As such, UNICOR workers can earn several hundred dollars per month, a handsome sum by prison standards.

On the downside, the wait for UNICOR employment can be several months to several years. It also is dependent on the inmate being housed at a UNICOR-equipped facility. Hiring is conducted via four lists: prior UNICOR experience (for those who worked for UNICOR at a previous institution); IFRP priority (inmates who owe a significant financial obligation are given priority hiring under the IFRP, where they agree to contribute 50 percent of their pay toward that obligation); Veteran priority (inmates who are veterans of the armed forces); and general hiring (usually the longest list). As a matter of fairness, some factory managers will hire inmates from all three lists in one group. Policy also allows for inmates with "special skills" to bypass the usual waiting lists.[16]

How to Request a Job

Upon arriving at a federal prison, it will be up to each inmate to quickly search out a preferred work assignment.

The first step, therefore, is to seek out a job. If an inmate has a special skill (like plumbing, electrical work, woodworking, painting, etc.) and wants to utilize it, they should find that office and a person who works there.

Step two is either to speak with the guard in charge of that work detail and emphasize their specialized skills and training, or to speak with an inmate who works there to learn who is the head inmate. If the guard is open to the inmate being assigned to his work detail, the inmate should present a cop-out for them to sign.

This process is followed regardless of whether the inmate already has an assigned work detail. If they don't, they will most likely be assigned to an undesirable detail such as the kitchen. Initiative is a must.

If an inmate can't get in touch with the guard in charge of the work detail or if they don't seem amenable, they should speak with the number one. The head inmate can make things happen. If that person isn't open to the suggestion, the inmate will need to simply submit a cop-out and hope for the best.

If the inmate receives a signed cop-out back, the final step is to respectfully hand the signed cop-out to their unit counselor and request assignment to the desired work detail. If he or she is amenable, the inmate will be assigned their chosen work detail. If not, they won't.

How to Influence Work Assignments

While not a policy-approved method of obtaining employment, many inmates obtain specific jobs by influencing inmate decision-makers (the number one for a particular work detail). Influencing this person typically happens through connections or through a transaction.

Influencing the number one through connections is probably more challenging but is also more common. In this method, the inmate asks friends and associates if anyone knows the number one for a particular work detail. Even if they don't, they can probably introduce the inmate to someone who does.

The person with the connection then introduces the inmate to the number one and asks that they place the inmate on the work detail. While this person won't make employment decisions, they can go to their boss – one of the guards – and ask them to make it happen by signing a cop-out authorizing the work detail assignment.

Monetary means, while less common, is the easier route. In this model, the inmate asks around to find out who is the number one for the desired work detail. Then the inmate asks what it would take to make the hire possible. If the person can make it happen, they will respond with a dollar amount. This will typically be in the $5.00 range. While not the most savory avenue, it is effective.

Notes

1. Program Statement 5251.06, Inmate Work and Performance Pay; 28 C.F.R. § 545.20.
2. Program Statement P4200.10, Facilities Operations Manual.
3. Program Statement P1600.09, Occupational Safety, Environmental Compliance, and Fire Protection.
4. Program Statement 4700.06, Food Service Manual.
5. Program Statement 4500.11, Trust Fund/Deposit Fund Manual.
6. Program Statement P5370.11, Recreation Programs, Inmate.
7. Program Statement 5300.21, Education, Training and Leisure Time Program Standards.
8. Program Statement 6031.04, Patient Care.
9. Program Statement 5251.06, Inmate Work and Performance Pay.
10. Program Statement 8120.02, Work Programs for Inmates, FPI; 28 C.F.R. § 345.11.
11. *State of the Bureau 2010,* U.S. Dept. of Justice, Federal Bureau of Prisons (Washington, DC 2010).
12. Mary Bosworth, *The U.S. Federal Prison System*, (Thousand Oaks, CA: Sage, 2002), 4.
13. 28 C.F.R. § 345.51.
14. 28 C.F.R. § 345.53.
15. 28 C.F.R. § 345.52.
16. 28 C.F.R. § 345.33.

Eight

Inmate Economy

The Bureau operates a shop called the commissary where inmates can purchase a variety of food, clothing, and other useful items. Inmates have a separate system whereby different types of items and even services can be obtained. These separate systems are described in this chapter along with information on the accounts used to buy items and other ways inmates can finance their purchases.

Commissary

In each prison within the FBOP is a prison store called the commissary. This is typically a building or part of a building where inmates shop once a week or once a month. The commissary is the only authorized store on the prison compound.

The Store

FBOP inmates are typically allowed to shop once a week at the commissary. This will be on an assigned day set by the prison administration. Usually, the day of the week that is assigned will correlate with the inmate's register number. General population inmates are allowed to spend up to $360.00 per month.[1]

The $360.00 limit applies to most commissary items. This includes all food, beverages, and condiments; hair, shaving, hygiene, and dental supplies; electronics; religious items; clothing; and sundry items. At most federal prisons postage stamps, copy cards containing a number of copy credits, and over-the-counter medications will not apply to the limit.

At present, the $360.00 limit has been increased to $410.00 during the period that begins in November to allow for holiday shopping. Most institutions offer a few novel items during this period such as fancy cookies, flavored coffee creamers, etc.

On their designated shopping day, inmates fill out a Commissary Sales Sheet. This is an order form provided by the prison administration that lists all items available for purchase and their cost. The inmate takes this completed order form to the commissary building. Once there, the inmate should check the out-of-stock items list to make last-minute adjustments.

At the beginning of the month, the commissary line will be longer (because everyone has been paid for their work assignment), while at the end of the month it will be much shorter. At most facilities the wait will be between five minutes and one hour in line to turn in a commissary slip.

After turning in a commissary slip, the inmate must wait until the commissary staff fills the order and calls their name. Inmate commissary workers will prepare the orders and deliver bins full of products to the guards. Sales will be processed by guards who stand behind reinforced windows with a chute for item delivery (picture a drive-through window at a local bank).

Once a name is called, the inmate will either have to hand the guard their inmate identification card, which has a bar code on it, or there will be a thumbprint scanner. One of these methods will be used to verify identity.

After the inmate's identity has been confirmed, the guard will scan each item and pass the order through the chute. Most inmates load their purchases into a mesh laundry bag, the preferred method of commissary transportation in the FBOP. When sales are completed, the guard will issue a receipt. If an inmate runs out of money or exceeds his or her spending limit during the transaction, the guard will inform them and have the excess items restocked by the inmate commissary workers.

When buying a lot of items, inmates should bring a friend to help carry the items back to the housing unit. It is customary to offer the friend an ice cream or other commissary items for the assistance. Even if help isn't necessary, it's nice to include a friend and give them an ice cream!

Commissary Items Available for Purchase

While each federal prison's commissary offerings will differ, all commissaries in federal prisons allow prisoners to purchase food items such as tuna, beef sausage, mackerel, salmon, chili, and others in foil packages; candy like Snickers, Milky Way, Twix, mints, and assorted candies; postage stamps, paper, envelopes, pens, and pencils; combination locks; sunglasses, clothing (t-shirts, shorts, boxers, briefs, socks, shoes, etc.); copy cards and typing supplies (typewriter ribbon, correction tape, typewriter wheel, typing paper, etc.); snacks (chips, crackers, popcorn, cheese, etc.); drinks (instant coffee, soda, drink mixes, tea, etc.); electronics (radios, MP3 players, batteries, clocks, etc.); over-the-counter medications; and more. Items are rotated on a quarterly basis to allow new items to be offered.

Appendix V illustrates a typical commissary list for a FBOP facility. Do note that each local institution's commissary offerings will be slightly different.

Commissary Restriction Status

If an inmate is issued an incident report for a disciplinary infraction, they run the risk of being placed on commissary restriction status. This is a sanction imposed by a disciplinary body for anywhere from one month up to several years.[2] The inmate will be restricted as to what they can buy and how much they can spend.

On commissary restriction status, inmates are limited to $25.00 per month, which can be used on the following items (this is an example from a federal prison):

AA or AAA Batteries
Balsam shampoo and conditioner
Pro-Line moisturizing conditioner
Hair brush or afro comb
Heritage roll-on deodorant
Toothbrush
CloseUp toothpaste
Denture cleanser
Chap-It lip balm
Dove or Dial soap
Soap dish
Shower shoes
Reading glasses
Master lock
Black ink pen
Effergrip
Denture cup
Cotton swabs
Dental floss
Nail clippers
Shaving cream
Disposable razor
Nextl skin lotion
Copy paper
Writing pads
Envelopes
Print wheel
Correctable ribbon
Correction tape

Inmates will also be able to purchase the following spending-limit-exempt items:

Postage stamps (up to $9.40 in postage)
Copy cards (up to three cards)
Over-the-counter medications

IFRP Refusal Status

Inmates who refuse to participate in the Inmate Financial Responsibility Program when directed to do so might face a reduced commissary monthly spending limit as a sanction. See Chapter 23, Inmate Financial Responsibility Program, for a full description of the IFRP. Generally, these inmates are restricted to a $25.00-per-month spending limit with exceptions for postage stamps and a few other items. The restriction also leaves one ineligible to make special purchase orders for recreation and religious items.[3]

Protecting Yourself and Your Purchases

Prison is populated by people who have been convicted of crimes and sentenced to confinement because of those crimes. This isn't to say that all people in prison are bad – the author has known many decent inmates – but that the criminal element is alive and well in American prisons. As such, constant vigilance is required to protect oneself and one's property.

In most federal prisons, inmates won't have much of a problem returning to the housing unit with their commissary purchases. Sadly, this is not the case in all federal prisons. While it is more typically a problem in state prisons, people do get robbed, held up, and even assaulted for what they have in their commissary bag.

At certain prisons in the North Carolina Department of Corrections, I had to go to commissary with several buddies. When problems arose, I had three or four people behind me ready to fight. While violence was unusual – if a group was involved – there were times when fights took place. This is a fact of life in some prisons.

In the FBOP, most inmates shouldn't have to deal with such issues. Instead, the biggest concern will be the sneak thief, the person who notes what one guy has and breaks into his locker while the victim is at chow or who grabs a radio left on a chair. The good news is that with a big lock and constant vigilance, the sneak thief will be thwarted.

With this caution in mind, inmates can take several actions to protect themselves and their property. First, each inmate should buy the biggest and strongest lock available. If the prison offers the $17 heavy duty lock, buy it! Second, inmates should never tell others how much money they have or what is in their locker. These are private concerns. Lockers should be kept shut and locked at all times when they are not in use.

Lastly, stagger purchases; there is no reason to spend $360 in a single week. For those who are going to spend the limit, it is suggested that they spend $80 to $100 a week and put it away ASAP. One should never leave items unattended or spread them on the floor for others to see. By following this advice, every inmate should ward off most commissary-related issues.

Underground Economy

Alongside the official commissary store is the inmate-to-inmate underground economy. When Jeff Smith, a former Missouri State Senator found guilty of obstruction of justice, entered prison, he was most surprised by the intricacies of the underground economy and the "tremendous entrepreneurial aptitude" displayed by the individuals who participated.[4]

He recognized that most prisoners were destitute when they entered the system. Although prison was supposed to provide everything they need, to live a "halfway decent existence" and buy enough hygiene items to stay healthy, they have to hustle. He saw individuals with artistic talent drawing portraits of people's family members alongside many other available services.[5]

This section offers detailed information and advice on how the underground economy works, different payment methods, and the risks involved.

The Black Market

Every prison has a black market that involves unauthorized commerce. Typically this operates out of a prisoner's locker or cell. The black market, which most inmates engage in to some degree, is the buying, selling, or trading of items outside of the institutional commissary, and it is a violation of the rules. It is a system of barter and trade that doesn't necessarily involve contraband or illegal substances. The trade can be as simple as borrowing a candy bar and paying for it later, or as nefarious as buying heroin or cocaine, which must be paid for in full prior to product delivery.

Stamps and Mackerel: Common Currencies

In most federal prisons, postage stamps and packages of mackerel are the common forms of currency. They replace money, which federal prisoners are not allowed to possess. Both can be purchased through the institutional commissary and can be used to buy products and pay for services.

TIP: In some federal prisons, depending on local market preference, items other than stamps or packets of mackerel are used as currency (e.g., foil packets of tuna from the commissary). Prices will equate to some multiple of those items.

As it pertains to stamps the federal prison marketplace only recognizes mailing stamps as a form of currency. Compound stamps, worn-out stamps that can no longer be used for mailing, are no longer deemed appropriate for prison commerce. Mailing stamps are worth their face value and can be used to mail out a one-ounce, first-class letter.

TIP: One-dollar stamps are often a prisoner's best buy since they retain their exact value at some institutions. If purchasing stamps from the institutional commissary for prison trade, it is recommended that an inmate buy one-dollar stamps if they are available.

Mailing stamps, as previously mentioned, can be purchased from the institutional commissary. However, as of 2013, the Federal Bureau of Prisons changed its national policy to limit the number of postage stamps prisoners can purchase on their shopping day. They are only allowed to purchase up to twenty first-class stamps or their equivalent value in higher or lower denomination stamps.[6] As such, many prisoners purchase the maximum amount allowed each week and stock up to use when needed. National policy allows inmates to retain sixty first-class stamps.

Mailing stamps can also be purchased from a fellow prisoner who runs a store in the housing unit or from someone who operates an internal gambling business (often called a "ticket"). Typically, this person will ask the inmate to go to the commissary to purchase $5.00 worth of goods. When the inmate brings these items back to the person (often called a "store man"), they will receive either five $1 stamps (the equivalent of $5.00) or 15 mailing stamps. Five $1 stamps are commonly referred to as a "book;" for mailers, fifteen is a book since, at many institutions, three mailing stamps equate to $1.00 regardless of their face value.

TIP: It is a smart idea to buy mailing stamps from fellow prisoners, especially from those who operate stores, because they will often sell books at a discount compared to what would be paid at the commissary. When doing so, be sure to verify that the mailing stamps are unused and that the book contains the correct total. Sometimes stamp sellers will short the buyer a stamp or two, or try to pass off used stamps as new ones to increase their profit.

The Convict Store

A convict store is not the institutional commissary. It is an unauthorized enterprise typically operated by what is known as a "store man" out of their locker or cell. These stores typically stock cold sodas along with various foods, snacks, candy, and chips. Convict stores and other underground commerce operate on a different set of rules than the institutional commissary. Inmates will need to know how to safely engage in this commerce.

The Markup

So that the owner of the convict store can make a profit, prices are higher than what an inmate would pay in the official commissary. The original cost of the item is added to the owner's cut and then typically rounded up to the closest full stamp amount (in denominations of 25 cents). The markup for convict store items varies from one state to another, one prison to another, and even store to store within the same prison.

At FCI Petersburg, a 25- to 50-cent markup is common. In the North Carolina Department of Corrections, the markup is based on a 2-for-1 model. So for every item purchased, two are owed (a 200 percent return!). The buyers pay the bill by going to the commissary on their assigned day with a list from the store man or obtains the prescribed number of currency items (i.e., stamps or packets of mackerel) to settle the bill.

With such high inflation rates, it is smart to keep one's locker stocked with what is needed and patronize a convict store as seldom as possible.

Some might ask why an inmate would pay a markup to the store man, especially when paying the bill is often done by visiting the commissary with the store man's list. Why pay a markup when you have to go to the commissary to pay the bill anyway?

Good question.

An inmate can pay less at the institutional commissary. But this assumes that the day they want the item(s) is their shopping day, and that they have money in their commissary account. Inmates can only shop on one assigned day each week. This is one reason why many inmates shop at a convict store on days when they cannot go to the commissary.

Here is another example: an inmate wants to buy a couple of sodas, which sell in packs of twelve for $4.85 at the commissary. At the convict store, the sodas are already cold, so the buyer doesn't need to obtain ice. Nor do they have to store bulky twelve-packs in their locker. But the store man charges a markup on the sodas. In the end, it's up to each prisoner to decide if the convenience is worth the higher cost.

Buyers pay the store man when they get paid for their institutional job (once a month – on "post"), when they receive money from family or friends, or when they go to the commissary. In this way, store men are somewhat like loan sharks.

What happens too often is that an inmate runs up a tab for items he or she can't afford and then has to work out a payment plan ... at an enhanced rate, of course. On several occasions, I've had to speak with a friend's store man to calm the guy down (violence for nonpayment is always a possibility). Usually this involves sitting down with both of them and creating a reasonable payment plan both can live with – and guaranteeing the debt if my friend doesn't cover his obligations. While I have done this in the past, it is almost universally a bad idea.

The convict store sells convenience. Inmates can walk up to the convict store anytime and get what they want when they want it. The convict store is much more accessible than the commissary, and costs a little extra.

TIP: It is more economical to plan ahead and buy what one needs from the institutional commissary than to rely on the convict store's inflated rates. Keep purchases from the convict store to a minimum.

Shopping: Buyer Beware

To better explain how the convict store model of shopping works, let's walk through a typical purchase. First, an inmate needs to locate a store man they like. Since the use of a convict store is so commonplace, and since specific stores are widely known and frequented, it is fine to ask around about which is the best. Then speak with the various store men to find the best fit.

> *TIP: Shop with the most reputable store man available. By finding the most established store, an inmate is more likely to build a long relationship and encounter fewer problems with credit if the store folds.*

After settling upon a vendor, the inmate will need to come to an agreement as to how they will pay, whether with stamps, other currency items like tuna or mackerel, or credit. If credit is the agreed-upon method, firmly establish the limit so there are no surprises.

Regardless of the payment method, the store owner will open his or her locker to show the shopper what is currently available. If they select an item (or several), the store man will tally the total owed. Payments made with stamps or packets of mackerel need to be provided at this juncture. If the buyer is paying on credit, the store man will record the purchase in a ledger. The debt will be paid off on the buyer's next shopping day or on the day the prison posts inmate pay for work details.

> *TIP: Pay careful attention to any tab with a store man or anyone else in prison. Always ask what the totals are and jot down purchases, the totals, when payments are made, and in what currency. Keep a record! Sadly but not surprisingly, store men do rip customers off from time to time. When this occurs, it's usually by making little additions to lists of purchases. It is hard to prove if the shopper is guesstimating totals.*

When engaging in any kind of commercial transaction in prison, and especially when using credit, make sure that all parties are absolutely clear on debts and agreements. Inmates should show the store men the recorded lists and get their agreement. This will foster a healthier, more open relationship and minimize future problems. Misunderstandings do occur and everything should be done to minimize them so confrontations and disagreements can be avoided.

Credit Carries Danger

If credit is the agreed-upon method of payment at a convict store, two methods of fulfilling the obligations are generally available: 1) buying items from the commissary to fulfill the bill, or 2) having someone outside of prison send money to the store man's commissary account. Inmates will find it best to pay their debt through the commissary and only in the amount which is currently owed.

For many reasons, inmates should avoid sending funds to a store man's account. Most importantly, it is against prison disciplinary regulations to give or receive anything of value to or from a fellow prisoner. If an inmate sends money to a fellow inmate, they run the risk of receiving an incident report for violating FBOP disciplinary regulations.[7]

This risk is significant. The FBOP constantly monitors prisoner accounts and tracks who sends money to which accounts. Inmates also must not disclose personal information to anyone in prison (such as the names, phone numbers, and addresses of family members or outside friends), and they should not be connected financially to anyone in prison.

Remember: people are in prison for violating the law. The last thing a convict store shopper wants is for their store man to buy dope or use their funds for illegal purposes and have those funds traced back to them, even if they had nothing to do with the illegal transaction.

TIP: If one person outside of prison deposits money on multiple prisoners' accounts, it sets off red flags and launches investigations. If a "send in" is the chosen method of paying for convict store purchases, use multiple parties and complete transactions in the quietest way possible (remember that letters, phone calls, and emails are monitored).

The safest way is to have someone outside of prison send money to the store man's family, which their family then sends to the store man. This might protect all parties involved except that this incurs an extra level of risk. Inmates now have additional parties involved, and they don't know if they can trust those parties. Possibly, they might want to keep the money for themselves.

Keep in mind that inmates never want to have too much credit with a store man. When hundreds or even fifty or so dollars are at stake, it creates motivation to either rip the customer off or force that person to "check in" (request to be placed in solitary confinement for protection). It's much smarter to pay the store man through commissary purchases – in the amount owed only, nothing more and nothing less. This will greatly reduce the potential for problems. And because it is common for inmates to check in to solitary because they owe large store bills, running up a bill can give a store man cause to question motivations.

Be forewarned: running up a bill and not being able to pay can be hazardous to an inmate's health.

TIP: Remember that doing business in prison is a violation of the rules. If caught, it can cause everyone engaged in those activities to receive incident reports despite the widespread nature of prison commerce. Be very careful to not get caught. Keep no formal record of commercial transactions, only a sheet of paper with a dollar total, no names, and only abbreviations for items purchased. Do not talk about transactions on the phone, in a letter, or via email, as all of these communications are actively monitored.

Be smart. Do not trust anyone in prison because, generally, everyone has a criminal mindset. Common sense and a bit of imagination can go a long way.

Other Prison Commerce

Federal prisoners engage in commercial transactions on a daily basis. These can be as simple as purchasing stolen hamburgers and fries, or as complex as retaining someone to stand in line for commissary, craft origami flowers to send a loved one on Valentine's Day, or borrow money to pay bills on the outside.

Prison is the Wild, Wild West: if someone is willing to pay for it, they can probably find someone to provide it. What follows are some common examples of services and products offered in the underground prison economy. Keep in mind that this is nowhere near a comprehensive accounting.

The Kitchen

The black market is alive and well in all areas of prison life but the kitchen holds a preeminent place in prison commerce. Since the federal prison commissaries often lack fresh meats, cheeses, and vegetables, inmates working in the kitchen steal onions, peppers, meats, cheeses, and anything they can get their hands on and cart out the door for sale to other inmates.

When an interviewer asked Matthew Kluger how inmates could steal from the kitchen when the food wasn't wrapped, he detailed some of the common methods. "[Y]ou can take a bread bag and put chicken in it," he said. "You can steal ten hamburgers. You can steal boiled eggs. You can steal bags of bran flakes. In the morning we get little breakfast bars. Those are wrapped, so they'll take those out like crazy. You're allowed a piece of fruit here. You weren't at Butner. People will steal extra fruit."[8]

An onion or pepper typically goes for around $1. Two eggs go for $0.50, while an entire bread bag of hamburger meat might cost up to $2.50. A hamburger patty typically costs $0.50 to $1 but if fries or another patty are added, the cost could increase to $2 to $2.50, and loaves of bread are practically a steal at $1 to $1.50. There is always a federal prisoner working in the kitchens who will steal and sell whatever can be slipped away.

The Laundry

The laundry is another black market hotbed. From the laundry comes bleach, laundry bags, towels, sheets, t-shirts, belts, new pants, and new button-up shirts (with or without identification labels affixed). An eight-ounce bottle of bleach will typically fetch $2.50. A new t-shirt will run around $1.00 while a new large towel goes for around $5.00.

Although federal prisons do issue clothing to new arrivals and officially reissue clothes at six-month or annual intervals, they are often used or of the lowest possible quality. These items wear out and become shabby quickly, so the market for them is healthy.

> *TIP: A word of caution regarding the purchase of bleach: bleach can be considered a weapon and is prohibited from unauthorized inmate possession. Buy only enough for immediate need. Keeping a supply of it around is asking for trouble, and it can result in an incident report.*

Laundry facilities vary in different federal prisons. Some prisoners must use a central laundry for washing and drying their clothes; others use machines in their housing unit. Because the FBOP has implemented a water-reduction policy that reduced the availability of in-unit washers and dryers, chances are good that most inmates will have to use the central laundry at some point. Centralized laundries are notorious for producing dingy, smelly clothes – after they've been washed – so demand for special services is high.

The centralized laundry employs inmate workers, so the opportunity is always available to pay (under the table) to have clothes washed separately or to have worn clothing replaced. This kind of service can run from $5 to $10 a month, depending on the going rate at a particular facility.

In facilities utilizing in-unit washers and dryers, inmates might be able to pay the unit's laundry operator to push their clothes to the front of the line, fold the laundry after it is washed, or allow for additional bags of dirty laundry to be cleaned each week.

Clerks Hustle, Too

Clerks in various departments are usually the head inmates for a particular work detail under the supervision of staff members. They have their own hustle, a way to make money outside official channels. Those who work in the electrical shop, for example, might sell wire, solder, or services repairing radios, headphones, clocks, and MP3 players. Clerks who work in the chapel, law library, prison staff areas, or education departments often steal and sell office supplies (highlighters, sticky notes, pens, pads of paper, etc.) at the going rate. As in the world outside of prison, existing relationships or bulk purchases might result in discounts.

> *TIP: When selecting a fellow prisoner to work on an electrical device, make sure to ask one or two of their former clients about their ability and examine the work product prior to coming to an agreement. There are always a few idiots in prison who are more than happy to be paid to rip apart a radio, headphones, or MP3 player and try to fix it. Don't be fooled. Use only a reputable person who has a proven track record of successful projects. And stick with this person as long as they are incarcerated at the same prison.*

Clerks in various areas of the facility who have access to a staff copier might sell copies on the black market. The fee for this depends on the number of copies needed and what is being copied (gambling tickets and pornography would most certainly earn a surcharge) but generally copies on the black market will cost less than copies made legitimately using the copy cards from the institutional commissary.

Barbers

Besides stolen property or the unauthorized use of laundry or copy machines, the black market offers a plethora of services. For example, inmates in the housing units might offer grooming services using moustache scissors and beard trimmers. The official option for haircuts is the facility's barber shop where the barber is paid a work assignment wage from the prison administration. They also expect an informal, under-the-table tip. Around $1.50 to $2.00 is customary.

Services of Convenience

Countless other services of convenience are available. Washing and ironing clothes are popular hustles. If a prisoner doesn't want to wake up early on a Saturday morning to sign up for a DVD slot in the chapel or education department, someone is probably willing to do it for a fee. If a prisoner doesn't want to get up early in the mornings to take their dirty clothes to laundry services, fellow prisoners would certainly be open to making the trip for a few stamps. The same is true for cooking all sorts of food.

Teresa Giudice located the services that were important to her ... namely, spa treatments. She paid other inmates to do her nails, style her hair, tailor her clothes, and give her massages.[9] As long as the prisoner has the money and is willing to spend it, a fellow prisoner will almost always be available to perform whatever services are required.

Protecting Oneself

In prison, inmates live with unpredictable people. Never forget that. Although there are some good people in prison, most inmates have a propensity to engage in shady dealings, to lie, cheat, steal, and much worse should the opportunity arise.

Kluger echoed this sentiment when he was interviewed. "Be careful about trusting people," he said. "You know, for the most part, these are criminals that you're with, and you're not going to get a straight story from a lot of them. So be careful how much faith you put in the things that you hear."[10]

One more thing regarding the prison trade and the convict store: a prisoner should never lend anything to anyone unless the prisoner is prepared to never see it again or to never see it operable again (as with electronics). Fellow prisoners will often dodge a creditor for a tab of less than $1.00. If they rack up a huge debt, they are likely to check in to avoid that debt.

The bottom line regarding commercial transactions in the prison marketplace is this: do not make oneself a target, and think transactions through before engaging in them.

> *TIP: Generally speaking, people act in a way that is advantageous to their personal interests. So, do what can be done to make others' personal interests the same as one's own. For example, a kitchen worker or store man is more likely to deal honestly if they know the agreement is for the long term. They are looking for a continuous stream of profit,*

and they know that responsible and honest business practices are the way to keep them.

Sending and Receiving Funds

Work details aren't the only way for inmates to access funds. Friends and relatives can send money to inmates using special FBOP accounts. Additionally, inmates can send funds to individuals outside the prison. Here's how.

Trust Fund/Commissary Account

Inmates in the FBOP are not allowed to possess actual money. Instead, they are assigned a trust fund account that is used for all monetary needs.[11] This central institutional account – which acts much like a checking and savings account – is used for commissary purchases, "TRU" purchases (email and MP3s), telephone minute purchases, and postage costs.

Inmates can have funds deposited through outside family, friends, and others, or through the prison administration for institutional work details and other incentives. Outside sources can deposit funds through the mail, Western Union, and MoneyGram. FBOP institutions deposit funds near the beginning of each month for work performed at institutional work details.[b]

Depositing Funds

Depositing Funds via U.S. Mail

Funds can be deposited to a trust fund account through the FBOP's National LockBox via U.S. Mail. No fee is charged for this service. To deposit funds via LockBox, the outside party must mail a U.S. Treasury, state, or local government

[b] *The exception to the two deposit methods noted above occurs when a self-surrendering inmate (one who turns themselves in to a specific prison at a specific time in accordance with a court order) arrives at the prison with money on their person. It is advised that inmates bring funds in cash or a U.S. Postal Service money order made out to their full committed name and inmate number.*

check, U.S. Postal Service money order, or foreign negotiable instrument payable in U.S. currency to:

Federal Bureau of Prisons
(Inmate's Committed Name)
(Inmate's Eight-digit Register Number)
Post Office Box 474701
Des Moines, Iowa 50947-0001

Regardless of the kind of negotiable instrument (personal checks are not permitted), it must be made out with a full committed name and register number. The sender's contact information must appear on the envelope, and nothing but the negotiable instrument is to be enclosed. Letters, pictures, and other items in the envelope will be returned to the sender.

Depositing Funds via Western Union

Funds can be deposited to an inmate's account through Western Union's Quick Collect program. Funds sent between 7:00 a.m. and 9:00 p.m. EST will be deposited to the account within two to four hours. If funds are sent after 9:00 p.m. EST, they will be deposited to the account by 9:00 a.m. EST the following morning. This includes weekends and holidays.

Western Union charges a fee that fluctuates depending on the amount of funds being sent. Family and friends have three ways to send funds via the Quick Collect program:

1) They can go to a Western Union location and complete a blue Quick Collect form using cash or a debit/credit card. To find a location, call 1-800-325-6000 or go to www.WesternUnion.com.
2) They can call 1-800-634-3422 (using option 2) to deposit funds via telephone. This method utilizes credit/debit cards only.
3) They can go to www.WesternUnion.com and deposit funds to an inmate's account via the automated transaction system. This method also utilizes credit/debit cards.

Regardless of the inmate's location – as long as they are in federal custody – the following information must *always* be provided when sending funds through Western Union:

- The inmate's committed name
- The inmate's registration number
- City code: FBOP
- State code: DC

When the time for Kristin Davis' incarceration approached, she sent herself money through Western Union three days before her intake date. She found that because the funds were there when she arrived, she was able to access her funds more quickly. The process of setting everything up inside the facility still took four days but once it was finished, she could use the funds.[12]

Depositing Funds via MoneyGram

Funds can also be deposited to an inmate's account through MoneyGram's Express Payment program. Funds sent between 7:00 a.m. and 10:00 p.m. EST will be deposited to the inmate's account within two to four hours. If funds are sent after 10:00 p.m. EST, they will be deposited to the inmate's account by 9:00 a.m. EST the following morning, including weekends and holidays. MoneyGram charges a fee of up to $9.95 for U.S. cash transfers of up to $5,000.00.

MoneyGram's Express Payment program is only available at MoneyGram locations. It does not allow funds to be sent to inmates via telephone or a website. To find a MoneyGram location, call 1-800-926-9400 or go to www.MoneyGram.com.

Regardless of an inmate's location – as long as he or she is in federal custody – the following information must *always* be provided when sending funds through MoneyGram:

- Company name: Federal Bureau of Prisons (FBOP)
- City & State: Washington, DC
- Receive code: 7932
- Account number: Inmate's last name and register number (no spaces)
- Message to Biller or Beneficiary Name: Inmate's Full Committed Name

A Cautionary Note

The FBOP is constantly on the lookout for disciplinary infractions involving the transfer of money between confined inmates because it is a prohibited act.[13] As such, prison authorities pay close attention to who sends money to which inmates. They also attempt to identify persons outside of the prison who deposit money into multiple inmates' trust fund accounts. This is a telltale sign of one inmate having someone outside of prison place funds into another inmate's account.

With this in mind, do not ask a family member or friend to place funds into another inmate's trust fund account. If a person does so of their own accord, it is arguably permissible … though they might consider having someone else do it or placing a different sender's name on the negotiable instrument. If someone outside of prison is placing funds into two different inmates' trust fund accounts, both prisoners run the risk of being flagged for potentially engaging in prohibited conduct.

Likewise, prisoners should not ask anyone to place funds into anyone else's trust fund account. Even suggesting a prohibited act can be construed as attempting to engage in a prohibited act, which is a disciplinary violation.

Sending Money to the Outside

With the advent of the TRULINCS computer system has come two new methods that allow inmates to send money from their trust fund accounts to outside recipients: BP-199s/U.S. Treasury Checks and MoneyGram.

BP-199s/U.S. Treasury Checks

This first method occurs through the use of electronic BP-199s (the FBOP document used to authorize the withdrawal of funds). No longer do inmates fill out a "green form" bubble sheet; the majority of the process is now handled electronically.

In order to send money from their trust fund account, the inmate must first log onto a TRULINCS computer. Once at the welcome screen, they will find a link entitled "Manage Funds." When selected, a new screen allows the inmate to send funds, view pending transfers, or review rejected transfers. In order to open each window, the inmate must select the applicable link (either "Send Funds" or "View Pending/Rejected BP-199s").

TIP: All outgoing funds sent via BP-199s are in the form of a U.S. Treasury Check.

When sending funds, the inmate first selects if the withdrawal is a one-time event or is to be executed monthly. If monthly, a start and end month and year will need to be inputted.

TIP: Monthly transfers are processed on the 15th of each month. If the monthly BP-199 isn't processed by the 15th of the start month, the first transfer will occur on the 15th of the following month.

Next, the inmate will select the reason for the withdrawal (i.e., the "Withdrawal Type") followed by the amount of the check and memo, if desired.

Last, the inmate selects the payee (where the check is to go). Only existing contacts are listed as valid payees, so the inmate must have already added them as a contact prior to initiating the transaction.

If the inmate desires to have the check placed in an envelope at their institution (a stamped and preaddressed envelope the inmate must furnish) – as in the case of a book order or a magazine subscription – they must select the "c/o Cashier" box located under the payee contact information on the lower right-hand side.

TIP: The "c/o Cashier" box will only illuminate when one of the following withdrawal types is selected: Books, Gov't Doc Required, Headphones, Outside Savings, Release Funds, Subscriptions, and Tuition.

Once all the applicable information has been entered, the inmate will click the "Save and Print" link located at the bottom right-hand corner. After acknowledging the confirmation message, the inmate will need to go to their prison library and print off the new BP-199. They will then sign this form and turn it in to either their counselor or unit secretary for processing.

TIP: By turning in the BP-199 to the secretary, the inmate might find that it goes through less scrutiny and is processed more quickly. All BP-199s for $500 or less will be sent directly to the Trust Fund office for processing. These typically take around a week or two to process.

All BP-199s for over $500 are first sent to an associate warden for signature. The AW then forwards the signed BP-199 to Trust Fund for processing. The AW step usually adds an additional two weeks.

From the moment the inmate confirms the transaction, it will be listed in the Pending/Rejected BP-199 window along with the commissary transaction window within the account transactions folio. To cancel a pending BP-199, the inmate must select the pending transaction in the "View Pending/Rejected BP-199s" window. At this point, a link titled "Cancel BP-199" will illuminate. Once this link is clicked – and confirmed – the encumbered funds will be released and the transaction will be cancelled.

TIP: Once the inmate inputs the information for the BP-199 to be processed – by clicking "Save and Print" – the funds to be withdrawn become encumbered. The funds will remain encumbered until the BP-199 is processed by the trust fund office. At that point, the encumbrance is released and the funds are withdrawn.

MoneyGram

As with the above protocols for BP-199/U.S. Treasury check money transfers, inmates can follow the same basic principles to electronically send funds to a community contact from their contact list. This is accomplished by going to the "Manage Funds" screen and clicking on the MoneyGram tab. The inmate will be able to select a recipient and the dollar amount. They will also have to agree to the terms of service. Inmates are only permitted to send $100 at a time through this service and only one MoneyGram per day. A $4.95 fee is assessed per transaction.

Once the prisoner has sent the funds, the recipient will receive an email containing the authorization code. They then locate a MoneyGram location where the funds will be collected in person. MoneyGram locations can be found by calling 1-800-926-9400 or visiting www.moneygram.com.

Notes

1. Program Statement 4500.11, Trust Fund/Deposit Fund Manual at Chapter 3.
2. Program Statement 5270.09, Inmate Discipline Program; 28 C.F.R. § 541.3.
3. Program Statement P5380.08, Financial Responsibility Program, Inmate at § 8; 28 C.F.R. § 545.1.
4. Zengerle, Jason, "What a Jail Sentence Taught One Politician About Prisons." *GQ*. November 12, 2015.
5. *Id.*
6. Program Statement 4500.11, Trust Fund/Deposit Fund Manual.
7. Program Statement 5270.09, Inmate Discipline Program; 28 C.F.R. § 541.3.
8. Roberts, Daniel, "Life Behind Bars: Matthew Kluger Reveals All." July 7, 2014. *Fortune.*
9. McShane, Larry, "'Real Housewives of New Jersey' Star Teresa Giudice Reveals the Details of Her Year Spent Behind Bars in New Book — Including Lots of Lesbian Sex." *NY Daily News.* January 30, 2016.
10. Roberts, Daniel, "Life Behind Bars: Matthew Kluger Reveals All." July 7, 2014. *Fortune.*
11. Program Statement 4500.11, Trust Fund/Deposit Fund Manual.
12. Davis, Kristin, "I Am Now Property of the Federal Government, Inmate 69007-054." XOJane. Jan 21, 2015. Retrieved from http://www.xojane.com/it-happened-to-me/kristin-davis-prison-journal.
13. Program Statement 5270.09, Inmate Discipline Program; 28 C.F.R. § 541.3.

Part IV – Medical/ Psychological Care

Nine

Health Services

Healthcare for Bureau inmates is an entitlement guaranteed by U.S. Supreme Court decisional law and other law. The denial of adequate care for a serious medical need can constitute grounds for a claim under the Eighth Amendment's cruel and unusual punishments clause.[1]

At the end of 2003, 28 percent of all inmates in the U.S. were between the ages of 40 and 54, an increase of 22 percent in less than a decade. Inmates 54 and older increased nearly 85 percent in the same period.[2] Our nation spends more than $16 billion annually to care for aging inmates.[3]

Elderly or not, inmates have greater medical needs than the population outside prison walls. The National Commission on Correctional Health Care reported in 2002 that federal prisoners suffer asthma at about 4 percent of the population, diabetes at 4 percent, and hypertension at 8 percent.[4] Because these numbers are self-reported, the commission felt that the data might underestimate the incidences of certain medical conditions, "especially those that require more sophisticated diagnosis."[5]

As might be expected in a population confined in crowded conditions, communicable diseases also thrive. Sexually transmitted diseases (STDs) are among those; other common illnesses are Hepatitis B and C, with rates among federal prisoners ranging from 8 percent to 43 percent in 2005, and tuberculosis

(TB) rates ranging from 2.9 percent to 11.8 percent. HIV/AIDS rates run more than twice as high in prison populations than in the general U.S. population. AIDS is, in fact, the second leading cause of death in prisons.[6]

These elements make for additional burdens on a system that is primarily focused on incarceration rather than medical assistance. Additionally, doctors are used to issuing orders, directing care, and operating in the best interests of the patient, whereas correctional administrators might view medical procedures as distractions from safety and security.[7] To ensure that inmates receive the best available care, this chapter lays out the services, facilities, and procedures for requesting and obtaining care in federal prison.

Triage and Access to Care

Medical care in the FBOP is provided through a triage system, which is a classification of patients "according to priority of need for examination and/or treatment."[8] According to the Bureau, this system "allows truly urgent conditions to be addressed adequately on the same day, while also allowing more routine conditions or concerns to be addressed at a scheduled appointment."[9]

In practice, many facilities use preprinted forms called Inmate Request for Triage Services. The triage form is filled out by the inmate and placed in a mailbox in the health services lobby. This practice has replaced the more traditional method of triage that involved a quick consultation with a health care provider at a morning "sick call" held several days a week. Dental sick call is an exception to this rule, with inmates being briefly evaluated by a dentist and then being scheduled for an appointment to address the issue.

Experience reveals that at institutions using the triage form rather than sick call, a same-day visit for care is rare. Unless thc inmate is in dire condition or is referred to medical staff for emergency care, he or she will wait several days to several weeks for an appointment.

Categories of Care

The Bureau of Prisons provides five defined levels of care to inmates.[10]

Medically Necessary - Acute or Emergent

This level is for medical conditions that are of an "immediate, acute, or emergent nature and which, without care, would cause rapid deterioration of the inmate's health, significant irreversible loss of function, or may be life-threatening."[11] Examples of conditions considered acute or emergent include but are not limited to:

- Myocardial infarction (heart attack);
- Severe trauma such as head injuries;
- Hemorrhage;
- Stroke;
- Status asthmatics;
- Precipitous labor or complications associated with pregnancy; and
- Detached retina or sudden loss of vision.

Treatment for conditions in this category is necessary to sustain life or function and warrant immediate attention.[12]

Medically Necessary - Non-emergent

These medical conditions are "not immediately life-threatening," but without care the inmate runs a significant risk of:

- Serious deterioration leading to premature death;
- Significant reduction in the possibility of repair later without present treatment; and
- Significant pain or discomfort which impairs the inmate's participation in activities of daily living.[13]

Examples of medically necessary, non-emergent conditions include but are not limited to:

- Chronic conditions (diabetes, heart disease, bipolar disorder, schizophrenia);

- Infectious disease in which treatment allows for a return to a previous state of health or improved quality of life (HIV, tuberculosis); and
- Cancer.[14]

Medically Acceptable - Not Always Necessary

In this category are medical conditions considered to be "elective procedures" or treatments that "may improve the inmate's quality of life."[15] Examples in this category include but are not limited to:

- Joint replacement;
- Reconstruction of the anterior cruciate knee ligament; and
- Treatment of noncancerous skin conditions (skin tags, lipomas).

These therapeutic interventions always require review by the Institution Utilization Review Committee. Factors considered for approval of the proposed treatment include, but are not limited to:

- The risks and benefits of the treatment;
- Available resources;
- Natural history of the condition; and
- The effect of the intervention on the inmate's functioning in his or her activities of daily living.[16]

Limited Medical Value

These are medical conditions for which treatment provides "little or no medical value" and "are not likely to provide substantial long-term gain, or are expressly for the inmate's convenience."[17] Procedures in this category are usually excluded from the scope of services provided. Examples in this category include but are not limited to:

- Minor conditions that are self-limiting;
- Cosmetic procedures such as blepharoplasty; and
- Removal of non-cancerous skin lesions.

Any treatment in this category recommended by a health care provider and that the clinical director feels is appropriate will require a review by the Institution Utilization Review Committee.[18]

Extraordinary

Medical intervention is deemed extraordinary if it affects the "life of another individual, such as organ transplantation" or if it is "considered investigational in nature."[19] Any treatment in this category requires the medical director's review and approval with notification to the regional director.

Ambulatory Care: The FBOP's Healthcare Model

The FBOP's primary model for delivering healthcare services utilizes "primary care provider teams" (PCPTs), which are "designed to function in the same manner as a medical office in a community setting."[20] In most instances, this model means that inmates will not see a traditional doctor or even a nurse when seeking medical services. Instead, their primary contact will be a midlevel practitioner (MLP) or a physician's assistant (PA). Referrals to higher-level caregivers are made only when deemed necessary. Members of the PCPT are detailed in this section.

Physician

A physician will "provide clinical oversight for multiple provider teams." The physician, as the licensed provider of the team, is responsible for the care the team delivers. As such, it is the physician's responsibility:

- To consult with the other team members;
- To provide training and mentoring; and
- To directly evaluate and treat severely ill and medically complex inmates.

While the MLP is the PCPT's primary care provider, physicians are also responsible for providing direct patient care. Physicians will medically manage inmates with complex conditions on an ongoing basis notwithstanding the assignment of that inmate to an MLP. At least one physician per 1,000 general population inmates is required under FBOP policy.[21]

Mid-level Practitioner (MLP)

The MLP will serve as the primary point of contact for inmates assigned to their caseload. They will serve as the primary provider for:

- Routine requests for evaluation of new complaints;
- Ongoing management of reoccurring conditions; and
- Emergencies when clinically indicated.

At least three MLPs per 1,000 general population inmates are required under FBOP policy.[22]

Clinical Nurse (RN)

The clinical nurse will serve as the coordinator for the outpatient area. Duties will include but not be limited to:

- Managing patient flow and triage;
- Responding to institution emergencies with MLP or physician backup;
- Coordinating the workload and duties of the licensed practical/vocational nurse (LPN/LVN);
- Screening new arrivals and assessing inmates returning from consultant visits or hospitalizations; and
- Providing patient education, etc.

At least one clinical nurse per 1,000 general population inmates is required under FBOP policy.[23]

Licensed Practical/Vocational Nurse (LPN/VPN)

The LPN/VPN is accountable to the RN and provides healthcare support for the other clerical staff. LPN/VPN duties include but are not limited to:

- Collecting patient information including vital signs and blood pressure checks;
- Providing dressing changes;
- Administering treatments and/or medications; and
- Performing EKGs, etc.

At least one LPN/VPN per 1,000 general population inmates is required under FBOP policy.[24]

Health Information Technician (HIT)

The HIT will obtain medical records for healthcare providers. Other duties include:

- Entering Sensitive Medical Data (SMD) data;
- Filing lab/x-ray/consultant reports; and
- Scheduling consultant visits, etc.

At least two HITs per 1,000 general population inmates are required under FBOP policy.[25]

Medical Clerical Staff

Clerical staff is responsible for:

- Ordering and stocking forms and supplies in the examination and treatment rooms;
- Entering Sensitive Medical Data (SMD) data;
- Filing lab/x-ray/consultant reports;
- Answering the telephone; and
- Locating inmates who do not report for scheduled appointments.

At least one medical clerical staff per 1,000 general population inmates is required under FBOP policy.[26]

Care Levels

The Federal Bureau of Prisons uses an inmate's medical fitness as a factor in their institutional placement and the manner in which medical care will be delivered. While not described in published policies or regulations, the Bureau now classifies inmates according to medical needs. This can play a role in where the inmate is designated.

Care Level 1 inmates are characterized as generally healthy with no special needs. Level 2 inmates are those with chronic conditions that are relatively well controlled with periodic review. Examples are a high blood pressure condition regulated by medication, those on antidepressant medications, and high-functioning diabetics.

Care Level 3 inmates are those with chronic conditions or who need regular assistance with daily living activities. Often cancer treatment survivors, inmates with severe cardiac issues, and the like are deemed Level 3 inmates. Level 4 inmates are those with grave medical issues requiring inpatient medical care.

The difference between a Care Level 1 and a Care Level 2 facility is usually determined by the institution's location. Level 1 facilities are located more than an hour from a major medical center. Level 2 facilities are closer, allowing for more utilization of outside assistance. Care Level 3 facilities are somewhat rare, and usually are located adjacent to a Bureau medical center that has greater medical capabilities. Care Level 4 facilities are the Federal Medical Centers.

While a care level assignment is not the determining factor in inmate placement, it can influence where the inmate is placed. As such, it is important for those newly entering the system to be complete and forthcoming about their medical conditions.

Utilization Review Committee

Each FBOP institution has a Utilization Review Committee (URC) chaired by its clinical director. The URC considers the allocation of resources for outside medical, surgical, and dental procedures; specialist evaluations; escorted medical trips; and other nonstandard medical services.[27] At some institutions, the URC is engaged in day-to-day decision-making; at other facilities, they consider only major decisions. In general, inmates simply need to be aware that every request for a special review is scrutinized.

Pill Line/Insulin Line Procedures

General population inmates who require medications obtain them via one of several methods.

Non-insulin Medications

Many non-insulin medications can be dispensed via a regular prescription the inmate picks up at the institutional pharmacy, which is usually adjacent to the health services area. The inmate is authorized to "self-carry" the medicine and store it in his or her locker or on their person.[28] Refills are made the same way.[29]

Certain medications are administered only at "pill line," which occurs several times a day at most facilities. Generally, mind-altering medications, medications that tend to be abused, or medications that require strict monitoring will be dispensed only at pill line. Inmates are required to appear at the pharmacy window with an ID card or other authorized identification. The inmate is required to swallow the medication and drink water in the presence of the pharmacy technician.

At some facilities, staff will ask the inmate to open their mouth to show that the medication has been swallowed.[30] At some facilities, pharmacy staff will allow an inmate to self-carry certain medications that would otherwise be dispensed at pill line if that inmate demonstrates regular and consistent medication usage; for example, after fourteen consecutive days of attending pill line.

TIP: The FBOP uses a National Drug Formulary for medications which does not list many common medications. Inmates who require non-formulary medications might have to be diligent in requesting them. An example would be Ritalin to treat ADHD; the Bureau does not usually dispense Ritalin.

Insulin Procedures

Inmates needing regular insulin are required to appear at insulin line, which is usually held twice a day. Inmates requiring injections will perform the injection themselves at the window with a syringe prepared by staff. Strict monitoring of needles and syringes is common, and syringes are returned immediately after use. Most facilities also supply insulin-dependent inmates with portable blood sugar testers like finger-stick monitors and other equipment.

Inmate Copay Program

Per the Medical Copay Act,[31] most inmates confined in the FBOP must pay a copay fee of $2.00 per visit for health care. Inmates confined at Medical Referral Centers are exempt from this requirement.[32] Services exempt from the copay requirement include:

- Healthcare services based on staff referrals;
- Staff-approved follow-up care for a chronic condition;
- Preventative healthcare;
- Emergency services;
- Prenatal care;
- Diagnosis or treatment of chronic infectious diseases;
- Mental healthcare; and
- Substance abuse treatment.[33]

Inmates without funds who are deemed indigent are not assessed the copay fee. Indigent inmates are those who have not had a trust fund balance of more than $6.00 for the past thirty days. All other inmates will be assessed the copay fee. If sufficient funds are not in the inmate's trust fund account at the time, the inmate's account will be levied until the debt is paid.[34]

Refusal of Treatment

Inmates may refuse medical treatment subject to certain exceptions. As a general rule, medical and dental treatment, including medication, is given "only when the inmate consents."[35] Exceptions might be made when medical staff determine that refusal of treatment "would result in danger to the life of, or serious permanent injury to, the inmate" or that the inmate "poses a serious risk to others by refusing treatment" (as with infectious tuberculosis, for example). An exception might be made if there is a court-ordered evaluation or treatment.[36]

In addition, inmates might be required to participate in diagnostic procedures relating to communicable diseases, including but not limited to tuberculin screening tests, chest x-rays, and blood specimens for hepatitis or HIV (post-exposure incident). An incident report might be issued for refusal of such testing.[37]

Emergency and Urgent Care

While all FBOP facilities have a plan for twenty-four-hour medical emergency and urgent care, the manner by which such services are delivered can vary from one institution to another.

American Correctional Association standards require that prisons be able to respond to a life- or limb-threatening medical emergency within four minutes.[38] To meet this requirement, every institution has a team of "first responders" established for each shift. These individuals hold documented training in first aid and CPR.[39] Most FBOP facilities have a medical specialist on call at all times, who might be a physician, an MLP, or an EMT.

An inmate who feels that they are in need of immediate medical attention can approach any available staff member for assistance. Should an inmate need care beyond that available at the institution, emergency transport to an outside medical facility will be arranged.

TIP: Experience reveals that some line-level staff members are hesitant to contact medical staff for less than life-threatening matters when asked by an inmate, as in the case of respiratory distress or chest pains. An inmate in distress should make efforts to speak to a lieutenant or other senior officer if a line officer appears unwilling to help. Usually these senior officers are more willing to contact medical staff.

Eye Care

The FBOP permits inmates to retain their prescription eyeglasses upon admission. Prior to 2013, inmates could order replacements or new glasses from outside vendors. Presently, however, after admission, inmates who need new or replacement eyeglasses (or repairs to existing glasses) must obtain them from Bureau suppliers. The current FBOP vendor is FCI Butner. While hardly fashionable, the standard plastic frames are sturdy and functional.

Inmates are not authorized to use contact lenses unless they meet a narrow standard determined by the Bureau's doctors or contract doctors. Generally, contact lenses are only permitted with a diagnosis of keratoconus or for inmates with artificial lens implants.[40] Inmates who do not meet the standard will be scheduled for an eye exam for prescription eyeglasses and will be required to send their contact lenses home when their glasses arrive. Bureau policy does require that facilities "ensure adequate contact lens supplies are available" for inmates awaiting eyeglasses.

Deafness and Hearing Aids

As with eyeglasses, inmates who enter the Bureau with personal hearing aids are permitted to keep them. Replacements and new issuances are made only via Bureau vendors.[41] Policy requires that the Bureau supply inmates with hearing aid batteries.

Advance Healthcare Directives and "Do Not Resuscitate" Orders

When it comes to advance directives, inmates may direct, in advance, to withhold or withdraw certain medical treatments when recovery or cure is not possible. Inmates may appoint, in advance, proxy decision-makers who will make critical decisions for them should they become incapacitated and unable to make such decisions for themselves.[42]

According to policy, "the Bureau's withholding or withdrawal of resuscitative or life-support services pursuant to an Advance Directive or DNR order, is consistent with sound medical practice and is not associated with assisting suicide, voluntary euthanasia, or expediting the inmate's death. The patient's right to refuse medical treatment is not absolute and, in all cases, will be weighed against legitimate governmental interests, including the security and orderly operation of correctional institutions."[43]

As to "do not resuscitate" (DNR) orders, the Bureau allows inmates to request that a DNR be placed in their medical file *only* when they are housed at a Bureau medical center or an outside hospital. "DNR orders *will never* be invoked while an inmate is housed at a general population institution. Emergency resuscitative measures must always be performed on an inmate who suffers cardiopulmonary arrest at a general population institution."[44]

Hospice and End-of-Life Care

As inmates age, the average cost of housing them in federal facilities nearly doubles from $27,549 per year to $58,956 including prescription drugs and elder-care treatments. The situation is so severe that at some facilities, healthy inmates are paid to work as companions for others who need assistance.[45] These elderly inmates can also never be assured that they will have access to the right specialists or medical assistance that arrives quickly enough.[46]

One step being taken to address end-of-life care is the opening of prison hospice programs. Hospice care provides palliative care, which is the relief of pain, stress, physical distress, and anxiety that comes with serious illnesses or the death process. Rather than treating only the body, hospice care tends to emotional and even spiritual needs.

The Federal Medical Center at Fort Worth, Texas is one of six federal prison medical centers and has an inmate hospice program first introduced in 1994. The facility focuses on palliative care, which is provided for the patient and their disease when there is no cure. Inmate volunteers sit with the patients, read to them, and write letters when they are too weak to do so themselves. In addition to easing individuals into the final stage of their lives, the program has considerably reduced the cost of caring for terminally ill inmates.[47]

Since America has a large number of prisoners who will die of old age behind bars, these new facilities are critically important. When they first opened, referrals could only be made at the last six months of life. The programs have since evolved to accept patients when it is deemed appropriate by their doctors. Inmates can be referred by their regular physician. Prisoners who wish to volunteer as assistants must go through a 30-hour training program.[48]

Female Medical Care

Beyond the care given to all inmates, female inmates confined in the FBOP are entitled to other, gender-specific medical care. The following elements apply to routine physical examinations of female inmates:

- A gynecological and obstetrical history, including sexual activity and any recent rape history;
- A pregnancy test for females of childbearing age (urine or serum) and other tests as clinically indicated;
- A breast and pelvic examination. A female staff member will be present when a male provider performs breast and pelvic examinations (except in emergency situations when a female staff member is not available). Annual breast examinations will be made available to inmates upon request. Self-examination instructions will be given to all females at the time of the breast examination;
- Pap smears and collection of chlamydia, gonorrhea, and/or endocervical cultures from vaginal and/or anal orifices when clinically indicated;
- Mammograms are also offered to female inmates over forty years of age as a baseline diagnostic tool. Inmates are permitted to refuse a mammogram; and
- Prescription birth control is generally not offered to inmates unless required for hormone manipulation as treatment for menstrual irregularity or for post-menopausal women as clinically indicated.[49]

Inmates entering the Bureau with IUDs or other implanted contraceptive devices can have them removed upon request.[50]

Inmates are entitled to a full spectrum of healthcare if they become pregnant while in FBOP custody.[51] At present, pregnant inmates are permitted to bring their child to birth or to have an abortion; the choice is solely the inmate's. However, unless an abortion is required because "the life of the mother would be endangered if the fetus is carried to term, or in the case of rape," government funds cannot be used to pay for the abortion. In all other cases, non-Bureau funds must be obtained to pay for any abortion procedure, or else the planned abortion may not be performed.[52]

Regarding childbirth, Bureau policy is that prior to an inmate giving birth, the warden will ensure that the person or agency taking custody of the child takes responsibility for all medical expenses from the time of delivery (including the first three days after birth). Unit management, or a social worker if available, will obtain a signed statement of responsibility from whoever receives custody of the child to confirm that the signing party accepts financial responsibility for the child's medical expenses. A copy of the signed statement of responsibility will be sent to the Health Services Administrator for placement in outside hospitalization.

Administrative discretion to pay for the immediate postnatal care of a child born to a female inmate is authorized when no other resource can be compelled to pay. Legislation is not required to authorize payment for the child's immediate medical needs. It is reasonable for the Bureau to provide for the child's medical expenses for the first three days following routine vaginal delivery, or for up to seven days following delivery by Cesarean section.

The regional director can extend this an additional seven days for extenuating circumstances on a case-by-case basis. Any further extension will require approval from the medical director.[53]

Gender Identity Disorder

In 2012, in response to a settlement in *Adams v. Federal Bureau of Prisons*, 716 F.Supp.2d 107 (D. Mass. 2010), the Bureau changed its policy regarding inmates diagnosed with gender dysphoria, called Gender Identity Disorder (GID) within the FBOP. The new policy requires that inmates diagnosed with GID (or transsexualism) be given treatment consistent with that given in the community at large.

Program Statement 6031.04, Patient Care, § 30 provides that "inmates with a possible diagnosis of Gender Identity Disorder (GID), including inmates who assert they have GID, will receive thorough medical and mental health evaluations from medical professionals with basic competence in the assessment of the DSM-IV/ICD-10 sexual disorders and who have participated in BOP's GID training, including the review of all available community health records.

"The evaluation will include an assessment of the inmate's treatment and life experiences prior to incarceration as well as experiences during incarceration, including hormone therapy, completed or in-process surgical interventions, real life experience consistent with the inmate's gender identity, private expressions that conform to the preferred gender, and counseling.

"If a diagnosis of GID is reached, a proposed treatment plan will be developed which promotes the physical and mental stability of the patient. The development of the treatment plan is not solely dependent on services provided or the inmate's life experiences prior to incarceration. The treatment plan may include elements or services that were, or were not, provided prior to incarceration, including, but not limited to elements of the real life experience consistent with the prison environment, hormone therapy, and counseling. Treatment plans will be reviewed regularly and updated as necessary.

"Current, accepted standards of care will be used as a reference for developing the treatment plan. All appropriate treatment options prescribed for inmates with GID as currently accepted standards of care will be taken into consideration during evaluation by the appropriate medical and mental health care staff. Each treatment plan or denial of treatment must be reviewed by the Medical Director or BOP Chief Physician. Hormone therapy must be requested through the non-formulary review process and approved by the Medical Director and/or Chief Psychiatrist. Consultation with the Chief of Psychology prior to such approval may be appropriate in some cases.

"In summary, inmates in the Bureau's custody with a possible diagnosis of GID will receive an individualized assessment and evaluation. Treatment options will not be precluded solely due to level of services received prior to incarceration."

Infectious Diseases

FBOP policy dictates that its control of infectious diseases can include voluntary, mandatory, and involuntary testing when required.[54]

Generally, voluntary testing for HIV, hepatitis, and certain other diseases is provided upon inmate request. Mandatory testing for diseases is performed "when there are risk factors and the test is clinically indicated and/or surveillance testing is required."[55] An example of such testing would be for tuberculosis, which is mandatory for all inmates, usually annually. Likewise, an inmate might be required to undergo "clinically indicated" testing for a disease when evidence indicates a need. An example would be HIV testing for an inmate who has been deemed high risk pursuant to Center for Disease Control (CDC) guidelines. A refusal would result in an incident report.[56]

Involuntary testing will be performed following a documented "exposure" incident when there is a "well-founded reason to believe that the inmate may have transmitted [a disease such as HIV], whether intentionally or unintentionally, to Bureau employees . . . Exposure incident testing does not require the inmate's consent."[57] Involuntary testing may be conducted via use of force.[58]

In rare instances, an inmate or group of inmates might be placed in isolated quarantine status when an infectious disease is detected.

Notes

1. *Estelle v. Gamble,* 429 U.S. 97, 104 (1976).
2. Today's Prisoners: Changing Demographics, Health Issues, and the Current Research Environment. Available from: http://www.ncbi.nlm.nih.gov/books/NBK19877/.
3. Vestal, Christine, "For Aging Inmates, Care Outside Prison Walls." *Stateline.* August 12, 2014.
4. National Commission on Correctional Health Care (NCCHC). 2002.
5. *Id.*

6. *Id.*
7. Dubler, Nancy, "Ethical Dilemmas In Prison And Jail Health Care." Health Affairs Blog. March 10, 2014. Retrieved from http://healthaffairs.org/blog/2014/03/10/ethical-dilemmas-in-prison-and-jail-health-care/.
8. Program Statement 6031.04, Patient Care at § 17.
9. *Id.*
10. *Id.* at § 7.
11. *Id.* at § 7(a).
12. *Id.*
13. *Id.* at § 7(b).
14. *Id.*
15. *Id.* at § 17(c).
16. *Id.*
17. *Id.* at § 17(d).
18. *Id.*
19. *Id.* at § 17(e).
20. *Id.* at § 12(a).
21. *Id.* at § 12(a)(1).
22. *Id.*
23. *Id.*
24. *Id.*
25. *Id.*
26. *Id.*
27. *Id.* at § 8.
28. Program Statement P6360.01, Pharmacy Services.
29. *Id.*
30. *Id.* at § 9(d).
31. 18 U.S.C. § 4048.
32. Program Statement P6031.02, Inmate Copayment Program at § 6.
33. *Id.* at § 7; 28 C.F.R. § 549.72.
34. *Id.* at § 10.
35. Program Statement 6031.04, Patient Care at § 44.
36. *Id.*

37. *Id.*
38. *Id.* at § 9.
39. *Id.*
40. *Id.* at § 27.
41. *Id.* at § 29.
42. *Id.* at § 24.
43. *Id.* at § 24(c).
44. *Id.* at § 24(d).
45. Levine, Sam, "Federal Prisons are Failing Aging Inmates, Justice Department Says." *The Huffington Post.* May 6, 2015. Retrieved from http://www.huffington-post.com/2015/05/06/aging-inmates-federal-prisons_n_7225674.html.
46. Dubler, Nancy, "Ethical Dilemmas."
47. "A Model for the Future?" National Prison Hospice Association. Retrieved from http://npha.org/npha-articles/models/a-prison-hospice-model-for-the-future/.
48. Gaseau, Michelle, "Hospice Programs Growing in Corrections, New Guidelines Being Created." Corrections.com. November 13, 2000. Retrieved from http://www.corrections.com/articles/7097.
49. Program Statement 6031.04, Patient Care at § 20.
50. *Id.*
51. Program Statement 6070.05, Birth Control, Pregnancy, Child Placement and Abortion at § 6; 28 C.F.R. § 551.22.
52. *Id.* at § 7.
53. Program Statement 6031.04, Patient Care at § 20(e).
54. Program Statement 6190.04, Infectious Disease Management at § 7.
55. *Id.*
56. *Id.* at § 7(a); 28 C.F.R. § 549.12(a).
57. *Id.* at § 7(a).
58. *Id.* at § 7.

Ten

Psychological Services

Inmates confined within the FBOP have the right to mental health treatment and services. This right is guaranteed by Supreme Court decisional law, federal statutes, and numerous regulations. See e.g. *Bell v. Wolfish*, 441 U.S. 520 (1979), *Gates v. Cook*, 376 F.3d 323 (5th Cir. 2004).

Mental healthcare (prescription medication and psychiatric care) within the Bureau is usually delivered by the psychology department with medical assistance provided by the health services department. According to the FBOP, the psychology department's primary mission "is to provide appropriate psychological, psycho-educational, and consultative services to inmates and staff."[1]

The Need

The Urban Institute found that nearly half the inmates in federal facilities have mental problems, with 40 percent exhibiting symptoms and roughly 15 percent having recently experienced mental or mood issues.[2]

As might be expected in an environment where freedoms are restricted, depression is the leading issue and is suffered by 21 percent of the population. Manic-depression, bipolar disorder, and mania come in second and hover around the same rate. General anxiety disorders, post-traumatic stress disorder (PTSD), and personality and psychotic disorders are also prevalent.[3]

Unfortunately, significantly more female inmates than male inmates are mentally ill. This is thought to be because women are more likely than men to report extensive histories of abuse ranging from physical to sexual and emotional violence. Female offenders are typically poor, women of color, unemployed, and care for young children. The struggles they engage with while trying to survive pushes them closer to the edge.[4]

Male and female inmates should seek the help they need. Prison is difficult enough without adding undiagnosed and untreated psychological illness to the mix.

Service Priority

Psychology services operates on a tiered priority basis. Pursuant to Bureau policy, first priority services include:

- Acute crisis intervention (suicidal, dangerous, or psychotic inmates);
- Suicide Prevention Program;
- Treatment of mentally ill inmates;
- Employee Assistance Program (staff crisis intervention);
- Court-ordered evaluations and reports;
- Special psychological reports (U.S. Parole Commission, DHO, hospital referrals, Witness Protection evaluations, etc.);
- Initial psychological screening evaluation of newly admitted inmates;
- Detention/segregation unit visits and periodic assessments;
- Psychological reports; and
- Assuring compliance with professional, correctional, and other applicable standards.[5]

Second priority services include:

- Brief counseling activities;
- Individual psychotherapy or psychoeducational therapeutic group programs with treatment plans;

- Maintenance of treatment notes in psychology files;
- Staff training in psychological areas;
- Personnel interviews for all new Bureau applicants;
- Attending institutional meetings;
- Special treatment programs (as in drug abuse programs);
- Maintenance of psychological entries in medical and central files; and
- Recruitment of psychologists and psychology interns and residents.[6]

Third priority services are:

- Program consultation for UDC and DHO;
- Unit Team consultation regarding inmate classification and program review;
- Consulting with other institutional departments;
- Institutional program development, program evaluation, and research projects; and
- Participation in seminars, conferences, and community programs.[7]

In reality, the level of psychological care delivered to a particular inmate is commensurate with the requirements of law and policy. Any additional (non-emergency) care is largely dependent on the level of staffing at an institution and the level of initiative taken by the staff. For example, at some high-security facilities, crisis intervention and SHU rounds consume psychology staff resources. At other facilities with drug treatment and sex offender programs, access to traditional group therapy and other programs is more common.

Staffing

Psychology services is usually headed by a chief psychologist who handles various administrative duties in addition to traditional caregiving. One or more staff psychologists are also usually present. They hold some coordination and supervisory responsibility for specific program missions like sex offender treatment, drug treatment, suicide prevention, etc. The psychology staff may also include drug treatment specialists, a department secretary, and occasional interns.

Staff "Dual Role" Conflict

The patient-therapist relationship in the prison setting has some marked differences from the relationship experienced in the outside community. The FBOP maintains that its psychologists generally adhere to professional standards like the guidelines established by the American Psychological Association (APA).[8]

Nevertheless, the Bureau also recognizes that critical issues "have, on occasion, surfaced" when psychologists are asked to function in other correctional roles.[9] An instance where a conflict might occur is when a psychologist is asked to work as a housing unit officer. This might occur during periods of annual training and other times of short staffing. The Bureau makes it clear that in "emergency situations" the psychology staff "are expected to assume duties wherever needed and assigned."[10]

Inmates should be mindful of the fact that their mental health providers are, at least on some level, correctional employees. Indeed, the Bureau spells this out by noting that psychology staff "work for many 'clients' within the Bureau of Prisons, including the Courts, the Parole commission, Wardens and other administrative staff, institutional staff, and inmates."[11]

Duty to Warn

Psychology staff have a mandate to break a client's confidentiality when there is a "duty to warn" which "arises when a therapist determines that a client presents a serious danger of violence to another."[12] There are other instances when a therapist is required to break confidentiality and report the content of communications with an inmate to law enforcement authorities. For example, state and federal laws require that suspected child abuse be reported.[13] Inmates should also be advised that psychology staff report misconduct and issue incident reports for misconduct.

Seeking Treatment

Notwithstanding the warnings listed above, every inmate should be aware that they have the established right to seek mental health assistance. Treatment usually begins when the inmate asks to be seen by the psychology staff. This can be effectuated via a paper cop-out (Request to Staff form), by email, or by appearing at a psychology "open house" at the appointed time. If emergency care is required, the inmate can approach any staff member and ask for psychology to be radioed. This can result in an immediate evaluation.

In addition, all inmates will be seen at least once by psychology staff as part of the Bureau's intake program. Inmates may request treatment at their intake interview as well. Be aware that any statements to staff that indicate suicidal ideations can cause an inmate to be placed on "suicide watch" in an isolation cell under direct observation at all times.[14]

Once contact has been made with psychology, non-emergency treatment usually occurs via scheduled appointments. Generally, most FBOP facilities do not offer one-on-one therapy due to limited resources, but such therapy is offered when required. In addition, some facilities offer limited group therapy or treatment programs. Inmates seeking mental health assistance should be diligent in seeking help.

In all instances, the Bureau uses cognitive behavioral therapy (CBT) as its theoretical model. In this approach, "a person's feelings and behaviors are influenced by his or her perceptions and core beliefs. By helping inmates perceive events objectively, and modify their irrational beliefs, they may become more successful in achieving pro-social goals."[15]

Suicide

Compared to the outside community, prisons have suicide rates far higher than usual. It is the third leading cause of death behind natural causes and AIDS, and so should be taken seriously. For a time, in fact, the rate of suicide in prison was 50 percent higher than the national average. It is particularly striking to note that suicide is so prevalent in an environment intended to control every movement and activity.[16] Inmates who are suffering enough to contemplate suicide should reach out for help.

Mental Health Step Down Program

In late 2013, the federal government began a new experiment called the Mental Health Step Down program. This is the first federal prison program to provide long-term care for mentally ill inmates at the high-security level. Most of the original sixteen prisoners were transferred from ADX or from the federal mental health prison hospital in Springfield, Missouri. An additional four were added to start with a test group of twenty.

"What's different here," wrote Andrew Cohen in *The Atlantic,* "what has not happened before in any federal prison, is that the new program is adequately staffed with mental health professionals who have designed a treatment-focused program intended to enable high-security prisoners eventually to 'step down' from solitary confinement to less restrictive environments."[17]

The other primary difference is the level of care. These individuals received direct, around-the-clock access to health professionals. Five medical staff helped the initial twenty, resulting in a high ratio of caregivers to patients. Compare that to the three mental health practitioners available to the 450 inmates available at ADX when a civil right suit was first filed against the prison, and the degree of involvement with this new program becomes clear.

The program is intended for inmates who don't need inpatient care but who lack the skills needed to function in a general prison population. The program lasts twelve to eighteen months, and can be accessed at any point during an inmate's sentence. Formal activities consume half days five days a week; the remaining time is spent in work assignments or other programming as the inmate is able.

All participants must volunteer for the program. The approach uses cognitive-behavioral therapies, cognitive rehabilitation, and skills training. Medications are provided as needed. The programs are available at FCI Butner, USP Atlanta, and USP Allenwood.[18]

Residential Drug Abuse Program (RDAP)

The FBOP offers a Residential Drug Abuse Program (RDAP). The live-in residential program lasts six to nine months and takes place in a housing unit dedicated to RDAP.[19] Qualified inmates who complete the program might be eligible for up to one year of sentence reduction under 18 U.S.C. § 3621(b) and as applied by Program Statement P5331.02, Early Release Procedures Under 18 U.S.C. § 3621 (e). See Chapter 11 for more on RDAP.

Sex Offender Treatment

The Bureau offers a variety of sex offender education and treatment programs. These range from outpatient groups to residential programs. The programs are governed by Program Statement 5310.12, Psychology Services Manual at § 5.2 and Program Statement 5324.10, Sex Offender Programs. Currently, none of the Bureau's sex offender programs offer a sentence reduction. See Chapter 12 for more on sex offender programs.

Notes

1. Program Statement 5310.12, Psychology Services Manual at § 1.1.
2. Kim, KiDeuk, Becker-Cohen, Miriam and Serakos, Maria, "The Processing and Treatment of Mentally Ill Persons in the Criminal Justice System." The Urban Institute. April 7, 2015.
3. Khazan, Olga, "Most Prisoners are Mentally Ill." *The Atlantic*. April 2015.
4. Bloom, Barbara E. and Covington, Stephanie S, "Addressing the Mental Health Needs of Women Offenders." Department of Criminal Justice Administration, Sonoma State University and Center for Gender & Justice. 2008. Retrieved from http://www.stephaniecovington.com/assets/files/FinalAddressingtheMentalHealthNeeds.pdf.
5. Program Statement 5310.12, Psychology Services Manual at § 1.3(A).
6. *Id.* at § 1.3(B).
7. *Id.* at § 1.3(C).
8. Program Statement 5310.12, Psychology Services Manual at § 2.1.
9. *Id.* at § 2.4.
10. *Id.* at § 2.4(D).
11. *Id.* at § 2.2(C).
12. *Id.* at § 2.3.

13. *Id.* at § 2.2(B).
14. Program Statement P5324.08, Suicide Prevention Program.
15. Program Statement P5330.11, Psychology Treatment Programs at § 1.2.
16. "No Escape: Male Rape in US Prisons." VI: Body and Soul: The Physical and Psychological Injury of Prison Rape. Human Rights Watch. 2001.
17. Cohen, Andrew, "An Experiment in Atlanta May Transform Care of Mentally Ill Prisoners." *The Atlantic.* Feb 11, 2014.
18. "A Directory of Bureau of Prisons' National Programs." BOP. May 22, 2015.
19. Program Statement P5330.11, Psychology Treatment Programs at § 2; 28 C.F.R. § 550.50.

Eleven

Residential Drug Abuse Program

The purported crown jewel of the FBOP's rehabilitative efforts is the Residential Drug Abuse Treatment Program (RDAP). This is the program most commonly prescribed by federal judges when sentencing offenders. RDAP is also the most commonly misunderstood program. Anyone seeking to participate in it and reap the potential benefits should pay close attention to its requirements.

RDAP is a unit-based residential program that involves daily group programming activities, individual counseling, and a great deal of peer-based interaction.[1] It is also the fabled "one year off" program. Eligible inmates might receive up to a one-year sentence reduction for successful completion pursuant to 18 U.S.C. § 3621(e)(2)(B), which is applied through Program Statement P5331.02, Early Release Procedures Under 18 U.S.C. § 3621(e). However, who is eligible and how the program is completed are left to the Bureau, which is empowered with vast discretion. See *Lopez v. Davis*, 531 U.S. 230, 237 (2001) wherein FBOP's wide discretion was upheld by the U.S. Supreme Court.

Generally, RDAP is offered at institutions within the FBOP. At present, the program is offered only to medium and lower custody level inmates. Ordinarily the program takes nine to twelve months to complete and involves a follow-up period in community confinement (a halfway house). The FBOP therefore generally requires that an inmate have at least twenty-four months remaining on their sentence to be considered.

Eligibility for RDAP

According to regulations governing the FBOP's operations of RDAP, inmates seeking admission to RDAP must meet all of the following criteria:

- Have a verifiable substance abuse disorder;
- Sign an agreement acknowledging the terms of the program; and
- Be able to complete all three of the program's phases.[2]

Admission to RDAP is extended to a far wider pool of inmates than those whose participation would make them eligible for a sentence reduction under § 3621(e). For all inmates, though, these three criteria apply.

A "verifiable" substance abuse disorder is usually established by a reference to substance abuse in the Presentence Report.[3] Generally, documentation is required as to "a substance abuse disorder within the 12-month period before the inmate's arrest on his or her current offense."[4] An inmate with multiple convictions for driving while intoxicated can also suffice. As such, it is critical that criminal defendants seeking treatment while incarcerated ensure that their Presentence Report explicitly depicts such information; without it, RDAP eligibility will be in grave doubt.

Exclusion from Sentence Reduction Eligibility

Not everyone admitted to RDAP is eligible for a sentence reduction. To be eligible for a sentence reduction under § 3621(e) requires far more and is determined by the FBOP in accordance with 28 C.F.R. § 550.55 and Program Statement P5162.05, Categorization of Offenses. As a general matter, any inmate with a prior conviction for homicide, forcible rape, robbery, or another offense deemed a "crime of violence" is excluded. Likewise, inmates whose current offense involves such conduct are also excluded.

The list of excludable convictions for a current offense also includes crimes that involved "the carrying, possession, or use of a firearm or other dangerous weapon or explosives (including any explosive material or explosive device)."[5] Other expansions on the classic definition of a "violent crime" are included and can determine eligibility as a fact-specific endeavor. The FBOP has at times removed such violent crime determinations from the local level, relegating all decisions to a single national location. In most cases, a two-point enhancement of sentencing offense level for possession of a firearm – for a defendant or codefendant – will be cause for exclusion.

Completing the Program

Inmates who successfully navigate the main unit-based section of RDAP must then participate in community-based drug abuse treatment to successfully complete RDAP.[6] This Transitional Drug Abuse Treatment (TDAT) component is usually performed at a halfway house prior to release or during home confinement. This requirement can prove troublesome for an inmate whose release destination is a halfway house that will not accept that inmate or for an inmate who discovers a long-forgotten warrant or detainer that precludes placement. Failure to complete the TDAT phase will preclude RDAP completion, as well. Until 2009, inmates housed in or sentenced in the area covered by the U.S. Court of Appeals for the Ninth Circuit could receive a reduction in such a case but the FBOP has since changed its regulations to eliminate any disagreement. See *Peck v. Thomas*, 697 F.3d 767, 772 (9th Cir. 2012).

Notes

1. Program Statement P5330.11, Psychology Treatment Programs at § 2.
2. 28 C.F.R. §§ 550.53 (b)(1)-(3).
3. Program Statement P5330.11, Psychology Treatment Programs at § 2.5.8.

4. *Id.*
5. 28 C.F.R. § 550.55(b)(5)(ii).
6. Program Statement 7430.02, Community Transitional Drug Abuse Treatment; 28 C.F.R. § 550.53(a)(3).

Twelve

Sex Offender Programs

Representing one of the fastest-growing segments of the federal prison population, inmates convicted of sex offenses and related crimes have become the focus of intensive programming within the Bureau. Several levels of programs are now offered, and the FBOP has designated several prisons as primary housing sites for sex offenders. Because an inmate's post-release quality of life might very well depend on his or her sex offender treatment while in prison, each inmate must take special care to ensure that they make informed choices at every juncture.

Eligibility for Sex Offender Programs

The FBOP casts a wide net in labeling inmates as sex offenders for purposes of classification and treatment. Beyond offenders convicted of any one of the growing list of federal sex offenses, those whose criminal history includes a sex offense are subject to a sex offender designation, a "Public Safety Factor" (PSF) label that precludes them from certain programs and housing security levels.

Likewise, the mention of sexual misconduct in a presentence report or a prison disciplinary matter can lead to assignation as a sex offender.[1] The imposition of a sex offender PSF will often result in an inmate being assigned to one of the Bureau's dedicated sex offender prisons. These institutions include USP Marion, USP Tucson, FCI Petersburg, FCI Elkton, FCI Englewood, FCI Seagoville, FCI Marianna, FMC Devens, and FMC Carswell.

Title 18 of the United States Code now lists several dozen sex-related offenses from crimes against the person (rape, kidnapping, etc.), to pornography and internet crimes, to sex offender registration offenses. The number of such federal offenses has quadrupled since the 1980s.

Participation in the Sex Offender Management Program (SOMP)

All inmates meeting the criteria for designation as a sex offender are evaluated for an "initial risk assessment" by staff within thirty days of arrival at an institution offering Sex Offender Management Programs (SOMPs).[2] This assessment might include a voluntary interview with a FBOP psychologist or SOMP specialist.

The initial risk assessment is a component of the FBOP's discharge evaluation, which might include a referral for civil commitment proceedings under 18 U.S.C. § 4248 and Program Statement 5324.10, Sex Offender Programs. During the initial risk assessment process, designated inmates will be informed as to their eligibility for SOMP participation. All programs are voluntary.

SOMP Programs

The Bureau's SOMP programs consist of a high-intensity Residential Sex Offender Treatment Program (SOTP-R) and nonresidential programs of varying levels of intensity and duration.

Residential Treatment Programs (SOTP-R)

The residential SOTP programs are of the unit-based, "modified therapeutic community" type.[3] The FBOP uses the Cognitive Behavioral Therapy model for SOTP programs. SOTP-R participants live in dedicated, separate units that are often more restrictive than those housing general population inmates. Such programs typically last twelve to eighteen months and are divided into several phases of treatment.

At least 400 hours of programming is required to complete SOTP-R, which is usually provided for ten to twelve hours per week. Generally, participation is limited to offenders determined to be at high risk to reoffend using actuarial risk assessments, the Static-99R, and other standardized ratings systems. However, it is not uncommon for moderate risk inmates to participate upon referral.

In Phase I, inmates are assessed in more detail using commercial tests such as the MMPI-II, intensive psychosexual interviews, and history recording.[4] In Phase II, the core treatment phase, members participate in process groups requiring an "appropriate level of self-disclosure."[5] Phase III, the transition phase, involves further intensive treatment. Participants "remain in this phase until they complete objectives specified in their treatment plan."[6]

While some graduates of the program remain housed in the dedicated program unit, policy permits the transfer of graduates to other institutions based on institutional need.[7] Further treatment might be ordered as an aftercare condition, including community-based treatment in prerelease halfway houses and thereafter.[8]

Nonresidential Treatment Programs (SOTP-NR)

The most intensive of the nonresidential sex offender treatment programs is the formal, three-phase SOTP-NR program, which is offered at most FBOP SOMP facilities. Designed for "low- to moderate-risk sexual offenders,"[9] SOTP-NR mirrors the residential program in many respects. It lasts nine to twelve months with a minimum of 144 hours required for completion.

Ordinarily, SOTP-NR entails four to six hours of programming per week.[10] SOTP-NR is also used to provide services to high-risk offenders preparing to transfer to a residential program; in some cases, inmates might be expected to complete Phase I in SOTP-NR before transferring to SOTP-R.[11]

Adjunctive Nonresidential Treatment Programs

In addition to the above programs, SOMP staff are empowered to offer additional adjunctive treatment groups. Often these are for inmates with "too much time remaining in their sentences, or who do not have enough time left on their sentences" to complete SOTP-R or SOTP-NR.[12] The specific content of such adjunctive programs is based on local decision-making at the institutional level.[13]

The Decision to Engage in Sex Offender Programming

Participation in a FBOP treatment program is voluntary. A long-held belief of inmates assumes that participating in SOTP programming can lead to undesired outcomes such as civil commitment and increased monitoring on supervised release. Such beliefs are not without foundation. In many cases where an inmate was civilly committed, records from that inmate's treatment participation have been used against them.[14] Moreover, none of the sex offender programs offer a sentence reduction. If possible, consultation with counsel is strongly advised prior to participation.

Correctional Management Plans

The Bureau now utilizes a policy that might assign a "Correctional Management Plan" (CMP) to a sex offender if he or she "is detected to have engaged in possible risk-relevant behavior."[15] The CMP is applied at the discretion of the psychology department if delegated to do so by the warden.[16] While the CMP program does not set forth sanctions for offenders who violate a CMP, disciplinary proceedings are sometimes initiated against them for violation of *Code 306, Refusing to Work or Accept a Program Assignment.*

The CMP process usually involves the issuance of a formal written notice that a CMP is being applied. In many cases, CMPs are applied with specific restrictions for the inmate. These might include restrictions on personal property, including photos and magazines, etc.[17]

A CMP can be modified or terminated at the warden's discretion. Inmates who are subjected to a CMP are advised to maintain clear conduct for six months or more. An inmate may then approach psychology services staff to discuss a plan to be removed from the program. Anecdotal evidence suggests that psychology staff are often willing to remove restrictions in steps until the entire CMP is rescinded.

Notes

1. Program Statement P5100.08, Inmate Security, Designation and Custody Classification at Ch. 5.
2. Program Statement 5324.10, Sex Offender Programs at § 2.1.1.
3. *Id.* at § 3.1.
4. *Id.*
5. *Id.*
6. *Id.*
7. *Id.* at § 3.6.2.
8. *Id.*
9. *Id.* at § 3.4.1.
10. *Id.* at § 3.4.4.
11. *Id.* at §3.4.2(b).
12. *Id.* at § 3.4.5.
13. *Id.*
14. Program Statement 5394.01, Certification and Civil Commitment of Sexually Dangerous Persons.
15. Program Statement 5324.10, Sex Offender Programs at § 4.3.
16. *Id.* at § 4.5.
17. *Id.* at §§ 4.6.1 - .3.

Thirteen

Transgender Inmates[c]

Against the backdrop of changing social attitudes about the lesbian, gay, bisexual, and transgender (LGBT) segment of American society, the FBOP now houses a growing number of transgender and gender nonconforming inmates. These prisoners bring with them unique needs and unique challenges that are slowly being addressed.

Identifying Transgender and Gender Nonconforming Inmates

Anecdotal evidence suggests a growing number of transgender inmates in the FBOP. Several hundred inmates meet the criteria for gender identity disorder (GID). GID is a medical diagnosis for persons who indicate that their birth sex does not match their perceptions of themselves.

For example, a genetic male may perceive himself as a female, or a genetic female may perceive herself as a male. The perception often leads to serious risks for self-harm and social dysfunction. GID therefore requires treatment by psychological and medical professionals. This treatment might include hormone

[c] *The term "transgender" encompasses a wide variety of persons and various gender expressions. For the sake of brevity, "transgender" is used in this text to describe all gender nonconforming persons.*

therapy, "real life experience," and surgical procedures designed to assist with transition to the desired expression of gender.

For obvious reasons, this type of treatment regimen is difficult to realize in prison. As indicated in the landmark Supreme Court decision, *Farmer v. Brennan*, 511 U.S. 825 (1994), transgender (sometimes called transsexual) inmates face significant challenges in receiving appropriate medical treatment. Their status as women among men or vice versa also leaves them at serious risk for attack and exploitation.

This is in large part because the FBOP, like most American correctional agencies, categorizes prisoners based on their genital status rather than on their perceived gender identity. This often leaves transgender women, regardless of their presentation, physical appearance, or attributes, imprisoned among men and vice versa.

Medical and Psychological Treatment for Transgender Inmates

In the FBOP, transgender inmates diagnosed with GID have the right to medical and psychological treatment. This includes assistance in transitioning from their assigned sex and gender to another. The FBOP's general policy reads as follows:

> INMATES WITH GENDER IDENTITY DISORDER
>
> Inmates with a possible diagnosis of Gender Identity Disorder (GID), including inmates who assert they have GID, will receive thorough medical and mental health evaluations from medical professionals with basic competence in the assessment of the DSM-IV/ICD10 sexual disorders and who have participated in BOP's GID training, including the review of all available community health records. The evaluation will include an assessment of the inmate's treatment and life experiences prior to incarceration, as well as experiences during incarceration (including hormone therapy completed or in-process surgical interventions, real life experience consistent with the inmate's gender

> identity, private expressions that conform to the preferred gender, and counseling).
>
> If a diagnosis of GID is reached, a proposed treatment plan will be developed which promotes the physical and mental stability of the patient. The development of the treatment plan is not solely dependent on services provided or the inmate's life experiences prior to incarceration. The treatment plan may include elements of the real life experience consistent with the prison environment, hormone therapy, and counseling. Treatment plans will be reviewed and updated as necessary. Current accepted standards of care will be used as a reference for developing the treatment plan. All appropriate treatment options prescribed for inmates with GID in currently accepted standards of care will be taken into consideration during evaluation by the appropriate medical and mental health care staff. Each treatment plan or denial of treatment must be reviewed by the Medical Director or BOP Chief Psychiatrist. Hormone therapy must be requested through the non-formulary review process, and approved by the Medical Director and/or Chief Psychiatrist. Consultation with the Chief of Psychology prior to such approval may be appropriate in some cases.
>
> In summary, inmates in the custody of the Bureau with a possible diagnosis of GID will receive a current individualized assessment and evaluation. Treatment options will not be prescribed solely due to level of services received, or lack of services, prior to incarceration.[1]

Medical care for transgender inmates is provided on a case-by-case basis. Experience indicates that local policy is often a factor. Generally, the FBOP has mandated that a GID diagnosis by the psychology department be made before medical interventions like hormone therapy are provided.

At present, gender dysphoric inmates should expect extraordinary delays in the provision of care, especially when seeking hormone therapy. While the Bureau is still in the early stages of being willing to provide care, at some prisons transgender and gender nonconforming inmates are being granted access to female commissary products, electronic hair removal, and female garments.

Quality of Life for Transgender Inmates

Depending on the security level to which a transgender inmate is assigned, life in the FBOP has varying levels of safety and comfort. At most camps and low-security facilities, safety is generally provided to all; at the USP level, transgender inmates face serious safety risks if they are permitted on the compound. Each prison is different.

As to the "real life experience" component of care set forth in the World Professional Association for Transgender Health (WPATH) Standards of Care, treatment depends on local factors. Some institutions allow transgender prisoners the full complement of items permitted at institutions for inmates of their chosen gender. Others might receive only medically approved items (brassieres, etc.).

When it comes to housing assignments and other conditions, situations also vary. However, treatment of transgender inmates is now in flux due to the implementation of the Prison Rape Elimination Act of 2003 (PREA).

PREA and the Transgender Inmate

The Bureau's implementation of PREA is carried out through federal regulations and program statements such as Program Statement 5324.12, Sexually Abusive Behavior Prevention and Intervention Program. These policies provide transgender inmates with specific protections that every such inmate should be familiar with. These protections include the right to nonintrusive pat searches, the right to shower "separately from other inmates," and to not be "search[ed] or physically examined for the sole purpose of determining the inmate's genital status."[2] Transgender inmates in the FBOP also have the right to not be subjected to involuntary segregation on the basis of their gender status. Any decision to segregate such persons cannot be made without assessing all available alternatives.[3]

In the FBOP, transgender and gender nonconforming inmates have the well-established right to be free from assault and harassment. Every such inmate should familiarize themselves with their rights under PREA.

Notes

1. Program Statement 6031.04, Patient Care at § 30.
2. *Id.*
3. *Id.*

Part V – Contact with the Outside

Fourteen

Communication

Prison can feel like a desolate island far from family, friends, and familiar surroundings. In an institutional setting, outside influences are minimal. For the sake of an inmate's sanity and for their success after release it is essential that they stay connected with the world outside. Most prisoners do this through the use of postal mail, telephones, email services, visitation, and by reading books, newspapers, and magazines.

U.S. Postal Mail

Inmates in the Bureau are allowed to send and receive letters through the U.S. Postal Service.[1] This is a right guaranteed by both the First Amendment and FBOP policy, but it is not an absolute right. Inmate mail can be restricted for a variety of security reasons.

Monitoring of Correspondence

FBOP officials have an obvious interest in the security and orderly operation of their institutions. Therefore, all incoming mail is inspected by mailroom staff to ensure it does not contain illegal or disruptive material.[2] This could mean simply opening the correspondence or publication and verifying that no contraband is enclosed. It could also mean reading every word or looking at every photo for unauthorized content.

Inmates generally cannot be held responsible for what is sent to them, but they can, in some cases, be held responsible for requesting or ordering prohibited items. Inmates will be held responsible if contraband items are delivered to their possession.

> *TIP: When arriving at a federal prison for the first time, inmates are asked to sign a form that authorizes staff to open and inspect their incoming mail. They can refuse to sign this form but it will mean they can't receive postal correspondence. It is better to sign.*

Publications

Inmates can subscribe to and receive publications while in a federal prison, and they do not need advanced authorization. According to the FCC Petersburg institutional handbook, the term "publication" means "a book, pamphlet, or similar document, or a single issue of a magazine, periodical, newsletter, newspaper, or other materials addressed to a specific inmate such as advertising brochures, flyers, and catalogs."

All correspondence must weigh less than sixteen ounces (one pound). To receive a parcel weighing more than that, inmates have to apply for prior authorization. Only rarely will it be granted, except for books – a maximum of five in any one package – or preapproved college correspondence courses.[3]

At medium- and maximum-security prisons, books must come directly from the publisher or distributor (e.g., Amazon, Barnes & Noble, etc.). Although some low-security federal prisons still require hardcover books to be sent directly from the publisher, in most low- and camp-security levels, books can be mailed directly from friends and family. Inmates should request that book providers clearly mark each parcel with the words "Books from Publisher" or "Directly from the Publisher."

> *TIP: While the number of books within a single box or envelope must not exceed five, there is no restriction on the number of boxes or envelopes that*

can be sent. So, if an inmate wants ten books, they can be sent in two boxes, which can arrive on the same day.

Different prisons have different regulations regarding how many books inmates can keep in their cell. Most place a limit of five to ten books but prison staffers seldom bother to count unless they are prominently displayed (stacked to the ceiling, on a desk, or piled high under a bunk).

Rejection of Correspondence

Inmates should expect their mail to be regularly rejected by the FBOP if:

- It contains threats;
- It depicts or describes procedures for the construction or use of weapons, ammunition, bombs, or incendiary devices;
- It depicts, encourages, or describes methods of escape from correctional facilities or contains blueprints, drawings, or similar descriptions of Bureau institutions;
- It depicts or describes procedures for the brewing of alcoholic beverages or the manufacture of drugs;
- It is written in code;
- It depicts, describes, or encourages activities that might lead to the use of physical violence or group disruption;
- It encourages or instructs on how to conduct criminal activity;
- It is sexually explicit material that poses a threat to the security, good order, or discipline of the institution;
- It contains matter that is illegal to mail or that violates postal regulations;
- It contains information about escape plots, plans to commit illegal activities, or violation of institution rules; or
- It relates to the management of an inmate's business.[4]

TIP: Inmates in federal prison are not allowed to subscribe to publications that feature nudity like Playboy, Penthouse, Hustler, etc.; publications that feature drugs like High Times; or publications focused on martial arts or fighting techniques. However, some inmates subscribe to publications of the National Rifle Association (NRA) and other gun-focused publications without restriction.

In addition to parcels that weigh over sixteen ounces, books coming from a source not readily identifiable as a publisher and envelopes containing more than twenty-five photos are often rejected. When mail is rejected, both the sender and recipient are supposed to be notified (although this does not always happen). The inmate has the right to appeal the decision through the Administrative Remedy Program.

TIP: I have spent some time litigating the issue of mail that is not delivered. In my personal experience and that of inmates at other federal prisons, the staff at some facilities hold the position that not accepting mail (leaving it at the post office) and rejecting mail (inspecting and then returning mail to the sender) are two different concepts, and that the former requires no notice of rejection.

Inmates should be sure to tell all of their correspondents that items mailed to them at the FBOP must contain their full name as it appears on official records as well as their register number or it will not be accepted. Information regarding any federal inmate's current location is always available at www.bop.gov/inmateloc, a website the Bureau updates daily.

Receiving Mail

At most facilities, mail is delivered to each housing unit around 2:00 p.m. Monday through Friday. Policy dictates that mail be delivered within twenty-four hours of arrival during the evening shift but some officers pass it out immediately.[5]

TIP: Many unit officers, although not all, require that inmates present their identification card when receiving mail. It is a good idea to have the card handy at all times just in case.

Sending Mail

If an inmate is housed at a low- or minimum-security prison, they will be allowed to seal their mail before they place it in the institutional mail system. At a medium- or maximum-security prison, inmates place outgoing mail unsealed in the housing unit's mail receptacle. The third shift of staff, those working from 10:00 p.m. to around 6:00 a.m., inspect and possibly read the outgoing mail prior to sealing it. Some staff will actually seal outgoing mail; others just place a piece of tape on the back of the envelope and call it sealed. Some won't bother.

> *TIP: Staff read letters to gain intelligence on inmate activities and to spot violations of policy. Never mention names, fights, alcohol, drugs, or other prohibited acts. Write with an awareness that every word might be read by an investigator.*

TRULINCS Mailing Labels

In recent years, the computerized Trust Fund Limited Inmate Communication System (TRULINCS) was installed in the FBOP. One component of this system is the mail contact feature into which inmates input all their contacts' names, addresses, phone numbers, and email addresses. Inmates may input up to 100 contacts and generate mailing labels free of cost.

Every letter mailed out must have a TRULINCS mailing label affixed to it.[6] TRULINCS computers with label printers are usually located in all housing units, in the education department, and sometimes also in the recreation department.

> *TIP: At most facilities, inmates can print up to ten labels each day (five labels during a maximum of two sessions daily). A smart way to ensure that labels are available when needed is to print a number of labels for regular contacts and retain those labels in one's locker. As the supply runs down, print additional labels.*
>
> *In addition to affixing mailing labels to correspondence, inmates should be sure to write their full name, registration number, address, and the name of their prison on the return address section of every envelope. The*

Bureau now requires inmates to spell out "Federal Correctional Institution" or "United States Penitentiary" instead of using their abbreviations (FCI, USP, etc.).

Postage Stamps: A Limited Supply

Inmates with funds in their commissary account are allowed to purchase postage stamps on their day at the commissary. The allowable maximum can vary but national policy limits purchases to twenty first-class stamps per week. Inmates cannot possess more than the equivalent of sixty first-class postage stamps at any given time.[7] In some institutions where possession of postage stamps is prohibited, inmates must present each of their letters at a window for postage.

Inmates can also purchase writing and typing paper, pens and pencils, envelopes (large and small), and typewriter supplies at the commissary.

TIP: New arrivals who need typing supplies (like a typewriter ribbon, print wheel, correctional tape, etc.) should consider asking around in the law library if anyone is willing to sell a good, used set. Prisoners who engage in legal work often have serviceable items they are willing to sell at a substantial discount.

If an inmate lacks funds and is officially regarded as indigent, their unit team will be responsible for providing them with postage, writing materials, and typing supplies for legal work.

TIP: The staff member who issues postage stamps to an indigent inmate might be the inmate's unit manager or correctional counselor. Inmates should speak with this member of their unit team and ask how they should handle these matters. Some unit managers will provide five or ten first-class stamps at a time; others only provide postage for envelopes that have been addressed and that have letters enclosed.

Prison-Style Email

Forget Yahoo! Mail, Gmail, and Hotmail. If an inmate wants to send and receive email, they'll have to use the prison's monitored electronic messaging program, which is part of the TRULINCS system. The electronic messaging program provides an enormous benefit to federal inmates who want to communicate electronically.

Inmates can utilize the TRULINCS computers in the housing units to send messages to contacts through the website www.Corrlinks.com. The system allows inmates to correspond with a maximum of thirty email contacts in the outside world at any one time.[8] Inmates can, of course, delete existing contacts and add new ones.

TRULINCS electronic messaging is more like a message posting system than true email. Inmates do not have access to the internet or traditional email providers. Instead, they send messages to the website www.Corrlinks.com. When an inmate's authorized contact wants to return the message, they must log into the Corrlinks site.

TIP: Advise outside correspondents that email messages can only be sent to their Corrlinks.com account, and never directly to a personal email account. This is a common point of confusion because people in the outside world are accustomed to receiving messages in their personal email inbox. They forget to check their Corrlinks.com account.

How to Use TRULINCS Electronic Messaging

To utilize the electronic messaging service, inmates should log in at a TRULINCS computer in their housing unit and input their contact's information – their name, address, and email address. The system then generates an email to alert the contact that a message from a federal inmate awaits them at Corrlinks.com.

The system-generated message instructs the contact on how to become an approved messaging contact and provides an authorization code to activate an account. Once that is done, they can send and receive electronic messages as well as communicate with other federal inmates through a single Corrlinks.com email account.

To compose a message, outside contacts can either type directly into the window at Corrlinks.com or they can copy and paste messages from Word or another word processing program into the message window. They can also copy and paste plain text from a website.

TIP: Contacts should be advised to visit the Corrlinks.com FAQ (frequently asked questions) page to learn how the system works, how to use it effectively, and how premium options can add smartphone capabilities. They can also choose to receive an email alert when they receive a message by logging into www.corrlinks.com, clicking "Account Management," then clicking "Manage My Inmate List," and finally checking the box under "email alert."

Applicable Costs

The cost for using this system is entirely the responsibility of the inmate; the outside contact is never charged. Inmates pay five cents per minute for using any aspect of the electronic messaging service, whether that means composing a message, reading a message, or browsing old messages. An inmate is not charged for the time their contacts spend on the system.

To pay the fee, inmates buy "TRU-Units," which can be purchased for $0.05 each in groups of 40, 100, 200, 300, or 600. The inmate selects the amount of units they want to purchase on the welcome screen of the TRULINCS system. The cost is deducted from their commissary/trust fund balance. Printing out copies of emails costs 15 cents or 3 TRU-Units per page.

Time Usage and Message Limitations

To ensure equal access to the service, most Bureau facilities set a thirty-minute or one-hour time limit on public messaging. When an inmate has exhausted this time, the system will log them off. They will then have to wait thirty minutes before logging back on. If an inmate is in the process of typing a message when they reach the time limit, the message will be automatically saved in their drafts folder. They can always come back to finish it later by clicking on the save icon.

Each of the messages cannot exceed 13,000 characters, or roughly 2,000 words per email. As the inmate types, they will see a "Characters Remaining" countdown indicator on their composition screen advising them how many character spaces remain.

TRULINCS electronic messaging is a text-only communications medium. Plain, black text. No bold, no italics, no foreign symbols. No photos, no attachments. And messages can't be forwarded. In order to send the same message to multiple contacts, an inmate selects those contacts prior to sending the message. Except for the time limitation, there is no restriction on the number of messages that can be sent or received in a twenty-four-hour period.

TIP: Inmates and their outside electronic messaging correspondents often hit reply when responding to a message. This allows each party to read what the other party previously wrote but it also includes the prior emails in the 13,000-character limit. If this character limit has been reached – either by replying to several messages within the same string of emails or simply by writing a very long email – the inmate or the outside contact can start a new email to reset the character count to zero.

Monitoring of Electronic Messages

Just like the telephone and U.S. mail, prison staff also monitor electronic messages.[9] Certain keywords trigger more intense scrutiny. Staff are often looking to see if the names of other inmates are mentioned or if violations of disciplinary regulations are revealed.

Monitoring naturally slows down message delivery. Inmates might wait an hour or so to receive messages, while it takes around twenty minutes for an inmate's message to reach an outside contact. Messages might be obstructed if they contain anything determined to be "detrimental to the security, good order, or discipline of the institution, or a threat to the public and staff or if it might facilitate criminal activity."[10]

Anything that would be rejected by the prison's mailroom will be rejected by the electronic messaging system. If it is not rejected, an inmate might receive an incident report for engaging in a prohibited discussion. At worst, an inmate could be banned from the service, although this usually requires a very serious violation.

TIP: A word of caution: When sending a message to an approved outside contact, the outside contact is not allowed to forward that message to anyone else. If they do, the inmate risks receiving a disciplinary incident report for a Code 397 or 297 violation.

If an inmate receives a Code 397 or 297 violation for email abuse, they can expect to lose their public messaging privilege for several months. However, as long as this forwarding isn't mentioned in the emails, institutional staff will probably never know.

If an inmate discovers that an outside contact has done so out of ignorance, they should immediately tell them that they are not to do it again. This falls within the scope of plausible deniability and might help mitigate damaging consequences.

Restriction of Access to Service

Not all inmates in the Bureau are granted access to the public messaging feature of TRULINCS. A since-rescinded policy[11] explained that an inmate could be restricted from the public messaging system when:

1) They have a record (as determined by the presentence investigative report) that presents a threat to institutional security or to the public.

Policy states, "Inmates with a personal history of, or prior offense conduct or conviction for, soliciting minors for sexual activity, or possession/distribution of child pornography through the Internet or other means, are excluded from program participation based on their history. Likewise, an inmate with a personal history of special skills or knowledge for using computers/email/Internet or other communication methods as a conduit for committing illegal activities will be excluded."[12]

Not every person who fits this description will be excluded but they might be. Access privileges are determined on a case-by-case basis. Initially access is reviewed by the inmate's unit manager followed by a review by an associate warden. For example, some inmates who are incarcerated for possession of child pornography are granted access to public messaging as long as they didn't utilize email, instant messaging, or text messages to engage in these illicit activities.

2) They are currently under investigation for a potential disciplinary violation related to TRULINCS abuse or misuse.
3) They are being sanctioned for a disciplinary violation. Denial of access to public messaging is usually imposed in thirty-day increments.

Inmates have no constitutional right to email, but if prison authorities deny an inmate access to the service, they should provide the inmate with notice of the reason and the right to appeal the decision.

An *administrative restriction* can occur if an inmate has a criminal charge or has committed an offense, such as soliciting minors for sexual activity through email, texting, or instant messages. It can also apply if an inmate has the kind of specialized computer skills they could use to hack into the computer system. Should an inmate be barred from the email system for these reasons, they can file an administrative remedy (initially a BP-9) and attempt to reduce or reverse the decision on administrative grounds.

A *disciplinary restriction* – which is usually temporary and is meted out in thirty-day increments – will deny an inmate access as a form of discipline for misconduct or an infraction of rules. An inmate can also appeal a disciplinary restriction from email but the results might come in after they have undergone disciplinary proceedings or sanctions. Regardless, an inmate can still appeal disciplinary sanctions through the administrative remedy process. If they are successful, such sanctions will be rescinded.

The new policy[13] explains, "An inmate's exclusion from participation must be based on their individual history of behavior that could jeopardize legitimate penological interests[.]" The program statement further clarifies, "inmates must not be excluded from participation based on general categorizations of previous conduct."[14]

Whereas the same types of disciplinary and investigation restrictions still apply to program exclusion and suspension, the new policy provides clarification concerning sex offenders. "Inmates whose offense, conduct, or other personal history indicates a propensity to offend through the use of email or jeopardizes the safety, security, orderly operation of the correctional facility, or the protection of the public or staff, should be seriously considered for restriction." These inmates must be evaluated to see if they "pose a realistic threat."

Telephones

Inmates in the FBOP cannot have a personal telephone or cell phone. Instead, there are communal phones made available through the Inmate Telephone System (ITS). Inmates can place but not receive collect or debit calls.[15]

Telephones are placed in each housing unit, and enough are available to ensure that inmates have reasonable access. Inmates can use the phones during their nonworking hours between 6:00 a.m. and 9:30 p.m. or 10:00 p.m., depending on the facility.

> *TIP: Some facilities reduce the number of telephones available during the 7:30 a.m. to 3:30 p.m. work period to one per housing unit. All phones, four to six per unit, function at lunchtime and during nonworking hours.*
>
> *A line of inmates is usually waiting to place calls. Inmates should ask the person currently on the phone if anyone is waiting; do not assume there is not simply because no one is in line or near the phone. There is usually an unseen casual line of people scattered around the housing unit waiting their turn by watching TV or playing cards.*

Usage Limitations

Inmates can use a total of 300 minutes of phone time each month. On a specific date each month (called a "revalidation date"), this total will be reset to 300 minutes. In November and December, administrators allot 400 minutes to allow for more family contact during the holidays. If an inmate does not use all of their allotted telephone minutes in a given month, the minutes will not be credited or carried over to following months.

Each telephone call is limited to fifteen minutes. Inmates must wait thirty to forty-five minutes before placing another call.

Applicable Costs

Debit calls are paid for by inmates, who can transfer funds from their trust fund (commissary) account to their phone account. These are the current rates for inmate-dialed (debit) calls:

Local debit calls	$0.06 per minute
Long-distance U.S. debit calls	$0.21 per minute
Debit calls to Canada	$0.35 per minute
Debit calls to Mexico	$0.55 per minute
Debit calls to other countries	$0.99 per minute

Collect calls are paid for by an outside contact. Depending on the outside contact's carrier, they might need to set up an account with Value Added Communications, the Bureau's contractor, by calling 1-800-913-6097. But be aware that collect calls can be more than three times as expensive as debit calls. Because debit calls cost so much less, inmates should plan ahead and keep sufficient funds in their commissary account.

To reduce the cost of long-distance calls (300 minutes for $69.00) to the cost of local calls (300 minutes for $18.00), the people most frequently called might want to consider requesting an additional phone line for their current plan. Specify that the area code for the new line should be local to the prison. That way when the inmate calls on the new line, they are charged only the local rate.

TIP: Never use a call-forwarding service like Google Voice or the ones advertised in prison magazines. It is a major violation of FBOP disciplinary policy (a Code 297 violation). Even if these services advertise that they are permitted by policy, they are not.

Security Features: PAC Number and Voice Recognition

When an inmate is first confined, they will receive a nine-digit phone access code (PAC). This number will permit access to both the TRULINCS computers and the ITS. It should be memorized and never shared with others.

Before an inmate places their first telephone call, they must record their name on ITS. The recorded name can subsequently be heard by dialing 112 followed by the inmate's PAC number. This is a security feature. Inmates should state their name as clearly and as naturally as possible because they will have to match their voice to the recording every time they place a call.

This feature ensures that inmates cannot place calls using another prisoner's account. However, the high noise levels in the housing units can make it difficult to match one's voice to the recorded name. It might be necessary to repeat one's name several times to match it to the recording.

TIP: To make the voice-recognition process easier, inmates should use the shortest possible form of their name. For example, if their name is Christopher, they should probably record the name Chris. Avoid including a middle name because it provides an additional voice-recognition component that requires the vocal tones to match recorded ones.

Adding Phone Numbers and Placing Calls

Inmates can have up to thirty telephone numbers on their ITS account.[16] To add a new contact, inmates must login to a TRULINCS computer and input the name, address, and telephone number of the person they wish to call. They will have to wait approximately fifteen minutes for the new number to be approved and activated.

To place a call, an inmate must dial one of the telephone numbers they have listed in their TRULINCS account and then enter their PAC number and state their name when prompted. If all this information matches, the call will be placed with a message to the contact stating that the call is from a federal inmate. The recipient accepts the call by pressing the number 5.

Call participants will hear a warning beep when only sixty seconds remain of the allotted fifteen minutes and again at the thirty-second mark. When the fifteen minutes of call time have expired, the phone will automatically disconnect.

TIP: If an inmate has less than fifteen minutes remaining in their monthly telephone allotment, the sixty- and thirty-second beeps still occur. But if they don't have enough money in their ITS account for a complete fifteen-minute call, these beeps will not occur and the call will disconnect without warning when the funds have been depleted.

The ITS has several useful account-keeping features that can be accessed by dialing 118 followed by the PAC number. Inmates can choose from the following features:

#1: Current ITS account balance;
#2: Current commissary account balance;
#3: Transfer funds from a commissary account to an ITS account;
#4: The cost, duration, and phone number of the most recent call; and
#5: The number of phone minutes remaining for the current validation period.

Monitoring of Calls

As with postal mail and email, inmates should be very careful about what they say on the telephone. All calls are subject to monitoring and are recorded. References to violations of disciplinary regulations can cause investigations and incident reports. Inmates should not use the names of other inmates because that can cause problems for them. Suicidal statements should also not be made because they may result in the inmate being thrown into a suicide watch cell without any clothes.

Notes

1. Program Statement 5265.14, Correspondence; 28 C.F.R. § 540.
2. Program Statement 5800.16, Mail Management Manual.
3. *Id.* at § 1.7(c).
4. Program Statement P5266.11, Incoming Publications; 28 C.F.R. § 540.71.
5. Program Statement 5800.10, Mail Management Manual at § 304.
6. Program Statement 4500.11, Trust Fund/Deposit Fund Manual at § 14.10.
7. Program Statement 5265.14, Correspondence at §§ 13(a)(2)-(3).
8. Program Statement 4500.11, Trust Fund/Deposit Fund Manual at § 14.10(c)(3).
9. *Id.* at §14.10(j).
10. *Id.*

11. Program Statement P5265.13, Trust Fund Limited Inmate Computer System (TRULINCS) Electronic Messaging.
12. *Id.*
13. Program Statement 4500.11, Trust Fund/Deposit Fund Manual at § 14.9(a).
14. *Id.*
15. Program Statement P5264.08, Inmate Telephone Regulations; 28 C.F.R. §540.100.
16. Program Statement 4500.11, Trust Fund/Deposit Fund Manual at § 14.10(c)(2).

Fifteen

Visitation

Inmates in the FBOP enjoy visitation privileges at all general population facilities to "maintain the morale of the inmate and to develop closer relationships between the inmate and family members or others in the community."[1]

Who May Visit

Any person who wishes to visit a federal inmate must be approved by the Bureau and placed on the inmate's visiting list. Visitors fall into several categories.

Regular Visitors

Members of an inmate's immediate family are by regulation "placed on the visiting list, absent strong circumstances which preclude visiting."[2] These regular visitors are usually identified in the inmate's presentence report. Immediate family includes the inmate's mother, father, stepparents, foster parents, brothers and sisters, spouse, and children. Background checks might be completed for these visitors "when deemed appropriate."[3]

A "spouse" is one legally married to the inmate and "includes a common-law relationship which has been previously established in a state that recognizes such a status."[4d] "Other relatives," i.e., extended family members, can visit if there "exists no reason to exclude them."[5] In practice, these visitors are asked to fill out a BP-629 Background Check form, which includes a waiver allowing FBOP staff to perform a criminal background check (an NCIC check). The existence of a prior criminal conviction might be cause for a visitor to be denied, but wardens are empowered to allow such persons to visit when warranted.

> *TIP: It is possible that any visitor, including an immediate family member, can be excluded for a prior conviction. If any proposed visitor is under parole, probation, or court supervision, it is strongly advised that this fact be dealt with openly. It is a virtual certainty that attempts to avoid disclosure will result in exclusion.*

"Friends and Associates" is a visitor category that is generally limited to persons "having an established relationship with the inmate prior to confinement."[6] While wardens do have the authority to grant exceptions to the pre-confinement relationship requirement, these exceptions are rarely granted.

> *TIP: It is best that visitors be as inclusive as possible when describing their prior relationships with the inmate on the BP-629 form to avoid unwarranted exclusion.*

Children under the age of sixteen cannot visit "unless accompanied by a responsible adult."[7] Additionally, the child's parent or legal guardian must sign the BP-629 form on the child's behalf.

Some Bureau facilities are currently experimenting with video visitation. In this situation, visitors and inmates are not able to see each other in person, and are only able to talk and look at each other through a computer screen or other device. In 2010, Jodie Emery found this out only when she appeared at FDC SeaTac to visit her husband.

---

[d] *At the time of press, the FBOP had not yet issued guidelines as to same-sex marriages or civil unions. The author presumes the above policies apply.*

She waited for a very long time for the paperwork to be processed in a lobby filled with "so many broken-hearted parents, girlfriends, wives, and troubled children crying 'I want to see daddy.'" Finally she was told her visit would be conducted through video.

"I was stunned, trembling, and ready to burst into tears," she wrote, "because the thought of not being able to touch him in person was utterly devastating, especially after flying here from Vancouver … expecting to kiss, hug, and hold hands."[8]

The couple received a reprieve because the guard had gotten the date wrong. Video visits wouldn't begin until the next day. They met in a large visiting room with rows of plastic chairs and paintings of scenes from around Seattle. His hug lifted her from the floor. Their kiss lasted as long as the contact allowance (thirty seconds). Their time together felt even shorter because she knew it would be their last in-person visit for a while.[9]

Although visitations can be challenging because of the emotional elements, inmates should know that it won't always be difficult. Matthew Kluger found that visitations with his family, including three preteens, did get easier. Visits remained emotional, especially as Kluger felt guilty about how his incarceration had affected the family, but the visits were still an important way to stay connected.[10]

Special Visitors

Special visitors are described in FBOP policy as business visitors, consular visitors for foreign nationals, clergy, and representatives of community groups.[11] These visitors might be required to undergo background checks when warranted. Depending on circumstances, they might be permitted to visit with the inmate in a private area. During "times of personal or family emergencies," the inmate's minister of record might be allowed additional considerations.[12]

Inmates who would like to have a weekend religious crusade visit their facilities, including a former NFL player who can bring dozens of volunteers into institutions nationwide, should contact:

Mike Barber Ministries
PO Box 1086
DeSoto, TX 75123-1086
800-331-1253 or 972-223-3131
www.mikebarber.org

The "Mommy Read to Me" program takes volunteers into federal prisons, as well. A volunteer will visit an inmate (male or female, despite the name of the program) and provide a tape recorder and a Christian children's book the inmate reads aloud. The recording and the book are then sent to the child so that they can hear their parent's voice. Contact:

Mission Gate Ministry
PO Box 6644
Chesterfield, MO 63006
636-391-8560
www.missiongateministry.org

The Upaya outreach program visits prisons to teach mindfulness as a way to deal with feelings and develop emotional intelligence. Contact:

Ray Olson, Coordinator
Prison Outreach Project
Upaya Zen Center
1404 Cerro Gordo Road
Santa Fe, NM 87501
rayolson29@gmail.com

Inmates interested in Buddhism can have an instructor teach in their facility. Contact:

Liberation Prison Project
PO Box 33036
Raleigh, NC 27636
(415) 701 8500
mailinfousa@liberationprisonproject.org

Individuals can also be visited by the interfaith Prisoner Visitation & Support (PVS) program which was founded in 1968 by Quakers. More than 375 volunteers visit 102 federal prisons nationwide to support the development of constructive lives and encourage inmates to survive incarceration. They also recognize the importance of reconnecting prisoners with the outside world. Contact:

Prisoner Visitation & Support
1501 Cherry Street
Philadelphia, PA 19102
(215) 241-7117
PVS@prisonervisitation.org

Attorney Visits

Attorneys and paralegals are permitted to visit inmates without "auditory supervision."[13] The warden cannot limit the frequency of attorney visits but can stipulate that such visits occur during regular visiting hours. Generally, an advance appointment by the attorney is required, but regulations dictate that the warden "make every effort to arrange for a visit when prior notification is not practical."[14]

Attorneys might be required to indicate where they are licensed but cannot be questioned as to the subject matter of the visit.[15] Attorneys are subject to searches for contraband, and cannot exchange documents with an inmate without authorization.

Media Visitors

The FBOP also permits members of the media to visit if they are employees of a "general circulation" newspaper; a news magazine with "national circulation;" a national or international news service; or a radio or TV news program.[16] Other reporters and writers of books might be permitted to visit and interview inmates with permission from the warden, contingent upon verification of previously published works or a contract with a publisher, and subject to several restrictions.[17]

The media representative must initiate a written request for a visit in advance. The inmate must also give written consent to being interviewed before the visit. Additionally, the inmate "must authorize the institutional staff to respond to comments made in the interview and to release information to the news media relative to the inmate's comments."[18] Prior authorization is not required for interviews or other communications via telephone, email, or postal mail.

Visitor Admittance to the Institution

Once a visitor is approved, he or she need not give advance notice of intent to visit an inmate in general population. Inmates in special housing may be subject to special restrictions, which are addressed later in this section.

Before leaving for the prison, visitors should verify the inmate's current location one last time. The Bureau can move individuals with little notice. An inmate also might have become ill and be receiving treatment in a different facility; in this case, visitation is approved on a case-by-case basis. The facility might also restrict an inmate's contact for security reasons or if the inmate has had a number of visitors already that month.

It's also a good idea to check visitation days and hours again. Visitors should know the route they will take to the facility and one potential alternative route in case roads are closed or transportation is delayed or cancelled due to weather or equipment failure.[19]

All visitors are required to present valid identification, generally a current, valid photo identification card from a state or federal government source. Visitors are subject to a personal search before visiting, which can include a search of their belongings and of their person. The FBOP posts signs alerting all visitors that their entry into a facility constitutes implied consent to be searched. Refusal might be deemed cause to be barred from entry.[20] Such searches might be performed via electronic devices, including metal detectors and ion spectrometry devices that sense the presence of certain drugs.

TIP: Ion search machines are very sensitive. Inmates should advise their visitors to wash their hands thoroughly before entering the facility and to minimize their handling of personal medications before the visit. Even legally prescribed medicines can set off the machines. Visitors taking medications containing narcotics should try to make advance arrangements with the facility to avoid issues.

Pat searches might be conducted either on a random or reasonable suspicion basis. The refusal to be pat searched might bar a visitor from entry. Religious headwear is not ordinarily searched without cause.[21]

Strip searches of visitors, called "visual searches" in FBOP policy, are permitted "[only] when authorized by the Warden upon reasonable suspicion that the subject is engaged, or attempting to engage, in prohibited activities."[22] For the most part, visitors will not be subjected to visual searches.

The initial screening process for visitors can be time-consuming at certain facilities. Usually a visitor is required to fill out an application at the door and then wait while it is processed (notwithstanding that all visitors must be preapproved). Visitors must know the make, model, color, and license plate number of their car. At times, staff might run warrant checks on visitors. Generally, though, the process takes less than an hour.

Although pets are not allowed inside federal facilities for visitation, certified service animals can accompany visitors with disabilities. Visitors can take their photo ID, authorized money, baby care items, and certain medications into the visiting room. Gifts for the inmate must be approved in advance; the gifts should not be wrapped so that the items can be searched.[23]

Any money that a visitor wants to place in the inmate's Trust Fund account cannot be accepted by the staff on site. It must be deposited through the usual means.[24] Visitors can check Prisonpro.com for a list of visiting hours and visiting application forms for every correctional institution in the U.S.

Visitor Clothing

Visitor clothing is always an issue of great concern to staff. Visitors are routinely rejected for failing to comply with a particular facility's regulations on attire. Generally, the following items are listed as prohibited for visitors at most FBOP institutions:

- Military-type clothing;
- Khaki-colored or orange-colored clothing;
- Skirts and dresses shorter than three inches above the knee;
- Sleeveless shirts;
- Overly tight clothing such as tights, etc.;
- Tank tops; and
- Hats that are non-religious headgear.

This list is not exhaustive. Every visitor should *always* obtain a list of prohibited clothing articles either from the inmate or from the www.BOP.gov website. The website links to specific institutions and provides local regulations (called an "institutional supplement").

TIP: Staff enforcement of visitor clothing rules can border on the obsessive. It is highly recommended that visitors avoid clothing that could be interpreted as prohibited to avoid being turned away.

For example, women wearing short skirts can expect the possibility that staff will actually measure the hemline to ensure it does not rise more than three inches above the knee. Anything close to khaki or orange should be avoided. Experienced visitors often bring a change of clothes in the car in case their outfit is rejected.

Regrettably, it bears mentioning that staff sometimes attempt to reject visitor clothing as "too sexy" even if it otherwise meets regulations. Whenever a visitor feels that their clothing is being unfairly rejected, they should ask to see the duty officer, the final arbiter of visiting room matters.

Inmate Admittance to the Visitation Room

Inmates will be called for visits in the order their visitors are admitted. Most facilities try to call inmates to visits in a timely fashion. The exception might be shortly before institutional counts. Inmates on a visit are counted separately, and a list might be prepared as early as an hour before that count.

TIP: Whenever an inmate expects a visit, they should let the housing unit officer know where they'll be when visiting hours begin. They will usually be the one tasked with finding inmates when they are called to visitation. If not, the inmate runs the risk of leaving their visitor(s) sitting alone in the visiting room for quite some time. Inmates should be ready to go when they're called.

Inmates are subject to search when arriving at the "strip room" in visitation. At some facilities, inmates are required to change into visitation room clothing, a jumpsuit or hospital scrubs complete with a change of underwear and footwear. At other facilities, a simple pat search is conducted, and inmates are expected to wear only government-issued khakis and undergarments. Policies vary from one institution to another.

National Visitation Policies and Procedures

Generally, visits in the FBOP are "contact visits" in which there is no glass or telephone between the inmate and their visitors. Some facilities provide tables; others have rows of chairs. Some lower-security facilities even have outdoor picnic-type areas. According to federal regulations:

- The visiting room officer shall ensure that all visits are conducted in a quiet, orderly, and dignified manner. The officer can terminate visits that are not conducted in an appropriate manner.
- Staff shall permit limited physical contact such as handshakes, embracing, and kissing between an inmate and a visitor unless there is clear and convincing evidence that such contact would jeopardize the safety or security of the institution. Where contact visiting is provided, handshakes, embracing, and kissing are ordinarily permitted within the bounds of good taste and only at the beginning and end of the visit. The staff may limit physical contact to minimize opportunities for the introduction of contraband and to maintain the orderly operation of the visiting area.
- The visiting room officer cannot accept articles or gifts of any kind for an inmate, except packages that have been approved by the warden or a designated staff member.
- The visiting room officer shall be aware of any articles passed between the inmate and the visitor. If there is any reasonable basis to believe that any item being passed is contraband or is otherwise in violation of the law or Bureau regulations, the visiting room officer may examine the item.[25]

Penalties for Violation of Visiting Regulations

Inmates who violate any national or local policy on visits are subject to disciplinary action and, if applicable, criminal prosecution. Visitors might be barred for a period of time or indefinitely and can also face criminal prosecution, if applicable.

> *TIP: Every inmate and his or her visitor should be aware that staff are usually hyper-vigilant about detecting the introduction of contraband during visits. As such, keeping one's hands visible (and out of each other's clothing) is advisable. More than a few inmates have found themselves confined to a "dry cell" for several days after an innocent gesture like putting their hands in their pockets was deemed suspicious. Obey every visiting regulation to the letter.*

Notes

1. Program Statement 5267.09, Visiting Regulations; 28 C.F.R. § 540.40.
2. 28 C.F.R. § 540.44(a).
3. Program Statement 5267.09, Visiting Regulations at § 12.
4. *Id.*
5. *Id.*
6. *Id.*
7. 28 C.F.R. § 540.44(e).
8. Emery, Jodie, "My First US Federal Prison Visit With My Heroic Political Prisoner Husband, Marc Emery." June 19, 2010. Retrieved from http://www.cannabisculture.com/content/2010/06/19/my-first-us-federal-prison-visit-my-heroic-political-prisoner-husband-marc-emery.
9. *Id.*
10. Roberts, Daniel, "Life Behind Bars: Matthew Kluger Reveals All." *Fortune.* July 7, 2014.
11. 28 C.F.R. § 540.45.
12. Program Statement 5267.09, Visiting Regulations at § 9.
13. 28 C.F.R. § 543.13(e).
14. 28 C.F.R. § 543.13(c).
15. 28 C.F.R. § 543.13(d).
16. 28 C.F.R. § 540.2(b).
17. Program Statement 1480.05, News Media Contacts at § 8.
18. 28 C.F.R. § 540.63(e).
19. "General Visiting Information." Federal Bureau of Prisons. Retrieved from https://www.bop.gov/inmates/visiting.jsp.
20. Program Statement 5510.15, Searching, Detaining, and Arresting Visitors to Bureau Grounds and Facilities; 28 C.F.R. § 511.14.
21. Program Statement 5510.15, Searching, Detaining, and Arresting Visitors to Bureau Grounds and Facilities.
22. *Id.*
23. 28 C.F.R. § 540.51(h)(3).
24. Program Statement 5267.09, Visiting Regulations at § 14.
25. 28 C.F.R. §§ 540.51(h)(1)-(4).

Part VI – Personal Development

Sixteen

Educational Opportunities

Federal inmates have access to a variety of education materials and classes. These cover everything from traditional leisure reading to a variety of classes at different levels of sophistication. If an inmate has the will to improve their mind, the FBOP will usually provide a means to do so.

The prison community has little positive to say about the Bureau's educational efforts. At best, they call it substandard; at worst, a fraud. This is not the case. While federal prisoners will not earn an Ivy-league college education while incarcerated, motivated prisoners can find programs that will improve their level of education.

Those who put in the hard work at the Education Department can enjoy success. If one cannot read or write, they can learn to do so. Those who cannot speak or understand English will be tutored. Inmates who do not have a high school diploma or General Educational Development (GED) certificate will be provided the means to earn a GED.

Inmates who have achieved some level of education prior to incarceration will find that the Education Department offers something for them as well, whether it be teaching or studying.

TIP: The author's own education was obtained while behind bars. He earned a GED, a high school diploma, ministerial credentials, legal credentials, and his bachelor's degree. He is now a graduate student at Adams State University pursuing his MBA via correspondence education. He has even penned several books while incarcerated.

The prison itself might be a cage but the mind can roam free. Inmates should take advantage of what's available and become a better person for it.

An Overview of Educational Programs

Most federal facilities offer literacy classes, English as a Second Language (ESL) classes, GED classes, adult continuing education (ACE) classes, parenting classes, and Release Preparation Program (RPP) classes. By adding personal funding, every level of study is available including personal enrichment, high school, trade studies, religious, and college courses via correspondence education. While each institution's educational offerings vary, the programs listed in this section are typical.

English as a Second Language (ESL)

These classes are mandated by the Comprehensive Crime Control Act of 1990.[1] In these classes, non-English-speaking inmates learn to read and write in English. By law, they are required to participate in these classes until they pass a comprehensive skills test scored at the eighth-grade level. Those who qualify for this program should expect a traditional classroom setting managed by bilingual instructors.[2]

High School Equivalency (GED)

In the FBOP, inmates are not afforded the opportunity to earn a high school diploma. Instead, they are allowed to earn a GED certificate, the official high school diploma equivalent.[3] In fact, prisoners who don't already hold a high school diploma or GED are required to participate until they earn a GED or have spent a minimum of 240 hours in classroom instruction.[4] In the latter circumstance, they will be allowed to withdraw from school but they will not be allowed to earn and vest the maximum amount of good conduct time. This is a provision of the

Violent Crime Control and Law Enforcement Act (VCCLEA) and the Prison Litigation Reform Act (PLRA).[5]

GED classes are the most common and widely used type of education in the FBOP. This is because they are compulsory and the vast majority of prisoners are high school dropouts. As such, the need for these classes is widespread.

GED classes are much like those at a traditional high school, with a less diverse and less challenging curriculum. The tests are primarily based upon reading comprehension. Picture a teacher standing in front of a classroom presenting a general lesson followed by individual assignments. Instead of the teacher and the teacher's aide doing the bulk of the teaching, prisoners who typically have a higher education do most of the teaching through individual tutoring.

The FBOP also offers basic literacy classes designed for prisoners who can't read or write. These can be thought of as classes at the elementary and middle-school levels. Most federal prisons classify all general education courses below the GED level that prepare a student to obtain a GED to be GED courses. While different classrooms can be used for students at different education levels (first through fifth grade, sixth through eighth grade, or ninth through twelfth grade), these differences are not reflected in policy.

> *TIP: Inmates who need this level of education should do themselves a favor and make the most of it. A GED is the first step in the higher education process. Students must either hold a GED or a high school diploma to enroll in college.*
>
> *Similarly, a GED or high school diploma is a requirement for most entry-level employment. In fact, without a GED, inmates are restricted to the lowest pay grade and employment even while in the FBOP.*

Inmates are automatically placed in GED classes if they don't already have a GED or a high school diploma, although this takes time because of release date-related waiting lists. Those who are motivated can speed up the process by engaging in one of the following three actions: 1) speak with an Education Department staff member; 2) speak with the Supervisor of Education during the noon meal (turn in a cop-out to make the request formal); or 3) submit a paper cop-out or Electronic Request to Staff to the Supervisor of Education.

Parenting Classes

Most federal prisons offer some sort of parenting program.[6] These include classes designed to help inmates stay in contact with their families, strengthen parental bonds while incarcerated, and learn valuable parenting skills.

At some institutions, the classes are sponsored by the Education Department, Psychology Department, or Chapel. While offerings and formats differ, inmates with children are strongly advised to participate. These programs might help an inmate keep in contact with family and might help them demonstrate parenting skills.

Adult Continuing Education (ACE)

Beyond the GED level classes, the Bureau offers Adult Continuing Education (ACE) classes.[7] These classes are designed to give inmates an opportunity to receive an introduction to a number of disciplines. These are typically eight- to twelve-week classes that meet once a week for an hour or two and are taught by fellow prisoners. Examples of ACE classes include:

- Automobile sales
- Bookkeeping
- Business management
- Commercial driver's license (CDL)
- Money management
- NAPA vehicle repair
- Post-conviction remedies
- Spanish
- Writing and publishing

In addition to traditional ACE classes, many federal prisons also offer a Release Preparation Program (RPP) as well as self-paced ACE classes.[8] The former revolves around (sometimes mandated) classes on resume writing, interview skills, job searching skills, and job retention skills. The latter are based upon educational DVDs/VHS tapes in the library that correspond to written lessons.

> *TIP: While all of these classes have a GED prerequisite, they are not challenging. This is because of the low bar set by institutional staff. As a case in point, for over a year the author taught Writing and Publishing (an ACE course he developed). While he was eager to make it a beneficial course of study, he was instructed to lighten the load and "dumb down" the curriculum.*
>
> *In fact, instructors weren't even able to base grades upon a final project or essay. Instead, the only choice was a dumbed-down multiple choice examination. One would hope that FBOP institutions would allow their educators to actually challenge their students.*
>
> *ACE courses can be a great way for inmates to expose themselves to new ideas, concepts, and disciplines. As long as inmates are incarcerated, it can't hurt to sign up for as many classes as possible.*

Correspondence Education[e]

One of the most beneficial forms of education available to inmates is correspondence education, usually provided through the U.S. mail. While not the ideal format in this technological age, such classes offer real credentials and educational value. The breadth of correspondence educational opportunities is surprising.

Correspondence courses are available in the following areas: free and fee-based Bible studies, high school courses, personal enrichment courses, career/vocational courses, and college courses (both undergraduate and graduate). The options are virtually endless.

The only catch is the cost. While some of the programs in these fields are free or low-cost (usually Bible studies and personal enrichment courses), any

[e] *For a more in-depth look at higher education opportunities – including a complete correspondence education guide – purchase* Prison Education Guide *by Christopher Zoukis (Prison Legal News Publishing, 2016). In this book, see Appendix X for contact information for several quality correspondence programs.*

costs associated with a correspondence education program of study must be met by the inmate, not the FBOP.

TIP: Enrolling in a program of correspondence study is fairly simple. Locate a program of choice, fill out the application to enroll in the program, pay all the associated fees, receive and complete the coursework, and take any required examinations (which the education department will proctor if requested).

Inmates need authorization from their Education Department's College Coordinator prior to enrolling in any program of correspondence education with the sole exception of free Bible studies.

Library Services

The Education Department usually maintains a leisure library.[10] While the format of the library can vary, the principles are the same. All inmates will have access to a free selection of books, magazines, and newspapers that can be checked out or reviewed while in the library.

Selection will vary by the local prison but a few aspects are commonplace. For example, most federal prisons subscribe to *USA Today* and several other local and national newspapers. As for magazines, *Time, Rolling Stone*, and *People* are staples. Books are a bit more varied. While plenty of bestselling books find their way into the library, they could be there by donation or institutional purchase.

TIP: If inmates are interested in a specific text that is not offered in their prison's library, they might luck out with an interlibrary loan program. Some prisons engage in these programs while others do not.

If an inmate's prison does engage in such a program, they'll be able to submit a request for a specific book. If the text is available from a partnering library, they will be called to the Education Department several weeks later to pick up and check out their selections.

At most federal prisons, the library will stock select DVDs and VHS tapes that inmates can watch, free of charge, on specific TVs in the library. Typically this program is operated on a sign-up basis. As such, inmates must go to the library at a specific time to sign up for a specific time slot during the following week.

Notes

1. 18 U.S.C. § 3624(f).
2. Program Statement 5350.24, English-as-a-Second-Language Program (ESL); 28 C.F.R. § 544.40.
3. Program Statement 5350.28, Literacy Program (GED Standard).
4. 28 C.F.R. § 544.70.
5. 28 C.F.R. § 544.73.
6. Program Statement 5300.21, Education, Training and Leisure Time Program Standards; Program Statement 5355.03, Parenting Program Standards.
7. Program Statement 5300.21, Education, Training and Leisure Time Program Standards.
8. Program Statement P5325.07, Release Preparation Program; 28 C.F.R. § 571.10.
9. Program Statement P5354.03, Postsecondary Education Programs for Inmates.
10. Program Statement 1542.06, Library Services, Inmate; 28 C.F.R. § 544.100.

Seventeen

Entertainment

For a number of reasons, both pro-inmate and pro-administration, all federal prisons allow certain types of entertainment including TVs, radios, and MP3 players (a newer development). For the administration, these devices occupy and placate the incarcerated population. For the inmate, these devices help pass the time and provide enjoyment. Entertainment is a win-win proposition in a correctional setting.

> *TIP: The key with any form of entertainment is to utilize it as a tool, not an excuse. While entertainment in prison is invaluable, inmates should not allow their entertainment activities to interfere with constructive activities.*

Television

Television is by far the most common and widely used form of entertainment and is a primary pastime for incarcerated populations. Hundreds of thousands of prisoners regularly watch television programming. For some, this amounts to a mere passing of time. For others, it is an unhealthy religion. The largest number simply enjoy sports, movies, and the programs they can access.

TVs in federal prisons typically offer basic cable packages. Some packages allow for up to 100 channels while other prisons might only have 30 or so. Regardless of how many channels are included, a selection is available.

TVs are typically housed in two different areas: day rooms and TV rooms. In day rooms, they are mounted fifteen or twenty feet up on walls or support beams located in various places within a single housing unit. This allows many inmates to watch diverse programming. These TVs have had their speakers removed to cut down on noise. Instead, they utilize FM modulators, a technology that allows the inmates to tune into a specific FM frequency on a radio/headset to listen to a specific TV.

In TV rooms, the sets still have speakers. Typical housing units maintain two TV rooms with one TV in each. These rooms are usually smaller spaces that can comfortably hold ten to fifteen inmates in chairs. Inmates who don't have radios utilize TV rooms. While some institutions set TV schedules through an inmate programming committee, many do not. For those which do not, the inmate watching the individual TV decides on programming. See the "Housing Unit" section of Chapter 4 for information on TV politics.

A highlight of the week for many inmates is the institutional movie. These are commercial video releases obtained by the administration and shown via the institutional movie channel on the TVs. Most facilities provide three movies for each weekend. One will play on Friday nights at 5:00 p.m. and 7:00 p.m., another on Saturdays at 7:00 a.m., 1:00 p.m., 5:00 p.m., and 7:00 p.m., and the third on Sundays, following the Saturday schedule. Only movies rated PG-13 and lower are permitted, but exceptions are made for special events.

It is common for inmates to save specific seats for both regular TV watching and institutional movie watching. This is done by placing their chair – a plastic chair assigned to their cell or bunk – in a specific spot.

TIP: Specific spots for TV viewing are viewed much like traditional property. Fellow inmates will be very territorial of their spots. When an inmate first enters a prison, it is advised that they pick a spot with no other chair. Then, as people leave or go home, they can slowly take a better spot.

Radios

Within every FBOP facility, inmates have the option of purchasing a Walkman-type radio. While the model of radio and headphones can vary from prison to prison, all sell through the commissary. A typical model is the $41.60 Sony SRF-M35 radio, a clear AM/FM radio that operates on two AAA batteries. A variety of headphones might also be sold in the commissary, some of them very high quality.

TIP: A word of caution is required concerning radios. These small and expensive items are appealing to a thief. Inmates should never leave their radios out when they are not around. When inmates go to chow, their radios should be locked in their lockers. Inmates should never lend a radio out if they are not prepared for it to never come back or to come back broken.

If an inmate does not have enough money to purchase a new radio, other prisoners will often have used radios for sale. Typical prices range from $5.00 to $20.00. The key is to test and inspect it thoroughly prior to purchase. It is imperative to ensure that all of the features work, that the shell of the radio is intact, and that both the AM and FM channels work.

TIP: Some used radios are on the market because they've been dropped and the reception is compromised. As such, it is a good idea to first walk around and test the radio before purchase.

Owning a radio is a must in the FBOP. It helps to drown out all the noise, allows the user to listen to the mounted TVs, and helps pass the time. To be in prison for any amount of time is reason enough to buy one. Without it, a vast amount of contact with the outside world is cut off.

TIP: If a prisoner knows a talented electrician, they can have them convert a AAA radio into a AA radio. This will cut their battery costs in half. But beware: many prisoners who claim to be experts at radio repair will only be good at taking someone's money.

MP3 Players

In an innovative move, the FBOP is now allowing inmates to purchase MP3 players from the commissary and individual MP3 music files through the TRULINCS computer system.[1]

> *TIP: The FM radio reception and functionality of the SanDisk Clip+ and SanDisk Sport leave a bit to be desired. As such, it is recommended that inmates also purchase a regular radio.*

MP3 players allow inmates who have funds to enjoy personalized music selections. They also help the entire inmate population keep pace with the outside technological world. TRULINCS teaches inmates needed computer skills in this computer-driven world.

At present, the two MP3 players being sold in the FBOP are the SanDisk Clip+, which has 8 gigabytes of memory, and the SanDisk Sport, which has 16 gigabytes of memory. The former costs $69.20 while the latter runs $88.40. Both can be purchased at the commissary and come with a built-in clip and a set of ear buds. Their dimensions are approximately 2" high x 1 ¼" wide. Despite their small size, they hold approximately 2,000 and 4,000 songs, respectively and have an FM radio and rechargeable battery built in.

> *TIP: Because of the small size and fragility of the player, prisoners should go to the hobby craft area to ask about an MP3 player holder. Chances are somebody will make high-quality MP3 player holders to protect the device. These holders generally cost five to ten dollars.*

Upon purchasing the MP3 player in the commissary, an inmate must wait two hours before activating it on a TRULINCS computer. To activate the player, the inmate connects the device to the USB cord attached to a TRULINCS computer, logs on, and clicks the music icon. Once the music window opens, instructions will be given on how to activate the player. After activation, the player will display the inmate's name and register number at start-up.

TIP: The player must be revalidated every fourteen days or it will deactivate. A deactivated player will not allow use of the MP3 or FM radio functions. Each time new MP3s are purchased, the player is automatically revalidated. Additionally, an inmate can revalidate anytime by selecting the option in the music store.

After the player has been activated, the inmate has access to the store/library area of the music folio. Songs are located and purchased in the store. Inmates can search according to artist, album, title, and genre. Over 2 million songs are available for purchase through four major record labels. Songs with explicit lyrics are not available although many edited versions are.

Only individual songs can be purchased, though it is possible to purchase all of the songs on an album individually. Songs are purchased with TRU-Units and are priced in three tiers: $0.80 (16 units), $1.20 (24 units), and $1.55 (31 units). Available titles and prices are decisions made by the vendor, not the FBOP.

TIP: Refunds are not furnished for accidental song purchases. Inmates should make sure to preview each song prior to purchasing it to ensure that it is the song they want to download.

As the inmate browses, they can listen to thirty-second samples (a limit of thirty samples per day is imposed); add up to thirty songs to a wish list of desired music; and purchase up to fifteen songs per day (which is done by placing selections in the cart). The Bureau places strict limits on the amount of time inmates can spend on the music service each day. As of this writing, inmates can spend a total of sixty minutes per day in the music service with a fifteen-minute limit imposed on each session.

TIP: Since purchases are deducted from an inmate's TRU-Units balance, purchase TRU-Units from the TRULINCS home screen before selecting the music after. Once an inmate is in the music service, they will not be able to purchase more TRU-Units. If more TRU-Units are required, they would have to exit the music service, purchase more TRU-Units, log off the computer, wait thirty minutes, log back on, and then make the purchase.

Many songs are available for immediate download while some are not. Those that are not immediately available upon purchase will automatically download to the player once they are available (typically the following day) and the player has been connected to a TRULINCS computer and the music service opened. Notifications about which songs are available for immediate download are not currently available.

If music is waiting to be downloaded because it was not immediately available, the inmate will not be able to purchase any more music regardless of whether the fifteen-minute session limit has been reached.

TIP: If an inmate plans on purchasing fifteen songs on a certain day or any amount over one, they should first add the songs to their wish list. Then they can select all the songs they wish to buy that day and purchase them collectively. That way, all of the desired songs will be purchased and those immediately available will be downloaded.

When first using the player, the inmate should fully charge the battery and then use it until the battery is completely empty. Rechargeable batteries work best when fully charged, fully depleted, and then fully charged again. Short charge periods may harm the effective capacity of the battery.

Under the best of circumstances, the battery on the SanDisk Clip+ (8GB) and SanDisk Sport will last for up to fifteen hours of continuous use on a single charge. Players can be charged either at the charging station provided in each housing unit or at a TRULINCS computer with a USB cord. Typically, the charging station is where charging occurs. It takes between two and three hours to fully charge a completely depleted battery.

TIP: Inmates shouldn't leave MP3 players unattended even while charging. They are even smaller and more expensive than a radio. A good security device is a brightly colored string tied to the MP3 player holder. At a glance, an inmate can ensure that their player is still on the charging stand.

TIP: If an inmate uses a lot of email time, they could charge their player as they email. Thirty minutes of email plus fifteen minutes of music browsing is forty-five minutes of charging. Several of these sessions a day means charging won't be a problem.

As of this writing, the SanDisk Clip+ and SanDisk Sport appear to have software glitches. This isn't so much because of the product but because of the specialized programming installed by the vendor Advanced Technologies Group (ATG). Inmates should expect the player to freeze up from time to time. When this occurs, the inmate should hold down the power button for a full fifteen seconds. Then power on the player (allow it to fully turn on), power it off normally (not using the fifteen-second power off), and then power it on again. This should clear up the problem.

According to documents obtained from the Bureau, the FBOP is not responsible for broken or defective MP3 players. They will, however, allow the inmate to mail their player to ATG for warranty repair, after which it will be allowed back into the institution. The only local replacements done will be for players that were nonfunctional at purchase; that is to say, the player was never able to turn on or wasn't able to be activated.

TIP: If a problem arises, inmates should bring their player directly to the trust fund supervisor and explain the issue. They shouldn't speak with the commissary staff or other institutional staff. The trust fund supervisor will provide information on warranty processing.

Upon release, the player can be mailed to ATG with a $15 check. They will remove all of the customized software, disabling the requirement that the player be revalidated, and enabling the recording functions of the player. This essentially restores it to the state it would be in if it had been purchased from a store on the outside but with the purchased music intact.

Notes

1. Program Statement 4500.11, Trust Fund/Deposit Fund Manual.

Eighteen

Recreation

Every federal prisoner in a general population facility will have at least some time for recreation. How that time is spent can have a big impact on quality of life.

The Yard

At most FBOP institutions, the recreation department is a hub of activity and the yard is usually the epicenter of such activities. Many organized sporting and recreation activities occur, and the yard is a social gathering spot, for better or worse.

While construction and design techniques among the 200 or so federal prisons vary substantially, most general population institutions will have one or more recreation yards for inmate use. Generally, there will be one main yard that contains at least a soccer or football field with smaller areas for basketball courts, handball or tennis courts, and other activities. Many will have a free-standing softball field.

How these areas are divided depends largely on the security level of the facility. At the high security USP institutions, yards might be divided by fences that are gated and accessible only at ten-minute moves on the hour. Other prisons have one large yard in which inmates can move from one area of interest to another unimpeded. Again, configurations vary but inevitably there will be areas for chess and card games, Bocce courts, volleyball, etc.

At most Bureau facilities, the yard is open from 6:00 a.m. to 8:30 p.m. with periods of closure for the noon meal and counts.[f] This broad access allows inmates at least some outdoor recreation time regardless of work assignments and other programs. Some inmates spend a large chunk of their lives on the yard while incarcerated.

Inclement or extreme weather such as lightning storms can cause the yard to close. However, the extent to which weather is a factor depends on each institution's attitude. For example, at USP Tucson, AZ, where temperatures can reach 120°, the thirty-five-and-over basketball league will play in the afternoon sun. At FCI Petersburg, VA, no outside recreation is allowed if the temperature index reaches 100°. FCI Ray Brook, NY, has a strong tradition of enduring cold and snow, so the yard will usually stay open despite temperatures of negative 30° and several feet of snow.

> *TIP: Many institutions have outdoor weights and exercise equipment. While these items are ostensibly for everyone's use, inmates should make note of the local customs before jumping in and disrupting another inmate's routine.*
>
> *As with many things in prison, inmates can be attached to their routine and will not be happy if a new inmate gets in their way. Prisoners should observe and ask rather than merely do.*

The yard can be a challenging location for new inmates because supervision is significantly reduced in these large and populated areas. At a USP, a gun tower will loom overhead; at other institutions, staff is stationed on the ground. Generally there is a culture within the FBOP of leaving supervision a

[f] *Some facilities have reduced access due to security and staffing issues. Several USPs are "split yard" facilities, in which one side of the prison never "recs" with the other, to allow for more secure management.*

bit loose in the yard. As such, some inmates visit the yard only when forced to, for instance when their unit is being shaken down.

At some facilities, this reluctance is not without reason. At higher security-level institutions, the yard is where "prison business" is conducted, where friendships are forged, debts are paid, and conflicts resolved. As the yard is one of the few places where inmates from different housing units can meet, incidents involving violence are quite common in some places. Common sense and awareness of what's going on will allow an inmate to avoid trouble.

TIP: Many institutions have staffed gun towers in the yard, and virtually all of the medium-security or higher-security institutions have armed personnel outside the perimeter fence. Accordingly, when there is trouble in the yard – a fight or a disturbance – it is imperative that inmates move away from the problem calmly and obey any staff directives, especially orders to "get down on the ground."

FBOP staff are authorized to use lethal force to quell disturbances. Even nonlethal projectiles fired from the tower can kill or inflict permanent injury. It is not an inmate's business, they should stay away from it.

Indoor Recreation: The Gym and Hobby Craft

Most FBOP facilities have an indoor recreation area consisting of a gym or exercise area, a hobby craft room, and a passive recreation area.

The Gym

An indoor basketball gym is a common feature. The gym is used for organized sports (basketball, floor hockey, volleyball leagues, etc.) as well as for indoor handball/racquetball and pickup games. Some facilities will use the gym for yoga and exercise classes during the winter months.

If the facility is so equipped, the indoor weight room is a popular spot. Free weights, cable machines, and various benches and pull-up bars are common. Some facilities might not have weights; most of the newer institutions do not. Others might be equipped with a dedicated indoor area for exercise bikes, stair steppers, and the like. Still others might offer kettlebells, jump ropes, and other personal fitness accessories. Most such items are signed out from an inmate-staffed issue room on a first-come, first-served basis.

Hobby Craft

"Hobby craft" is the FBOP term for arts and crafts such as painting, leatherwork, pottery, and beading. Participation in these programs usually begins with enrollment in an art program, leather class, etc. Some institutions permit inmates to join hobby craft if space permits or if they demonstrate interest or proficiency.

Materials used in hobby craft might be issued to the inmate for classes or programs, or they can arrive through Special Purchase Orders (SPOs) at the institutional commissary. SPOs allow inmates to order arts and crafts supplies from a preapproved vendor through the recreation department. The items are then sold to the inmate at the prison's commissary with a markup of 5 to 30 percent depending on the type of material and local policy.[1]

Most facilities provide space for using arts and crafts materials as well as lockers to secure personally owned supplies. For leathercraft and other crafts involving tools, a secured room or cage might issue tools that are not authorized for personal possession, such as awls and hammers.

Participation in hobby craft permits an inmate to mail personally created items home as long as the address is on the inmate's visitation list. Inmates are permitted to sell their products to the public and Bureau staff only via a preapproved authorization process.[2] In practice, this is rarely permitted.

TIP: Nothing in FBOP policy prohibits family and friends from selling inmate-produced items. Many pieces of inmate art are sold on the internet and through other sources.

Art can provide more than the satisfaction of holding something an inmate has made themselves. The Prison Arts Resource Project, sponsored by the National Endowment for the Arts, looked at nearly 50 studies of how arts programs inside prisons can impact inmates.

The study found that art programs increased self-esteem and social behaviors while participants were still incarcerated. Prisoners also became more connected to their families because they could share something they had created. After release, art program parolees had a higher chance of favorable outcomes over a two-year period compared to those who did not participate in any arts-related projects.[3]

The Prison Arts Coalition (PAC) was established in 2008 to serve as a national network for prison arts. They provide support, information, and partnership opportunities. They can guide inmates to publications and programs that support their desires to go further with their art. Disciplines include writing and poetry, visual arts, drama, music, dance and, where possible, yoga, meditation, and horticulture. Contact PAC managers Becky Mer, Wendy Jason, or Freddy Gutierrez at PACoalitionadmin@gmail.com for more information.

Even if an inmate has only a slight interest in hobby craft activities, exploring the opportunities could pay off richly.

Passive Recreation

Most Bureau facilities offer a variety of passive recreational activities such as billiards tables, table tennis, and other diversions. A wide range of leisure activities can take place from Dungeons and Dragons groups to fantasy football leagues and drama clubs. Many recreation departments also offer television viewing, audio CDs and videos to check out, satellite libraries, and a host of classes, seminars, and groups on a variety of subjects.

Recreation departments are authorized to operate satellite radio services from commercial vendors to offer a wide range of programming beyond that available in the rural areas where some facilities are located. These services can be accessed throughout the institution's local FM broadcast stations.

FBOP policy also permits recreation departments to show commercially available movies to the inmate population. This usually occurs through an institution's closed-circuit television network. Federal regulations restrict the showing of movies as follows: "no movies rated R, X, or NC-17 may be shown to inmates, [but] institutions may show R and NC-17 movies that have been edited for general public viewing."[4] This restriction generally permits "airline edit" versions of popular films shown on commercial jets.

Foreign language movies are sometimes not rated. As such, they can be shown "if they do not include profanity, graphic violence, or nudity."[5]

Facilities are required to observe strict compliance with all licensing agreements and copyright requirements when showing movies to the inmate population. For this reason, some popular movies might not be available for viewing. Most institutions enter into licensing agreements through a distributor such as Swank Motion Pictures, Inc., which brokers the deals.

As to movie selections, many facilities show selections from the latest releases on commercial video or use an inmate request system to choose movies.

> *TIP: At the end of Program Statement P5370.11, Recreation Programs, Inmate is an extensive Q&A section that addresses the particulars of movie selection and viewing. It also addresses other recreation issues created by recent legislation that are intended to restrict inmate health and enjoyment programs.*

Music

Most facilities offer a music program. Inmates have access to musical instruments ranging from acoustic guitars they can play in the yard to fully equipped band rehearsal rooms complete with drum sets, amplifiers, and PA systems.

While recent legislation has resulted in a bar against "electric or electronic musical instrument[s],"[6] most institutions get around these restrictions by equipping acoustic guitars with electronic pickups or by "borrowing" instruments from the religious services department, which faces no such bar. At many institutions, high quality music is made and regular band shows are common. Inmates are not permitted to own or retain personal instruments with the exception of a harmonica.

Sports

Every general population prison in the FBOP system offers a variety of sporting events. There are organized leagues for basketball, softball, soccer, street hockey, and flag football; virtually every team sport is played somewhere in the system. These leagues can be highly organized with inmate coaches, referees, and commissioners. Often several levels of competition are set up for popular sports (A League; B League for those thirty-five and over; 5'9"-and-under basketball, etc.).

> *TIP: Team sports can be a ticket to instant acceptance at many institutions where sports are taken very seriously. Skilled inmates might even be offered contracts for compensation!*

Individual sports are also well funded. Tennis, handball, racquetball, and other individual sports are very popular. On holidays, most recreation departments sponsor tournaments for these sports as well as for team sports and other contests like fitness challenges.

> *TIP: Inmates in the FBOP have a long tradition of working very hard and resourcefully toward achieving high levels of physical fitness. While weight rooms are becoming a vestige of the past (no new facilities are permitted to have them), staff are usually committed to finding viable alternatives. They might order kettlebell-style weights (which are not explicitly prohibited) or simply look the other way while inmates lift homemade sandbags or dirt bags.*

Notes

1. 28 C.F.R. § 544.35.
2. Program Statement P5370.11, Recreation Programs, Inmate at § 14.
3. Taohil, Kathleen, "Why Arts Programs in Prisons Are So Important." June 21, 2015. Retrieved from http://csgjusticecenter.org/corrections/media-clips/why-arts-programs-in-prisons-are-so-important/.

4. Program Statement P5370.11, Recreation Programs, Inmate at § 11; 28 C.F.R. § 544.33.
5. *Id.*
6. *Id.* at § 15.

Nineteen

Religious Services

Inmates confined within the FBOP have the right to practice the religion of their choice. This is guaranteed by a host of constitutional, statutory, and regulatory provisions. Correctional chaplains shoulder quite a bit of the burden, providing services, outreach, and information. The history of religious protections in prison spans centuries because churches were among the first institutions to provide sanctuary for the accused. The religious Order of the Misericordia was founded in the late 1400s specifically to console prisoners condemned to death.

In previous times, chaplains provided programs and pastoral care, including delivering distressing news from home. Nowadays their role has expanded to coordinating facilities, finding volunteers for special programs, helping inmates secure religious furlough visits, connecting with religious organizations outside prison walls, and training administrators and staff about non-traditional faiths.[1]

Because of the work performed by a number of chaplains, religious groups, and because of legal protection, most inmates find an acceptable level of religious accommodation at most institutions.

Constitutional Guarantees

The Free Exercise Clause of the U.S. Constitution's First Amendment "requires government respect for, and noninterference with, the religious beliefs and practices of our Nation's peoples."[2] Those confined in prisons retain those First Amendment rights, notwithstanding some "necessary withdrawal or limitation of many privileges and rights, a retraction justified by" legitimate penal concerns.[3] Restrictions on religious freedoms in prison are subject to a "reasonableness" test that balances these competing concerns on a case-by-case basis.[4]

Statutory Protections

Federal prisoners enjoy protection of their religious rights under the Religious Freedom Restoration Act (RFRA) of 1993.[5] The RFRA forbids the government from "substantially burden[ing] a person's exercise of religion," including "any exercise of religion, whether or not compelled by, or central to, a system of religious belief."[6] Government burdens on such rights must be "in furtherance of a compelling governmental interest," and must be "the least restrictive means of furthering the governmental interest."[7]

Regulatory Protections

Religious practices for federal inmates are governed by 28 C.F.R. §§ 548.10 - .20 and Bureau program statements, most notably Program Statement P5360.09, Religious Beliefs and Practices, and Technical Reference Manual T5360.02, Ministry of BOP Chaplains.

Under Program Statement P5360.09 and 28 C.F.R. § 548.10(a), the FBOP pledges to provide "inmates of all faith groups with reasonable and equitable opportunities to pursue religious beliefs and practices within the constraints of budgetary limitation and consistent with the security and orderly running of [the] institution and the Bureau of Prisons."

While the FBOP does not require inmates to profess a religious preference, an inmate "may designate any or no religious preference" at any time.[8] In doing so, an inmate is then permitted to take advantage of an enhanced level of access to religious services.

Chapel Operations

Generally, most Bureau institutions offer access to an institutional chapel for the purpose of group worship activities, religious study, library access, and pastoral counseling from staff chaplains.

Most FBOP facilities employ several staff chaplains who participate in the activities listed above and supervise the day-to-day operations of the chapel. Some institutions also utilize contract clergy and community volunteers for conducting religious services and studies.[9] Staff chaplains are the primary contact with inmates for notifications of family deaths and serious illnesses in the community.

Most Bureau institutions offer a weekly worship or service period for each religious group authorized by the chapel. Such groups might include mainstream Christian, Jewish, and Muslim communities as well as smaller groups like Buddhists and Wiccans. Policy dictates that no religion can receive preferential treatment over another; however, experience dictates that this requirement is rarely observed. Some facilities might offer regular study periods, as well.

Many chapels also offer extensive libraries containing written and audiovisual resources. Books can be checked out, and movies and CDs can be used at the chapel.

Most FBOP institutions also offer one annual "ceremonial meal" for each recognized group.[10]

Most federal facilities will support at least a few of the four largest traditional groups: Catholic, Protestant, Muslim, and Jewish. Nowadays, a host of nontraditional groups are active inside correctional facilities. These include but are certainly not limited to Hinduism, Mormonism, Native American, Buddhism, Rastafarian, Santeria, Christian Scientists, and Wiccan.

No matter what religion an inmate subscribes to, services are generally considered safe havens because few attacks happen during worship. They also provide spaces where inmates can meet new people, enjoy regular social interaction, and find acceptance within a group. Individuals who actively participate in religious activities while in prison also have a lower rate of recidivism.[11]

Special Considerations

Inmates whose religious beliefs require special considerations not extended to the general population may or may not find those needs accommodated. Whether such considerations are provided is often determined by the relative establishment of the tradition.

For example, the FBOP allows Jewish, Muslim, and Native American inmates to wear religious headgear throughout the institution. The same accommodation is also extended to Rastafarians and Sikhs.[12] Other groups might be permitted to wear headgear during religious services. Likewise, items like prayer beads, religious medallions, and prayer rugs can be retained as personal property.[13]

When it comes to holidays and holy days, the Bureau often permits inmates to enjoy a work proscription provided they are listed under that particular religious preference. Events like Ramadan, Passover, and other festivals are also routinely honored.[14]

Religious dietary matters are dealt with in a similar fashion. For example, Jewish and Muslim inmates often participate in the Certified Food program, an alternative diet that meets Kosher and Halal certifications. Conversely, inmates whose religious beliefs require vegetarianism are required to "self-select" foods from the general population menu.[15]

Inmates whose religious beliefs are not well known might be required to produce documentation from a recognized source to obtain special consideration.[16]

Notes

1. "Religion in Corrections." *The Encyclopedia of Crime and Punishment,* Vol. 3. (Sage, 2002). Pg. 1375.
2. *Cutter v. Wilkerson*, 544 U.S. 709, 719 (2005).
3. *O'Lone v. Estate of Shabazz*, 482 U.S. 342, 348 (1987).
4. *Turner v. Safley*, 482 U.S. 78, 89 (1987).
5. 42 U.S.C. §§ 2000bb – 2000bb-4.
6. *Id.*
7. *Id.*

8. Program Statement P5360.09, Religious Beliefs and Practices; 28 C.F.R. § 548.10(a).
9. 28 C.F.R. § 548.14.
10. 28 C.F.R. § 548.20(c).
11. "Religion in Corrections." *The Encyclopedia of Crime and Punishment*, Vol. 3 (Sage, 2002). Pg. 1375.
12. Program Statement P5360.09, Religious Beliefs and Practices at § 14.
13. *Id.*
14. 28 C.F.R. § 548.18.
15. Program Statement T5360.02, Ministry of BOP Chaplains at § (B)(5).
16. *Id.* at § (B)(12).

Part VII – Disciplinary Program

Twenty

Inmate Discipline Program

All inmates confined within the FBOP are required to abide by the disciplinary program authorized by 18 U.S.C. § 4042(a)(3). According to 28 C.F.R. § 541.1, the disciplinary program "helps ensure the safety, security, and orderly operation of correctional facilities, and the protection of the public, by allowing Bureau staff to impose sanctions on inmates who commit prohibited acts."

This disciplinary policy is contained in Program Statement 5270.09, Inmate Discipline Program. It is highly recommended that every federal inmate and attorney who handles in-detention concerns become familiar with this policy. According to section 3(b) of the program statement, "staff take disciplinary action at such times and to the degree necessary to regulate an inmate's behavior within Bureau rules and institutional guidelines and to promote a safe and orderly institutional environment[.]" The disciplinary program is a significant and ever present aspect of life in the Bureau of Prisons.

As outlined in Program Statement 5270.09 § 3(a) through (e), four principles are said to apply to every disciplinary action: (1) every FBOP employee or contractor can initiate incident reports; (2) inmate behavior is controlled by staff in an impartial and consistent manner; (3) disciplinary action is never to be capricious or retaliatory; and (4) corporal punishment of any kind is never imposed or allowed.

Within Table 1 of the same Program Statement is a list of all prohibited acts. According to 28 C.F.R. § 541.3(a), "[these] acts are divided into four separate categories based on severity: greatest [100 series]; high [200 series]; moderate [300 series]; and low [400 series]." Sanctions progressively become more serious as the severity level increases. See Appendix II for a complete list of currently prohibited acts.

Note that an inmate need not succeed in committing a prohibited act to be charged with a violation. Policy stipulates that "[a]iding, attempting, abetting, or making plans to commit any of the prohibited acts is treated the same as committing the act itself."[1]

Overview of Disciplinary Process

The disciplinary process is initiated when a staff member has reason to believe a prohibited act has been committed. The staff member first writes an incident report that describes the incident and prohibited act(s). The report is forwarded to the institution's lieutenant's office for processing. The inmate is to be issued a copy of the incident report by the lieutenant on duty within 24 hours ("ordinarily," according to 28 C.F.R.. § 541.5(a)).

During this stage of the disciplinary process, the inmate is allowed to make an initial statement and can enter an initial pleading of innocence or guilt. This inmate retains the right to remain silent but should be advised that "[the inmate's] silence may be used to draw an adverse inference against [him or her] at any stage of the process."[2]

If an alleged prohibited act is of a greatest (100) or high (200) severity, the lieutenant has the authority to immediately place the inmate in the Special Housing Unit (SHU) on administrative detention status pending resolution. While this can also occur if the inmate is charged with a moderate (300) or low (400) severity prohibited act, it is far less common.

Within five working days of receiving the incident report ("ordinarily," according to 28 C.F.R. § 541.7(c)), the inmate will be called in front of the

Unit Disciplinary Committee (UDC). At this hearing, the inmate has the right to make a further statement and present documentary evidence of his or her innocence. The committee then makes one of three dispositions.

- The inmate committed the charged prohibited act(s);
- The inmate did not commit the charged prohibited act(s); or
- The charges are to be referred to the disciplinary hearing officer.[3]

If the committee finds that the inmate committed prohibited act(s), they will immediately impose sanctions. Typical sanctions include loss of phone, email, visitation, commissary, work assignment, or preferable housing for a specified period of time (fifteen days, thirty days, sixty days, ninety days, etc.). Notice of the findings and sanctions will be issued to the inmate by the close of the next business day.[4] Once notice is received (in the form of the completed incident report form), the inmate can appeal through the Administrative Remedy Program.

If the UDC finds that the inmate did not commit the charged prohibited act(s), all charges and record thereof will be expunged. If the alleged prohibited act is of greatest (100) or high (200) severity, or if the Disciplinary Hearing Officer (DHO) has already suspended a previous sanction, the committee must refer the incident report to the DHO.[5] If the alleged prohibited act is of a repetitive nature, the committee can refer the incident report to the DHO for a hearing.

If the charges are referred to the DHO, the inmate has the right to request a staff representative to assist with their defense and/or to have witnesses called.[6] Inmates are also advised of their right to be present at the hearing (as well as the right to waive appearance), their rights surrounding the hearing itself, and are provided with notice of the hearing.

This notice must be issued at least twenty-four hours before the disciplinary hearing officer's hearing.[7] Those who remain in general population will typically wait a few weeks before their hearing while those housed in the SHU may wait a month or more.

Once in front of the DHO, the inmate will be allowed to have their staff representative and witnesses present.[8] The inmate will also be allowed to present documentary evidence of innocence and make an official statement.[9] The inmate retains the right to remain silent but, as previously stated, silence can be used "to draw an adverse inference."[10]

The officer then makes one of four dispositions:

- The inmate committed the charged prohibited act(s);
- The inmate committed a similar prohibited act(s);
- The inmate did not commit the charged prohibited act(s); or
- The incident report requires further investigation/review.[11]

If the inmate is found to have committed a prohibited act(s), the DHO will immediately impose sanctions. These may include loss of privileges (commissary, phone, visitation, email, etc.), monetary restitution, and/or disciplinary segregation.

Unlike the notice provided in UDC hearings, the DHO's notice is much more detailed. It is supposed to be issued within fifteen days, but this is often not the case. Typical wait times range from two months to six months. Once the report is issued, the inmate can appeal through the Administrative Remedy Program.

If the inmate is found not to have committed the charged prohibited act(s), all charges and records thereof will be expunged. If the incident report is referred for further investigation/review, the investigating lieutenant will continue the investigation based on the disciplinary hearing officer's directives. Also at this stage, the DHO can remand the incident report back to the UDC for rehearing.

Incident Reports

According to 28 C.F.R. § 541.5(a), "The discipline process starts when staff witness or reasonably believe that [the inmate] committed a prohibited act.

TIP: Chapter 2 of Program Statement 5270.09 states that staff "must" complete an incident report when warranted. The policy also states that the reporting employee must "immediately" complete part 1 of the incident report. While this is a way of ensuring accurate evidence, it is also helpful to the inmate. Reporting officers cannot hold a past incident as a coercive tool.

"A staff member will issue [the inmate] an incident report describing the incident and the prohibited act(s) [the inmate is] charged with committing.

TIP: A more detailed description can be of use when appealing because there is more opportunity to poke holes in the allegations. On the flip side, a less detailed description can help since circumstances might not fit the limited scope of the description.

"[The inmate] will ordinarily receive the incident report within 24 hours of staff becoming aware of [the inmate's] involvement in the incident."[g]

TIP: If an inmate has been caught red-handed by an officer, it is advised that they immediately engage in damage control. This means presenting mitigating thoughts or ideas to the reporting officer. The officer might let the issue go. The author has seen officers let fights, recent tattoos, tattoo equipment, and even large quantities of booze go with effective mitigation techniques.

The inmate will be called to the lieutenant's office to receive the incident report. Once there, the inmate will be greeted by the investigating officer (the lieutenant currently on duty).[h] Once the lieutenant has verified the inmate's identity (using the identification card or recital of registration number), they

[g] *While 28 C.F.R. § 541.5(a) states that the twenty-four hour limit is "ordinarily" imposed, generally a justification is required for going beyond this time limit. If an incident report isn't issued within twenty-four hours of staff becoming aware of a prohibited act, the inmate is advised to state this to the investigating officer and pursue this during their appeals.*

[h] *Program Statement 5270.09, Chapter 2 clarifies, "The Investigating Officer is an employee at the supervisory level who conducts an investigation of alleged inmate misconduct. The Investigating Officer must be IDC-certified, and may not be the employee reporting the incident or otherwise be involved in the incident."*

will inform the inmate of the charge(s) leveled against them. This is done by reading the description of the alleged prohibited act(s) contained in the incident report.

After reading the description of the incident report to the inmate (a requirement of 28 C.F.R. § 541.5(b)), the investigating officer is required to inform the inmate "that [he or she] may remain silent at all stages of the discipline process, but that [their] silence may be used to draw an adverse inference against [them] at any stage of the process. [Their] silence alone, however, cannot be the basis for finding [they] committed the prohibited act(s)."[12]

At this point, in accordance with 28 C.F.R. § 541.5(b)(2), the investigating officer will inquire if the inmate desires to make a statement, explain the incident, request any witnesses to be consulted, and/or request any additional evidence to be obtained and reviewed.[i] This is a crucial point, so each component is discussed below.

> *TIP: This is a very stressful experience. Often the lieutenant (the allegedly impartial investigating officer) will attempt to intimidate the inmate into complying with their wishes ... in other words, admitting to the incident report. At times, this is done by having several compound officers surround the inmate or even slam them against a wall under the guise of a personal search for contraband. Whatever they do, the inmate should not falsely admit. At this point in time, silence is the inmate's point of strength.*

Statement/Explanation

Generally speaking, if the inmate is in the lieutenant's office to receive an incident report, staff already has all the information they need to find the inmate guilty. In the vast majority of cases, the only evidence is an officer's word against the inmate's. Even if the officer is proven to have provided false testimony in a

---

[i] *If the incident report is being referred to an outside agency for potential criminal prosecution, a statement will not be requested and the internal disciplinary proceedings will be halted pending the result of the criminal investigation.*

portion of their statement, the Bureau tends to use the allegedly truthful portions as a basis for a guilty finding.

The reporting officer's statement is often all the evidence needed to convict an inmate of a disciplinary infraction. This is evidenced by the staggering rate of guilty findings. So, it stands to reason that the inmate can't talk their way out of an incident report. The goal of the inmate at this juncture, therefore, is to not provide additional evidence. It is strongly advised that the inmate simply state "I contest all charges against me" and leave it at that.

If the inmate in question is substantially familiar with the Inmate Discipline Program,[13] it might be a good idea to contest the charged code violation. In other words, an inmate can attempt to convince the lieutenant to change the charge to a lower security violation.

This is especially effective when the reporting officer has improperly charged the inmate with a higher severity code violation than is warranted. If this technique is utilized, the inmate should not address the offense. Instead, they should speak only about policy: what the charge should be if the act had been committed.

> *TIP: It's always a good idea to be friendly and inquiring with the investigating officer to mitigate charges and obtain background information. While in the lieutenant's office, the inmate should ask questions but not answer any pertaining to the incident report. By obtaining additional incident report information, the inmate will be better able to prepare a defense.*

Witnesses

In the prison culture, calling witnesses can be challenging. Inmates typically don't appreciate fellow inmates mentioning their name in front of FBOP staff, much less being called in to testify or answer questions. Therefore, inmates are advised to only call inmate witnesses who have already agreed to be called.

Staff witnesses are a completely different matter. If the inmate feels that a particular staff member – or even several – can provide honest mitigating evidence, the inmate should call as many as possible. Any staff witness who supports or corroborates the inmate's situation or assertions will be a very valuable asset. A staff statement will be deemed truthful, whereas an inmate's statement will be deemed inherently untruthful.

Evidence

At this point of the disciplinary process, inmates generally don't have much of an opportunity to gather evidence much less review it to determine if it furthers their cause. In fact, presenting evidence can be a bad idea; it helps the Bureau create a record from which to convict and contest appeal attempts. Even evidence that somewhat verifies the inmate's position can be used against the inmate. This goes back to the reporting officer's statement being all the evidence needed to convict. As such, an abundance of caution is required.

At this stage of the process, two types of evidence typically come into play: camera and radio recordings. Both of these can be of use to inmates who are either innocent or guilty of the charges.

If the inmate is innocent and cameras are present in the area of the alleged incident, the inmate should insist that the recordings be reviewed if the footage could prove their innocence.[j] However, if the inmate was engaged in any kind of prohibited act – charged or not – at the time of the offense, he or she should not request video evidence.

If the inmate is guilty, camera evidence – or lack thereof – can still be useful. The lack of audio or video evidence can help muddy the waters and cast some doubt on the allegations. As long as the camera recording does not prove guilt, it can be used to support an accused inmate's claim of innocence.

Radio recordings can be useful in cases involving out-of-bounds allegations. At times, an inmate will be released from their unit for a variety of reasons. When this occurs, often the unit officer will radio the compound officer or the inmate's destination to alert them to the inmate's movement. When this radio transmission occurs, a recording that can be entered into evidence is made. The recording can prove that the inmate was authorized to

---

[j] *Program Statement 5270.09, Chapter 2 states that "If the inmate requests exculpatory evidence, such as video or audio surveillance, the investigator must make every effort to review and preserve the evidence." Requesting it means it should be retained for future appeals and litigation. If it is disposed of, a great point of appeal results.*

be released from their unit and/or to be in a specific area. Again, this kind of evidence can be used for inmates who are either innocent or guilty.

Another official form of evidence (besides phone call recordings, emails, letters, etc.) that can be requested are unit log books and work logs. These documents can help prove or disprove an incident through the record or lack of record. Work logs are primarily of use when contesting incident reports written by officers who claimed to have been on duty at a particular time but were not.

This typically occurs when it's almost shift change and the arriving officer writes the incident report – with the correct times – as if they were the officer on duty. They claim to have been the responding officer when they weren't. The lieutenant's work logs and housing unit log books can prove when officers actually arrived at the institution and at specific housing units.

The point of presenting any form of evidence at this stage is to either prove one's innocence, if the inmate is indeed innocent, or to prove qualifying factors – aspects of truth – which prove part or parts of a guilty inmate's position. The goal of the wrongfully accused inmate is to prove absolute innocence through evidence. The goal of a rightfully accused inmate is to prove surrounding aspects so that doubt and conflicting truths muddle the issue and yield a not guilty finding.

After the inmate has made or declined to make the applicable statements, the lieutenant issues the inmate a copy of the incident report.[k] The incident report must record the date and time of the issuance. At this time, the investigatory phase of the disciplinary process continues outside the inmate's presence. The investigating officer has twenty-four hours to speak with witnesses and the reporting officer, review evidence, and draft their conclusion for the UDC and/or the DHO.[141]

According to Program Statement 5270.09, Chapter 2, "[U]nder Comments and Conclusions, the investigator may include:

---

[k] *Program Statement 5270.09, Chapter 2 clarifies: "The incident report should be delivered to the inmate within 24 hours of the time staff become aware of the inmates* [sic] *alleged misconduct." As such, the incident report should be for conduct allegedly committed within twenty-four hours. If it is not, the inmate has a strong point of appeal. At a minimum, the Bureau must draft a memorandum explaining why this time limit was not met.*

[l] *Typically the investigating officer spends between twenty minutes and one hour in their investigation. Rarely do they do more than read the incident report's description and check to see if the inmate has prior incident report convictions. Anything more than this would be the exception to the rule.*

- Comments on the inmate's prior record and behavior,
- Analysis of any conflict between witnesses,
- Conclusions regarding what happened.

The investigator must record all steps and actions taken on the incident report and forward the relevant materials to staff holding the initial hearing." While the inmate is not allowed to receive a copy of the investigation,[m] if the incident report is forwarded to the disciplinary hearing officer, the inmate's staff representative can review it along with all other relevant investigatory materials.

Informal Resolution

Prior to forwarding the incident report to the committee for processing, the lieutenant has the option of informally resolving it. According to 28 C.F.R. § 541.5(b)(3), "[T]he incident report may be informally resolved at any stage of the disciplinary process, except for prohibited acts in the Greatest and High-severity levels, or as otherwise required by law or these regulations. If the incident report is informally resolved, it will be removed from [the inmate's] records."

Program Statement 5270.09, Chapter 2 states: "The Bureau encourages informal resolution of incidents. However, prohibited acts in the Greatest-severity level (100 level) and High-severity level (200 level) may not be informally resolved, and must be referred to the [DHO]. Moderate-severity level (300 level) and Low-severity level (400 level) offenses can be informally resolved at any stage of the process. A record of any informal resolution is maintained in SENTRY, the Bureau's staff computer system. However, the incident report is not filed in the inmates [sic] central file. . . [T]he determination to informally resolve an incident report is solely at the discretion of staff."

---

[m] *If the inmate subsequently becomes convicted of the infraction they can submit a request for their case manager to review their central file. During the review, the inmate should come across the investigating officer's report documenting the incident report. While not specifically authorized by policy, this is a common oversight by the case manager. Requesting copies of the disciplinary materials can give the inmate fuel for their appeals.*

Clearly, policy provides a basis for informal resolution of incident reports. Unfortunately, this avenue is rarely pursued. Much more often, an inmate will go in front of the UDC and be formally sanctioned.

> *TIP: If an inmate receives a 300 or 400 series incident report, it can't hurt to seek informal resolution. This is done by suggesting to the lieutenant that the conduct doesn't warrant formal sanctions, and that extra duty (several hours of menial labor) is better suited to the infraction. For lesser offenses, the lieutenant might grant the request.*

Administrative Detention Pending the DHO Hearing

If the inmate is charged with a 100 or 200 series incident report, the lieutenant has the authority to place the inmate in the SHU pending a hearing before the DHO. This "administrative detention" is an allegedly non-punitive form of solitary confinement. While this form of prehearing confinement is allegedly utilized for the safety and orderly operation of the institution, many inmates charged with nonviolent prohibited acts like conducting a business or failing to show up at an appointment find themselves in the SHU pending disciplinary hearings. See Chapter 21 for more information on administrative detention in the SHU.

Building a Defense

The inmate should consider the incident report not simply as a "shot" or "write up" but as a charge akin to an indictment. They should closely review every aspect of the incident report to find as many faults as possible. These faults can become the basis for a successful defense or appeal.

Factual Errors

The first area to address is basic information. Are the inmate's name and register number correct in every listing within the document? Was the incident report delivered within twenty-four hours from the time staff alleges the prohibited act took place or when they became aware of it? Did the lieutenant sign and date the report, and note the time the incident report was issued? These are fundamental questions. While a misspelled name or an incorrect inmate number is probably not a huge concern, missing or incorrect dates and times can be fodder for appeals. They can also lay the groundwork for establishing other errors.

Another important concern at this stage is ensuring that the inmate has been charged appropriately. In their zest for punishment, staff sometimes charge the inmate with an overly severe disciplinary code violation. One of the inmate's first jobs is to locate the actual wording of the charged code violation and compare it to the allegations in the incident report.

During this stage, the inmate should also review the entire table of disciplinary code violations to see whether a lower severity prohibited act is more in line with the alleged conduct. This can become a sound basis for an initial statement at the UDC hearing or the DHO hearing, and can be a worthwhile point on appeal.

Description

The description of the alleged incident is always a primary focal point. This is where the majority, if not all, of the Bureau's evidence is asserted. Ensure that the locations are correct, that the people are correct, the times are correct, and the statements are correct. If inconsistencies are present, note them. These are points of attack during the hearing and on appeal. Even a prohibited act that was committed must be properly charged and described. Otherwise the incident report is not proper and can be challenged.

More often than not, the description of the incident will be mostly accurate. Typically, the description will provide a generally supportable depiction of the conduct at issue. The name of the game isn't proving the reporting officer wrong but presenting the facts and circumstances in the light most likely to lead to a not guilty finding.

The worst set of circumstances for the accused is when the incident report is completely factual, and camera evidence and staff witnesses back up the accusation. If this is the case, it might be wise not to bother poking holes in the report's description. Instead, focus on mitigating evidence that can limit the sanctions.

Developing an Argument

Every statement and every sentence in the report can and should be attacked. This is a principle from which an inmate cannot deviate. To successfully defend themselves, the inmate must often challenge every assertion made by the Bureau in the description box of the incident report. The inmate should literally go sentence by sentence and try to either prove or disprove it with evidence. If the allegation is easily and completely provable, it should be left alone. But whenever proof can show a particular allegation to be incorrect, a challenge should be made and that challenge should be supported with proof.

The inmate should take careful notes on ideas concerning each point in the report. In the next stage, the inmate will search for evidence to back up relevant facts. By presenting a position with strong supporting evidence, the inmate can be on their way to acquittal or perhaps to having the charges expunged.

Evidence

Depending upon the circumstances, many kinds of evidence can be presented. This could include the actual incident report, video camera recordings, inmate and staff witnesses, recordings of telephone calls, radio recordings, log books from housing units, staff, or the lieutenant's office, confiscated items, any evidence collected by the reporting officer or investigating officer, and even statements made by persons outside of the prison. Case law, policy, and memos can also be presented by an inmate. Anything that supports their position should be considered. The best way to present the evidence is through a written statement and attachments.

To locate evidence, the inmate can make a request to the investigating lieutenant, members of their unit team, their staff representative (only in a DHO hearing), and even the DHO. When the inmate makes the request, they should log the request, note to whom the request was made, and the date and time of the request. Detail is necessary since the inmate might utilize this request as a basis for appeal.

The inmate should review all evidence obtained to ascertain if it is of use. The goal is to present a succinct but detailed argument before the UDC or DHO. An onerous, jumbled folder of evidence won't do the trick. The inmate needs to think like a legal professional who is presenting a specific – and provable – case to a judge.

Writing the Argument

Because the central evidence against an accused inmate is the incident report and its description of the alleged violation, the inmate doesn't necessarily need to prove where they were, what they were doing, or how they are innocent. They might instead prove that the proffered description of the conduct is incorrect. This gives the inmate the best shot at winning either during the UDC hearing, the DHO hearing, or an appeal.

As the inmate goes through the incident report and finds allegations that can be challenged, each should be written down. Then, with the points of attack in place, the inmate should make a list of all available evidence that can refute each accusation. By having everything in writing, the inmate will be able to easily draft their written statement.

A one-page statement of defense is ideal. This statement should start with the inmate's best argument, supported with evidence. After the first point, the inmate should list and support the other arguments in descending order of importance, while always providing evidence.

A very strong method of presenting evidence is to make assertions in the written statement and cite an attachment as evidence. This way the evidence is directly in front of the UDC chairperson or the DHO. This method is hard to ignore and ensures that an accurate record of the inmate's defense is memorialized.

Ideally, the inmate's statement should be typed. This can either be done by counsel, family or, best of all, the inmate, since this is the most expedient method. As a typed statement is a bit of a rarity in this realm, it helps to set the inmate apart from most others and make the argument look more professional. A neatly compiled document is better received than a messy one regardless of its merits.

The Complete Defense Document

The complete defense document is made of the one-page typed statement on top with all applicable attachments behind it. This way everything is neat and together, and the inmate can turn in a professional submission. Copies should be made prior to the hearing to avoid having to rely on staff to locate and copy documents later.

The Unit Discipline Committee

After the inmate has been issued the incident report by the lieutenant, he or she will typically appear before their UDC.[n] From the inmate's perspective, this is not a scheduled event; the only notice might be a page over the public address system to report to the unit team area. If the inmate is in the SHU, the UDC hearing will be held there. The UDC hearing begins the disciplinary tribunal.

Timing

According to 28 C.F.R. § 541.7(c), "[T]he UDC will ordinarily review the incident report within five working days after it is issued, not counting the day it was issued, weekends, and holidays. UDC review of the incident report may also be suspended if it is being investigated for possible criminal prosecution." If an extension is needed, the warden's approval is required and must be documented in the disciplinary record. It is not uncommon for such delays to occur, and for staff to cite scheduling conflicts and other nonemergency reasons for the delay.

TIP: If an inmate does not go in front of the UDC within five working days of the incident report being issued, they should raise this complaint on appeal. At a minimum, if any required extensions are not documented or not issued at all, the process will be remanded.

[n] *The inmate does have the right to waive an appearance but this is rarely done and is not recommended. It is always best for the inmate to participate – at least in an observational capacity – in every hearing. This way a record is always being created and the inmate will be privy to Bureau employee actions that could be challenged on appeal.*

The UDC Hearing

Although inmates do not attend UDC deliberations, they are allowed to go before the UDC during its review of the incident report. This appearance is the actual UDC hearing.

> *TIP: Being brought before the UDC can be nerve-wracking for those who have never been in trouble before. Panic is common. Inmates should try their best to keep a level head and present their case as effectively as possible. Remember, the most the UDC can do is take a privilege or two (or a few) away. They can't place anyone in the SHU and they can't take good conduct time.*

Inmate Appearance

It is specified in 28 C.F.R. § 541.7(d)(1) that the inmate "may appear either in person or electronically (by video or telephone conference) at the UDC's discretion." Almost categorically, the inmate will appear at the UDC hearing in person.

The inmate can choose to waive their appearance, in which case the UDC will document the waiver using a Waiver of Appearance form (BP-A0307).[15] In this case and in the case of an inmate who has escaped from custody, the UDC will conduct the hearing in the inmate's absence.

> *TIP: Inmates shouldn't waive their right to be present at any hearing. To do so predisposes the hearing body to assume guilt or that the inmate is troublesome. Either conclusion can only harm the inmate's case and potentially increase their sanctions.*

Evidence

During the hearing, the inmate is "entitled to make a statement and present documentary evidence to the UDC on [their] own behalf. The UDC will consider all evidence presented during its review. The UDC's decision will be based on at least some facts and, if there is conflicting evidence, on the greater weight of the evidence."[16] It is further clarified in Program Statement 5270.09, Chapter 4, "The phrase 'some facts' refers to facts indicating the inmate committed the prohibited act. The phrase 'greater weight of the evidence' refers to the strength of the evidence."

Effectively presenting evidence is vital for the accused. Evidence is useful for the hearing at hand as well as for an appeal. Every action must have as its goal the creation of a record of mitigating evidence so the inmate has a chance of winning on appeal. This is imperative because the vast majority of charged inmates are found guilty by the UDC and DHO.

Regardless of what the inmate is charged with or the facts surrounding the alleged misconduct, the inmate should prepare a written statement to be presented during the UDC hearing. This statement should address the intended defense as succinctly as possible (one typed page is best) and have as attachments anything in writing that supports the inmate's position.

The written statement is of particular use during the appellate stage of the process. Typically, the UDC will find the inmate guilty and base its decision on the "greater weight of the evidence." Rarely will the UDC take the inmate's statement into consideration when making a finding. Even if they do – they must, after all, summarize the inmate's statement on the incident report (two lines' worth of space) – they will not include the inmate's full statement. Regardless, the full written statement is essential for creating a record and proof that objections were raised during each stage of the process.

> *TIP: When asked for a statement at the UDC hearing, inmates should present the written statement for them to read. By asking the UDC chair to read the statement themselves, they won't be able to ignore it as they could if it was read to them.*

Available Dispositions

After the UDC reviews the incident report, they will make one of the following decisions:

1) [The inmate] committed the prohibited act(s) charged, and/or a similar prohibited act(s) as described in the incident report;

2) [The inmate] did not commit the prohibited act(s) charged; or
3) The incident report will be referred to the Disciplinary Hearing Officer (DHO) for further review based on the seriousness of the prohibited act(s) charged.
4) If [the inmate is] charged with a Greatest or High severity prohibited act, or [is] an inmate covered by 541.4, the UDC will automatically refer the incident report to the DHO for further review.[17]

Sanctions by the UDC

If the UDC finds that the inmate committed the charged prohibited act(s), they can impose sanctions.[18] These sanctions can vary greatly depending on whether the charged act is a moderate (300) or low (400) severity act, the inmate's past, and who is on the UDC. Generally speaking, the UDC will take some form of privileges in thirty-day increments. For example, a *Code 334, Conducting a Business*, could result in the inmate receiving a loss of commissary for one to six months alongside other sanctions. There is no typical privilege loss.

Note that the UDC cannot impose the sanctions of disciplinary segregation, monetary fines, or good conduct time loss.[19] A UDC sanction, while possibly annoying and even impeding, is not life-altering.

The inmate might be able to mitigate potential sanctions. It can't hurt to ask the UDC to leave a certain privilege for a specific reason. For example, if the inmate regularly has visits, they might consider voicing how much their visits mean to them. Likewise, if the inmate is housed far away from their family, they might state how the loss of the phone would cut off contact with their family.

These actions need to be weighed at the time of the hearing, and will depend on how the hearing has transpired and the inmate's relationship with the UDC members. Regrettably, such overtures can sometimes cause the opposite effect: the imposition of the undesirable sanction.

Referral to the DHO

If the charged prohibited act is of the greatest (100) or high (200) severity, the UDC has no choice but to refer the incident to the DHO for review.[20] If the charged prohibited act is of the moderate (300) or low (400) severity, the UDC can refer the incident report to the DHO (typically in cases of repeated misconduct). If this occurs, the inmate will be advised of their rights pertaining to the DHO hearing. See 28 C.F.R. § 541.8 for these rights.

Program Statement 5270.09, Chapter 4 provides:

> The UDC forwards copies of relevant documents to the DHO with a statement of reasons for the referral, along with recommendations for sanctions if the DHO finds the inmate has committed the act or another prohibited act. The UDC Chair records reasons for the referral and recommendations for disposition in the 'Committee Action' section of the incident report. Recommendations are contingent upon a DHO finding that the inmate committed the act.[o]
>
> When charges are referred to the DHO, the UDC advises the inmate of the rights afforded at the hearing. The UDC asks the inmate to choose a staff representative,[p] if any, and the names of witnesses the inmate wishes to be called to testify, and what testimony they are expected to provide. The UDC advises the inmate that he or she may waive the right to be present at the hearing, but still have witnesses or a staff representative appear on his or her behalf.

If an inmate waives the right to appear at the UDC hearing, the UDC ensures that the inmate is advised of the rights afforded at the hearing before the DHO.

[o] *Even the most casual observer would find this aspect of the process flawed. After all, how can an allegedly impartial hearing body, the UDC, recommend an appropriate sanction for acts they don't even take under advisement? When incident reports are referred to the DHO because they are in the greatest (100) or high (200) category, the UDC doesn't even hold a full hearing. They do not review the evidence and do not allow the inmate to present a full defense. Yet they recommend sanctions if the DHO finds the inmate guilty.*

[p] *Program Statement 5270.09, Chapter 5 clarifies the matter. It reads: "The executive staff, the DHO or alternative DHO, reporting officer, witnesses to the incident, and UDC members involved in the case may not be staff representatives. The Warden may exclude other staff in a particular case or when there is a potential conflict. If the inmate continues to select staff which are not available, the Warden may select a staff representative for the inmate."*

This is done through forms titled: "Inmate Rights at Discipline Hearing" and "Notice of Discipline Hearing Before the Discipline Hearing Officer (DHO)."

This is all performed extremely quickly. If there is even the most remote chance the inmate could go in front of the DHO, they should be prepared by having a staff representative and all applicable witnesses in mind.

> *TIP: The inmate should select a staff representative that is familiar with FBOP policies concerning disciplinary adjudication. Lieutenants are great selections, particularly if the inmate already has a decent rapport with them.*

Written Report

The UDC must create a record of the proceedings.[21] This record typically consists of the completed incident report and any documentary evidence. This record is then placed in the inmate's central file. According to Program Statement 5270.09, Chapter 4, "[T]he UDC gives the inmate a written copy of the decision and disposition by the close of business the next work day." Once this copy is delivered, the inmate can appeal through the process described below. It is imperative that the inmate retain copies of all disciplinary documents. These are necessary for appeals and potential litigation.

Appeal

Appeals of UDC action are pursued through the Administrative Remedy Program.[22] Once the inmate receives the completed incident report from the UDC (their copy of the decision and disposition), an appeal can be started with a BP-9 (an appeal to the warden).

The inmate has twenty days from the date of the hearing to file a BP-9, and the warden is permitted twenty days to respond, along with a twenty-day extension. If the warden denies relief, the inmate can appeal to the applicable regional office, which is permitted both a thirty-day response period and a thirty-day extension. The final level of appeal is to central office, which is permitted forty days to respond and a twenty-day extension but they usually take upwards of a year or more.

The DHO Hearing

If the incident report has been referred to the DHO, the DHO hearing is the next step. According to 28 C.F.R. § 541.8(b), "[T]he [DHO is] an impartial decision maker who [is] not a victim, witness, investigator, or otherwise significantly involved in the incident."

Further, "The term Discipline Hearing Officer (DHO) refers to a one-person, independent officer who conducts hearings and imposes sanctions for incidents of misconduct referred by the UDC. A DHO may not conduct hearings without receiving specialized training and passing a certification test. If the institution's assigned DHO is unavailable to conduct hearings, the Warden arranges for another DHO, who must be certified."[23]

As far as inmates are concerned, the DHO should be viewed as an adverse staff member who almost always finds the accused inmate guilty. The accused inmate must expect the DHO to find them guilty and be prepared to battle the issue on appeal. This is why it is so important to create a record.

Timing

The inmate is entitled to receive written notice of the charges lodged against them at least twenty-four hours prior to the DHO hearing.[24] This is fulfilled through form BP-A0294, "Notice of Discipline before the Discipline Hearing Officer (DHO)." This notice is signed by the inmate at the conclusion of the UDC hearing.

> *TIP: If the DHO hearing is initiated before twenty-four hours of receipt of the notice, it is well within the inmate's right to demand that the hearing be delayed until twenty-four hours have transpired. By doing so, not only will the inmate document flaws with the process that can be utilized on appeal, but they will also have more time to prepare.*

The DHO Hearing

The DHO hearing can be held at any number of locations throughout the prison. Typical ones include the lieutenant's office, the inmate's unit team area, and the SHU (for inmates being housed in the SHU pending disciplinary action). Regardless of where the hearing is held, the DHO, the accused inmate, the inmate's staff representative (if applicable)[q], and any witnesses for the inmate will be present. Unless the inmate is in the SHU, he or she will not be handcuffed.

> *TIP: At all times after the UDC hearing, inmates should be prepared to go in front of the DHO with little advance notice. They should create a file of defense materials that includes their written statement, the written statements of others, and any documentary evidence. Always be prepared. The DHO probably won't grant an extension.*

Inmate Appearance

Almost universally, the inmate will be allowed to go to the DHO hearing in person to state their case. 28 C.F.R. § 541.8(e) defines the parameters as follows:

> (1) [The inmate] may appear either in person or electronically (for example, by video or telephone conferencing), at the DHO's discretion;[r]
>
> (2) [The inmate's] appearance may be prohibited during the DHO deliberations when [the inmate's] presence would jeopardize institution security, at the DHO's discretion;

[q] *Rarely will the staff representative even speak with the inmate they are representing prior to the hearing. If the inmate doesn't seek out their staff representative, they will receive no assistance. Even if the inmate does seek out their staff representative, that person might not even know what to do or how to help. An inmate should request a lieutenant as a staff representative since they know the investigatorial process and are familiar with inmate discipline.*

Often the staff representative will not show up to the hearing. When this occurs, the DHO typically tries to pressure the inmate into waiving their right to staff representation. This is never a good idea. The inmate is strongly advised to assert their right to a staff representative and to have the proceedings delayed.

[r] *Almost universally, the inmate will be allowed to appear at the DHO hearing in person to state their case.*

(3) [The inmate] may waive [their] appearance before the DHO. If [the inmate] waive[s] [their] appearance, the DHO hearing will be conducted in [their] absence;[s]

(4) If [the inmate] escape[s] or [is] otherwise absent from custody, the DHO will conduct a hearing in [their] absence at the institution where [they] were last confined.[t]

TIP: It is never a good strategy to waive the right to appear. By doing so, the inmate prejudices the DHO and any appellate decision-maker. They also diminish their ability to create a record from which to appeal. Inmates should go to the hearing, attempt to defend themselves, and create a record from which to appeal regardless of the prospects for success.

Right to Present Evidence and Witnesses

According to 28 C.F.R. § 541.8(f), "[The inmate] is entitled to make a statement and present documentary evidence to the DHO on [his or her] own behalf. The DHO will consider all evidence presented during the hearing. The DHO's decision will be based on at least some facts and, if there is conflicting evidence, on the greater weight of the evidence."[u] Witnesses can appear at the DHO hearing as follows:

(1) Witnesses may appear before the DHO either in person or electronically (for example, by video or telephone conferencing) at the DHO's discretion.[25]

---

[s] *If inmates waive their right to be present at the DHO hearing, their staff representative and witnesses can still appear at the inmate's request.*

[t] *According to Program Statement 5270.09, Chapter 5, if "an inmate returns to custody following an absence during which sanctions were imposed by the DHO, the Warden has the charges reheard by the DHO, ordinarily within 60 days after the inmate's arrival at the institution to which he/she is designated after return to custody, following an appearance before the UDC at the institution."*

[u] *Program Statement 5270.09, Chapter 5, "The phrase 'some facts' refers to facts indicating the inmate committed the prohibited act. The phrase 'greater weight of the evidence' refers to the strength of the evidence, not to its quantity or to the number of witnesses testifying."*

> (2) The DHO will call witnesses who have information directly relevant to the charge(s) and who are reasonably available. However, the DHO need not call witnesses adverse to [the accused] if their testimony is adequately summarized in the incident report or other investigation materials.[26v]

The "directly relevant" information is a common point of contention between jailhouse litigators and DHOs. DHOs tend to view direct witnesses as relevant, any staff member as relevant, and any witness who corroborates a small portion of the inmate's defense as irrelevant. The inmate might have to assert their right to their witnesses.

If the DHO excludes a witness, the inmate should ask that the DHO make their reasoning a part of the record for future appeal. The inmate should lay out a defense when pondering which witness to call. It will be necessary to prove certain facts if the inmate is to have a chance at an acquittal at the DHO hearing or on appeal. The inmate should try to structure witnesses to support their defensive strategy. Since most incident reports are based on some amount of fact, the inmate needs to maintain a chance of success at the hearing and on appeal.

> (3) [The accused inmate] or [their] staff representative may request witnesses [to] appear at the hearing to testify on behalf of the accused. [The inmate's] requested witnesses may not appear if, in the DHO's discretion, they are not reasonably available, their presence at the hearing would jeopardize institutional security, or they would present repetitive evidence.[27w]

---

[v] *According to Program Statement 5270.09, Chapter 5, "The statement of an inmate requesting a witness is not enough to mandate the witness's appearance. There must be an indication that the witness has information directly relevant to the charges."*

[w] *Program Statement 5270.09, Chapter 5, asserts, "There is no minimum or maximum number of witnesses who may be called; the number should be based on the situation and the information to be presented. While several eyewitnesses may be called, it is expected that the number of character witnesses would be limited, at the discretion of the DHO."*

All desired witnesses should already have been requested through the documents signed at the end of the UDC hearing when the incident report was referred to the DHO. If this did not occur, or if the inmate did not request any witnesses, this should immediately be brought to the DHO's attention and witness requests made.

If the inmate is not yet in front of the DHO, they should email their unit team with their list of witnesses and what each can attest to, or immediately speak with their staff representative or a lieutenant. Witnesses are necessary. They greatly assist in creating a record from which to appeal. As such, obtaining witness statements and calling witnesses in general is a top priority.

> (4) If [the inmate's] requested witnesses are unavailable to appear, written statements can be requested by either the DHO or staff representative. The written statements can then be considered during the DHOs hearing.[28x]

This is a key area for the accused. By and large, written statements are preferable to any witness, those who can appear and those who cannot. Written statements can say what they need to and not get bogged down in irrelevant or harmful testimony. Plus, a written statement can't be antagonized, intimidated, or tricked by the DHO (or threatened with an incident report for not answering a question, as is the case with in-person inmate witnesses). As such, the best witness is a properly written and targeted statement.

It is important for the inmate to explain the situation to their witnesses, share what a good statement would be from the particular party, and receive two copies of the signed statement (one for themselves and one for the DHO).

---

[x] *If a witness is not available, according to Program Statement 5270.09, Chapter 5, "[t]he DHO ordinarily allows time for the written statement of the witness to be received, if he/she is expected to have relevant information. . . If an extension is not granted, the DHO must clearly state in the record reasons for not granting it."*

This section also clarifies that "The DHO may not refuse to call a witness who is reasonably available (e.g., on a different shift) and has information relevant to the charges solely because the witness (staff or inmate) does not wish to appear."

Then, during the hearing, the inmate can present the DHO with their own copy of the well-crafted witness statement.

This witness statement will support the inmate's defensive efforts and will become part of the record. By having a detailed, concrete, and specific witness statement added to the record – as opposed to a bad summarization of a verbal statement by the DHO – the inmate will have concrete evidence for the appeal.

> (5) Only the DHO may directly question witnesses at the DHO's hearing. Any questions by [the accused inmate] or [their] staff representative must be submitted to the DHO, who will present the question to the witness at his or her discretion."[29y]

Clearly, the inmate cannot question witnesses or directly confront – or even necessarily hear – adverse witnesses. Ideally, the Bureau will fail to bring any adverse witnesses. This is because they already have all they need in the incident report. As for supportive witnesses, it is always best to speak with them beforehand to explain what would be helpful in their testimony. Suggestions and parameters can work wonders since many witnesses will find the experience jarring.

If the inmate must contend with adverse witnesses, he should ask to step out into the hall with his or her staff representative to request a delay. This way the inmate can present the representative with a list of questions to ask when the next hearing occurs. If not, the inmate should scribble down questions and explain them to the staff representative. Some direction is much better than none at all.

> (6) The DHO may consider evidence provided by a confidential informant (CI) that the DHO finds reliable. [The inmate] will not be informed of the CI's identity. [The accused inmate] will be informed of the CI's testimony to the extent it will not jeopardize institutional security, at the DHO's discretion.[30]

---

[y] *Program Statement 5270.09, Chapter 5, further clarifies that "The inmate's staff representative, or the DHO, when the inmate waives staff representation, questions witnesses requested by the inmate who are called before the DHO. An inmate who waives staff representation may submit questions for requested witnesses in writing to the DHO. The inmate may not question witnesses."*

Confidential Informants

A sad truth is that in prison, informants are everywhere. Some call them "snitches," "rats," "stool pigeons," or "Inmate Task Force members." Regardless of what they're called, they all do the same thing: inform Bureau staff when fellow prisoners engage in prohibited conduct.

Since a number of such individuals exist in every prison, the Bureau has promulgated significant policy on how to utilize their testimony and how to protect their identities. It helps to know what testimony from a confidential informant (CI) is allowed to prove, not prove, and how the accused inmate can defend against a faceless accuser whom they cannot confront and whose testimony they cannot know.[31]

Program Statement 5270.09, Chapter 5, states, "[W]hen a discipline decision is based on confidential informant information, the UDC or DHO must document, ordinarily in their hearing report, their findings as to the reliability of each confidential informant and the factual basis for that finding." If the report would identify or place the informant in danger, a special report must be created which will not be issued to the inmate.

CIs won't necessarily be mentioned if other evidence supports the report. Thus, even if a CI is the reason for the investigation, this fact won't necessarily be disclosed. The same program statement continues, "[O]rdinarily, the finding that an inmate committed a prohibited act must be supported by more than one reliable confidential source. If there is only one, the confidential information must be corroborated by independently verified evidence linking the inmate to the prohibited act."[32]

Uncorroborated confidential information from a single informant is insufficient as the sole basis for a finding "unless the circumstances of the incident and the knowledge possessed by the informant are convincing enough to show that the information must be reliable. In an assault with no witnesses, for example, the statement of a seriously injured assault victim could be sufficient to support a finding without corroborating evidence."[33]

In order for a CI to be deemed reliable, the informant must either have a history of reliably informing or must convince the DHO or UDC of their reliability. When CIs are utilized, "the staff member providing information to the DHO must include a written statement of the frequency with which the informant provided information, the period during which the informant provided information, and the information's accuracy. If reliability is based on other factors, they must be clearly specified."[34]

Staff must determine if the CI's testimony is truthful, because they can only use that testimony if they believe it is truthful. However, one can imagine that a Bureau official would be hard pressed to set aside information if it furthers the investigatory process. Also, policy clarifies that CIs cannot receive favors for supplying such testimony, yet such favors are commonplace ... whether explicit or implicit.

When CI testimony is utilized, it must be in writing and it must present the circumstances leading up to how the CI obtained the information. The statement is to be signed. Staff can write a statement in place of the informant as long as they write it in "language as close to the informant's as possible."[35] In this case, the staff member would sign the statement.

In cases of referrals to the DHO, the UDC does not need to be made aware of the CI's identity or what the information might be. Only the DHO needs to know.

The inmate cannot know the CI's identity or the substance of their testimony. The inmate's staff representative (at the DHO level) is sometimes allowed to see the CI's allegations and can challenge them but only if the DHO allows either to occur. The staff representative is not allowed to know the CI's identity and can't question the reliability of the CI since the DHO – the officer charged with adjudicating guilt, the allegedly impartial FBOP employee – judges the CI's reliability.

In cases where the staff member writes the statement, it follows that it might be difficult for the DHO to find the statement unreliable since it comes from a fellow Bureau employee. If CI testimony is in direct conflict with that of other witnesses, the DHO must indicate in the record "the reason for believing the testimony of one witness over another or otherwise resolve the conflict."[36]

If the DHO determines that including references to the CI's testimony would not reveal their identity, this information is included. If it would reveal the CI's identity, specific testimony will be included in a special confidential report not made available to the inmate. The confidential report will not be placed in the accused inmate's central file; instead it goes to a secure location and is retained for later administrative and judicial review.

Since the Bureau allegedly strives to utilize independent information over CI testimony, it's more likely that the Bureau will not disclose a CI's involvement in the first place. If that evidence is relied upon, a small notation is made in the DHO report. Further, policy dictates that if information is received anonymously, it "does not meet the necessary reliability standard [and] may not be used as evidence in making a finding. Such information, however, may be used in the investigation."[37]

The Process

When an inmate is called in front of the DHO for a hearing, the DHO will read the incident report aloud to all present (the inmate, their staff representative, and any witnesses). After the DHO reads the description of the alleged prohibited act, they will ask the inmate if they would like to make a statement.

> *TIP: The staff representative might not know what to do if they haven't been part of a disciplinary proceeding before. If this is the case, the inmate is advised to use this person as a witness rather than an advocate; they won't function as an advocate anyway.*
>
> *The assumption that a staff representative will defend an inmate or act like an attorney is incorrect. The only real reason to have a staff representative present is to use them as the witness guaranteed to be present, or to allow the inmate to delay the proceeding until they are present.*
>
> *But, it is never a good idea to waive the right to a staff representative. At a minimum, this person's actions or the DHO's actions towards them can cloud the matter and create another avenue for appeal. If they don't act according to policy, another ground for appeal can be created.*

Before the inmate does anything else, even before presenting their statement, they should say, "I raise procedural complaints as to the disciplinary process thus far." This way it becomes a part of the record from the start. If the DHO asks what specifically the inmate finds fault with, the inmate should state something along the lines of, "I find fault with numerous due process and evidentiary errors in the process thus far." If the inmate has specific complaints, they should state each one. If not, further explanation is not necessarily needed or required.

The next step is for the inmate to hand the DHO their statement and attached documentary evidence. It is important that the inmate *not* read aloud their statement or those of their witnesses. Having the DHO read the statements increases the likelihood that they will retain what is being said.

If the DHO casually glances or doesn't even look at the statements, or does it so quickly they couldn't possibly have read them, this issue should be raised on appeal. The inmate can state that all evidence was not taken into account. If the DHO does not review all of the evidence, they have no way of judging the "greater weight of the evidence." This is a terrific point to present on appeal and has been successful in challenging proceedings that otherwise were legal.

After the DHO has the statements – and ideally has read them – the inmate should insist that the packet become part of the record. If necessary, this can be done by refusing to accept the packet back.

If any staff witnesses are present the DHO will question them.[38] Ideally, the DHO will ask the inmate what each witness can attest to. The inmate should state what the staff member can attest to. By doing so verbally and directly, the witness will have specific parameters within which to testify. The inmate's verbal reply might lead the witness into making a similar statement.

The inmate is not allowed to directly confront any witnesses but they are allowed to respond to the DHO about witness statements. This isn't a formal process but one that can be asserted by the inmate. While it is not a good idea to contest everything an adverse witness states – or clarify everything a supporting witness offers – it can be helpful to do so on certain points and when significant oversights are an issue.

After the DHO has reviewed all of the evidence, the inmate will step outside of the room so that they can deliberate and privately question witnesses. The DHO will then pronounce a verdict. They will say something like, "I'm finding the inmate (guilty/not guilty)" or "I'm remanding this back to the UDC for further review."

If the DHO finds the inmate guilty, the inmate can ask to be heard before the imposition of sanctions. At that point, the inmate can attempt to mitigate sanctions. Or, if the inmate has just "gone to war" with the DHO, they could say, "If you would, please make the record as detailed as possible so that when litigation occurs, clarifications from your office won't be needed."

The final step, if found guilty, is the sanction. The DHO will state what the sanctions are and the period of time for which they apply. While the DHO will read the sanctions aloud, what really counts is what they place in the report. Often the DHO will sanction the inmate to more punitive measures than they remember to place in the report. If this occurs, only the sanctions listed in the report are applicable. If the DHO increases the sanctions in the DHO report, this can be a good point of appeal.

Available Dispositions

According to 28 C.F.R. § 541.8(a), the following dispositions are available at the close of a DHO hearing:

(1) [The inmate] committed the prohibited act(s) charged, and/or similar prohibited act(s) as described in the incident report;
(2) [The inmate] did not commit the prohibited act(s) charged; or
(3) The incident report will be referred back for further investigation, review, and disposition.

Sanctions

If the DHO finds that the inmate committed the charged prohibited act(s) or similar ones, sanctions will be immediately imposed. The DHO can impose any and all sanctions available (sanctions are listed in 28 C.F.R. § 541.8(g)). As with UDC findings of guilt, the DHO will typically take away a particular privilege or several privileges for a specific period of time. Unlike the UDC, however, the DHO can also impose periods of disciplinary segregation and/or loss of good conduct time.

Since DHO matters are of a more serious nature, the sanctions tend to be more severe. For example, instead of losing commissary privileges for one to three months, the DHO might impose loss of commissary for six months or a year.

It might be possible to mitigate the sanctions. The inmate can make a case for not imposing a particular sanction such as telephone or email. For example, when the inmate's family lives far away or current court proceedings require regular contact with an attorney or family members or others outside the prison, the inmate can request that telephone and email privileges remain intact.

Note that some DHOs have been known to take such privileges specifically because they are more valued.

Written Report

According to 28 C.F.R. § 541.8(h), "[The inmate] will receive a written copy of the DHO's decision following the hearing. The DHO is not required to prepare a verbatim record of the hearing." The written report will document the following:

(1) Whether [the inmate was] advised of [his or her] rights during the DHO process;
(2) The evidence relied on by the DHO;
(3) The DHO's decision;
(4) The sanctions imposed by the DHO; and
(5) The reason(s) for the sanction(s) imposed.

Program Statement 5270.09, Chapter 5 clarifies, "[T]he DHO prepares a record of the proceedings. The evidence, decision, and reasons for actions taken must be specific, unless this would jeopardize security. The DHO gives the inmate a written copy of the decisions and disposition."

Policy dictates that the report be issued within fifteen work days.[z] The DHO signs the report, certifying that it accurately reflects the proceedings, and a record of the hearing and supporting documents are kept in the inmate's central file.

The written report itself is a fill-in-the-blank, box type of report that most likely will be between two and four pages long. Some can be upwards of six pages if the case is complex. The report explains what the inmate was charged with, the facts surrounding the incident, who the staff representative and

[z] *While policy dictates that the DHO report will be issued within fifteen work days of the decision, practice is vastly different. In actuality, reports tend to take between two and six months. Once they are issued, the appellate process can begin.*

witnesses were (if applicable), evidence relied upon in deciding the verdict, the inmate's statement, applicable dates, and so on. It is essentially a summary of what occurred.

While a detailed incident report can be bad for the accused, a detailed DHO report is always good. Typically, the DHO will not do a complete job detailing the report. He or she will misquote the inmate and their witnesses, fail to note all of the evidence relied upon (such as the inmate's statement), fail to note evidence the inmate presented (i.e., their statement or those of the inmate's witnesses), include a plethora of grammatical and spelling errors, and generally do a very unprofessional job. This is good for the inmate because this report is a basis for appeal.

Challenging the DHO Report

Much like building a defense by poking holes in the description of the incident report, the inmate now pokes holes in the DHO report. Instead of dealing with an allegation and finding proof that an event didn't occur or presenting mitigating facts, the inmate can directly attack the report and its allegations. The focus shifts from the facts of the original incident to whatever the report states. Common points of attack might include:

(1) Evidence excluded: Often the DHO will state in the report that the inmate didn't present any evidence. While it could be true that the inmate didn't produce any new tangible evidence of innocence, even the inmate's written statement becomes evidence once submitted to the DHO. As such, if the DHO did not acknowledge the inmate's written statement, this can create a basis for appeal.

(2) Misquotes or incomplete quotes: Often the DHO will grossly fail to note or only briefly summarize statements by the inmate's witnesses. This could include the DHO producing a very small (one- or two-sentence) summary of each witness' verbal statement. The DHO might also fail to note who the witnesses were. This is one of the reasons why it is important to have written witness statements. If the DHO states something incorrect or fails to record testimony, the inmate will have a copy of the statement to submit on appeal.

(3) Blatant falsehoods: At times, the DHO will make completely untruthful and nonfactual statements. This might be a claim that the inmate admitted to the conduct when the inmate did no such thing. Or the DHO might make untrue statements about witnesses or even with basic facts. If this occurs, the inmate is strongly advised to appeal the issue with documentary proof. This could overturn the entire case.

(4) Incorrect charges: Bureau employees will sometimes charge an inmate with an overly severe charge when a lower charge is more appropriate (e.g., 197 instead of 297 or 296 instead of 396). If this occurs, it is important to bring up on appeal because it can substantially reduce sanctions. It can also result in a rehearing or even expungement of the charge.

(5) Improper sanctions: If the DHO stated during the hearing that the inmate will receive certain sanctions but the report increases the sanctions, this can be brought up on appeal. It would be smart to suggest that a particular individual who was present could testify about the DHO's statements.

Review the Appeals section below for more information on challenging a UDC/DHO finding of guilt.

Sanctions

Available sanctions are enumerated in 28 C.F.R. § 541.3(b) and are also presented in this section.

A. RECOMMEND PAROLE DATE RESCISSION OR RETARDATION: The DHO can recommend that an inmate's parole date be rescinded or retarded. Only military inmates and inmates sentenced before 1987 are eligible for federal parole and are subject to this sanction.

B. FORFEIT EARNED STATUTORY GOOD CONDUCT TIME, NON-VESTED GOOD CONDUCT TIME, OR TERMINATE OR DISALLOW EXTRA GOOD CONDUCT TIME: This represents the loss of good conduct time classified as "earned statutory good conduct time" or "extra good conduct time." If the DHO imposes this sanction, the inmate's projected release date will be pushed back.

This sanction does not apply to inmates who committed their crimes before the passage of the Comprehensive Crime Control Act (CCCA) of November 1, 1987, or after the passage of the Violent Crime Control and Law Enforcement Act (VCCLEA) of September 13, 1994. For all inmates sentenced after September 13, 1994, the applicable good conduct time sanction is Disallowance of Good Conduct Time [see B.1 below].

Forfeited good conduct time cannot be restored. However, for pre-CCCA and military inmates, statutory good time can be restored after a period of clear conduct. If the warden or their designee denies restoration, the unit team notifies the inmate and sets a new restoration eligibility date. This date is not to exceed six months from the date of the denial.

Vested good conduct time – good conduct time already earned – cannot be rescinded. Only the current amount of non-vested time can be forfeited, for example, the fifty-four days of good conduct time per year allowed for inmates who committed their crimes on or after November 1, 1987, and who are sentenced under the Sentencing Reform Act provision of the Comprehensive Crime Control Act. For inmates to whom this applies, the maximum amount of good time that can be taken is calculated by multiplying the months served at the time of the prohibited act by the applicable monthly rate specified in 18 U.S.C. § 4161 minus previous forfeitures and withholdings.

The maximum amount of extra good conduct time that can be disallowed is capped at the amount associated with the particular month in which the prohibited act occurred.

B.1 DISALLOWANCE OF GOOD CONDUCT TIME: This, as with the above, is effectively the loss of good conduct time. The inmate will be released a set amount of days later than originally expected; specifically, the number of days specified in the sanction.

According to Program Statement 5270.09, Chapter 1, all inmates "sentenced under the Sentencing Reform Act provisions of the Comprehensive Crime Control Act (having committing a crime on or after November 1, 1987) may not receive statutory good conduct time, but [are] eligible to receive 54 days [of good conduct time] each year."[39] Once awarded, the credit is vested, and may not be disallowed.

This means that an inmate can only lose up to fifty-four days of good conduct time for the year in which a prohibited act occurs. If multiple acts occur within a particular year, the maximum amount of sanctionable good conduct time loss remains fifty-four days.

The same program statement notes that for "crimes committed on or after September 13, 1994, and before April 26, 1996, (VCCLEA) credit is not vested unless the inmate has earned, or is making satisfactory progress toward, a high school diploma or equivalent degree – or [that the prisoner is exempt] because of a learning disability."

Typically, inmates who go in front of the DHO lose good conduct time. The following figures apply to VCCLEA inmates (rated "violent") and those subject to the Prison Litigation Reform Act (inmates who committed their offense on or after April 26, 1996) in accordance with Program Statement 5270.09, Chapter 1:

- GREATEST-SEVERITY PROHIBITED ACTS: Minimum of forty-one days of good conduct time (minimum of 75% of available good conduct time if less than fifty-four days are available) for conviction of each prohibited act.
- HIGH-SEVERITY PROHIBITED ACTS: Minimum of twenty-seven days of good conduct time (minimum of 50% of available good conduct time if less than fifty-four days are available) for conviction of each prohibited act.
- MODERATE-SEVERITY PROHIBITED ACTS: Minimum of fourteen days of good conduct time (minimum of 25% of available good conduct time if less than fifty-four days are available) for conviction of each prohibited act only if the inmate has committed two or more moderate-severity prohibited acts within the past twelve months.
- LOW-SEVERITY PROHIBITED ACTS: Minimum of seven days of good conduct time (minimum of 12.5% of available good conduct time if less than fifty-four days are available) for conviction of each prohibited act

only if the inmate has committed two or more low-severity prohibited acts within the past twelve months.

Good conduct time is only applied to inmates who are sentenced to more than twelve months of incarceration. As such, this sanction (and the previous one, "B") does not apply to inmates sentenced to twelve months or less. Inmates with less than twelve months remaining can only have the remaining amount of non-vested good conduct time sanctioned.

C. DISCIPLINARY SEGREGATION: The inmate is removed from the general population and placed in the SHU for disciplinary reasons. Only the DHO can impose this sanction – the UDC can only recommend it. Typically, disciplinary segregation time is issued in blocks of fifteen or thirty days.

If an inmate is sanctioned to disciplinary segregation time, they will immediately be walked to the SHU to start serving their time. All of their property will be packed for them by their unit officer. Upon return to the general population, they will be placed in the least desirable housing. This sanction is a particularly bad one.

The following are allowable guidelines for terms of disciplinary segregation. Repeated violations can increase these sanctions:

- GREATEST-SEVERITY PROHIBITED ACT (100): Up to twelve months.
- HIGH-SEVERITY PROHIBITED ACT (200): Up to six months.
- MODERATE-SEVERITY PROHIBITED ACT (300): Up to three months.
- LOW-SEVERITY PROHIBITED ACT (400): No time unless repeated violations occur.[40]

D. MONETARY RESTITUTION: If an inmate destroys or damages government property while committing a prohibited act, the DHO can sanction them to restitution for the damages. The UDC is not allowed to impose this sanction but can recommend it. If the inmate lacks funds in their prison trust fund account to make reparations, commissary privileges will be suspended until full restitution is made.

E. MONETARY FINE: According to Program Statement 5270.09, Chapter 1, the Bureau can now fine inmates for disciplinary infractions. This sanction, unlike the previous one, is never to be utilized as a method of restitution for damage to U.S. Government property. This sanction is purely punitive. Only the DHO can impose this sanction. In accordance with policy, the following figures apply:

- GREATEST-SEVERITY PROHIBITED ACT (100): Up to $500 or 75% of the inmate's trust fund balance.
- HIGH-SEVERITY PROHIBITED ACT (200): Up to $300 or 50% of the inmate's trust fund balance.
- MODERATE-SEVERITY PROHIBITED ACT (300): Up to $100 or 25% of the inmate's trust fund balance.
- LOW-SEVERITY PROHIBITED ACT (400): Up to $50 or 12.5% of the inmate's trust fund balance.

If the inmate doesn't have enough funds, their commissary privileges will be suspended until the obligation is fulfilled.

F. LOSS OF PRIVILEGES: Both the DHO and the UDC can impose a loss of privileges. This form of sanction is the type most often utilized and typically include loss of telephone, email, visitation, and commissary privileges. Movies and recreation privileges can also be sanctioned. Usually this form of sanction is imposed in increments of thirty days. As such, for virtually any prohibited act, the inmate could lose one or more privileges for several months or even more than a year.

Ideally, sanctions are progressive in nature and in line with the severity of the prohibited act. Program Statement 5270.09, Chapter 1, specifies that loss of recreation privileges cannot be imposed on SHU inmates. Inmates in the SHU can be sanctioned to a loss of mattress but the mattress must be returned for overnight sleeping hours.

G. CHANGE HOUSING: Both the UDC and the DHO can sanction an inmate to the loss of their current housing. When this occurs, the inmate is typically placed in the least preferable housing available such as dormitory or housing with multiple inmates per room.

H. REMOVE FROM PROGRAM OR GROUP ACTIVITY: Both the UDC and DHO can remove an inmate from a specified program or activity for a specified period of time. This sanction is often utilized when an inmate has committed an offense pertaining to the program or activity.

I. LOSS OF JOB: Both the UDC and DHO can sanction an inmate to a loss of an institutional job for a specific period of time. Typically, this sanction is imposed when the inmate committed the prohibited act while in the course of their institutional job duties like stealing food while working in the kitchen.

J. IMPOUNDING THE INMATE'S PERSONAL PROPERTY: Both the UDC and DHO can sanction an inmate by impounding their personal property. This is typically utilized when the inmate has excessive property in their cell, as in the case of a store man, or when the inmate is in the SHU for a long period and has accumulated excessive property.

K. CONFISCATE CONTRABAND: Both the UDC and DHO can impose this sanction. In actuality it is rarely imposed because the contraband has already been confiscated by the reporting officer.

L. RESTRICT TO QUARTERS: Both the UDC and DHO can impose this sanction. If an inmate is restricted to his or her living quarters, they must remain in their cell or dorm unless going to the dining room, religious services, or a call-out. To not comply with this sanction would invite an "out of bounds" incident report (316) and/or a refusal to accept a program assignment incident report (306).

M. EXTRA DUTY: Both the UDC and the DHO can impose a period of extra work for a prohibited act. The sanction often provides for a specific number of hours of extra duty rather than a specific task. The inmate will have to complete the sanctioned number of extra duty hours within a specific time frame.

This is done by keeping an extra duty time log, asking various officers if they require assistance in some sort of activity (like picking up trash, cleaning, etc.), and having the officer sign the inmate's log sheet. After the extra duty has been completed, the inmate turns the log sheet in to the lieutenant on duty.

Suspended Sanctions

Both the UDC and the DHO can suspend some sanctions. This is done by the hearing body placing a hold on existing sanctions such as loss of commissary, email, telephone, or visitation for a specific period of time not to exceed six months. As long as the inmate maintains clear conduct during that period, the incident report remains in the inmate's central file but the sanctions are not activated.

If an inmate with previously suspended sanctions violates Bureau policy, is issued an incident report, and is found guilty, the suspended sanctions are activated and added to the sanctions imposed for the new incident. While the DHO can activate UDC-suspended sanctions, the UDC cannot activate DHO-suspended sanctions. The UDC can only activate UDC-imposed sanctions.

If an incident report is issued while the inmate currently has DHO-imposed suspended sanctions, the UDC can either informally resolve the incident report or forward the new incident report to the DHO for hearing. This is possible only in the cases of moderate-severity prohibited acts (300) and low-severity prohibited acts (400).

Regardless of the severity of the new incident report, however, if the inmate currently has DHO-imposed sanctions, the UDC cannot hear it. Once the DHO hears the new incident report, he or she can retain the existing suspended sanctions and remand the new incident report to the UDC for hearing. Any new sanctions would be added to the existing suspended sanctions but not necessarily suspended themselves.

The DHO can suspend all forms of sanction with the exception of those related to the loss of good conduct time [see B and B.1 above, and Program Statement 5270.09, Chapter 1]. The UDC can only suspend a loss of privileges (F), a change in housing (G), removal from a program and/or group activity (H), loss of a job (I), impounding an inmate's personal property (J), confiscation of contraband (K), restriction to quarters (L), and extra duty (M).

TIP: For all intents and purposes, only two categories of inmates receive suspended sanctions: informants and inmates who have never had previous incident reports (or when some time has passed since their last incident report). Inmates should therefore not go into a UDC or DHO hearing expecting to receive a suspended sentence.

If an inmate is an informant, perhaps they won't be discovered and will be able to pass the leniency off as luck. Do note that it is not advised to inform in order to seek suspended or lesser sanctions. Informants are almost always found out and are not dealt with kindly by fellow inmates.

Mentally Ill Inmates

When an inmate is not competent to participate in disciplinary proceedings and when the inmate was not mentally cognizant – or responsible – for their actions while committing a prohibited act, the Bureau cannot hold the inmate accountable.

According to 28 C.F.R. § 541.6(a), "[i]f evidence indicates that [the inmate] cannot understand the nature of the disciplinary proceedings, or cannot help in [their] own defense, disciplinary proceedings may be postponed until [the inmate is] competent to participate. The Unit Disciplinary Committee or Discipline Hearing Officer will make this decision based on evidence, including evidence presented by mental health staff."

Program Statement 5270.09, Chapter 3, clarifies what it means for an inmate to be incompetent. "A person is incompetent if he/she lacks the ability to understand the disciplinary proceedings, or to assist in his/her defense. When a person is determined incompetent, the disciplinary proceedings are postponed until the inmate is able to understand the proceedings and assist in his/her defense. If competency is not restored within a reasonable time, the incident report shows as a finding that the inmate is incompetent."

According to 28 C.F.R. § 541.6(b), the inmate "will not be disciplined for conduct committed when, as a result of severe mental disease or defect, [the inmate was] unable to appreciate the nature and quality, or wrongfulness of the act. The UDC or DHO will make this decision based on evidence, including evidence presented by mental health staff."

The program statement clarifies what it means for an inmate to not be responsible for their actions. "A person is not responsible for his/her conduct if, at the time of the conduct, as a result of severe mental disease or defect, he/she was unable to appreciate the nature and quality of the wrongfulness of his/her acts." Program Statement 5270.09 at Chapter 3 finishes the mental health discussion by describing the proper protocol when handling such situations. It reads:

> If it appears at any stage of the discipline process that the inmate is mentally ill, staff refers him/her to a mental health professional to determine whether he/she is responsible for his/her conduct or is incompetent. Staff may take no discipline action against an inmate who is determined by a mental health professional to be incompetent to participate in the disciplinary proceedings or not responsible for his/her behavior . . . Generally, the UDC initiates referral to a mental health professional. However, staff at any stage of the discipline process may make such a referral. The completed mental health evaluation is returned to the UDC, which then decides whether the incident may be handled by the UDC (other than Greatest or High-severity level), or referred to the DHO. In Greatest and High-severity level cases, the UDC may refer an inmate for a mental health evaluation along with referral to the DHO. The completed evaluation is returned to the UDC, which forwards it to the DHO.

TIP: It is a bad idea to present mental illness as a defense for committing a prohibited act. This defense is often a losing one. The bar for proving mental illness is so high that to succeed would almost certainly result in a very worrisome memorandum being placed in an inmate's central file. At worst, the inmate would be found guilty of the prohibited act and lose the opportunity to create a detailed record from which to appeal. Unless an inmate is truly severely mentally ill, they shouldn't utilize mental illness as a defense.

Additional Sanctions for Repeated Violations

If an inmate persists in engaging in prohibited conduct, the Bureau authorizes UDCs and DHOs to substantially increase applicable sanctions [see Program Statement 5270.09, Table 2]. This is a method of persuading the inmate to comply with Bureau disciplinary policy.

Low-severity prohibited acts (400): If the inmate receives two low-severity incident reports within six months, the additional sanctions of one-month disciplinary segregation becomes available. If the inmate receives three or more incident reports for low-severity prohibited acts within the six-month time period, additional sanctions of the loss of good conduct time (either 15% or up to fifteen days of non-vested good conduct time/statutory good time), disallowance of extra good conduct time, or the sanction of any applicable moderate-severity prohibited act (300) become available.

Moderate-severity prohibited acts (300): If the inmate receives two moderate-severity incident reports within twelve months, the additional sanction of six months disciplinary segregation becomes available. If the inmate receives three or more incident reports for moderate-severity prohibited acts within a twelve-month time period, the additional sanctions of loss of good conduct time (either 37.5% or up to forty-five days of non-vested good conduct time/statutory good conduct time), disallowance of extra good conduct time, or the sanction of any applicable high-severity prohibited act (200) become available.

High-severity prohibited acts (200): If the inmate receives two high-severity incident reports for prohibited acts within eighteen months, the additional sanction of twelve months of disciplinary segregation becomes available. If the inmate receives three or more incident reports for high-severity prohibited acts within the eighteen-month time period, additional sanctions of the loss of good conduct time (either 75% or up to ninety days of non-vested good conduct time/statutory good conduct time) or the sanction of any applicable greatest-severity prohibited act (100) become available.

Greatest-severity prohibited acts (100): If the inmate receives two or more greatest-severity incident reports for prohibited acts within twenty-four months, the additional sanction of eighteen months of disciplinary segregation becomes available.

TIP: Not only will these sanctions become applicable but the hearing body will substantially increase the sanctions for the underlying offense. While a moderate-severity prohibited act (300) might typically carry the loss of one or two privileges for up to six months, with repeated violations, the UDC or DHO might sanction one year loss of several privileges plus the applicable sanctions noted above.

Long story short, inmates shouldn't repeatedly engage in prohibited conduct. Once they get on the Bureau's radar, it's time to slow down and get back off it.

Appeals

The appeals process begins when an inmate receives the written report from either the UDC or the DHO.[aa] If the inmate is appealing a UDC decision, a BP-9 form (appeal to the institution's warden) is to be used. If the inmate is appealing a DHO decision, a BP-10 form (appeal to the regional office) is utilized.

Program Statement 5270.09, Chapter 5 provides that the reviewing official (warden, regional director, or general counsel) can approve, modify, reverse,[bb] or send back with directions, including ordering a rehearing, any action of the UDC or DHO but cannot increase a valid sanction. The decision of the DHO is final and subject to review only by the regional director to ensure conformity with the discipline policy by appeal through the Administrative Remedy Program. On appeal, pursuant to Program Statement 5270.09, Chapter 5, the reviewing authority considers:

[aa] *While the Bureau is required to present the inmate with the UDC's findings by the end of the next business day, DHO Reports typically take two to six months to be issued. This is despite the policy that states that the report is to ordinarily be delivered within fifteen work days.*

[bb] *Program Statement 5270.09, Chapter 5, states, "[i]f the DHO expunges an incident report [or if it is expunged while on appeal], unit staff must ensure the inmate's central file does not include the incident report and/or related documents."*

(1) Whether the UDC or DHO substantially complied with regulations on inmate discipline;
(2) Whether the UDC or DHO based its decisions on facts;
(3) If conflicting evidence was presented, whether the decision was based on the greater weight of the evidence;
(4) Whether an appropriate sanction was imposed for the severity level of the prohibited act and other relevant circumstances.

The reviewing official is limited to determining whether the UDC or DHO could have rationally concluded that the evidence supports the decision. They cannot necessarily determine whether the reviewing official would have made the same decision. Where a remand is directed, the UDC or DHO is bound by the original sanction(s) except where:

(1) The sanction is in violation of policy,
(2) The remand is made specifically because of the sanction, or
(3) The inmate's behavior since the first hearing is determined by the UDC or DHO to justify an increase in sanction(s). The intervening behavior or activity and the reasons for an increase or decrease in sanction(s) must be documented in the hearing record.

When an appeal results in the original sanction being replaced by a suspended sanction, the suspension runs from the date the original sanction was imposed.

Special Topics of Consideration

Telephone Recordings

The discipline process will at times utilize recordings of telephone conversations as evidence of an inmate having committed a prohibited act. If this is the case, the inmate should request transcripts of the calls. The Bureau will almost certainly refuse to produce such transcripts. If or when this occurs, it can be a point of appeal.

If the inmate wasn't provided with an opportunity to review the evidence and thus defend against it, then due process violations have occurred. Just because staff claims to have evidence of the inmate committing a prohibited act on the telephone, if they cite only specific phone calls and their times, they have proven only that the inmate placed phone calls, not that the content of the calls was a violation of the rules.

Urine Analysis and Breathalyzers

If an inmate is called for a breathalyzer test or to participate in the institution's urinalysis program and they have been drinking or using drugs, the inmate should refuse to provide a sample. While this is a certain way to be placed in the SHU and convicted of violating an order, there is some chance of success on appeal.

By comparison, to be found drunk or to have used drugs would result in a guilty verdict and could result in the inmate being placed in a restrictive drug/alcohol abuse program. For example, if an inmate is found to have abused substances or to have consumed alcohol three times, they are eligible for placement in a Special Management Unit (SMU), a very undesirable fate.[41]

If the inmate agrees to participate in the urine analysis program and is found to have utilized illegal substances, several specific avenues of appeal are noted in policy. Program Statement 5270.09, Chapter 2, states: "An inmate who receives an incident report based upon a 'positive' urine test may claim this result comes from either:

(1) Permissible medication he/she was given, or
(2) A combination of medications he/she is taking.

"In the first situation, the investigator must contact the Health Services staff to determine if the inmate is receiving medication that contains the compound found in the urinalysis. In the second situation, the investigator must confirm that the inmate is authorized to take the medications. When necessary, the testing laboratory is contacted to see if the combined medications could produce a 'false positive.'

"While an inmate can challenge the results of a urine test, and this may be considered by the DHO, the validity of the testing process is not at issue. Neither the investigator nor the DHO has the experience to assess the accuracy of the laboratory process."

Non-inclusive and Non-conclusive Evidence

Part of the inmate's job during disciplinary matters is to muddy the waters, usually with a request to obtain evidence that contradicts what the Bureau alleges. For example, if the Bureau alleges that an assault occurred, the inmate should request camera evidence if cameras were at the site. If they are innocent and cameras were recording, it will completely prove their defense. On the other hand if no camera recorded the event, the lack of camera footage can be utilized as evidence to defend the accused.

When the only form of evidence is an inmate or staff member's statement, the accused might attempt to disprove the accusations by calling into evidence the lack of other evidence. At times this will be the only defense available, and it can help support an otherwise mediocre defense.

Notice to Inmates of the Inmate Discipline Program

According to Program Statement 5270.09, Inmate Discipline Program, "[s]taff must give each inmate a copy of the following documents promptly after his/her arrival at an institution:

(1) Summary of the Inmate Discipline System (Appendix B [of program statement]),
(2) Inmate Rights and Responsibilities (Appendix C [of program statement]),
(3) Prohibited Acts and Available Sanctions (Table 1 [of program statement]).

Receipt of these documents must be noted on the intake screening form and maintained in the inmate's central file. The receipt is kept in the inmate's central file."

While this is fairly general information, it exposes a significant flaw in the Bureau's disciplinary policy. Most inmates spend a number of years in the FBOP. The only time an inmate signs an intake screening form is when they are being admitted to a new institution.

The disciplinary policy changes every few years; most recently in 2009 and 2011. An inmate very well might not sign a new copy of their intake screening form for a number of years (or ever), a period during which the discipline policy could change.

To compound matters, Admission & Orientation handbooks are often badly out of date and don't contain a current list of prohibited acts and sanctions. Inmates aren't provided with notice of a current or revised listing of prohibited acts. This lack of notice can be a violation of due process rights if the institution attempts to hold the inmate accountable for prohibited acts of which they are unaware. This is a very good argument to present either at the UDC or DHO hearing or on appeal.

If the inmate is facing such a situation, they should request a copy of their intake screening form to prove the date on which they were provided notice of the Bureau's disciplinary policy. To add to this, they should present a copy of the applicable pages from their institution's A&O Handbook from their date of admission.

By presenting both of these forms, an inmate found guilty of an infraction that did not exist when they were admitted and about which they were provided no advanced notice might win on appeal. Additionally, over time, certain prohibited acts become more severe (e.g., tattooing, drinking, drug use, etc.). If this is the case, an argument can be made for the inmate being charged and sanctioned according to past disciplinary policy rather than current policy.

Notes

1. Program Statement 5270.09, Inmate Discipline Program at §§ 3(a)-(e).
2. 28 C.F.R. § 541.5(b)(1)(B).

3. 28 C.F.R. § 541.7(a).
4. Program Statement 5270.09, Inmate Discipline Program at Chapter 4.
5. 28 C.F.R. § 541.7(a)(4).
6. 28 C.F.R. §§ 541.8(d)-(f).
7. 28 C.F.R. § 541.8(c).
8. 28 C.F.R. §§ 541.8(d)-(f).
9. *Id.*
10. 28 C.F.R. § 541.5(b)(1)(B).
11. 28 C.F.R. § 541.8(a).
12. 28 C.F.R. § 541.5(b)(1)(B).
13. Program Statement 5270.09, Inmate Discipline Program.
14. *Id.* at Chapter 2.
15. *Id.* at Chapter 4.
16. 28 C.F.R. § 541.7(e).
17. 28 C.F.R. §§ 541.7(a)(1)-(4).
18. 28 C.F.R. § 541.7(f).
19. *Id.*
20. 28 C.F.R. § 541.7(a)(4).
21. Program Statement 5270.09, Inmate Discipline Program at Chapter 4.
22. Program Statement 1330.18, Administrative Remedy Program.
23. Program Statement 5270.09, Inmate Discipline Program at Chapter 5.
24. 28 C.F.R. § 541.8(c).
25. 28 C.F.R. § 541.8(f)(1).
26. 28 C.F.R. § 541.8(f)(2).
27. 28 C.F.R. § 541.8(f)(3).
28. 28 C.F.R. § 541.8(f)(4).
29. 28 C.F.R. § 541.8(f)(5).
30. 28 C.F.R. § 541.8(f)(6).
31. *Id.*
32. Program Statement 5270.09, Inmate Discipline Program at Chapter 5.
33. *Id.*
34. *Id.*
35. *Id.*

36. *Id.*
37. *Id.*
38. 28 C.F.R. § 541.8(f)(5).
39. See also 18 U.S.C. § 3624(b).
40. Program Statement 5270.09, Inmate Discipline Program at Table 1.
41. Program Statement P5217.01, Special Management Units.

Twenty-One

Special Housing Unit

When inmates must be securely separated from the general inmate population, they are sent to the Special Housing Unit (SHU), sometimes referred to as "the Hole" or "the Bucket." The SHU is a secured cellblock that is effectively a prison within a prison.

At the end of the 18th century, solitary confinement began to be used as a replacement for corporal punishment. It was thought that solitude could calm prisoners much more effectively than whipping or stocks. The Pennsylvania System, implemented at Philadelphia's Eastern State Penitentiary, housed inmates in cells with skylights and access to private outdoor courtyards. Despite these small amenities, prisoners quickly fell into depression or became violent or suicidal … just as they do today.[1]

After falling out of favor for a time, the practice returned in the mid-1960s when Alcatraz closed. In 1983, USP Marion was the first federal prison to be converted to an all-lockdown facility. In 1986, the FBOP opened a unit specifically intended to house female political prisoners in the basement of the federal prison in Lexington, Kentucky.

Former political prisoner Susan Rosenberg described the unit in her memoir *An American Radical.* "It was a bright, gleaming artificial white," she wrote, "the kind of white that with any lengthy exposure could almost sear your eyeballs. It was the kind of white that can make you go mad."[2]

She recalled daily confrontations with guards to have every "human need" like water, showers, and going outside met. Marc Emery, who was incarcerated for his political activities, described the SHU as "just like solitary confinement in the movies, truly that horrible."[3]

In 2009, American facilities held at least 25,000 inmates in isolation inside supermax facilities. An additional 50,000 to 80,000 were held in isolated quarters in restrictive segregation units.[4]

Anthony Graves, a wrongly convicted ex-prisoner, said, "You have to rise above [solitary confinement] because if you can't you're going to be carried out of there not even knowing your name." He kept himself occupied by having friends send him pictures they had taken throughout the day, just as if they had been spending time with Graves in the outside world. The letters that went along with the photos helped him escape mentally.[5]

From the Inside

Several times while serving my sentence, I was sent to the SHU. The most recent incident was when prison officials falsely charged me with conducting a business while incarcerated, something that is against prison policy. None of it was true, however, and I was ultimately exonerated. Regardless, it cost my family a fortune in legal fees, and it cost me five months of my life in a small, dark hole. This section describes what it was like.

The typical SHU is a housing unit with secured hallways and rows and rows of locked cells. A typical cell holds two inmates. Single-man cells exist for prisoners who act up, while others can hold three or more when needed, often for prisoners on holdover status. Typically, approximately 200 inmates reside in a SHU.

In my case, I entered the SHU and was placed in a miniature holding cell where I had to strip and pass my clothes to the watching guard. It was the same routine as when I had first arrived at the prison: I stripped, ran my hands through my hair, opened my mouth and held up my tongue, raised my arms, and squatted and coughed. After this too-familiar ritual, they gave me a pair of boxers, a t-shirt, socks, a pair of blue bus shoes, and an orange jumpsuit.

I took in the lay of the land. A cube area for the guards was bordered by four gates. In the center was a second internal cube where the guards handled their paperwork and watched TV. I was in a prison within a prison, a jail cell within a bunker.

Suited up, I was escorted by the guards to a cell with my hands cuffed behind my back. We went up a stairwell through a gate and down a hallway filled with countless cells. The ceiling, walls, floors, and cell doors looked grim and grimy. I could not see into any of the cells but I could hear banging and yelling. It felt like the first day of county jail when I had imagined that monotony, boredom, and uncertainty might kill me. I was not to be disappointed.

I was placed in a cell by myself. Inside were a shower, a toilet-sink combo, and a bunk bed along with a large pile of trash. No toilet paper. I asked for cleaning supplies and scoured the cell, which only took about twenty minutes. Then I was left with myself. There was a Bible with print too small to read, a frosted window I couldn't see through, and lots of fruit flies. After a few do-nothing hours, I felt hopeless and lost. I didn't know what to expect, how anything worked, or what to do with myself for however long the ordeal would last.

The intense boredom was punctuated by meals, occasional clothing exchanges, and the 6:00 a.m. recreation call. With no warning, the small trap in the center of my cell door might open and something would happen: food was placed on the trap, a commissary form was passed inside, or an orderly asked if I wanted to change out my clothes or sheets.

The days were bad: long stretches with nothing to do except swat fruit flies and walk to my cell door when I heard keys in a lock. There was no educational or rehabilitative programming, nothing to occupy my time. Eventually I was able to procure a flexible, bendable pen and a few sheets of paper. I wrote letters. Well, I tried to write letters. Mostly I tried to get the damn pen to work or begged for a few more sheets of paper.

The nights were worse. I lay in bed praying for sleep, listening to other prisoners banging on their doors, rapping to others under their cell doors, and screaming into the vents. Nights were long and painful. I was constantly angry, frustrated, and bitter. I felt hopeless. I understood how these conditions could make someone want to kill themselves.

The guards were awful. Some were merely apathetic; others were sadistic. They were either kicking me or issuing incident reports or denying me toilet paper when I needed it – anything to destroy my few remaining strands of sanity. They found ingenious ways to make me feel lower than I already felt, and they inflicted their torment in a cold, calculated way, totally detached and uncaring. In their minds, they were not abusing prisoners, they were punishing wrongdoers. The system literally created sadists and condoned abuse. It validated cruelty and allowed the guards to feel righteous, as if they were making the world a better place one abused prisoner at a time.

The guards would say they would do something and then not do it, leaving me waiting at the door for something that would never come. Hope flared faintly when the next shift came on but it was only to be more of the same. Lies, always lies. Lies and deceit. It seemed to be a planned program of torture. But the deceit helped focus my resentment more on the guards and less on my depressing and extreme circumstance. Their mean-spirited behavior drove me to push forward to spite them.

Much of my time in the SHU was about struggling to get my most basic needs met. Simply obtaining toilet paper was a task. Obtaining pens, paper, envelopes, or anything else was a struggle. Getting to the law library was a joke.

It took a mental toll, as was evident in my letters, which radiated anger and hate. I'm sure those letters were disagreeable for my family and friends to read but they understood that the experience was distorting my natural disposition. Locked in a cage, my mind alternated between racing and stone-stillness. I was frustrated beyond imagining and completely despondent. I became a canvas of angry reds and bottomless blacks.

And this is how it was for one of the few who retained his sanity. Others started talking to themselves for something to do and for some level of social interaction. I preferred to quietly sing songs I remembered. One of my favorite bands, New Found Glory, played in my head to divert my attention when everything else was too much to take.

Books and letter writing were my salvation. In an environment of despair, hate, and nothingness, books were my lifeline. I asked friends and family to send books, lots of them. I read and read and read during my stay in the SHU.

Books helped keep my mind engaged but there was still so much time spent simply waiting. Waiting for a guard to bring paper, waiting for meals, waiting to fall asleep. Just waiting. Waiting became a serious mental assault. To counter this, I found ways to make the cell better, and scrubbed every inch with a toothbrush, paperclip, and a torn sheet. I used part of the sheet to make a line on which I hung a blanket to give me some privacy while using the toilet. I implemented a workout regimen. I found ways to fill the time. To keep my sanity.

Five long months. Then they called my name. The day had come for my release. After having done nothing but wait for so long, I now had to hurry up, pack, and be ready to leave in fifteen minutes. But the SHU guards were not yet done with their abusive games.

Standing in the central cube area, my personal belongings stacked before me in large green bags, I asked for a cart to transport my property to my housing unit. The SHU guards said to carry it all myself. They laughed and joked about how many trips it was going to take. After months of continual abuse, I had had enough. I called the head guard and told him I was going to walk my ass back to my cell and leave the stuff for him to deal with. It was now his problem. He was not amused. Within five minutes he had a cart brought over for me to use.

Carts and toilet paper. That sums up my SHU experience. Two insignificant objects wielded as weapons. Petty objects, but they symbolize the abuse of federal prisoners at the hands of their captors in the SHU.

Surviving the SHU is serious business, and there are serious consequences if no effort is made to safeguard one's sanity. Some of these units are so oppressive that the medical community now recognizes the mental health problems that result from long incarceration in such conditions. They call it "SHU Syndrome."

There were effects after I was released. I was jittery and anxious. I didn't like being around people and became very angry when there was loud noise. Some of these issues eventually abated; others did not. I am no longer the happy person I used to be. At times I am hateful and spiteful with regard to the prison administration despite my Buddhist cellmate's best efforts to right me again.

Time in the SHU creates a hard edge of frustration and anger for those who make it out. The key is to understand this and forgive oneself for it, so that the explosive anger can be mitigated before it becomes a problem. With God's help, I trust I will eventually recover my true nature.

Conditions of Confinement

In January of 2016, President Obama banned the use of solitary confinement for juveniles inside all federal prison facilities because it could lead to "devastating, lasting psychological consequences."[6] Any juvenile or inmate serving a disciplinary sanction for low-level infractions will no longer be subject to confinement in the SHU. As many as 10,000 inmates were expected to be impacted by being released from solitary confinement.

Federal regulations require that living conditions in the SHU meet or exceed minimum standards for "healthy and humane treatment."[7] They specify the following:

Environment

> "[Inmate's] living quarters will be well-ventilated, adequately lighted, appropriately heated, and maintained in a sanitary condition."[8]

In reality, cell floors and walls are often filthy. Windows, if there are any, are usually small slits, frosted so inmates cannot see through them. Ventilation is questionable, despite the presence of an air vent, and many SHU cells are plagued with cockroaches, fruit flies, and rodents.

> *TIP: When moving into a SHU cell, inmates should immediately ask for cleaning supplies. Before even making their bed, they should clean the cell thoroughly to prevent illness or disease.*

Cell Occupancy

> "[Inmate's] living quarters will ordinarily house only the amount of occupants for which it is designed. The Warden, however, may authorize more occupants so long as adequate standards can be maintained."[9]

Most SHU cells are designed for a single inmate but they usually house two or more. This means the lives of two SHU prisoners are contained within a six-foot radius. They shower, use the toilet, sleep, eat, and do all their living within a few feet of one another. The close quarters and limited movement often cause strife between cellmates. Sometimes the issues are resolved; at other times it ends in violence.

Clothing

> "[Inmates] will receive adequate institution clothing, including footwear, while housed in the SHU. [Inmates] will be provided necessary opportunities to exchange clothing and/or have it washed."[10]

SHU inmates are issued one institutional orange jumpsuit, two t-shirts, two sets of boxers, two pairs of socks, and a pair of slip-on shoes similar to those worn during their original transport on the bus. Typically, underclothes are exchanged twice a week and jumpsuits once a week.

> *TIP: If a SHU inmate's cellmate is being released, they should keep his or her clothing so they can have some extra fresh changes. This is especially useful if they exercise or work out. Extra clothing can also be used as a makeshift pillow, which is nice because SHU inmates don't get pillows.*

Bedding

> "[Inmates] will receive a mattress, blankets, a pillow, and linens for sleeping. [Inmates] will receive necessary opportunities to exchange linens."[11]

Program Statement 5270.10(12), Special Housing Units addresses particular concerns regarding bedding. First, the Program Statement interprets the requirements of providing inmates with a mattress and pillow to be fulfilled by issuing a "combination mattress with a pillow incorporated." This is a thin, dark green mattress that compresses with use.

Second, staff can remove an inmate's mattress during "non-sleeping daytime hours" if a UDC/DHO has sanctioned the inmate.

Third, "absent life or safety concerns as specifically documented and authorized by the Warden, or his or her designee," an inmate's mattress cannot be removed absent a disciplinary sanction imposed by the UDC/DHO.

All SHU inmates are issued bedding. Typically this includes a dark green mattress/pillow combination, two white sheets, two towels, and two washcloths. Linens are usually exchanged once a week and blankets once a month. As with clothing, inmates are advised to retain all excess linens if possible.

> *TIP: Inmates can place extra linens underneath their mattress to improve the padding. Since most federal prisons use slab-style metal bunk beds, this "ground pad" can make a huge difference in quality of their sleep and relaxation.*

Food

"[Inmates] will receive nutritionally adequate meals."[12]

Usually, except for soups, SHU inmates receive the same food served to prisoners in general population. But in the SHU, there is no chow hall. Food, juice, and small Styrofoam cups come in covered trays and are passed through the tray slot in the cell door.

> *TIP: If an inmate is in the SHU on disciplinary segregation (defined below), they won't be able to buy food from the commissary and they might get pretty hungry. They should save their Styrofoam cups and use them to store some of the food they get during meal times so they can snack between*

meals. If there is no food available, several cups of water can make them feel somewhat full.

Personal Hygiene

> "[Inmates] will have access to a wash basin and toilet. [Inmates] will receive personal items necessary to maintain an acceptable level of personal hygiene, for example, toilet tissue, soap, toothbrush and cleanser, shaving utensils, etc. [Inmates] will ordinarily have an opportunity to shower and shave at least three times a week. [Inmates] will have access to hair care services as necessary."[13]

In compliance with this requirement, SHU inmates typically receive a two-inch toothbrush, several one-inch by two-inch motel-sized soaps, mini toothpaste tubes, a mini deodorant, a black plastic comb, and single-blade Bic razors (issued and collected three times a week). Prisoners receive the non-razor items weekly – *if* the range officer decides to provide them. If not, the inmates go without.

Inmates have the option of getting a haircut once a month. An inmate barber from the general population barber shop visits the SHU to deliver this service.

> *TIP: As in general population, it is customary to tip the barber a dollar or two for a haircut using the equivalent of mailing stamps. See Chapter 8 on Underground Economy for stamp values.*

Toilet paper is always a challenge. Each inmate is supposed to receive one roll per week. That only happens *if* the range officer feels like passing it out. If an inmate needs more toilet paper, he has to beat on his cell door until the officer comes by. And then he's at the mercy of that prison employee's mood at that moment. I found it useful, whenever the shift changed, to ask the newly arrived range officer for a roll to avoid the ugly problem of running out when a range officer is on duty but refuses to provide more.

TIP: To obtain some privacy when using the toilet, inmates can hang up a sheet or blanket. At many facilities where toilets are equipped with flush timers, the toilets shouldn't be flushed more than once within a five-minute period or else it will not flush again for one hour. At some prisons, the guards flush remotely from outside the cell. If there is standing waste in the toilet, inmates have to beat on the door until the guard comes by or wait until they do their rounds. If the range guard is in a good mood, they might flush the toilet. If not, those confined therein will have to contend with the smell.

Working out a system between cellies for toilet use is a good idea; it can help reduce in-cell strife.

Exercise

> "[Inmates] will receive the opportunity to exercise outside [their] individual quarters at least five hours per week, ordinarily on different days in one-hour periods. [Inmates] can be denied these exercise periods for a week at a time by order of the Warden if it is determined that [their] use of exercise privileges threatens safety, security, and orderly operation of a correctional facility, or public safety."[14]

Recreation in the SHU consists of being placed in a cage resembling a large dog run for one hour per day, Sunday through Thursday. Four to ten inmates are in each cage. Some play handball if there is a solid wall; some work out; some walk; and some just sit and talk. It is not especially entertaining or fitness oriented, but the value of fresh air and sunlight is immeasurable. Being locked away for months or years on end with no sunlight or fresh air takes a heavy toll on a person's mental health.

TIP: If an inmate is in the SHU for protective custody as an informant or as a sex offender, recreation could be a problem. Many SHU inmates won't enter the same cage with an informant or a sex offender.

Inmates who want to express their contempt for such prisoners might wait until the cage door is locked and then attack the "offensive" individual. If this could be an issue, the inmate should only go into a recreation cage with people they know or with others who have a similar background.

Program Statement 5270.10(12) states that "[r]estriction or denial of exercise is not used as punishment ... [e]xercise periods are only restricted or denied when inmates [sic] activities pose a threat to the safety, security and orderly operation of a correctional facility, or health conditions of the unit."

TIP: By ripping off a two- to three-foot strip of sheet, an inmate can make a belt to tie around their waist. This turns their jumpsuit into pants.

In practice, the restriction of recreational privileges is not so limited. Such restrictions can happen if inmates don't have their beds made when recreation call is announced, if they aren't up at 5:30 a.m. to tell the range officer they want to go to recreation, or even if the range officer forgets to ask.

TIP: Don't be a "house mouse." Inmates should go to recreation if they believe they'll be safe. Lack of fresh air, sunlight, and social interaction is very harmful. Going to recreation even just to walk around will help maintain mental health.

Correspondence

"[Inmates] will receive correspondence privileges according to Part 540, subpart B."[15]

Inmates in the SHU have the same correspondence privileges as inmates in general population. Incoming mail is distributed Monday through Friday. Prisoners bring outgoing mail to the range officer by placing it under or in the side of their cell door.

The only additional restriction imposed upon SHU inmates is that they cannot receive or possess hardcover books. Hardcover books sent to a SHU inmate are placed in their property bin and will not be delivered until the inmate is released from the SHU.

The value of reading material in the SHU, where inmates experience a cruel form of sensory deprivation, cannot be overstated. Letters, books, magazines and newspapers are their only connection to the outside world. It is a good idea for the attorneys, family members, and friends of SHU prisoners to order a subscription to *USA Today* or another daily paper for them during their SHU confinement, and even after their release to general population. Two or three paperback books a week will help keep their minds alert, and frequent letters will let them know that they are cared about and remembered.

SHU inmates are not allowed to buy paper, envelopes, or writing utensils. They depend on the range officer to give them paper (usually ten to twenty pages a week), envelopes (five to seven a week), and bendable pens (if any are available). For those who want to write a lot, this is a real problem.

TIP: Inmates should try to stock up by asking for more paper, pens, and envelopes as each new shift comes on. Inmates are at the mercy of their keeper's mood of the moment.

The pens inmates receive in the SHU are challenging to write with because they aren't stiff like normal pens and they tend to have ink flow issues. If an inmate wants to write while in the SHU, they should make a pen holder to stiffen the pen.

TIP: To make a pen holder, seal an empty envelope. Then take a piece of tape or a sticker (like those on a deodorant label) and tape the short side of the envelope to the long side of the bendable pen. Roll the envelope very tightly around the pen several times. Rip off the excess envelope and secure the wrapping with more tape or sticker. This is the basic pen holder; it should last as long as the pen.

In the SHU, as elsewhere in prison, inmates purchase postage by ordering it on the commissary form. If an inmate qualifies as indigent, they should speak with their unit team and/or the SHU lieutenant about how to obtain postage.

Telephone

> "[Inmates] will receive telephone privileges according to Part 540, subpart I."[16]

The governing program statement, PS 5270.10(12), provides that "if an inmate has not been restricted from telephone use as a result of a specific disciplinary sanction, he/she is allowed to make one telephone call per month." In practice, most SHU lieutenants will allow inmates between one and three telephone calls each month. But telephone use in the SHU is much more limited than in general population where prisoners get 300 minutes per month.

Even more difficult is that the telephone is anchored to a small wheeled platform and must be brought to the SHU inmate – if the inmate can convince the range officer to bring it. At the cell, the officer opens the food slot and passes the handset through. The inmate reaches an arm through the slot to dial the required PAC and phone numbers.

> *TIP: Some inmates try to trick the range officer into giving them additional phone calls. It doesn't work. The officer can easily see a log of all calls placed from their range and who placed each call.*

Visiting

> "[Inmates] will receive visiting privileges according to Part 540, subpart D."[17]

As long as the inmate has not lost visitation privileges through a disciplinary sanction, visits are allowed while in the SHU and are similar to visits in general population. This may be accomplished through video visitation due to security considerations. The difference is that SHU inmates wear orange jumpsuits and must sit in a designated area of the visitation room close to the guards' platform.

> *TIP: Visitors should arrive at the institution as early as possible because it takes a longer time for SHU inmates to be delivered. Some prisons cut SHU visitation periods short by thirty or sixty minutes before the end of visitation times for the general population.*
>
> *Visitation, like correspondence, is very important for connecting SHU inmates with reality and showing them that someone cares. It goes a long way to helping an inmate retain their mental health.*

Legal Activities

> "[Inmates] will receive an opportunity to perform personal legal activities according to Part 543, subpart B."[18]

Inmates have limited access to legal activities. They can mail legal letters (which are sealed and placed under their cell door to be mailed), they can have attorneys visit and, at some institutions, attorneys can secure legal telephone calls to the prisoner through the inmate's counselor.

> *TIP: Inmates often find it difficult or impossible to make legal calls, whether in general population or in the SHU, because the FBOP is only required to provide a means of communicating with legal counsel. That can be satisfied by postal mail and visits.*
>
> *Staff is not required to allow calls to attorneys but attorneys have more success in calling in to the prisoner. If a legal telephone call is needed, it is more likely to take place if initiated by the attorney.*

SHU inmates must also be permitted access to a law library. In reality, however, inmates can spend weeks or even months requesting to go to the law library to no avail. Lack of access to SHU law libraries is inevitable. A SHU typically houses around 200 inmates but has only one law library that can be used by only one inmate at a time. SHU inmates attempting access to the courts are pursuing a mirage.

The SHU law library is a small room with a typewriter and a computer which, at some institutions, has a screen covered with a metal mesh. Inmates can't read even a tenth of a line of text through the mesh; they must angle the screen to see a few words at a time so that it's almost impossible to read a full page of case law. SHU typewriters aren't much better. Some of the typewriters are broken. Those that are functional often lack typing supplies (paper, typing ribbon, and correctional tape), which the SHU inmate cannot purchase.

> *TIP: If an inmate is experiencing problems getting to the SHU law library, they should first speak with the SHU lieutenant and attempt to resolve the issue. If that doesn't work, file a BP-8. The only way to ensure access to the courts while in the SHU is to go through the Administrative Remedy Program [see below].*
>
> *Inmates should be diligent about requesting an extension of time to file their pleadings with the court. Explain that they are in the SHU; it is usually sufficient reason to obtain more time but be sure to request the extension before the deadline. It won't be considered after the deadline has passed.*

Programming Activities

> "In administrative detention status [inmates] will have access to programming activities to the extent safety, security, orderly operation of a correctional facility, or public safety are not jeopardized. In disciplinary segregation status, [inmate] participation in programming activities, e.g., educational programs, may be suspended."[19]

That's the theory. In practice, there is no programming in a typical SHU. There are no courses, no athletic activities, and no religious services outside of occasional visits by a chaplain that take place through the crack of a locked cell door.

The closest thing to programming would be the book cart but it comes by infrequently (less than once a month at the FCC Petersburg SHU). Inmates on administrative detention status don't see the book cart any more often than those on disciplinary segregation status.

> *TIP: If an inmate is enrolled in college correspondence courses when they enter the SHU, they should immediately contact their school and request an extension for completion. They should explain that while they are in the SHU, they will not be allowed to sit for proctored examinations. If the inmate immediately requests an extension, they can hopefully extend the course long enough to finish when they leave the SHU.*

Administrative Remedy Program

> "[Inmates] can submit a formal grievance challenging any aspect of their confinement in the SHU through the Administrative Remedy Program. 28 C.F.R. part 540, subpart B."[20]

If conditions in the SHU are not what they are supposed to be according to regulations and the SHU lieutenant has failed to correct any concerns, inmates have recourse through the Administrative Remedy Program. It is never a smart idea to hassle the FBOP staff about frivolous matters, but legitimate complaints need to be put on paper and addressed.

If an inmate wants to submit a complaint through the Administrative Remedy Program, they should ask their counselor, case manager, or unit manager for the required forms when they make their regular SHU rounds. The inmate will need a BP-8 (local administrative remedy form) and a BP-9 (appeal to the warden) which are turned in to the counselor. The inmate also needs a BP-10 (regional appeal) and BP-11 (central office appeal), which are mailed to those respective offices.

Once a BP-8 has been filed, the counselor routes the complaint to the person involved or to their department head for a response. After receiving the response, the counselor fills out the form and speaks to the inmate. If the inmate feels the issue is resolved, that's the end of it. If not, the inmate has the right to appeal the ruling, including the action taken or lack of action taken, to the warden. From there, the inmate can continue to send appeals until they reach the central office level or a satisfactory response or resolution has occurred.

Prisoners in the SHU might be reluctant to file for an administrative remedy because they fear retaliation from prison guards. This does sometimes happen, although it is illegal. More often than not, retaliation simply means losing favor with a cop. Unless the issue is very sensitive, such as accusing a guard of making racist, sexual, or other harassing comments, the inmate does not risk anything more severe in the way of retaliation. Maybe the guard will write an incident report next time they catch them doing something wrong instead of letting it go, but they probably won't go out of their way to harass an inmate who files a grievance.

Personal Property

All SHU inmates are allowed to possess a certain amount of personal property, though the amount and kind of property differs depending on whether the inmate is on administrative detention status or disciplinary segregation status.

28 C.F.R. § 541.31(h) states that personal property can be limited for fire safety and sanitation purposes. "In administrative detention status [the inmate is] ordinarily allowed a reasonable amount of personal property and reasonable access to the commissary." This is markedly different than what is allowed for those on disciplinary segregation status. The relevant regulation states, "In disciplinary segregation status [the inmate's] personal property will be impounded, with the exception of limited reading/writing materials, and religious articles. Also, [the inmate's] commissary privileges may be limited."[21]

To clarify the matter, the FBOP promulgated Program Statement 5270.10(12), Special Housing Units, which identifies items inmates on administrative detention status are ordinarily allowed to retain. These items include:

- Bible, Koran, or other scriptures (1)
- Paperback books (5)
- Prescription eyeglasses (2)

- Legal materials
- Magazines (3)
- Mail (10)
- Newspaper (1)
- Personal hygiene items (1 of each type but no dental floss or razors)
- Photo album (25 photos)
- Authorized religious medals or headgear (e.g., kufi)
- Shoes for the shower (1 pair)
- Shoes for walking (1 pair)
- Snack foods without aluminum foil wrappers (5 individual packs)
- Powdered soft drinks (1 container)
- Stationary and stamps (20 each)
- Wedding band (1)
- Radio with ear plugs (1)
- Watch (1)

The program statement goes on to state that "[t]he Warden may modify the quantity and type of personal property allowed. Personal property may be limited or withheld for reasons of security, fire safety, or housekeeping." Note that the housekeeping aspect of this statement is merely the FBOP's interpretation of the Code of Federal Regulations, not actual federal regulatory law.

The personal property section of the program statement concludes by addressing reading materials. It reads, "[The inmate] will receive a reasonable amount of non-legal reading material, not to exceed five books per inmate at any one time, on a circulating basis. Staff shall provide the inmate the opportunity to possess religious scriptures of the inmates [sic] faith."[22]

TIP: The SHU property officer has significant control over an inmate's quality of life, so it is always a good idea to be polite and patient with them. A happy property officer means inmates will get to retain more of their property, which means a higher quality of life. Also, always accept or ask for property that is offered or left behind by inmates who have moved on. No one knows how long they'll be in the SHU or if they'll eventually need a certain item.

As usual, policy and regulations provide only a dim view of reality. Because inmates must furnish personal property themselves, they often have very few of the allowable items, although most will have soap, toothbrushes, toothpaste, paper, pens, and envelopes. Book carts are theoretically available but are rarely accessible.

Most of a SHU inmate's personal property is what they had before they were confined in the SHU. When an inmate goes to the SHU, the unit officer inventories and packs the inmate's property into large property bags. After several days, the SHU property officer brings the allowable belongings to the inmate. After the first delivery of property, the inmate must wait thirty days before making another property request.

TIP: When prisoners are released from the SHU and are given a chance to dig through all of their belongings, they often discover that items are missing. They might have been stolen by other inmates or thrown away by a unit officer out of ignorance.

To avoid loss, inmates should carry their radio, headphones, and other valuables with them to the SHU. If this is not possible or if other property is missing, they should immediately file a tort claim when they are released from the SHU. They have only six months from the date of property loss to file the tort claim.

Commissary

SHU inmates have limited access to the commissary. If they are on administrative detention status, they can order food, coffee and powdered drink mixes, hygiene items, over-the-counter medications, and allowable electronic items on a weekly order form the commissary staff fulfills.[23] Inmates on disciplinary segregation status are limited to over-the-counter medications and a few hygienic items; no food, drinks, or other purchases are permitted.[24] Inmates on both statuses are allowed to purchase postage stamps.

Many SHUs house inmates on administrative detention status together with those on disciplinary segregation status or, if not in the same cell, then on the same hall. Therefore, prisoners on disciplinary segregation status often try to buy food and drinks from inmates on administrative detention status by exchanging postal stamps. Inmates on disciplinary segregation status should purchase the maximum amount of stamps each week if their trust fund account has enough money.

Staff Monitoring

A number of FBOP staff members are charged with monitoring the SHU inmates.[25] At the most basic level is the range officer assigned to each specific hall or range. This officer typically does rounds every half hour or hour (after 11:00 p.m., rounds become more sporadic).

Above the range officer is the "number one" for each shift, the top-ranking, frontline SHU officer who oversees the range officers. At times this person might make rounds.

> *TIP: If an inmate has a problem with the range officer or a decision they've made, they can request to speak with the "number one," whose objective is to make things run smoothly. The number one might be more agreeable than the range officer.*

Senior to the number one for each shift is the SHU lieutenant who is supposed to do rounds daily on all ranges. Some do and some don't. Often, they do rounds at a time when inmates won't notice (during recreation or in the early morning when inmates are asleep) so they can walk through without offering an opportunity for inquiry.

According to PS 5270.10(12), the institution duty officer is also supposed to "[v]isit each inmate daily, including weekends and holidays." To state it bluntly, this does not happen. At best, the duty officer sprints down each range while inmates beat on their doors trying to catch their attention. If this occurs, one or two inmates might get to speak with them. Sometimes the duty officer literally holds their keys so they can slip by without making a sound. Either way, nowhere near each inmate is visited.

The program staff and unit team staff typically do a collective walkthrough at a scheduled hour once a week to speak individually with the inmates on their caseloads.

In many SHU cells there is a duress button which, if pushed, sets off an alarm in the control and the central staff areas of the SHU. Inmates are only to sound these duress buttons for emergencies. An inmate who repeatedly presses the duress button for trivial reasons will be subject to disciplinary action.

TIP: The SHU staff might ignore the duress alarm. If an inmate or their cellmate is experiencing a medical emergency, they should press the duress button repeatedly, beat and kick on their door, and scream under their door for medical staff. This is sometimes the only way to receive emergency medical attention.

Medical and Mental Healthcare

Federal regulations mandate that inmates in the SHU have access to both medical and mental health staff. According to 28 C.F.R. §§ 541.32(a)-(b), "[a] health services staff member will visit [each inmate] daily to provide necessary medical care. Emergency medical care is always available. After every 30 calendar days of continuous placement in either administrative detention or disciplinary segregation status, mental health staff will examine [each inmate] including a personal interview. Emergency mental health care is always available."

In real life, the idea of a medical staff member visiting each inmate daily is preposterous. What actually happens is that a Physician's Assistant screams down each range, "Sick call!" Inmates can state their medical issue on a piece of paper and slip it in their cell door for the PA to collect. After a period of time, those who submit a complaint are brought out to see their assigned PA. Only inmates who must receive medications get to see a medical staff member daily, and this is only for medication, not to discuss other matters.

Emergency Medical Care: If an inmate pushes the duress button and speaks with the range officer, the range officer contacts the health services department. If the concern is not life-threatening, the inmate will be instructed to wait until the PA does sick call the next morning. If the inmate is having a heart attack, stroke, or seizure, medical personnel will see them to evaluate the need for emergency medical care. If they do not deem the situation an emergency, the inmate will be told to turn in a sick call request the following morning.

Mental Health: Federal regulations claim that mental health staff will examine and personally interview each inmate every thirty days of continuous confinement.[26] This does not happen. The fifteen- to thirty-second "examination" and "personal interview" takes place through a locked steel door on a noisy hall where a member of the psychology department asks two questions:

- "What is your name?" and
- "Are you okay?"

This comprises the entire evaluation process. Then the staff member from the psychology department makes an assessment and reports on:

- How the inmate is adjusting to his or her surroundings, and
- If the inmate poses a threat to self, staff, or other inmates.

Emergency mental health care works the same way as emergency medical care, the difference being that the inmate is instructed to submit a cop-out to the psychology department. Even inmates who are screaming and crying and out of control must submit a cop-out and wait a week or more until a member of the psychology department comes by.

21-Day Cell Rotation

SHU inmates must change cells every three weeks. Inmates who refuse are forcibly moved. As the final day approaches, the range officer knocks on the cell door and tells the occupants to pack up their property for a move.

TIP: Because SHU inmates have to change cells every twenty-one days, they learn to keep their property in a semi-packed state, always ready to move with only a few minutes notice.

Some SHUs provide Rubbermaid plastic containers to store personal property when prisoners are admitted to the SHU or when a prisoner requests them from the range officer. Seek out these containers; they make packing and moving much easier.

For moving, property can also be tied up inside sheets and placed on a mattress that the range officer can place on a shower curtain and drag to the new cell.

Once the property is packed, the occupants are handcuffed and led to their new cell. During the move, the range officer usually rifles through the inmate's property in search of contraband. For prisoners on disciplinary segregation status, contraband can be a radio or food. Many inmates on disciplinary segregation status try to hide those items on their person or in their mattress.

TIP: It might not be a good idea to hide contraband in a mattress because the range officer might not allow the mattress to be taken to the new cell. If an inmate is on disciplinary segregation status and their cellmate is on administrative detention status, the one on administrative detention status can move the other's radio and food along with their own property. Or, if the contraband is small enough, the inmate can try sending it to someone on the hall whom they trust via "fishing."

"Fishing"

SHU "fishing" is the act of passing items between cells using a system of lines and weights that anchor the lines.

One inmate sends his line down the hall by throwing it under his door. A second inmate throws a line over the first inmate's line. The weight on the end of the second inmate's line hooks and pulls on the first line. The second inmate then pulls the line under his or her cell door. In this way, two inmates can tie notes or small items to their lines and pass them back and forth.

Inmates use ripped sheets, string from institutional blankets, or mattress threading to create their lines, which average twenty-five to fifty feet in length. At the end of the line, the inmate attaches a weight so the line can be thrown. Some inmates will tie on a pack of two batteries, a pack of tuna, or an empty pack of tuna with mashed-up soap in the packet to add weight. That way the line can be slung under the crack of their cell's door and sent down the hall.

TIP: If an inmate doesn't have a sharp object with which to cut a sheet, they can use nail clippers or a pen or comb to create a hole they can tear further. Strong teeth help in creating a fishing line.

To ensure that the line will hook another line, wind paperclips or staples through the packaging surrounding the weight or even within the line to increase efficiency and speed.

To be sure my line reached the inmate for whom it was intended, I would yell his name under my door and tell him to throw his line. He would then throw a line down the range and I would throw mine. I'd continue to throw mine until I managed to hook it on his and pull it under my cell door. Then I would tie our lines together and yell, "Okay, pull."

Once my recipient had the lines under his door, he would untie the objects I had fastened to my line, or he would tie objects on and yell for me to pull the line back and retrieve his objects. After some time, those in the SHU can distinguish different people's voices.

If I only needed to send something to someone else, I could simply pull their line in, tie the object to it, and tell them to pull it back. I would not have to tie my line to theirs.

TIP: To be sure the guards don't see the lines floating around, inmates should wait until they are off the range. Most of the time they are watching TV or hanging out in the guards' cubicle where they don't have a direct line of sight to the range, which at FCC Petersburg was up a flight of stairs. They only generally came around for meals, recreation call, walk-throughs, or to pass out clothing and other items. They were not often on the range.

Surviving the SHU Experience

Any FBOP prisoner who has served a lengthy sentence will most likely have spent time in the SHU. They will recall it as the most depressing, dangerous, and painful part of their prison journey. It might help to be aware of several common pitfalls.

Dangerous Situations

Situations that are inherently dangerous to inmates in the SHU involve cellmates and recreation cages.

Cellmates: FBOP policy does not allow inmates to pick or choose their cellmates. Even in the SHU, an inmate who refuses to cell with another inmate or who refuses to allow an inmate into the cell they are occupying faces disciplinary action (often a Code 306 violation, "Refusing to work or accept a program assignment"). Nonetheless, there are occasions when an inmate has to stand their ground and refuse to cell with another particular inmate.

For instance, if residents of a cell say they will not accept a new cellmate, the newcomer might be better off refusing that particular cell assignment regardless of pressure from staff. This is especially true when a triple-bunk situation involves multiple cellmates. Cell residents who don't want another cellmate might attack the newcomer upon entry and force the administration's hand. Case law has determined that staff are responsible for protecting inmates from assault by other inmates, especially when they have "knowledge of a substantial risk of harm."[27] This, of course, does not necessarily stop an attack by a fellow inmate.

TIP: Inmates are usually handcuffed when placed in a SHU cell. It is always advisable for each inmate to try to be first in line so they can be uncuffed before the others. Assaults sometimes occur at this time.

The odds of a safe cell situation increase if inmates observe the maxim that it is best to cell with someone who looks like them. If a prisoner is a middle-aged schoolteacher doing time for possession of child pornography, throwing him in a cell with a tattooed young guy with a shaved head is asking for trouble. This is a broad generalization, of course, but such maxims exist for good reason.

Fights in Recreation Cages: It is a reality of prison life that fights occur, sometimes for no rational reason. In SHU recreation cages, assaults occur often.

As previously mentioned, the one-hour daily exercise accorded to SHU inmates generally takes place outdoors with several inmates in large "dog-run" type enclosures. The SHU rec cages are particularly violent because they are the only place where inmates are able to interact.

Many facilities have rec cages that adjoin and are separated only by a chain-link fence. Inmates involved in gang activity might be put on the spot by peer pressure and forced to commit violent acts, sometimes on total strangers against whom they have nothing personally. Rec cage assaults are common, so inmates should pay careful attention to the demeanor of other inmates in the same cage.

> *TIP: Here, too, it's a good idea for inmates to try to be first in getting uncuffed before entering with other inmates. If an assault occurs, they have a much better chance to protect themselves.*

Mental Stability: The "SHU Syndrome." Living in a SHU environment for any appreciable amount of time can be a genuine hazard to an inmate's emotional and mental well-being. Indeed, while medical professionals have debated whether the effects of SHU confinement constitute a diagnosable condition, a vast body of evidence addresses what has become known as SHU syndrome. See, for example, *The SHU Syndrome and Community Mental Health*, American Association of Community Psychiatrists Newsletter, Summer, 1998, which describes symptoms common in many SHU inmates.

David Cloud of the Vera Institute of Justice said that "The research is pretty conclusive: Since people started looking at this, even 200 years ago, when a guy named Francis Gray studied 4,000 people in 'silent prisons,' the studies have found that the conditions themselves can cause mental illness, stress, trauma."[28]

SHU syndrome consists of symptoms "made up of official diagnosis such as paranoid delusional disorder, dissociate disorder, schizophrenia, and panic disorder."[29] Notably, this phenomenon strikes not only inmates with prior histories of mental illness but also prisoners who have no such history.[30]

SHU syndrome is rooted in the extreme isolation and lack of stimulation present in contemporary SHU settings that, in the opinion of one expert, "borders[s] on barbarism."[31] Courts have found that the FBOP's standard SHU practices are inhumane. In *United States v. Brooks*, 2008 U.S. Dist. LEXIS 85658 (E.D.N.Y. 2008) the court had this to say about an inmate held in the SHU for ten months: "[T]he impact on his mental health has been severe. Defendant's description of the negative psychological consequences he has suffered comport with cases and studies addressing the harsh impact that prolonged solitary confinement may have on an inmate's mental health."

The inmate in *Brooks* faced the same restricted living conditions virtually every FBOP prisoner confined in the SHU faces: being "confined to his cell for 23 hours a day, only permitted one hour per day of outdoor exercise in a cage, [with] no contact with other inmates, restricted commissary, family and religious visiting, and telephone privileges."

These conditions can be toxic to an inmate's mental health, particularly if that inmate has preexisting mental health issues.

> [I]solated confinement intensifies symptoms for those prone to mental illness. The almost total isolation and inactivity deprives seriously mentally ill inmates of reality checks; they receive no feedback to keep their psychosis in check. Seriously mentally ill inmates in isolated conditions lost total control of their lives. They feel incapable of being an active agent in their lives; this feeling exacerbates depressive tendencies. Without intervention and without diurnal rhythms provided by light, seriously mentally ill inmates lose their sense of time and of the future, leading to great despair and hopelessness. This sense of doom is compounded when seriously mentally ill inmates are not capable of following the rules necessary to earn their way out of [the SHU].[32]

While many inmates might survive a long stay in the SHU without developing such symptoms, many inmates leave with problems relating to post-traumatic stress disorder (PTSD). *Comer v. Stewart*, 230 F.3d 1016, 1040-43 (D. Az. 2002) describes the symptoms. It is therefore important for inmates, counsel, and family members to be mindful of the mental health hazards associated with living in a SHU setting. Care should be taken to maximize the inmate's contact with the outside world, with special attention paid to providing them with reading material and other forms of stimulation.

The bottom line is that SHU placement is an inherently challenging part of prison life. Special efforts should be made to avoid some of the difficulties whenever possible.

TIP: Experienced inmates seeking to maintain a mental balance ask family and friends to mail them frequent letters, books, crossword puzzles, and other paper-based stimulating games. Although different SHUs have different interpretations of property restrictions, there is usually enough leeway to provide opportunities for the inmate to remain connected to the world outside.

Federal Regulations Governing SHU Placement

According to federal regulations, SHUs exist to "ensure the safety, security, and orderly operation of correctional facilities, and to protect the public, by providing alternative housing assignments for inmates removed from the general population."[33]

Inmates can find themselves segregated in the SHU either on administrative detention status or on punitive disciplinary segregation status. These labels and official definitions might have different meanings relating to correctional policy; however, to the inmates who find themselves in the SHU on administrative detention status or on disciplinary segregation status, the effect of the living conditions is the same.

Notwithstanding the official distinctions, inmates housed in the SHU on both statuses typically live in two-man cells and have many of the same restrictions (except that those who are there for disciplinary reasons are also denied access to the commissary). They live by the exact same schedule and under the same conditions.

Disciplinary Segregation

Disciplinary segregation status is "a punitive status imposed only by a Discipline Hearing Officer (DHO) as a sanction for committing a prohibited act(s)."[34] Disciplinary sanctions can involve an extended period of time in disciplinary segregation: up to twelve months for Greatest Severity Prohibited Acts, up to six months for High Severity Prohibited Acts, and up to three months for Moderate Severity Prohibited Acts.[35]

Administrative Detention

Administrative detention is "an administrative status which removes [the inmate] from the general population when necessary to ensure the safety, security, and orderly operation of correctional facilities, or protect the public. Administrative Detention Status is non-punitive, and can occur for a variety of reasons."[36]

Inmates can be placed in the SHU on administrative detention status if they find themselves in any of the following situations:

Pending Classification: New arrivals might be placed in the SHU while awaiting classification, reclassification, placement in a housing unit, or before completing their interviews with department representatives prior to being released to the general population. This group also includes inmates whose security level is being reclassified or who are awaiting transfer to another institution.[37]

Holdover Status: Inmates who are in transit might be temporarily placed in the SHU. It often takes days or even weeks to transfer a prisoner from one prison to another, and the Bureau will sometimes keep an inmate in the SHU of an interim federal prison as they travel to their ultimate destination.[38]

Removal from General Population: Prisoners whose "presence in the general population poses a threat to life, property, self, staff, other inmates, the public, or to the security and orderly running of the institution"[39] can be segregated if:

1) They are under investigation or awaiting a hearing for having allegedly violated a FBOP policy or criminal law.[40] However, the investigative staff can only hold an inmate in the SHU for ninety days. Each additional ninety-day period must be approved by the warden;
2) An inmate is awaiting transfer to another location because the current facility cannot meet their needs, or because their classification score has changed and an institution of a different type or security level is required to manage the inmate;[41]
3) The inmate is confined to the SHU for their own protection either because they requested the protection, or because it was recommended by the prison staff;[42] or
4) An inmate has completed a term of disciplinary segregation but it has been determined that their "return to the general population would threaten the safety, security, and orderly operation of a correctional facility, or public safety," in which case they can be subject to post-disciplinary detention.[43]

If detention and removal from general population extends beyond the completed term of disciplinary segregation, the segregation review official (SRO) must inform the inmate of the determination and the reason for it. This is done by issuing an administrative detention order (ADO) on a BP-A0308 form. The decision requires a separate review; it cannot be determined only by the DHO hearing that brought about the initial period of disciplinary segregation.[44]

TIP: If FBOP staff do not officially notify an inmate of their specific category of administrative detention, they should respectfully ask the SHU lieutenant about it during their daily rounds.

If the SHU lieutenant is not helpful then the inmate should file an administrative remedy and state that they haven't been notified of the reason for their administrative detention. For resolution, they should request to receive an administrative detention order (BP-A0308).

Once a prisoner is placed on post-disciplinary detention, the staff have ninety days to either return the inmate to general population, or to initiate a transfer proceeding by submitting a Request for Transfer/Application of Management Variable (form EMS-A409). If ninety days is insufficient, the regional director can approve a ninety-day extension. Any additional extensions of sixty days each must be ordered by the assistant director of the Correctional Programs Division.

If an inmate is placed in the SHU on an administrative status but they do not meet any of the above conditions, they can immediately initiate administrative remedy filings. They should quote these requirements. Inmates should let the staff know that this is specific FBOP policy, not an opinion. This way staff are put on notice that they are violating Bureau policy. See Chapter 22 for more on the Administrative Remedy Program.

Notice of Review of SHU Placement

When a prisoner is placed in the SHU, a lieutenant or other correctional supervisor prepares and distributes an administrative detention order (ADO) that states the reason(s) for the detention. Inmates placed on administrative detention status should receive a copy of the ADO within twenty-four hours.[45] However, inmates pending classification or on holdover status will not receive an ADO.

Prisoners on disciplinary segregation status are notified by the DHO, not an ADO, at the end of their hearing.[46]

> *TIP: If an inmate is on administrative detention status and does not receive an ADO within twenty-four hours, they should file a BP-8 form to put pressure on those who are detaining them. This could motivate the FBOP to review the case and release the inmate from SHU if errors are found. If the inmate is not released, their response will at least provide information on the inmate's status.*

There are various kinds of reviews for inmates placed on administrative detention in the SHU:

A *three-day review* must be completed within three working days of the inmate's admittance. This review includes the supporting records being reviewed and is not a formal hearing the inmate can attend. This review does not apply to inmates on disciplinary segregation status.[47]

Seven-day review: Inmates on both administrative detention status and disciplinary segregation status will have their SHU placement reviewed within seven days of admittance at a formal hearing the inmate is entitled to attend. Subsequent seven-day reviews will occur in the inmate's absence.[48]

Thirty-day review: Inmates on both administrative detention status and disciplinary segregation status will have their SHU placement reviewed after thirty days of continuous confinement. This, too, is a formal hearing the inmate may attend.[49] The SRO must provide the following documents:

- The SHU record (form BP-A0292);
- All available memoranda from staff; and
- All available investigatory memoranda.

After each review, the SRO must complete a Special Housing Review form (BP-A0295).[50]

TIP: While inmates technically have the right to attend the seven-day and thirty-day SHU placement reviews and hearings, staff will do all they can to prevent them from being there. Often they won't inform the inmate that reviews are taking place or that they can attend.

Instead of holding a formal hearing, some of the SROs will just walk by and ask, through the locked cell door, if the inmate is okay. If the inmate desires to attend reviews and hearings related to their detention, they should tell the SHU lieutenant directly during his or her rounds. As with most matters in the SHU, the inmate might have to be persistent.

Protective Custody

Inmates who are at risk of assault, have been assaulted, or fear for their safety can be placed in the SHU on administrative detention status for protective custody. However, these prisoners will live with the exact same conditions as those on administrative detention status and disciplinary segregation status.

The FBOP's way of protecting those who need or think they need protection is to lock them in a cell for days, months, or years. If an inmate is thinking about "checking in" for protection they should first try to resolve whatever problem they have. Living in the SHU is difficult and dangerous in itself. Some would say it's better to live in general population with some fear or the occasional need to fight than to have themselves locked in a SHU cell for twenty-three to twenty-four hours a day. It's a serious decision. Of course, if an inmate reasonably believes they're going to be killed or badly injured, the SHU could be a viable option.

TIP: Some inmates think if they check in they will be transferred to another prison. This rarely happens. The truth is that most inmates who check in are eventually released back into the same compound. If they are going to be transferred, they often sit in the SHU for up to a year awaiting transfer review proceedings.

According to 28 C.F.R. §§ 541.27(a)-(d), a prisoner can be placed in the SHU for protective custody if he or she is:

- A victim of assault or is threatened with assault;
- An informant who provided – or is believed to have provided – information to FBOP staff or law enforcement;
- Refusing to enter general population because of coercion or threats, even if the inmate refuses to specify the threat or reason; or
- Subject to the staff's belief that the inmate's safety is at risk in general population.

TIP: Protective custody can be just as dangerous as general population. In the SHU, those on administrative detention and disciplinary segregation are often celled together. The FBOP is notoriously lax about keeping inmates who should be separated apart.

Any time inmates are placed in the SHU for their own protection, PS 5270.10(9)-(11), Special Housing Units and 28 C.F.R. §§ 541.28-30 mandate a review of the situation that led up to it. This is how the process unfolds:

1) *Staff Investigation*: Within two working days of being placed in the SHU, the warden or captain will review the inmate's situation to verify the reason for protective custody.[51] Staff will attempt to unravel the situation that led to the need or perceived need for protection.[52] If, after investigation, the staff confirms the need for protection, the inmate either remains in the SHU at the current institution or is transferred to another institution where the threat does not exist.[53] On the other hand, if staff fail to verify the need, the inmate is often issued a direct order to return to general population. If the inmate refuses, they will be subject to disciplinary actions.[54]
2) *Hearing*: Within seven calendar days of admittance, the staff holds a hearing regarding the need for protection. While this is like the seven-day review, in this case the inmate is usually retrieved to attend so they can be asked why they are seeking protection.[55]
3) *Periodic Review*: If the inmate desires to stay in the SHU after the seven-day review, their case will be reviewed every thirty days as with all other SHU inmates.[56]

Inmates in protective custody have been known to spend months on end in the SHU. Even if the staff verifies their need for protection, they might be kept in the SHU indefinitely rather than transferred. The long stay is sometimes used as a deterrent to having prisoners "check in" for protection.

TIP: If at any time an inmate decides that they no longer need to be in protective custody, they can request a hearing to discuss and possibly terminate their protective custody status.

Staff will sometimes pump inmates for information when they check in. If an inmate goes to the SHU for protective custody, they should expect this and not turn over. If an inmate does "debrief" or provide information, whether they are transferred or not, they could earn a reputation as a snitch. This is a "bad jacket" that can follow them to any other facility for the rest of their incarceration.

TIP: Some inmate informants check in to the SHU for protection and think they can claim they are there for disciplinary reasons. This subterfuge often does not work because other inmates will insist on seeing their DHO report. Only a DHO can place an inmate in the SHU for disciplinary reasons, so anyone who is in the SHU for disciplinary reasons will have a DHO report.

The only exceptions are prisoners awaiting their DHO hearings. But if a hearing is pending, they would still have been given an administrative detention order (ADO), which is proof of the reason for SHU confinement, and they can show that to other inmates.

Release from the SHU

The protocol for getting released from the SHU is different for inmates on administrative detention status and those on disciplinary segregation status. Regulations state that inmates "will be released from administrative detention status when the reason[s] for [their] placement no longer exist."[57] On the other hand, inmates "will be released from [disciplinary segregation status] after satisfying the sanction[s] imposed by the DHO. The SRO may release [the inmate] earlier if it is determined they no longer require disciplinary segregation status."[58]

Program Statement 5270.10(14) clarifies release from disciplinary segregation thus: "When considering release from disciplinary segregation, the SRO first consults with the Captain and must notify the DHO of the inmates [sic] release from disciplinary segregation status before satisfying the imposed sanction." However, the SRO is not permitted to increase any previously imposed sanction(s).

Since the SHU lieutenant has the authority to release an inmate from disciplinary segregation prior to fulfilling a sanction, inmates should try to speak with them a couple of weeks before the end of their sanction about an early release. In some SHUs, it is common to be released a few days early. At others it might be a week or two early.

> *TIP: Once the range officer tells an inmate to pack their property for release, they should leave behind sheets, clothing, and other supplies for the next person who inhabits the cell. If they have a cellmate, they should give everything to him or her.*

Inmates leaving the SHU should remember that they are leaving a high-stress environment that, in many cases, can alter their attitude and demeanor. These prisoners might need time to readjust to general population with its increased stimuli before some of these symptoms abate.

In order to get used to being around others again, it might be helpful to join a low-intensity, low-energy class. Yoga, painting, and other mellow classes can ease a former SHU resident into normal prison life and might foster positive interactions with others again.

Notes

1. Binelli, Mark, "This Place is Not Designed for Humanity." *The New York Times*, March 29, 2015.
2. Law, Victoria, "Women in Solitary Confinement: Buried Inside the Federal Prison System." Solitary Watch. Jan 24, 2014. Retrieved from http://solitarywatch.com/2014/01/24/women-solitary-confinement-buried-inside-federal-prison-system/.
3. Emery, Jodie, "My First US Federal Prison Visit With My Heroic Political Prisoner Husband, Marc Emery." June 19, 2010. Retrieved from http://www.cannabisculture.com/content/2010/06/19/my-first-us-federal-prison-visit-my-heroic-political-prisoner-husband-marc-emery.
4. Gawande, Atul, "Hellhole." *The New Yorker.* March 30, 2009.
5. Fuchs, Erin, "How To Survive Life In Solitary Confinement." *Business Insider.* September 5, 2013.
6. Shear, Michael D. "Obama Bans Solitary Confinement of Juveniles in Federal Prisons." *The New York Times.* January 25, 2016.
7. Program Statement 5270.10, Special Housing Units at § 12; 28 C.F.R. § 541.31.
8. 28 C.F.R. § 541.31(a).
9. 28 C.F.R. § 541.31(b).
10. 28 C.F.R. § 541.31(c).

11. 28 C.F.R. § 541.31(d).
12. 28 C.F.R. § 541.31(e).
13. 28 C.F.R. § 541.31(f).
14. 28 C.F.R. § 541.31(g).
15. 28 C.F.R. § 541.31(i).
16. 28 C.F.R. § 541.31(j).
17. 28 C.F.R. § 541.31(k).
18. 28 C.F.R. § 541.31(l).
19. 28 C.F.R. § 541.31(n).
20. 28 C.F.R. § 541.31(o).
21. 28 C.F.R. § 541.31(h)(2).
22. Program Statement 5270.10, Special Housing Units at § 12.
23. 28 C.F.R. § 541.31(h)(1).
24. 28 C.F.R. § 541.31(h)(2).
25. 28 C.F.R. § 541.31(m).
26. Program Statement 5270.10, Special Housing Units at § 13; 28 C.F.R. § 541.32(b).
27. *Farmer v. Brennan*, 511 U.S. 825, 828 (1994). See also *Carter v. Galloway*, 352 F.3d 1346, 1349 (11th Cir. 2003).
28. Binelli, Mark, "This Place is Not Designed for Humanity." *The New York Times*. March 29, 2015.
29. *Jones 'El v. Berge*, 164 F.Supp. 2d 1096, 1101 (W.D. Wis. 2001).
30. *Id.* at 1102.
31. *Id.*
32. *Id.* at 1103.
33. 28 C.F.R. § 541.21.
34. 28 C.F.R. § 541.22(b).
35. 28 C.F.R. § 541.3 (Table 1).
36. 28 C.F.R. § 541.22(a).
37. 28 C.F.R. § 541.23(a).
38. 28 C.F.R. § 541.23(b).
39. 28 C.F.R. § 541.23(c).
40. 28 C.F.R. § 541.23(c)(1).
41. 28 C.F.R. § 541.23(c)(2).
42. 28 C.F.R. § 541.23(c)(3).

43. 28 C.F.R. § 541.23(c)(4).
44. Program Statement 5270.10, Special Housing Units at § 4.
45. 28 C.F.R. § 541.25(a).
46. 28 C.F.R. § 541.25(b).
47. 28 C.F.R. § 541.26(a).
48. 28 C.F.R. § 541.26(b).
49. 28 C.F.R. § 541.26(c).
50. Program Statement 5270.10, Special Housing Units at § 7.
51. *Id.* at § 9.
52. 28 C.F.R. § 541.28(a).
53. 28 C.F.R. § 541.29.
54. 28 C.F.R. § 541.30.
55. 28 C.F.R. § 541.28(b).
56. 28 C.F.R. § 541.28(c).
57. 28 C.F.R. § 541.33.
58. 28 C.F.R. § 541.33(b).

Part VIII – Legal Activity

Twenty-Two

Inmate Legal Activities

The FBOP is required to permit inmates access to legal materials and counsel so they can prepare and present legal documents.[1] Regulation of inmate legal activities is governed by 28 C.F.R. §§ 543.10-.16 and Program Statement 1315.07, Legal Activities, Inmate.

Law Libraries, Research, and Preparation of Legal Documents

Consistent with *Bounds v. Smith* and its progeny, each institution "must establish a main law library" that contains a long list of legal materials for use by inmates.[2][cc] Most Bureau facilities use the TRULINCS computer system to provide an electronic law library from which inmates can read and print documents.[3] The law library is based on the LexisNexis system, and generally includes the following items:

- FBOP program statements in English and Spanish
- United States Code, Titles 1 through 51 (Annotated)

[cc] *This section deals with general population law libraries.*

- United States Sentencing Guidelines (current and previous editions dating back to 1994)
- United States Constitution (Annotated)
- Federal Court Rules
- United States Code Service Tables
- District of Columbia Code and Rules
- Code of Federal Regulations
- Decisions of the United States Supreme Court (with annotated articles and tables)
- Decisions of the United States Courts of Appeals (including Federal Reporter)
- Decisions of the United States District Courts (including Federal Supplement)
- Decisions from the Military Courts
- District of Columbia Decisions[4]

The TRULINCS library also contains a number of commercially available legal reference texts including *Shepard's Federal Citations; BNA Criminal Law Reporter; Federal Habeas Corpus Practice and Procedure; Constitutional Rights of Prisoners*; and others. The system is updated every month or so to include the latest court decisions.

The law library is also required to provide the text of Federal Register materials as well as postal information and equipment like mailing scales. Most law libraries include copy machines for which inmates can purchase copy cards, typically at $0.13 per copy, from the commissary.

According to 28 C.F.R. § 543.11(g), staff is required to "duplicate legal documents if the inmate demonstrates that more than one copy must be submitted to court and that duplication cannot be accomplished by the use of carbon paper." Inmates who are not deemed indigent are generally required to buy copy cards. Indigent inmates can usually request free copies of legal documents from unit staff; however, inmates are not entitled to free copies of court decisions and other materials.

TIP: When the library copier is out of service, unit staff will generally copy legal documents upon request. While policy requires that staff charge inmates for such copies, most staff don't wish to bother with the paperwork!

Typewriters and Word Processors

Many courts have ruled that there is no constitutional right to typewriters and word processors,[5] but 28 C.F.R. § 543.11(h) provides that unless it is "clearly impractical, the Warden shall allow an inmate preparing legal documents to use a typewriter or, if the inmate cannot type, to have another inmate type his documents."

Generally, FBOP law libraries contain a few to several dozen electric typewriters for inmate use with ribbons available in the commissary. Some facilities offer indigent inmates the use of a ribbon without charge. In the last decade, several Bureau facilities have offered the use of cordless word processors like Alphasmart's Neo, which can be plugged into a central printer station. There is no cost to the inmate, save for paper expenses, and the units can be used anywhere. Moreover, the TRULINCS system has word processing capabilities in use as a pilot program at several institutions.

TIP: Inmates under a deadline can always type a legal document in an email and then print the document. While not a cost-effective measure, this method can be used as a last resort.

Legal Assistance from Other Inmates

The United States Supreme Court has ruled that prison officials cannot actively interfere with an inmate assisting others with the preparation of court documents.[6] As such, federal regulations expressly provide that, subject to some restrictions, "an inmate may assist another inmate in the same institution . . . with legal research and the preparation of legal documents for submission to a court or other judicial body."[7] However, "[b]ecause an inmate may not conduct a business, the assisting inmate may not receive compensation."[8]

There are several rules applicable to one inmate assisting another with legal documents. First, inmates confined in different institutions cannot assist each other in legal matters except where written permission has been granted by the wardens of the respective institutions, and the inmates are family members, co-defendants, etc.[9]

Second, an inmate can only possess another inmate's legal documents "while assisting the other inmate in the institution's main law library and in another location if the Warden so designates."[10] The assisting inmate is not permitted to remove the other inmate's legal materials from the law library, including photocopies. However, an "assisting inmate is permitted to make handwritten notes and to remove those notes from the library . . . if the notes do not contain a case caption or document title or the name(s) of any inmate(s)."[11]

Third, while FBOP policy does not require that the inmate remain present in the law library while assistance is being rendered, "that inmate is responsible for providing and retrieving his or her legal materials from the library or other designated location."[12]

TIP: Policy dictates that an inmate "with an imminent court deadline may request a brief absence from a scheduled program or work assignment in order to provide or retrieve legal materials from the assisting inmate."[13] Using this provision can ensure that the assisting inmate is not punished for leaving the law library with another's legal materials.

Assistance with Filing a Federal Lawsuit

Inmates who wish to file a federal lawsuit over prison conditions or abuse by prison staff should seek out a copy of *The Jailhouse Lawyers Handbook.* Published by the Center for Constitutional Rights, the handbook is free to anyone, including prisoners, their family members and friends, activists and lawyers. In addition to teaching inmates how to protect their civil rights through a lawsuit, the work also includes general information about the American legal system. Contact:

The Center for Constitutional Rights
666 Broadway, 7th Floor
New York, NY 10012
www.jailhouselaw.org to download a free copy

Notes

1. *Bounds v. Smith,* 430 U.S. 817, 821 (1977).
2. Program Statement 1315.07, Legal Activities, Inmate.
3. Program Statement 4500.11, Trust Fund/Deposit Fund Manual at § 14.10(d).
4. Program Statement 1315.07, Legal Activities, Inmate at Attachment A.
5. *Taylor v. Coughlin*, 29 F.3d 39, 40 (2d Cir. 1994).
6. *Johnson v. Avery,* 393 U.S. 483, 489 (1969).
7. 28 C.F.R. § 543.11(f)(1).
8. Program Statement 1315.07, Legal Activities, Inmate at §10.
9. *Id.*
10. 28 C.F.R. § 543.11(f)(2).
11. 28 C.F.R. § 543.11(f)(2)(i).
12. *Id.*, 28 C.F.R. § 543.11(f)(2)(ii).
13. *Id.*

Twenty-Three

Inmate Financial Responsibility Program

The FBOP operates the Inmate Financial Responsibility Program (IFRP) to "encourage each sentenced inmate to meet his or her legitimate financial obligations."[1] The program was introduced in federal prisons to support the Victim and Witness Protection Act of 1982, the Victims of Crime Act of 1984, the Comprehensive Crime Control Act of 1987, and the Federal Debt Collection Procedures Act of 1990.[2]

The "encouragement" inmates are given to participate is carried out by offering contracts to those with financial obligations or debts. Through the contract, the inmate agrees to allow the Bureau to remove funds from their commissary account on a monthly or quarterly basis; the money will be used to pay down their financial obligation.

While participation in the IFRP is "voluntary," inmates who decline to enroll are deemed "refusal" cases. They face numerous sanctions from poor classification and Parole Commission recommendations, to commissary, work, and housing restrictions. They might even face exclusion from drug treatment and community-based programs.[3]

On the other hand, compliance can help create a favorable parole recommendation. Requests for things that make life in prison more comfortable like a new cell assignment, work performance pay raises, and eligibility to participate in community based programs can also be positively impacted.[4]

Statutory Authority

Prisoners owing various financial obligations can be considered for the IFRP program. These obligations include special assessments imposed under 18 U.S.C. § 3013 applicable to all inmates, as $100.00 per felony count of conviction and $50 per misdemeanor count of conviction is a mandatory sentencing sanction; court-ordered restitution under the Mandatory Victim Restitution Act (MVRA),[5] and other provisions; fines, and other court costs. State and federal court obligations including tax liabilities, student loans, and even child support enforcement orders are also collectible through the IFRP.[6]

While scores of published court cases record inmates and others calling the IFRP extortion [see, e.g., *Duronio v. Gonzales*, 293 Fed. Appx. 155, 157 (3d Cir. 2008)], the fact that none of the sanctions implicate constitutional entitlements or liberty interests has allowed the IFRP to withstand judicial scrutiny.[7]

Payment Plan Computations

The IFRP process usually begins at the inmate's initial classification at their designated institution. Unit staff will "help" the inmate develop a financial plan by offering the inmate a payment plan based on their financial status. Such payments can be made on a one-time basis (say, for a $100.00 special assessment obligation), or on a monthly or quarterly basis.[8]

A minimum payment of $25.00 per quarter is required for IFRP participation.[9] However, this is the *minimum* payment; at some facilities, inmates are "asked" to make payments of several hundred dollars a month [see, e.g., *United States v. Lemoine*, 546 F.3d 1042, 1044 (9th Cir. 2008), inmate challenging payment of $132.00 per month]. [dd] Great variances in the payment requested

[dd] *I have personally witnessed payments by other inmates at FCC Petersburg in excess of $300.00 per month.*

by staff can occur depending on the region the inmate is housed in, the institution, and even the inmate's housing unit.

A basic formula computes the payment listed in the IFRP program statement. First, staff computes "the total funds deposited into the inmate's trust fund (commissary) account for the previous six months."[10] This base figure is not computed solely from the inmate's institutional work assignment pay, as some purport; rather, it includes *all* funds received regardless of their source or how those funds were ultimately spent.

From that six-month figure, staff must subtract the IFRP payments made by the inmate during the previous six months. They then subtract $450.00 for a phone allowance exclusion of $75.00 per month.[11] This adjusted figure is used to calculate payments. According to the program statement:

> Any money remaining after the above computation may be considered for IFRP payments, regardless of whether the money is in the inmate's trust fund or phone credit account. The Unit Team has the discretion to consider all monies above that computation to adjust the inmate's IFRP payment plan.
>
> The Unit Manager is the determining authority when it comes to deciding whether an inmate's IFRP payments are commensurate with his/her ability to pay. This decision is solely at the discretion of the Unit Manager and is to be decided on a case-by-case basis. Variations in what is considered a commensurate payment are expected and are appropriate since the determination of commensurate payments is based on individual circumstances.[12]

"Commensurate" Payments

The above "commensurate" passage is interpreted in an inconsistent manner by the Bureau and is often misunderstood by inmates. Some staff interpret it to mean that all funds left after the computations are "available" as the basis for evaluating a monthly payment. See *Bonneau v. Thomas*, 2012 U.S. Dist. LEXIS 106672 (D. Ore., July 27, 2012), ("potential monthly payment of

$663" established by dividing adjusted total by six; staff accepting contract for $450.00 per month). Others simply request that the inmate submit half of his or her work assignment pay or even the minimum payment permitted.

The minimum payment required for IFRP participation is as follows: "Ordinarily" (for all inmates other than UNICOR factory workers and UNICOR workers at Grade 5, the lowest grade), the minimum payment is $25.00 per quarter.[13] UNICOR workers in pay Grades 1 through 4 "will be expected to allot no less than 50% of their monthly pay to the payment process."[14]

Notably, the courts have granted the Bureau unilateral discretion as to what constitutes a "commensurate" payment plan. See *Bramson v. Winn*, 136 Fed. Appx. 380, 381 (1st Cir. 2005), where the court upheld the Bureau's unilateral payment determination.

> *TIP: Anecdotal evidence suggests that it can be fruitful for inmates to challenge IFRP determination by arguing that policy requires staff to "assist the inmate in developing a financial plan."[15] The idea that the Bureau's interpretation of 28 C.F.R. § 540.10 is an unreasonable one has not been litigated in a published opinion but, given the regulation's language, such a challenge could be valid.*

Sanctions for Refusing to Volunteer

While the FBOP calls the IFRP a "voluntary" program, it also provides a list of sanctions applicable to those inmates who decline to volunteer:

- Where applicable, the Parole Commission will be notified of the inmate's failure to participate;
- The inmate will not receive any furlough (other than possibly an emergency or medical furlough);
- The inmate will not receive performance pay above the maintenance pay level, bonus pay, or vacation pay;
- The inmate will not be assigned to any work detail outside the secure perimeter of the facility;

- The inmate will not be placed in UNICOR. Any inmate assigned to UNICOR who fails to make adequate progress on their financial plan will be removed from UNICOR. Once removed, they cannot be placed on a UNICOR waiting list for six months. Any exceptions to this require approval of the Warden;
- The inmate is subject to a monthly commissary spending limitation more stringent than the limitation set for all inmates. This shall be at least $25 per month, excluding purchases of stamps, telephone credits and, if the inmate is a common fare participant, Kosher/Halal certified shelf-stable entrees to the extent that such purchases are allowable under pertinent Bureau regulations;
- The inmate will be quartered in the lowest housing status (dormitory, double bunking, etc.);
- The inmate will not be placed in a community-based program;
- The inmate will not receive a release gratuity unless approved by the warden; and
- The inmate will not receive an incentive for participation in residential drug treatment programs.[16]

Notes

1. 28 C.F.R. § 545.10.
2. Watkins, Emma, "Inmate Financial Responsibility Program." eHow. Retrieved from http://www.ehow.com/about_6162870_inmate-financial-responsibility-program.html.
3. 28 C.F.R. § 545.11(d).
4. Watkins, Emma, "Inmate Financial Responsibility Program." eHow. Retrieved from http://www.ehow.com/about_6162870_inmate-financial-responsibility-program.html.
5. 18 U.S.C. § 3663A.
6. 28 C.F.R. § 545.11(a).
7. *United States v. Lemone,* 546 F.3d 1042, 1049 (9th Cir. 2008).
8. 28 C.F.R. § 545.11(b).

9. 28 C.F.R. § 545.11(b)(1).
10. Program Statement P5380.08, Financial Responsibility Program, Inmate at § 8.
11. *Id.*
12. *Id.*
13. 28 C.F.R. § 545.11(b)(1).
14. 28 C.F.R. § 545.11(b)(2).
15. 28 C.F.R. § 540.10.
16. Program Statement P5380.08, Financial Responsibility Program, Inmate at § 8(d); 28 C.F.R. § 545.11(d).

Part IX – Prison Culture

Twenty-Four

Fights

Fights happen in prison. This is a reality. At some facilities they are rare, particularly at the FBOP's lower-security prisons. At higher levels of security where the population is "harder" and usually serving long sentences, violence is routine and occurs daily.

Prison fights can be fistfights, group attacks on one or more inmates, or wild melees involving weapons. More than a few inmates are killed through inmate-to-inmate violence each year. Thousands more are injured, many of them severely. The threat is real.

It is important for all inmates – particularly those new to the system – to be aware of the potential for violence and to act with vigilance, confidence, and common sense.

Why Fights Happen

Prison violence has many causes including gang disputes, illicit trade in gambling, drugs or sex, and other matters often depicted in movies. Sometimes larger issues like racial tensions or overcrowding cause one prisoner to attack another.

In general, though, most prison fights happen simply because one party feels insulted or "disrespected." Most longtime prisoners can attest to witnessing or being involved in physical confrontations that arose from simple misunderstandings. One prisoner cuts in front of another in the chow line. A chair is moved without permission. Gossip and other careless speech escalate. Two men bump into each other accidently in a doorway, and one does not apologize.

Kristin Davis had been assigned to a camp but spent seven weeks in a standard FCI facility. Among the differences she noticed between the two was that the women in the higher-security facility "like to fight and start trouble." They had an "aggressive sense of ownership of their rooms, and they are easily angered or provoked."[1]

Simply put, virtually any innocuous confrontation can cause violence. Most prison fights are sparked by seemingly minor offenses.

Those new to prison often find themselves in peril because they don't understand prison's unique value system where respect is more important than anything else. The concept of respect in prison differs from that on the outside; virtually *any* affront, no matter how seemingly insignificant, can be cause to "defend one's honor," so to speak. For this reason, many prisoners who attack another feel they have no choice.

Peer pressure is the cause of many such confrontations. Whereas an accidental bump in line at Burger King might bring an angry glare, the same incidental contact might be grounds for attack – regardless of intent – in a crowd of prisoners who are quick to ridicule one who is "soft."

How to Avoid Fights

Avoiding violence in prison comes down to some basic strategies: be polite to everyone, keep that temper in check, pay attention, and mind one's own business. Even the greenest newbie can find life a lot more tolerable by observing these simple principles.

Courtesy is key. Prison is the most polite society on earth, and for good reason. An inmate who is quick to apologize gracefully for minor mistakes – even when it might not be their fault – stands a better chance of avoiding problems. This is not to say that one should roll over and take all blame – weakness is as dangerous as rudeness – but common courtesy and civility go a long, long way.

For example, being a gentleman (or lady) and simply saying, "Excuse me," when approaching other inmates who are involved in a conversation can avoid the perception of eavesdropping or not minding their own business. A friendly "I'm sorry," or, "My bad!" when accidently brushing against someone on the stairs can avoid conflict. It sounds simplistic but politeness matters. Even the most hardened, tattooed convict appreciates being treated civilly.

In addition to the use of common courtesy, keeping one's temper in check can be a literal life saver in the explosive world of prison. In the free world, a dirty look or mumbled epithet is rude; in prison, such behavior can result in being maimed or killed. While at times assertive action might be required, it is never fruitful to create confrontations through angry stares or annoyed gestures. Experience teaches that prisoners who can't keep their temper in check have far more problems than those who can.

Paying attention at all times is essential. A good rule of thumb is that whenever it feels like the tension level has gone up, get out of the way. When inmates seem to be bunching up according to race or geographical group, leaving the area might be a good idea.

On a smaller scale, it is never advisable that an inmate "sleep on" someone they had a confrontation with, even a minor one that seems resolved. Some inmates will pretend to resolve a confrontation only to initiate a sneak attack later. It pays to keep one's head up and eyes open.

Minding one's business is another strategy that goes a long way in keeping one in good health. Avoid injecting oneself into troublesome events. Standing near while a casual acquaintance is having an argument is a surefire way of being identified as a potential threat.

When a Fight Cannot Be Avoided

Unfortunately, even those inmates who do everything they can to avoid confrontations are sometimes left with no choice but to defend themselves. While it would be impossible to comment on every permutation of these situations, some general rules apply when a confrontation can't be avoided.

First, if someone must fight, fight. There is no upside to allowing someone else to assault you without fighting back. There are no referees in a prison fight: no one will stop the fight because one party is losing or even losing badly.

Most prisoners will fight until they are tackled by guards or pepper-sprayed. Curling up on the floor will most often simply allow one party to repeatedly kick the other party, which can cause serious injury or death. Even if fighting skills are poor or non existent, repelling an attack with weak punches or kicks will still dampen an assailant's enthusiasm.

Second, in the FBOP, virtually every participant will receive an incident report for the fight, win, lose, or draw. There is no advantage to not fighting back. It is a basic human right to do so.

Third, if someone is engaged in a fight and staff order them to stop, face a wall, or get on the ground, *they should not comply unless they can do so safely.* That is, they should make sure that other combatants have been secured. Often one inmate will attack another after the latter has been handcuffed and immobilized. Better to endure some flak from the guards than be kicked while lying helpless on the ground. Staying safe is paramount.

As a final matter, keep in mind that the vast majority of all federal prisoners, particularly those in lower-security facilities, will never be in a physical confrontation during their imprisonment. As a general matter, serious injuries from fights are quite rare. By following the above principles, most men and women can avoid trouble without much difficulty.

Notes

1. Davis, Kristin, "I've Been Moved 'Inside the Wall' In Federal Prison." XOJane, May 1, 2015. Retrieved from http://www.xojane.com/issues/on-going-inside-the-wall-in-federal-prison.

Twenty-Five

Gangs

The social structure of prison is usually defined by group behavior. Beyond the divisions created by official action – assignments to particular institutions, housing units, jobs, etc. – many align themselves in groups with varying organizational structures.

Within the FBOP, these groups include gangs like the Bloods, Aryan Brotherhood, Texas Syndicate, etc.; "cars," or groups formed around a common hometown or area (the "Boston car," etc.); and other affiliations based on race, nationality, or religion. The choices are many, and they are sometimes fluid.

Gang Influence and Culture in Prison

The influence such groups have on daily prison life depends primarily upon a particular facility's security level. In USPs, where many prisoners are serving life sentences or long terms of imprisonment, gangs and other organized groups affect virtually every aspect of daily life. At lower-security facilities, their influence is far less.

At the USP level and at many mediums, for example, group politics determine at which table one may sit in the chow hall. It is a serious matter; prisoners have been killed over who sits where, and violent disputes arise regularly as the populations of different groups rise and ebb.

Groups also control cell assignments. As implausible as it might seem to a civilian, most staff members will consult the relevant group leader, or "shot caller," before assigning an inmate to one of "their" cells. Racial mixing in cells is relatively unheard of at the USP level, along with at many rougher mediums.

The primary reason why groups and gangs hold so much sway is that their members are often deeply committed to the group identity. Some groups include members who are never going home or who have decades left to serve with no real hope of reaching a lower-security prison. They are fully invested in the group identity, and will often do whatever needs to be done to protect it, regardless of the consequences.

In easier medium- and lower-security facilities, group and gang identities are less critical, likely because inmates at those facilities have more to lose. While group dynamics might come into play in certain instances, such as a fight between prisoners from different areas, it is rare that groups "run" cell assignments and other areas of concern.

Designation as a Gang or Group Member

The Bureau of Prisons collects and applies as much data as it can when it comes to classifying inmates as members of a group. When an inmate is thought to be a member of a gang, he or she is logged as a Central Inmate Monitoring (CIM) case.[1] Inmates assigned a CIM designation for gang reasons are subject to increased scrutiny and monitoring. Beyond those deemed gang members, others considered a threat to security, like members of a "disruptive geographical group," can be subject to being housed only in high-security facilities and, in some cases, in Special Management Units.[2]

The process used for identification or validation as a gang or group member is less than scientific. Staff might designate an inmate based on information contained in the presentence report, official intelligence reports, and in some cases, informant information and rumor. Because of this, inmates entering the Bureau for the first time sometimes find themselves tagged as a member of a particular group based on flimsy information. Because that information falls within the Bureau's definition of privileged "security" data, access to the information is limited. Removing such a designation from an inmate's file is very difficult.

TIP: Counsel for a newly convicted defendant should advise the client to avoid making any remark, even the most casual, about any affiliations in their presentence report interview with U.S. Probation. Long experience demonstrates that many new prisoners make this mistake.

The consequences of a gang or group designation are many. On the official end, such a designation can be used to keep an inmate in high security through application of a Public Safety Factor in their classification scoring.[3] Identification as a gang or group member can also result in assignment to a Special Management Unit or the SHU – even for events occurring at another institution – or in being removed from a facility without explanation. Affiliation with a gang or group can even lead to inclusion in a new indictment for acts primarily committed by others.[4]

On the unofficial side, inmates identified as gang or group members often experience great difficulties. A transfer to a prison where the inmate's group is not in favor or one populated by a rival group can result in unprovoked, violent attacks. Likewise, membership almost invariably involves performing "missions," acts of violence on behalf of the group, even when detection by authorities is probably assured.[4] When an inmate decides to leave the group, in some cases, it is akin to a death sentence.[5]

Avoiding Gang/Group Affiliations

For those not yet affiliated with a gang or group when entering prison, most will, if assigned to a "hard" facility like a USP, be asked to declare themselves as belonging to one group or another. If they are not affiliated with a group, the pull to join can be quite strong. At some prisons, no "independents" are allowed; at others, even the "independents" are organized in a hierarchy to some degree.

Inmates who desire to avoid joining a gang or group can face great difficulties going it alone. Consequences might include being "run off the yard" (threatened with or visited with violence). Inmates who "refuse to program" might seek protection by remaining locked up in the SHU until a transfer to another facility is arranged. However, such transfers can take up to two years. None of the options are good.

Still, many prisoners do manage to negotiate the USP system without formally joining a gang or a group. They develop a reputation as a non-controversial, "solid" prisoner who minds his own business.

> *TIP: Inmates new to the system often panic and refuse to leave the SHU for fear of having to declare an affiliation or otherwise being dragged into the gang/group culture. Such inmates should be advised that this tactic is sure to destroy any chance of "making it" at another institution because they will be tagged as a "check in" prisoner too afraid to walk the yard.*
>
> *Unless they have special issues or are serving a sentence in excess of 20 years imprisonment, most inmates will be designated to a low-security facility within a year or two if they maintain clear conduct. As such, most should be advised to do their time, avoid controversy, and mind their own business to increase their chances of avoiding conflict.*

Notes

1. 28 C.F.R. § 524.72(d).
2. Program Statement P5217.01, Special Management Units at § 2.
3. Program Statement P5100.08, Inmate Security Designation and Custody Classification at Chapter 5.
4. See *United States v. Bingham*, 653 F.3d 983, 988 (9th Cir. 2011)(racketeering indictment charging 40 gang members).
5. *Id.* at 988.
6. *Id.* at 987.

Twenty-Six

Vices

Prison, just as regular life, offers plenty of opportunity for vices, activities that are illegal or against the rules or that flout social conventions. In the outside world, many vices like drinking too much are merely frowned upon. In prison, vices can become a way of life and can have significant official consequences such as sanctions for disciplinary policy violations. Each federal prisoner must determine which vices they can live with and which ones they cannot.

Asking for forgiveness rarely works in prison. A price has to be paid, and it is often high.

Contraband

The most common vice in which almost every prisoner engages to some degree is that of contraband. Officially, contraband is anything not authorized for inmate retention or any authorized item obtained through an unauthorized means. So, both prison-made alcohol and a candy bar purchased through a convict store qualify as contraband. The difference is found in the type of contraband and the severity of sanctions if possession is uncovered by the administration.

Hard and Soft Contraband

Contraband is categorized as either "hard contraband" or "soft/nuisance contraband."[1] Hard contraband includes weapons, alcohol, drugs, or other unauthorized, mind-altering substances like prescription medications that do not belong to the person possessing them, and more serious items.

Soft contraband consists of everything else. Cardboard, extra books, clothes, sheets, modified or repaired electronics, and other non-hazardous items such as homemade weight bags or altered clothing all qualify.

As with every area of prison life, there are many gray areas. Pornography is one example. Some prison guards consider pornography to be hard contraband that requires official confiscation, a possible referral to the psychology department, and an incident report. Others consider it soft contraband and just throw it away without further action.

> *TIP: If caught with something arguably deemed to be soft contraband, it is never a bad idea to speak informally with the confiscating prison guard and ask if they would be willing to just throw the item(s) away. At best, this can result in the loss of the item and no incident report. At worst, an incident report will be issued but nothing has been lost attempting to resolve the matter informally.*

Contraband Risk Threshold

Each prisoner will have to determine their threshold for the risk contraband entails. Many prisoners are willing to risk being caught with stolen kitchen food. Most prison guards will merely throw it away, and having it adds a whole new dimension to eating in prison.

But the risk of possessing anything unauthorized (a prohibited act of moderate severity) or of stealing (a prohibited act of high severity) is present. On the other hand, most prisoners wouldn't run the risk of being caught with heroin, which would most certainly result in a prohibited act incident report of the highest severity and a referral for outside criminal charges. Prisoners must determine what they are willing to risk and accept whatever responsibility comes with that risk.

TIP: Best practice says that prisoners should always avoid possessing hard contraband. It simply brings more worry and risk than it is worth.

Soft contraband is a different story. If a prisoner needs a highlighter or paperclips for their college correspondence classes then they should go for it. At worst, the highlighter or paperclips are confiscated.

The risk/reward tradeoff is what matters.

Gambling

Gambling is alive and well in American prisons. Prisoners bet on anything and everything. Football and basketball are favorites but baseball, hockey, soccer, NASCAR, and other lesser-known sports also hold interest. Bets are even placed on the intramural sports leagues at the prison. Gambling occurs through "tickets," a term used for gambling forms in prison. These tickets are owned and operated by groups of prisoners who are often of the same gang or race, or who are from the same geographic area.

Gambling in prison works much the same way as it does in Vegas. Prisoners locate a "ticket man" (the person who operates the ticket) or one of their "runners" (the person who collects bets and returns the bets back to the ticket man). They ask for a ticket (the slip of paper with the odds and available bets placed on them) and hand over funds for the bet. These funds could be in the form of stamps or commissary items.

TIP: Prisoners should never save old betting slips or other notes which have both bets and the lines (odds) on them. If this "gambling paraphernalia" is ever found, it may result in an incident report being issued. Some guards consider tickets soft contraband that can merely be thrown away, while others always issue incident reports.

Bets in prison are almost never placed on margin since collection is always a matter of concern. After the game is over, the ticket owners pay out any winners as soon as possible and keep the profits.

Inherent Risks of Gambling in Prison

While gambling is widespread in prison, it comes with inherent risk on the official and unofficial sides. From the official side, prisoners run the risk of being issued an incident report if they are found with "gambling paraphernalia" or engaged in a transaction related to gambling.[2] Additionally, federal prisoners are not allowed to give or receive anything of value to or from other prisoners.

On the unofficial side are a plethora of potential problems. Placing a winning bet can be problematic if the winnings are significant. At a certain point, a ticket man might find it more advantageous to not pay out to large winners. In prison, there are no police to ensure that the unspoken rules of the gambling trade are followed. If a ticket man refuses to pay out, it is up to the winner to take their earnings by force. This is a cost many are not willing to pay.

Gambling falls right in line with the other kinds of vices. A risk/reward calculation is necessary to determine if the risk of gambling in prison is worth the reward. Many find the risk within reason and gamble. Others don't. This is a question that every federal prisoner must answer for him or herself. As with all vices in prison, prisoners should put some thought into gambling decisions. Unexpected issues do present themselves, and unfortunately prisoners often resolve issues with violence.

Alcohol and Substances

Alcohol and drugs, both legal and illegal, have a special place in the prison culture due to the number of alcoholics and addicts. The common belief that there are tons of drugs and alcohol in prison is correct; one just has to have the money to spend and know where to look. Due to the character of the prisoners who brew and sell the substances, and the official response to being caught possessing or using the substances, this is a serious vice that carries significant consequences.[3]

Alcohol

Alcohol is more common than hard drugs. Prison alcohol is usually made out of sugar, water, citrus fruit, and a bit of bread (for the yeast). Oranges, potatoes, and tomato paste are staples. This mixture is placed in a gallon-sized milk bag from the kitchen or in a trash bag and left to sit and brew.

Due to simple recipes and a relative ease of storage, more than a few inmates constantly brew prison wine (often called "hooch"). The trick is not getting caught obtaining the ingredients, brewing the mixture, or drinking it. The official reaction is severe. The administration regularly breathalyzes the prison population at random to catch those under the influence.[4]

If a person is found under the influence or manufacturing alcohol, they are immediately locked in the SHU and issued a high-severity prohibited act incident report. The inmate can plan on spending a month or so in the hole, and the likely loss of privileges like commissary, phone, email, visitation, etc. Repeated alcohol-related offenses can land one in a Special Management Unit (SMU).[5]

The reason the alcohol trade is so widespread has to do with the number of alcoholics in prison and the vast profits garnered through the sale of prison wine. Brewers of prison alcohol might spend $20 to $30 on supplies and reap $5 in profit for every bottle sold. A trash bag of alcohol could result in over $300 worth of profits, a sum many prisoners would have to work over a year to earn through their work assignment.

Most adults in the world outside of prison enjoy a good beer, a glass of wine, or a shot or two every now and then to relax or blow off steam. The same is true with those in prison. But in an environment where the population is much more prone to violence, inhibitions are a good thing. They generally keep groups of prisoners from beating one another or attacking staff. The FBOP has a great interest in deterring alcohol use.

Drugs

Drugs, both legal and illegal, are another staple. Just because someone goes to prison for being a drug addict does not mean that their addiction magically leaves them once they are incarcerated. Plenty of prisoners are able to nurture a strong addiction behind bars. This is managed through the use of illegal drugs and the abuse of prescription medications.

Of all the illegal drugs, marijuana is probably the most commonly available in American prisons. Heroin is second but any recreational drug can be found if a prisoner is willing to pay the price. These illegal drugs are either brought in by dirty guards connected with gangs inside the system, smuggled in through new arrivals or during visitation, or, if the prison is close enough to a street or highway, thrown over the fence.

Regardless of how they are introduced, drugs are available to those who want them and can afford them. The prison drug culture is also rife with informants, snitches, and undercover operatives. Consequently, when engaging in prison drug transactions, most experienced prisoners know that facing legal troubles is a question of when, not if.

The abuse of prescription medications is also a part of the prison culture. While prison pharmacies do not frequently dispense narcotic pain killers, they do issue other medications that can be abused. For example, an odd trend in recent years is the abuse of "blues." This is medication for irritable bowel syndrome (IBS) which, when crushed and snorted in a high enough quantity, results in a feeling of being in a daze.

While most certainly not a good idea, many inmates abuse medications like these. The prison administration attempts to put a stop to the abuse, but prisoners will snort just about anything. It really doesn't matter what the medication is for; they'll try to see if it alters their mood, mind, or perception. Prozac, Zoloft, and other seemingly harmless drugs are abused in prison through "saving up" doses and other techniques.

Profits garnered through the sale of illegal substances and prescription medications are significant, even more significant than the sale of prison alcohol. A dime bag of marijuana, which runs $10 outside of prison, could cost $25 to $50 inside. A hit of heroin, as low as $10 to $20 outside, could easily cost $50 to $80.

On the other hand, a handful of IBS pills could run as low as a few stamps a pill, which is why they appear to be so popular at the moment. The low cost of prison alcohol at $5 a bottle is also appealing since it only takes two or three twenty-ounce bottles to become visibly drunk, a far cry from the expense of a joint of marijuana or a dose of heroin.

TIP: If a prisoner is shooting drugs intravenously, they should always obtain their own needles and other rig components regardless of the cost. Once the needles and the complete rig are obtained, the prisoner shouldn't share it with anyone else. HIV and Hepatitis C are easily passed through shared needles. Prisoners should be adamant about using only their own rig.

Drug use in prison is a risky business. As with prison alcohol, if a prisoner is found to be using illegal drugs or abusing prescription medications, they will be subjected to either a high severity prohibited act or a greatest severity prohibited act incident report. In the case of illegal drugs, if the drugs are found, the prisoner in possession of them may possibly receive a new criminal charge (called a "street charge" in the prison culture).

To combat the prison drug trade, prison administrators regularly employ drug testing.[6] This can be done through random testing or through targeted testing of those suspected of being under the influence. Regardless of the type of testing, if a prisoner is found to be dirty, they will be subjected to at least a month in the SHU and will lose several privileges. Additionally, when it comes to intravenous drug use, the risk of infections from HIV and Hepatitis B and C is obvious given the high-risk pool that prisoners inhabit.

Minimizing the Risk of Alcohol and Substance Abuse

When using either alcohol or prohibited substances in prison, it is vital for prisoners to protect themselves. First and foremost, inmates should keep the use of such substances to themselves and as few other people as possible. The more people who know, the greater the risk of someone snitching to the administration.

Similarly, prisoners should vary their routines so planned snitching can't occur. They should also do what they can to minimize their exposure to others while engaged in such activities. A good place for a prisoner to drink – from a risk-mitigation standpoint – is in his or her own cell after the doors have been locked for the night. Prison guards won't see it or smell it, and fellow prisoners who see it won't be able to snitch in time for the user to be caught (in the case of alcohol).

TIP: Prisoners should not alert their alcohol connection to an order in advance. This disallows the connection to snitch on the purchaser in advance or to let slip to a fellow prisoner who the customer is, who then can tell the prison administration. By trusting no one when using alcohol or prohibited substances, the prisoner's risk can be substantially cut.

The long and short of alcohol and prohibited substance use in prison is that it is a big risk … particularly with substances, since they remain in the system for a period of time. Prisoners who decide that the risk is worth the reward should take every preventative step to minimize their exposure. To be caught using alcohol or drugs is a big issue and comes with significant sanctions.[7] Before engaging in these activities, the prisoner should think long and hard about whether the benefit outweighs the cost.

Tattoos

Tattoos are synonymous with prison culture. Most prisoners have at least one or two, some many more. While some come to prison with tattoos, others get work done while there. It doesn't matter whether prison culture pushes prisoners toward a propensity for body art or whether those who go to prison are more likely to have impulse control and decision-making troubles. What does matter is that tattoos obtained in prison can be dangerous.

Research the Tattoo Artist

Prisoners who want to get a tattoo in prison must first locate a talented and reputable tattoo artist. This can be done easily enough by asking around. In prison, tattoo artists, especially talented ones, are well-known and well-liked. It's easy to locate a few that fellow prisoners will swear by. Once several tattoo artists are known, the prisoner should find a few people who have recently had work done. This is the quality assurance stage. Prisoners are advised to find a tattoo artist who has done the type of work they desire to have tattooed on them.

TIP: Prisoners should always review previous work done by a tattoo artist prior to allowing the artist to start tattooing on them. Tattoos are permanent. Be smart and do some research prior to moving forward with a tattoo.

Obtaining the Required Materials

Once the tattoo artist has been settled upon, the prisoner needs to be concerned with obtaining all required materials. These generally include a tattoo motor, ink, and needles. Luckily for the tattoo recipient, the tattoo artist will usually have all or most of these materials already. If not, they should have a line on where to obtain them.

The motor is the most expensive piece of equipment. It can easily run upwards of $30 to $50 or more. It is the central piece of equipment tattoo artists must have to work. As such, the artist should have their own motor. These motors are made out of cassette tape players, beard trimmers, hair clippers, CD players, portable or handheld fans, and anything else with a motor. The motor is what drives the tattoo gun or rig. Batteries tend to be the power source.

The next most challenging component is the needle. Unlike in the outside world, needles are very difficult to obtain inside prison. The best way to find suitable needles is probably through a music program. Smaller guitar strings can be cut up and used as needles. This is the preferable tattoo needle for many prison artists.

If these strings aren't available, the small springs out of typewriter ribbons can do the trick. Open the plastic typewriter ribbon assembly, remove the smallest-width spring, and use a flame to straighten it out. Some tattoo artists use other materials like welding wire that has been filed down to a point.

TIP: Due to the risk of infection, it is always smart for prisoners to obtain their own needles. In fact, this is so important that it might be worth the effort to locate a needle outside of the tattoo artist/client relationship. This way the prisoner knows the needle is new. This degree of separation can be the difference between infection with HIV and remaining clean.

The final material required is tattoo ink. Tattoo ink is not sold in the prison commissary – the prison administration strongly objects to prisoners obtaining new tattoos – so prisoners often have to make their own.

In prison, ink is most often "burned." Burning involves a prisoner taking either a Styrofoam cup or baby oil and burning it in a locker to create soot.

This soot becomes the tattoo ink. While different tattoo artists have different preferences, baby oil is generally the better method since it is healthier than Styrofoam, relatively cheap to purchase, and easy to make. If a prisoner is lucky enough to obtain a Liquid Espresso ink pen, this is the ink they should use. It is much cleaner than soot and is of a higher quality.

> *TIP: Never use the ink out of a Bic pen. Only AP non-toxic ink and ink proven to behave well and stay when injected into the body should be used.*
>
> *The selected tattoo artist should be able to help with ink selection if pen ink is being used. Often this will include placing an order for a pen through the hobby craft program or locating a fellow prisoner who is already a part of such a program who sells pens.*

Getting the Tattoo: Safety and Caution

When it finally comes time to get the tattoo, the prisoner should be extra careful. As with drinking and drug usage, receiving a tattoo is a violation of the FBOP's disciplinary code.[8] In fact, it is a high severity prohibited act. While not necessarily an offense that will result in time in the SHU, there is a possible sanction.

To mitigate the risks, prisoners receiving a tattoo should pay attention to which prison guard is working their housing unit when tattoos are administered. They should also pay a lookout who can alert the artist and the prisoner when the guard is making rounds. These two steps can greatly reduce the risk of being caught obtaining a tattoo.

> *TIP: Always require the tattoo artist to wear latex gloves when working. When the needle is digging into the prisoner's arm or other body part, an open sore is created. This creates an easy point of entry for all sorts of diseases and bacteria such as staph and MRSA.*

Tattoo Aftercare

After the tattoo has been completed, the risk of infection has not ceased. Until the tattoo has healed, there is a significant risk of infection. In fact, many tattoo recipients in prison contract a staph infection directly afterward. While a tattoo artist on the street might recommend that a client use unscented A&D ointment, such products aren't normally available at the commissary. What is available, however, is triple antibiotic ointment. Prisoners with fresh tattoos should place this antibiotic ointment on the tattoo several times a day until the tattoo has fully healed.

Outside of the antibiotic ointment, prisoners should also gently clean the tattoo with soap and water or even anti-bacterial soap such as Safe Guard. At first this should be done without a wash rag because that could damage a fresh tattoo. Extreme sunlight and the rub of clothing when working out should also be avoided for a week or two after receiving the tattoo.

Keeping It Quiet

Much like when a prisoner has been drinking or using illegal drugs, prisoners who obtain new tattoos need to keep that knowledge under their hat until the tattoo has healed. Prisoners who are caught may be subject to a high severity prohibited act incident report. This risk is run both during the process of obtaining a tattoo and while it heals.

Technically, an incident report can be issued at any point when staff becomes aware of the new tattoo. They usually don't recognize the tattoo as new unless it is fresh, though.

> *TIP: After receiving a new tattoo, prisoners should attempt to cover the tattoo at all times so staff will not see it. This can be done with long sleeves, by keeping one's shirt on, or by finding other creative ways to hide the tattoo (e.g., placing a bandage over it).*

Pornography

The final major vice for most prisoners is pornography. While not unexpected, considering that prisons are full of men or women who are kept away from the opposite sex, what is surprising is that this vice can be one of the most dangerous depending on what the inmate is in prison for.

Rules and Regulations

Today's prisons are not the same as prisons of the past. In prisons of the past, *Hustler* magazine was available, though it has since been banned in favor of less explicit adult magazines such as *Playboy* and *Penthouse*. The pendulum has continued to swing toward conservative policies.

Presently, all pornographic magazines and photos are by and large barred in federal prisons.[9] The most adult-focused materials allowed are magazines such as *Maxim* and those suggestive but non-nude photographs sold in the prison press. But this doesn't cover the full picture of pornography in prison.

Pornography on the Black Market

Pornographic images and magazines can be purchased in prison on the black market. Most such images are of poor quality, the black-and-white variety copied on the inmate copier rather than color adult magazine photos. While this sort of contraband isn't as prevalent as, say, prison alcohol, it is around enough so that a prisoner can find it without much effort. Costs for such photocopied pages vary but $1.00 per page is not uncommon. A complete color magazine could run $150 to $200 if a prisoner can find one for sale.

Risks of Possessing Pornography

The penalties for possessing pornography are surprisingly harsh, especially for those who are in prison for sex offenses. To start, when a prisoner is caught with pornography, the pornography is generally seized and sent to the lieutenant's office for review.[10] If it is found to be actual pornography (not just girly pictures that can be purchased through the mail), an incident report will likely be issued for possession of anything unauthorized, a moderate severity prohibited act.[11]

This infraction will most likely result in the loss of a few privileges including, phone, email, visitation, commissary, and so forth but will not result in placement in the SHU. It can brand the prisoner a fiend or a pervert, something that could harm their reputation while in prison.

TIP: If a prisoner is caught with pornography, it is the best practice to try to talk the seizing guard into destroying the pornography and not issuing an incident report. An argument could be made for the pornography being soft contraband that can be informally resolved by throwing it away. At best, this will be the end of the matter. At worst, the prisoner is still going to receive an incident report.

Of greater concern to prisoners caught with pornography is what follows after the incident report. Sometimes the pornography is referred over to the psychology department for them to review, photocopy, and place in the inmate's psychology file. This record can be particularly problematic when the prisoner is seeking halfway house placement or placement in a special rehabilitation program.

For sex offenders, this can result in the issuance of a Correctional Management Plan (CMP), a special program that subjects the prisoner to additional psychology supervision and places the sex offender at a greater risk of civil commitment.[12] As such, even the mere possession of real, adult pornography can be exceptionally damaging to a prisoner's future and problematic to their eventual release from prison.

Mitigating the Risk of Pornography Usage

Pornography is yet another area where a risk/reward analysis is required, but if a prisoner determines it is worth the risk, steps can be taken to mitigate the risk. For example, there are prisoners whose hustle is to rent pornography by the hour or by the day. This enables a prisoner to use the pornography and return it upon fulfillment of its usage, greatly reducing the risk of being caught with the pornography in their locker.

While not the most tasteful idea, renting pornography does reduce the risk of being caught. Another technique is the purchase of the girly photos or Penthouse Letters books. Neither of these will result in an incident report, and they can help fulfill sexual desires.

Notes

1. Program Statement 5580.08, Inmate Personal Property at § 4.

2. Program Statement 5270.09, Inmate Discipline Program at Table 1.
3. *Id.*
4. Program Statement 6590.07, Alcohol Surveillance and Testing Program.
5. Program Statement P5217.01, Special Management Units at § 2.
6. Program Statement 6060.08, Urine Surveillance and Narcotic Identification; 28 C.F.R. § 550.30.
7. Program Statement 5270.09, Inmate Discipline Program at Table 1.
8. *Id.*
9. Program Statement P5266.11, Incoming Publications; Program Statement 5265.14, Correspondence; 28 C.F.R. § 540.72.
10. Program Statement 5580.08, Inmate Personal Property at § 5; 28 C.F.R. § 553.13.
11. Program Statement 5270.09, Inmate Discipline Program at Table 2.
12. Program Statement 5324.10, Sex Offender Programs at Chapter 4.

Twenty-Seven

Sex and Sexual Assault

Sexual activity takes place in America's prisons, including in facilities within the FBOP. On many levels, sexual contact between inmates or between inmates and staff is viewed as problematic for all involved in the correctional field.

Sexual activity in prison falls within two broad categories: "consensual" relations between two persons, and nonconsensual contact, also known as sexual assault. Inmates newly committed to the Bureau should be mindful of some general guidelines.

Consensual Sexual Relations

Sexual activity between two or more inmates is a violation of Bureau policy. When such activity does not include coercion or force, a *Code 205 Engaging in Sexual Acts* violation might be applied. However, sexual activity between staff and an inmate is never consensual.[1] Sex between inmates and staff can result in criminal prosecution for the employee. See 18 U.S.C. § 2243(b), which criminalizes sexual acts between federal prisoners and staff.

Despite the consequences, many inmates still choose to engage in voluntary sexual relations with others. In women's prisons, for example, the saying is, "Gay for the stay, straight at the gate." The prevalence of relationships imbues every interaction with additional meaning.[2] Most longtime observers agree that such activity is ill-advised and to be avoided for a number of reasons.

First, it is virtually impossible for an inmate to engage in safe sex practices. Within the FBOP, condoms and other contraceptive devices are not distributed. Those who do try to engage in safe sex often steal latex gloves from the guards and use them as protection. Those confined in America's prisons and jails have a far higher infection rate than the general population for HIV/AIDS, hepatitis, and other sexually transmitted diseases. Some sources cite the prisoner rate at six times that of the general population.

Prison populations also include a greater percentage of prisoners who have engaged in substance abuse, IV drug use, and sexually irresponsible conduct. Simply put, it is difficult for any inmate to find a safe partner for sexual activity or to protect themselves if they do engage in sex.

Further, sexual relations in prison are not recommended due to the interpersonal difficulties that often arise as a result of sexual activities. Prisons are volatile places where strong emotional responses can lead to unfavorable results. The drama that often accompanies a sexual relationship almost always ends badly in relationships between prisoners.

Moreover, the predatory nature of some prisoners can make anyone who engages in consensual sexual relations a target for sexual abuse and assault. Some inmates might perceive such activity as a license for attack. Others assume that he or she wanted it. In a women's facility, Teresa Giudice knew prisoners who sold their bodies for commissary money.[3] Matthew Kluger talked about the same type of decisions made by some inmates in FCI Butner.[4]

Finally, voluntary sexual relationships can cause serious difficulties in official matters like classification and transfers. While the outside world has become more accepting of alternative sexual lifestyles, this tolerance has not yet permeated the insular world of prison. Many staff members view inmates who engage in sex as management headaches and troublesome to supervise; they often discriminate against them. Prison is difficult enough. Sexual activity between inmates is usually a poor choice.

It can also lead to a number of misunderstandings that have dramatic consequences. The complex system of norms in prison culture can mean that an act one person views as sexual assault can be viewed quite differently by another. How others interpret the act can depend on the victim's behavior before the assault as well as the perceived cause for the sexual violence.[5]

Likewise, sex with staff is always a bad idea. Kendrick Desmond Brooks, an employee at the federal prison camp in Bryan, admitted to engaging in intercourse with a female inmate in the commissary and the boiler room of the facility where he worked. As a result of this sexual activity, Brooks faced fifteen years in a federal prison and a $250,000 fine.[6]

It is not easy to stay under the radar in prison. Beyond the legal and disciplinary consequences that can result, any inmate found to have been having sex with staff will usually face increased scrutiny by security personnel, retaliatory transfers to other facilities, and other difficulties. Inmates who are perceived as having coopted a staff member will face many hurdles for the remainder of their incarceration.

And sex with staff members can negatively impact fellow inmates. Kristin Davis wrote that when this type of relationship was revealed in her facility, the entire population was punished. The administration took away "the small comforts that make us feel like a human," in this case makeup and hair dye.[7]

Moreover, sex with staff members can result in an inmate being falsely accused of sexual assault. It must be remembered that any staff member found to have had sex with an inmate can expect termination from employment, even if criminal charges do not ensue. Given the poor judgment such a person demonstrates, it should be no surprise that he or she might accuse an inmate of force or coercion under pressure. Accordingly, sex with staff should be avoided.

"Individual sexual masturbation is the sex act accepted in prison," notes Prison Justice for America. Engaging in this activity in private is possible in showers stalls, toilet stalls, and bunks after dark.[8]

Sexual Assaults and Abuse

Sexual assaults in prison are quite prevalent. Indeed, in promulgating the Prison Rape Elimination Act (PREA), Congress found that "experts have conservatively estimated that at least 13 percent of inmates in the United States have been sexually assaulted in prison."[9] Although the law also created an independent

National Prison Rape Elimination Commission,[10] "Like many ambitious pieces of legislation," Maurice Chammah writes in *The Atlantic,* "its promise has proven difficult to realize. Adoption of guidelines is painfully slow."[11]

Chammah's article quotes Wilbert Rideau's 1980 article, "The Sexual Jungle," where Rideau defined rape in prison as not a sexual crime but one based in power, violence, and politics. Unfortunately, that attitude seemed for a long time to have been adopted by administrators who not only made little effort to stop rape but responded with indifference. When Human Rights Watch released their 2001 expose on rape in prison, enough pressure was finally placed on the government to force action.

In August, 2012, the Bureau issued a comprehensive update to its sexual abuse protocols.[12] The new policy established a National PREA Coordinator, Regional PREA Coordinators, and Institutional PREA Compliance Managers at each facility. In addition, the Bureau has special rules for grievances on sexual abuse matters, including a waiver of the usual time limits for filing such complaints.[13]

Rape is known to be underreported outside of prison walls, and the same is true inside prisons. In fact, the reporting of rape inside prisons is assumed to be much lower because inmates might face retaliation from other prisoners and staff.[14] The Bureau's inmate email system, TRULINCS, has provisions for inmates to contact the Department of Justice or Inspector General directly and anonymously.

Despite the Bureau's apparently serious approach to preventing sexual assaults, the reality is that such assaults do occur. Some inmates contract HIV during rape while others are seriously injured or even killed due to the violence of the attacks. Obviously, all suffer psychological wounds. The extreme mental distress results in a condition called rape trauma syndrome; victims report nightmares, depression, feelings of shame and self-hatred, and loss of confidence. Some even consider suicide.[15]

Inmates in general believe that rape undermines the social order inside the prison community and therefore police themselves to some degree.[16] Anyone incarcerated within the Bureau should take steps to protect themselves.

First, inmates new to the system should observe the classic prison advice of never accepting anything of value from other inmates lest they put themselves in a position of debt. Second, inmates should do their best to be aware of their surroundings and avoid placing themselves in compromising situations such as isolated places or near groups that appear menacing.

Third, it is important that inmates who are unsure of their surroundings or new to prison respect their instincts about potentially dangerous situations. Navigating the world of prison successfully is, for the most part, based on using common sense to avoid trouble. If being in the presence of certain inmates makes one uncomfortable, that gut feeling should be heeded.

What to Do in the Case of Sexual Assault

In most FBOP facilities the likelihood of being sexually assaulted is remote, particularly in lower security level institutions. Nonetheless, any inmate who is sexually assaulted should immediately report the incident to staff.

Whether the assailant is a staff member or another inmate, victims have the right to be treated respectfully and as confidentially as possible. Usually, an inmate reporting a sexual assault will be placed in a safer environment (medical unit, SHU or, if necessary, outside hospitals). After receiving medical attention, the inmate will be referred to the on-call psychologist. At some point thereafter, investigative personnel will probably interview the inmate.[17]

Any inmate who fears sexual assault is entitled to protection. Beyond Bureau policies intended to reduce the possibility of assault and those that address treatment should an assault occur, the federal courts have been vigilant in imposing upon prison officials a duty to protect inmates, especially from sexual assault. See *Farmer v. Brennan*, 511 U.S. 825, 834 (1994), where the court said, "[b]eing violently assaulted in prison is simply not part of the penalty that criminal offenders pay for their offense against society."

Inmates who become victims of rape should never blame themselves. Even when groups of perpetrators overpowered them or extreme violence was used, some still feel shame unnecessarily. Many become obsessive about figuring out ways they could have avoided or stopped the rape. In cases where guards are not supportive or imply that the sex was consensual, particularly with openly gay men, maintaining a strong sense of self can be even more difficult.[18]

It is essential that every inmate know how to avoid sexual assault. Combined with a measure of common-sense behavior, this knowledge can ensure that an inmate lives more safely.

How to Report Sexual Assault

Generally speaking, inmates in the FBOP have four avenues for reporting sexual harassment and assault. The easiest is to simply tell any staff member. This should be a psychology department staff member or another FBOP employee the inmate trusts.

The inmate can also file an administrative remedy. Whereas informal resolution (BP-8) is usually the first step in the grievance process, when it comes to sexual assault where the inmate fears staff retaliation, they are permitted to file a "sensitive" BP-10 administrative remedy directly to the applicable regional office.[19]

Perhaps the most confidential method of reporting abuse is to log into a TRULINCS computer, click on "Request to Staff," and send an email to the DOJ Sexual Abuse Reporting Mailbox. Inmates should be advised that they must request to remain anonymous in any emails or else their identity will be disclosed to Bureau personnel.

Last, inmates can write a letter directly to the office of the Inspector General at this address:

Office of the Inspector General
U.S. Department of Justice
Investigations Division
950 Pennsylvania Avenue, NW
Room 4706
Washington, DC 20530

Notes

1. Program Statement 5324.12, Sexually Abusive Behavior Prevention and Intervention Program; 28 C.F.R. § 115.6.
2. Blakinger, K.L., "Is Prison Scary." Nov 30, 2014. Retrieved from http://www.gorillaconvict.com/2014/11/prison-scary/.
3. McShane, Larry, "'Real Housewives of New Jersey' Star Teresa Giudice Reveals the Details of Her Year Spent Behind Bars in New Book — Including Lots of Lesbian Sex." *NY Daily News*. January 30, 2016.
4. Roberts, Daniel, "Life Behind Bars: Matthew Kluger Reveals All." *Fortune*. July 7, 2014.
5. Kaufman, Pat, "Prison Rape: Research Explores Prevalence, Prevention." National Institute of Justice. *NIJ Journal* No. 259. June 1, 2010. Retrieved from http://www.nij.gov/journals/259/pages/prison-rape.aspx.
6. "Former Bryan Federal Prison Guard Pleads Guilty to Sex Crime Charges." KBTX TV. Jan 29, 2016. Retrieved from http://www.kbtx.com/content/news/Former-Bryan-federal-prison-guard-pleads-guilty-to-sex-crime-charges-367041671.html.
7. Davis, Kristin, "This Is Prison." XOJane, May 8, 2015. Retrieved from http://www.xojane.com/it-happened-to-me/kristin-davis-this-is-prison.
8. "A Few Notes About Federal Prison Camps." Prison Justice for America. Retrieved from http://prison-justice.org/news-editorials/172-a-few-notes-about-federal-prison-camps.
9. 42 U.S.C. § 15601(2).
10. Kaufman, Pat, "Prison Rape: Research Explores Prevalence, Prevention." National Institute of Justice. *NIJ Journal* No. 259. June 1, 2010. Retrieved from http://www.nij.gov/journals/259/pages/prison-rape.aspx.
11. Chammah, Maurice, "Rape in the American Prison." *The Atlantic*. Feb 25, 2015.
12. Program Statement 5324.09, Sexually Abusive Behavior Prevention and Intervention Program, which has since been replaced by Program Statement 5324.12.
13. Program Statement 1330.18, Administrative Remedy Program at § 16; 28 C.F.R. § 115.52(b)(1).
14. Chammah, Maurice, "Rape in the American Prison." *The Atlantic*. Feb. 25, 2015.

15. "No Escape: Male Rape in US Prisons." VI: Body and Soul: The Physical and Psychological Injury of Prison Rape. Human Rights Watch. 2001.
16. Kaufman, Pat, "Prison Rape: Research Explores Prevalence, Prevention." National Institute of Justice. *NIJ Journal* No. 259. June 1, 2010. Retrieved from http://www.nij.gov/journals/259/pages/prison-rape.aspx.
17. Program Statement 5324.12, Sexually Abusive Behavior Prevention and Intervention Program at § 10.
18. "No Escape: Male Rape in US Prisons." VI: Body and Soul: The Physical and Psychological Injury of Prison Rape. Human Rights Watch. 2001.
19. Program Statement 1330.18, Administrative Remedy Program at § 8; 28 C.F.R. § 542.14(d)(1).

Part X – Preparing For Life Outside

Twenty-Eight

Shaping A New Life

"I've come to realize being sentenced in the U.S. criminal justice system, for anything, is a life sentence," said Bernie Kerik, who was imprisoned for tax fraud and false statements. "It's not about the time they give you. You receive a punishment of imprisonment and then a lifelong sentence of collateral punishment."[1]

In *The Prison Community*, sociologist Donald Clemmer noted that "the prison experience is neither normal nor natural, and constitutes one of the more degrading experiences a person might endure."[2] Inmates may find their mental acuity deteriorating, experience apathy that was unusual before incarceration, and become uncertain about who they actually are. Incarceration is a punishment that involves much more than a loss of freedom.[3]

Finding meaning behind bars is no easy task. Inmates are surrounded by negative influences from inmates and staff. When the often treacherous prison culture interacts with these negative influences, it turns into a breeding ground that begets criminal-minded malcontents. This leads regular prisoners into becoming convicts. But it doesn't have to be this way.

After serving time in federal prison, former senator Jeff Smith said, "I think you need a total shift in the worldview of the prison system, and it's more like some prison systems in Scandinavia, where it's viewed as: 'You fucked up, and now you're going to take a break, and you're not going to be able to see your loved ones, but we're going to try to equip you with the skills in life and the ability to navigate the world, such that you never come back here again.' So there's a truly rehabilitative mindset."[4]

Smith's statement is aspirational in nature. Presently, in U.S. facilities, only the inmate can chose to create that mindset for themselves. Generally, three types of people are found in prison: the lazy, who watch TV for years on end; the convicts, who can often be found drinking, getting high, or engaging in sundry acts of criminality; and the focused, who turn their time into a stepping stone to success. While the first group lacks any real self-direction, the other two have some to spare. The question is the direction in which they apply their energies.

Time spent in prison can be either a detriment or an asset to post-release success. Michael Santos, who served forty-five years in federal prison for drug trafficking, said, "The entire journey for me has been hyper-deliberate. It has all been in preparation for this period of time when I can emerge into society with opportunities to live as a contributing person. Nothing distracts me from what I need to do."[5]

Santos did that by educating himself. He found a way to contribute to society once he was released. And before he got out, he began building a network of individuals who could guide him through the process of transitioning back into the free world.

While it is easy to fall into a funk of do-nothingness, there are some spectacular stories of amazing success. It all comes down, rather unsurprisingly, to the choices inmates make.

In the 1980s, Paul Wright, a young man living in Washington State, killed a drug dealer in a robbery that went poorly. He was subsequently sentenced to twenty-five years, four months in state prison. His time there was eventful. A constant thorn in the side of prison officials for his writing, advocacy and litigation activities, he founded the magazine *Prison Legal News*.

Twenty-six years later, *Prison Legal News* is the largest prison law monthly in the world with over 9,000 paid subscribers across all fifty states and an estimated readership of 100,000 monthly. Paul Wright, once a new fish sentenced to a lengthy term of imprisonment, now sits at the head of the most influential prisoners' rights and prison law publication the world over.

Another tremendous transformation is that of Jon Marc Taylor. Convicted in both Indiana and Missouri of a string of home invasions and other serious crimes as a teenager, Taylor earned his high school diploma, associates, bachelor's, master's, and even a doctorate degree while behind bars. He is also the author of the well-respected *Prisoners' Guerrilla Handbook to Correspondence Programs in the U.S. and Canada* (Prison Legal News Publishing, 2009). Once cast off as deserving decades in custody, Jon Marc Taylor reinvented himself and led the call for enhanced educational opportunities in prison even as he served time. Sadly, he died of a heart attack in December 2015. Prison doesn't have to be a barrier to life or success.

While a criminal conviction will endear no one to the world or society at large, what one does in prison can mitigate a criminal history … and effectively overcome it. The question is how to use one's time in prison as a stepping stone to something greater. Simple. Prisoners have one asset those on the outside often find in short supply: time. With a few years to spend behind bars, anyone can become an expert in an area that interests them.

Federal prisoners lack the ability to head out to their local library or surf the internet but they do have access to their prison's library and law library. They can also have books mailed to them by friends and family members. Reading is the key. A substantial portion of college consists of reading from a text and writing expository essays about the readings.

If a prisoner has access to funds for college correspondence courses, great. But if, like most, they don't have such access, cutting out the tuition and buying used textbooks can save thousands of dollars. With time, inexpensive books, and some self-determination, anyone in prison can prepare themselves for their eventual return to society. They can come out of prison an expert in the field they'd like to pursue.

The concept is easy to grasp but its application is not. Self-directed study is not fast or easy. No professor or instructor doles out assignments or provides encouragement. But if a prisoner is hungry enough, they will find a way to succeed.

Standing on the precipice of total social and professional failure is sobering. Regardless of whether a person is eighteen or eighty, being sentenced to a term of imprisonment is like being doused with a cold bucket of water. Somehow it takes away all past accomplishments and leaves one forever marked. From this point, it is possible to dig deeper into the hole of failure. It is also possible to stand tall and start the climb back to success, or even to build success for the first time.

Being in prison is not an excuse. Choices are choices, whether it involves turning in a term paper, showing up to work, or walking away from a prison TV to study or plan for release. By making the right choices, one will succeed in prison and post-release. The inverse is also true.

Every new arrival who stands at the prison gate has a choice. They can enter and become yet another drain on society, destined to remain a prisoner. Or they can put in the time and effort required for a remarkable transformation, one that sees them leave prison, realize their goals, and never return. The choice is there regardless of race, creed, social class, or even prior success or a lack thereof. It's just that simple.

As you stand at that prison gate awaiting entry into a culture to which no one wants admission, what choice will you make? Will you choose success or failure?

Notes

1. DePaulo, Lisa, "The Secrets of White Collar Prisons." DuJour. Retrieved from http://dujour.com/news/inside-white-collar-prisons-bernie-kerik-jack-abramoff/.
2. DeVeaux, Mika'il, "The Trauma of the Incarceration Experience." *Harvard Civil Rights-Civil Liberties Law Review,* Vol. 48. April 2013.
3. *Id.*
4. Zengerle, Jason, "What a Jail Sentence Taught One Politician About Prisons." *GQ.* November 12, 2015.
5. Whiting, Sam, "Inmate Shares Prison Survival Strategies." *San Francisco Gate.* Nov 24, 2012.

Appendices

Appendix I: Federal Bureau of Prisons Information and Addresses

This appendix contains the mailing addresses for the Federal Bureau of Prisons' Central Office and six regional offices. Below each regional office address is a listing of every federal prison located in that region. Also provided are each prison's security level and the city and state in which it is located. Most federal prisons also have an adjacent satellite prison camp. Listings with an asterisk have a satellite prison camp.

For a more comprehensive review, see *Federal Prison Guidebook* (Revision 3) (James Publishing, 2015) by Alan Ellis, Todd A. Bussert, and J. Michael Henderson. PrisonerResource.com also has an ongoing prison profile series that profiles every federal prison in the country.

Central Office
Federal Bureau of Prisons
320 First Street, NW
Washington, DC 20534
Phone: (202) 307-3198

Mid-Atlantic Region
Mid-Atlantic Regional Office
Federal Bureau of Prisons
302 Sentinel Drive, Suite 200
Annapolis Junction, MD 20701
Phone: (301) 317-3100

FPC Alderson (MINIMUM - Alderson, WV)
FCI Ashland (LOW - Ashland, KY)*
FCI Beckley (MEDIUM - Beaver, WV)*
USP Big Sandy (HIGH - Inez, KY)*
FCI Butner Low (LOW - Butner, NC)*
FCI Butner Medium 1 (MEDIUM - Butner, NC)*
FCI Butner Medium 2 (MEDIUM - Butner, NC)*

FMC Butner (ADMINISTRATIVE - Butner, NC)*
FCI Cumberland (MEDIUM - Cumberland, MD)*
FCI Gilmer (MEDIUM - Glenville, WV)*
FCI Hazelton Female (MEDIUM - Bruceton Mills, WV)
FCI Hazelton (MEDIUM - Bruceton Mills, WV)
USP Hazleton (HIGH - Bruceton Mills, WV)*
USP Lee (HIGH - Pennington Gap, VA)*
FMC Lexington (ADMINISTRATIVE - Lexington, KY)*
FCI Manchester (MEDIUM - Manchester, KY)*
USP McCreary (HIGH - Pine Knot, KY)*
FCI McDowell (MEDIUM - Welch, WV)*
FCI Memphis (MEDIUM - Memphis, TN)*
FCI Morgantown (MINIMUM - Morgantown, WV)
FCI Petersburg Low (LOW - Hopewell, VA)*
FCI Petersburg Medium (MEDIUM - Hopewell, VA)*

North Central Region
North Central Regional Office
Federal Bureau of Prisons
400 State Avenue, Suite 800
Kansas City, KS 66101
Phone: (903) 621-3939

MCC Chicago (ADMINISTRATIVE - Chicago, IL)
FPC Duluth (MINIMUM - Duluth, MN)
FCI Englewood (LOW - Littleton, CO)*
USP Florence - Administrative Maximum Facility (ADMINISTRATIVE - Florence, CO)
FCI Florence (MEDIUM - Florence, CO)*
USP Florence (HIGH - Florence, CO)
FCI Greenville (MEDIUM - Greenville, IL)*
USP Leavenworth (MEDIUM - Leavenworth, KS)*
USP Marion (MEDIUM - Marion, IL)*

FCI Milan (LOW - Milan, MI)
FCI Oxford (MEDIUM - Oxford, WI)*
FCI Pekin (MEDIUM - Pekin, IL)*
FMC Rochester (ADMINISTRATIVE - Rochester, MN)
FCI Sandstone (LOW - Sandstone, MN)
MCFP Springfield (ADMINISTRATIVE - Springfield, MO)
FCI Terre Haute (MEDIUM - Terre Haute, IN)*
USP Terre Haute (HIGH - Terre Haute, IN)*
USP Thomson Camp (MINIMUM - Thomson, IL)
FCI Waseca (LOW - Waseca, MN)
FPC Yankton (MINIMUM - Yankton, SD)

Northeast Region
Northeast Regional Office
Federal Bureau of Prisons
2nd & Chestnut Street, 7th Floor
Philadelphia, PA 19106
Phone: (215) 521-7301

FCI Allenwood Low (LOW - White Deer, PA)*
FCI Allenwood Medium (MEDIUM - White Deer, PA)
USP Allenwood (HIGH - White Deer, PA)
MDC Brooklyn (ADMINISTRATIVE - Brooklyn, NY)
FCI Berlin (MEDIUM - Berlin, NH)*
USP Canaan (HIGH - Waymart, PA)*
FCI Danbury (LOW - Danbury, CT)*
FMC Devens (ADMINISTRATIVE - Ayers, MA)*
FCI Elkton (LOW - Elkton, OH)
FCI Elkton Satellite Low (LOW - Elkton, OH)
FCI Fairton (MEDIUM - Fairton, NJ)*
FCI Fort Dix (LOW - Fort Dix, NJ)*
USP Lewisburg (HIGH - Lewisburg, PA)*
FCI Loretto (LOW - Loretto, PA)*

FCI McKean (MEDIUM - Lewis Run, PA)*
MCC New York (ADMINISTRATIVE - New York, NY)
FCI Otisville (MEDIUM - Otisville, NY)*
FDC Philadelphia (ADMINISTRATIVE - Philadelphia, PA)
FCI Ray Brook (MEDIUM - Ray Brook, NY)
FCI Schuylkill (MEDIUM - Minersville, PA)*

South Central Region
South Central Regional Office
Federal Bureau of Prisons
4211 Cedar Springs Road
Dallas, TX 75219
Phone: (214) 224-3389

FCI Bastrop (LOW - Bastrop, TX)*
USP Beaumont (HIGH - Beaumont, TX)*
FCI Beaumont Low (LOW - Beaumont, TX)
FCI Beaumont Medium (MEDIUM - Beaumont, TX)
FCI Big Spring (LOW - Big Spring, TX)*
FPC Bryan (LOW - Big Spring, TX)
FMC Carswell (ADMINISTRATIVE - Fort Worth, TX)*
FCI El Reno (MEDIUM - El Reno, OK)*
FCI Forrest City Low (LOW - Forrest City, AR)*
FCI Forrest City Medium (MEDIUM - Forrest City, AR)
FCI Fort Worth (LOW - Fort Worth, TX)
FDC Houston (ADMINISTRATIVE - Houston, TX)
FCI La Tuna (LOW - Anthony, TX)*
FCI La Tuna Satellite Low (LOW - Anthony, TX)
FCI Oakdale (LOW - Oakdale, LA)
FDC Oakdale (ADMINISTRATIVE - Oakdale, LA)*
FTC Oklahoma City (ADMINISTRATIVE - Oklahoma City, OK)
FCI Pollock (MEDIUM - Pollock, LA)
USP Pollock (HIGH - Pollock, LA)*

FCI Seagoville (LOW - Seagoville, TX)*
FCI Texarkana (LOW - Texarkana, TX)*
FCI Three Rivers (MEDIUM - Three Rivers, TX)*

Southeast Region
Southeast Regional Office
Federal Bureau of Prisons
3800 Camp Creek Park SW/Building 2000
Atlanta, GA 30331
Phone: (678) 686-1200

FCI Aliceville (LOW - Aliceville, AL)*
USP Atlanta (MEDIUM - Atlanta, GA)*
FCI Bennettsville (MEDIUM - Bennettsville, SC)*
FCI Colemna Low (LOW - Coleman, FL)
FCI Coleman Medium (MEDIUM - Coleman, FL)*
USP Coleman 1 (HIGH - Coleman, FL)
USP Coleman 2 (HIGH - Coleman, FL)
FCI Edgefield (MEDIUM - Edgefield, SC)*
FCI Estill (MEDIUM - Estill, SC)*
MDC Guaynabo (ADMINISTRATIVE - Guaynabo, PR)
FCI Jesup (MEDIUM - Jesup, GA)*
FCI Jesup Satellite Low (LOW - Jesup, GA)
FCI Marianna (MEDIUM - Marianna, FL)*
FCI Miami (LOW - Miami, FL)*
FDC Miami (ADMINISTRATIVE - Miami, FL)
FPC Montgomery (MINIMUM - Montgomery, AL)
FPC Pensacola (MINIMUM - Pensacola, FL)
FCI Talladega (MEDIUM - Talladega, AL)*
FCI Tallahassee (LOW - Tallahassee, FL)
FCI Williamsburg (MEDIUM - Salters, SC)*
FCI Yazoo City Low (LOW - Yazoo City, MS)*
FCI Yazoo City Medium (MEDIUM - Yazoo City, MS)

USP Yazoo City (HIGH - Yazoo City, MS)

Western Region
Western Regional Office
Federal Bureau of Prisons
7338 Shoreline Drive
Stockton, CA 95219
Phone: (209) 956-9700

USP Atwater (HIGH - Atwater, CA)*
FCI Dublin (LOW - Dublin, CA)*
FCI Herlong (MEDIUM - Herlong, CA)*
FDC Honolulu (ADMINISTRATIVE - Honolulu, HI)
FCI Lompoc (LOW - Lompoc, CA)*
USP Lompoc (HIGH - Lompoc, CA)*
MDC Los Angeles (ADMINISTRATIVE - Los Angeles, CA)
FCI Mendota (MEDIUM - Mendota, CA)*
FCI Phoenix (MEDIUM - Phoenix, AZ)*
FCI Safford (LOW - Safford, AZ)
MCC San Diego (ADMINISTRATIVE - San Diego, CA)
FDC Seatac (ADMINISTRATIVE - Seattle, WA)
FCI Sheridan (MEDIUM - Sheridan, OR)*
FCI Terminal Island (LOW - Terminal Island, CA)
FCI Tucson (MEDIUM - Tucson, AZ)
USP Tucson (HIGH - Tucson, AZ)*
FCI Victorville 1 (MEDIUM - Victorville, CA)
FCI Victorville 2 (MEDIUM - Victorville, CA)*
USP Victorville (HIGH - Victorville, CA)

Private Contract Facilities
Adams County Correctional Center (LOW - Natchez, MS)
Big Spring Correctional Institution (LOW - Big Spring, TX)
Cibola County Correctional Institution (LOW - Milan, NM)

D. Ray James Correctional Facility (LOW - Folkston, GA)
Dalby Correctional Institution (LOW - Post, TX)
Eden Correctional Institution (LOW - Eden, TX)
Great Plains Correctional Institution (LOW - Hinton, OK)
McRae Correctional Institution (LOW - McRae, GA)
Moshannon Valley Correctional Institution (LOW - Philipsburg, PA)
Reeves Correctional Institution (LOW - Pecos, TX)
Reeves Detention Center (ADMINISTRATIVE - Pecos, TX)
Rivers Correctional Institution (LOW - Winton, NC)
Taft Correctional Institution (LOW - Taft, CA)*

** Federal prisons with an adjacent satellite prison camp.*

Appendix II: Disciplinary Infractions

The Federal Bureau of Prisons' disciplinary code is contained within Program Statement 5270.09, Inmate Discipline Program, and 28 C.F.R. § 541. Federal prisoners who commit any of the listed infractions – or even attempt to commit any of them – are subject to disciplinary proceedings and sanctions as outlined in Chapter 20. In an effort to help readers understand conduct that is permissible and conduct that is not permissible, the various disciplinary code violations are contained below. For a more thorough review of the FBOP's disciplinary program, see Chapter 20.

Greatest Severity Level Prohibited Acts

100 - Killing.

101 - Assaulting any person, or an armed assault on the institution's secure perimeter. A charge for assaulting any person at this level is to be used only when serious physical injury has been attempted or accomplished.

102 - Escape from escort; escape from any secure or non-secure institution, including community confinement; escape from unescorted community program or activity; escape from outside a secure institution.

103 - Setting a fire. One is charged with this act in this category only when found to pose a threat to life or a threat of serious bodily harm, or in furtherance of a prohibited act of Greatest Severity, e.g., in furtherance of a riot or escape. Otherwise the charge is properly classified *Code 218 or 329.*

104 - Possession, manufacture, or introduction of a gun, firearm, weapon, sharpened instrument, knife, dangerous chemical, explosive, ammunition, or any instrument used as a weapon.

105 - Rioting.

106 - Encouraging others to riot.

107 - Taking hostage(s).

108 - Possession, manufacture, introduction, or loss of a hazardous tool, or tools most likely to be used in an escape or escape attempt or to serve as weapons capable

of doing serious bodily harm to others; or those hazardous to institutional security or personal safety; e.g., hacksaw blades, body armor, maps, handmade rope, or other escape paraphernalia, portable telephone, pager, or other electronic device.

109 - (Not to be used).

110 - Refusing to provide a urine sample; refusing to breathe into a Breathalyzer; refusing to take part in other drug-abuse testing.

111 - Introduction or making of any narcotics, marijuana, drugs, alcohol, intoxicants, or related paraphernalia not prescribed for the individual by the medical staff.

112 - Use of any narcotics, marijuana, drugs, alcohol, intoxicants, or related paraphernalia, not prescribed for the individual by the medical staff.

113 - Possession of any narcotics, marijuana, drugs, alcohol, intoxicants, or related paraphernalia, not prescribed for the individual by the medical staff.

114 - Sexual assault of any person, involving non-consensual touching by force or threat of force.

115 - Destroying and/or disposing of any item during a search or attempt to search.

196 - Use of the mail for an illegal purpose or to commit or further a Greatest category prohibited act.

197 - Use of the telephone for an illegal purpose or to commit or further a Greatest category prohibited act.

198 - Interfering with a staff member in the performance of duties most like another Greatest severity prohibited act. This charge is to be used only when another charge of Greatest severity is not accurate. The offending conduct must be charged as "most like" one of the listed Greatest severity prohibited acts.

199 - Conduct which disrupts or interferes with the security or orderly running of the institution or the Bureau of Prisons most like another Greatest severity prohibited act. This charge is to be used only when another charge of Greatest severity is not accurate. The offending conduct must be charged as "most like" one of the listed Greatest severity prohibited acts.

High Severity Level Prohibited Acts

200 - Escape from a work detail, non-secure institution, or other non-secure confinement, including community confinement, with subsequent voluntary return to Bureau of Prisons custody within four hours.

201 - Fighting with another person.

202 - (Not to be used).

203 - Threatening another with bodily harm or any other offense.

204 - Extortion; blackmail; protection; demanding or receiving money or anything of value in return for protection against others, to avoid bodily harm, or under threat of informing.

205 - Engaging in sexual acts.

206 - Making sexual proposals or threats to another.

207 - Wearing a disguise or a mask.

208 - Possession of any unauthorized locking device, or lock pick, or tampering with or blocking any lock device (includes keys), or destroying, altering, interfering with, improperly using, or damaging any security device, mechanism, or procedure.

209 - Adulteration of any food or drink.

210 - (Not to be used).

211 - Possessing any officer's or staff clothing.

212 - Engaging in, or encouraging a group demonstration.

213 - Encouraging others to refuse to work, or to participate in a work stoppage.

214 - (Not to be used).

215 - (Not to be used).

216 - Giving or offering an official or staff member a bribe, or anything of value.

217 - Giving money to, or receiving money from, any person for the purpose of introducing contraband or any other illegal or prohibited purpose.

218 - Destroying, altering, or damaging government property, or the property of another person, having a value in excess of $100.00, or destroying, altering, damaging life-safety devices (e.g., the fire alarm), regardless of financial value.

219 - Stealing or theft, including data obtained through the unauthorized use of a communications device, or through unauthorized access to disks, tapes, or computer printouts or other automated equipment on which data is stored.

220 - Demonstrating, practicing, or using martial arts, boxing (except for use of a punching bag), wrestling, or other forms of physical encounter, or military exercises or drill, except for drill authorized by staff.

221 - Being in an unauthorized area with a person of the opposite sex without staff permission.

222 - (Not to be used).

223 - (Not to be used).

224 - Assaulting any person. A charge at this level is used when less serious physical injury or contact has been attempted or accomplished by an inmate.

225 - Stalking another person through repeated behavior which harasses, alarms, or annoys the person, after having been previously warned to stop such conduct.

226 - Possession of stolen property.

227 - Refusing to participate in a required physical test or examination unrelated to testing for drug abuse (e.g., DNA, HIV, tuberculosis).

228 - Tattooing or self-mutilation.

229 - Sexual assault of any person, involving non-consensual touching without force or threat of force.

296 - Use of the mail for abuses, other than criminal activity, which circumvent mail monitoring procedures. Examples include the use of mail to commit or further a High category prohibited act, special mail abuse; writing letters in code; directing others to send, sending, or receiving a letter or mail through unauthorized means; sending mail for other inmates without authorization; sending correspondence to a specific address with directions

or intent to have the correspondence sent to an unauthorized person; and using a fictitious return address in an attempt to send or receive unauthorized correspondence.

297 - Use of the telephone for abuses other than illegal activity which circumvent the ability of staff to monitor the frequency of telephone use, content of the call, or the number called; or to commit or further a High category prohibited act.

298 - Interfering with a staff member in the performance of duties most like another High severity prohibited act. This charge is to be used only when another charge of High severity is not accurate. The offending conduct must be charged as "most like" one of the listed High severity prohibited acts.

299 - Conduct which disrupts or interferes with the security or orderly running of the institution or the Bureau of Prisons most like another High severity prohibited act. This charge is to be used only when another charge of High severity is not accurate. The offending conduct must be charged as "most like" one of the listed High severity prohibited acts.

Moderate Severity Level Prohibited Acts

300 - Indecent exposure.

301 - (Not to be used).

302 - Misuse of authorized medication.

303 - Possession of money or currency, unless specifically authorized, or in excess of the amount authorized.

304 - Lending of property or anything of value for profit or increased return.

305 - Possession of anything not authorized for retention or receipt by the inmate, and not issued to him through regular channels.

306 - Refusing to work or accept a program assignment.

307 - Refusing to obey an order of any staff member. This may be categorized and charged in terms of greater severity, according to the nature of the order being disobeyed (e.g., failure to obey an order which furthers a riot would be charged as 105, rioting; refusing to obey an order which furthers a fight would

be charged as 201, fighting; refusing to provide a urine sample when ordered as part of a drug-abuse test would be charged as 110).

308 - Violating a condition of a furlough.

309 - Violating a condition of a community program.

310 - Unexcused absence from work or any program assignment.

311 - Failing to perform work as instructed by the supervisor.

312 - Insolence towards a staff member.

313 - Lying or providing a false statement to a staff member.

314 - Counterfeiting, forging, or unauthorized reproduction of any document, article of identification, money, security, or official paper. This may be categorized in terms of greater severity according to the nature of the item being reproduced, e.g., counterfeiting release papers to effect escape (*Code 102*).

315 - Participating in an unauthorized meeting or gathering.

316 - Being in an unauthorized area without staff authorization.

317 - Failure to follow safety or sanitation regulations, including safety regulations, chemical instructions, tools, MSDS sheets, or OSHA standards.

318 - Using any equipment or machinery without staff authorization.

319 - Using any equipment or machinery contrary to instructions or posted safety standards.

320 - Failing to stand for count.

321 - Interfering with the taking of count.

322 - (Not to be used).

323 - (Not to be used).

324 - Gambling.

325 - Preparing or conducting a gambling pool.

326 - Possession of gambling paraphernalia.

327 - Unauthorized contacts with the public.

328 - Giving money or anything of value to, or accepting money or anything of value from, another inmate or any other person without staff authorization.

329 - Destroying, altering, or damaging government property, or the property of another person, having a value of $100.00 or less.

330 - Being unsanitary or untidy; failing to keep one's person or quarters in accordance with posted standards.

331 - Possession, manufacture, introduction, or loss of a non-hazardous tool, equipment, supplies, or other non-hazardous contraband. This includes tools not likely to be used in an escape or escape attempt, or to serve as a weapon capable of doing serious bodily harm to others, or not hazardous to institutional security or personal safety. Other non-hazardous contraband includes such items as food, cosmetics, cleaning supplies, smoking apparatus and tobacco in any form where prohibited, and unauthorized nutritional or dietary supplements.

332 - Smoking where prohibited.

333 - Fraudulent or deceptive completion of a skills test, including cheating on a GED, or other educational or vocational skills test.

334 - Conducting a business; conducting or directing an investment transaction without staff authorization.

335 - Communicating gang affiliation, participating in gang-related activities, possession of paraphernalia indicating gang affiliation.

336 - Circulating a petition.

396 - Use of the mail for abuses other than criminal activity which do not circumvent mail monitoring; or use of the mail to commit or further a Moderate category prohibited act.

397 - Use of the telephone for abuses other than illegal activity which do not circumvent the ability of staff to monitor frequency of telephone use, content of the call, or the number called; or to commit or further a Moderate category prohibited act.

398 - Interfering with a staff member in the performance of duties most like another Moderate severity prohibited act. This charge is to be used only when

another charge of Moderate severity is not accurate. The offending conduct must be charged as "most like" one of the listed Moderate severity prohibited acts.

399 - Conduct which disrupts or interferes with the security or orderly running of the institution or the Bureau of Prisons most like another Moderate security prohibited act. This charge is to be used only when another charge of Moderate severity is not accurate. The offending conduct must be charged as "most like" one of the listed Moderate severity prohibited acts.

Low Severity Level Prohibited Acts

400 - (Not to be used).

401 - (Not to be used).

402 - Malingering, feigning illness.

403 - (Not to be used).

404 - Using abusive or obscene language.

405 - (Not to be used).

406 - (Not to be used).

407 - Conduct with a visitor in violation of Bureau regulations.

408 - (Not to be used).

409 - Unauthorized physical contact, such as kissing or embracing.

498 - Interfering with a staff member in the performance of duties most like another Low severity prohibited act. This charge is to be used only when another charge of Low severity is not accurate. The offending conduct must be charged as "most like" one of the listed Low severity prohibited acts.

499 - Conduct which disrupts or interferes with the security or orderly running of the institution or the Bureau of Prisons most like another Low severity prohibited act. This charge is to be used only when another charge of Low severity is not accurate. The offending conduct must be charged as "most like" one of the listed Low severity prohibited acts.

Appendix III: Prisoner Publications and Pen-Pal Clubs*

GENERAL INTEREST PUBLICATIONS

What might be considered by many the most important of the publications is **Prison Legal News**. PLN is a top-quality monthly magazine distributed in prisons throughout the country. PLN was founded by Paul Wright, formerly a U.S. Army military policeman, then a convicted murder who became a jailhouse lawyer and, a prisoners' rights advocate. Battling public and private prison operators to gain reform and attention for human rights, PLN has focused on the need for protection against violence by other prisoners or guards, the right to adequate medical care, and the right of freedom of expression. The publication provides detailed information about political issues and news that affects the incarcerated directly, reporting on relevant court cases and educating prisoners about how to fight their legal battles to protect their legal rights. It has also long fought the financial exploitation of prisoners and their families by prisons, jails and corporations.

Publisher Wright has been battling prison censorship for a long time and has filed many lawsuits to preserve the publication in American prisons. Why does he put himself at risk to provide this information to prisoners? "Because," says Wright, "no one else will." An annual subscription is $30 for prisoners, $90 for attorneys and institutions, and $35 for other individuals. To subscribe, contact:

Prison Legal News
P.O. Box 1151
Lake Worth, FL 33460
Phone: (561) 360-2523
www.prisonlegalnews.org

Of equally significant importance is **The Journal of Prisoners on Prisons** (JPP). This Canadian-based non-profit is a distinguished academic journal publishing the work of convicts and ex-convicts since 1988. JPP earned its reputation as a clearing house of knowledge and academic studies produced

---

* *Reprinted from* College for Convicts: The Case for Higher Education in American Prisons *(McFarland & Co., 2014) with permission from the publisher.*

by imprisoned writers to enlighten the public about the current state of prison institutions. It creates an educational forum that allows "criminalized" men and women to develop research that concerns them directly.

Each issue focuses on a specific theme, such as *Education in Prisons* or *Women's Issues*. To maintain its high standards of quality, all writing submitted for publication undergoes a stringent peer-review process to select the finest articles from prisoners with strong academic backgrounds or advanced educational degrees.

The editors believe definitions of deviance are traditionally put forth, with few exceptions, by social scientists, media representatives, politicians, and people in the legal community who have no experience of prison life. As a result, true understanding of the people participating in those "deviant" acts is sadly lacking, and traditional analyses exclude the voices of the people most affected. Such a lack of understanding, the editors feel, may facilitate repressive and reactionary penal policies and practices. **The Journal of Prisoners on Prisons** serves, therefore, as a fresh, new source of information that counteracts popularly held stereotypes and misconceptions about those who face the deprivation of liberty. An annual subscription is $15 for prisoners, $30 for other individuals, and $60 for libraries and institutions. To subscribe, contact:

The Journal of Prisoners on Prisons
C/O University of Ottawa Press
542 King Edward Avenue
Ottawa, Ontario, Canada
K1N 6N5
Phone: (613) 562-5246
Email: jpp@uottawa.ca
www.jpp.org

The Prison Journal is the international and interdisciplinary Sage Publications periodical which presents a diversity of views from distinguished experts who explore various aspects of correctional punishment, new and progressive theories, research, policy, and practice. The **Journal** provides news about innovative programs, state-of-the-art surveys, and legal and historical analysis.

Special issues regularly supplement **The Prison Journal**'s coverage with articles offering in-depth analysis of a single topic, such as "*Women in Prison and Jails,*" "*Education in Correctional Settings,*" and "*Drug-Involved Offenders.*" Other topics include criminal justice administration and law, health and mental health, history, political science, psychology, public administration, public policy, and sociology.

Originally published by the Pennsylvania Prison Society, America's oldest prison reform organization (founded in 1787), **The Prison Journal** continues to gather vital insights and professional opinions on emerging trends, innovations, and developments in the rapidly changing world of corrections and alternative sentencing. Available from:

SAGE Publications
2455 Teller Road
Thousand Oaks, CA 91320
800-818-7243

Another **Prison Journal** is quite different. Edited by John and Ann Worley, this *Journal* publishes poetry, short essays, and art from prisoners with the intention of providing an outlet for creative expression. It is the belief of the editors that, "the presence of God resides in all people, and that everyone, even those incarcerated, can transform their lives in a positive direction." With no restrictions on professional standards except that the work be original, they invite submissions from inmates all over the country. To subscribe, contact:

The Prison Journal
C/O John Worley
6041 Watch Chain Way
Columbia, MD 21044-4107
Email: theprisonjournal@gmail.com

Cry Justice News is a newsletter publishing serious articles on imprisonment, poetry, and occasional art. One policy paper they published, *Calling for Sheepskins* by Dr. Jon Marc Taylor, had considerable influence in getting attention and initiating a grassroots lobbying campaign for allocating several million dollars a year to post-secondary correctional education for prisoners from the Inmate Collect Calling Phone System. Legislation was introduced in three General Assembly sessions of the Missouri Legislature. Although it was approved by committee, it was not passed by the full assembly. This is most unfortunate, because it would have been such an easy way to pay for getting on-site college programs back into that state's prisons. Moreover, had it been successful, it could have possibly worked for prisons in many other states, as well. To subscribe, contact:

Cry Justice News
P.O. Box 2525
New Bloomfield, MO 65063

Cell Door Magazine is written mostly by prisoners who describe the incarceration experience and how the ex-prisoner fares once back on the street. Content runs the gamut from poetry to short stories, and from art to op-ed commentary. Selected for quality and educational or entertainment value, the editors introduce the work of men and women behind bars. Articles range from self-help and self-pity to current topics, insight, empathy, and pathos. But the primary focus is always on how living behind bars affects a human life, revealing to those who don't already know, that prisoners can be intelligent, personable, and talented human beings. To subscribe, contact:

Mid-September to June:
Cell Door Magazine
12200 Road 41.9
Mancos, CO 81328
publisher@celldoor.com
www.lairdcarlson.com/celldoor/01002

July to mid-September:
Cell Door Magazine
6 Tolman Rd
Peaks Island, ME 04108
publisher@celldoor.com

The Pen, a publication originally created to give voice to the silenced, was similar to **Cell Door Magazine** in that it published prisoner-students expressing their trials, tribulations, hopes, dreams, frustrations, and fears, both in writing and through art. However, we do not know if this publication still exists, as no information can be currently located, and no address can be found.

Of interest to prisoners, but not actually targeted to an incarcerated readership, is the **Journal of Correctional Education.** The JCE is published by the Correctional Education Association, for professionals in the field of penal education. Articles concern post-secondary education, as well as ABE, ESL, pre-GED, and GED classes offered in prisons. The organization does not focus specifically on advanced academic education; however, it does emphatically support the concept of prison education as the most effective means to rehabilitation.

On the Association website, their stated position reads:

> "Since 1990, the literature has shown that prisoners who attend educational programs while they are incarcerated are less likely to return to prison following their release. Studies in several states have indicated that recidivism rates have declined where prisoners have received an appropriate education. Furthermore, the right kind of educational program leads to less violence by prisoners involved in the programs and a more positive prison environment. Effective education programs are those that help prisoners with their social skills, artistic development, and dealing with their emotions."

To subscribe, one must be a member of the Correctional Education Association. Annual membership fee is $65 for an individual. Contact:

Correctional Education Association
8182 Lark Brown Road
Suite 202
Elkridge, MD 21075
Phone: (800) 783-1232
Email: office@ceanational.org
http://www.ceanational.org/publicat.htm

FAMM-gram, published three times a year, is the email newsletter of Families Against Mandatory Minimums (FAMM) advocating for fair state and federal sentencing. Its colorful pages provide reports on FAMM's work to reform mandatory minimum sentencing laws and information about injustices resulting from mandatory minimum laws.

Articles are informative, ranging from the new crack law to the rumors of federal prisoners receiving increased time off for good behavior. The FAMMgram is free and does not accept prisoner submissions. At the current time, the printed newsletter is no longer sent to prisoners.

FAMM
1612 K Street NW, Suite 700
Washington, DC 20006
famm@famm.org
www.famm.org

Fortune News, published by The Fortune Society, is a quarterly dedicated to education, advocacy, and successful re-entry. Each issue includes *Justice Beat,* a summary of research in the field; *Lentes Latinos* ("Latin Lens"), a Spanish-language column about criminal justice issues faced by the Hispanic community; *New & Noteworthy Prison Programs,* a feature that highlights programs around the nation that are doing good work; *Center Stage,* a selection of poetry, comics, drawings, and other creative works from incarcerated or formerly incarcerated individuals; and more.

Sample topics in past issues have included *Re-entry, Immigration, and Detention, Giving Back, Crystal Meth, Aging in Prison, Alternatives to Incarceration, Prison Conditions, The Cost of Incarceration, Shattered Families, The Job Search, Hepatitis C: The Silent Epidemic, Voices from Death Row,* and *Youth.* The magazine is free to prisoners.

Founded in 1967, the Fortune Society is a Long Island, New York-based nonprofit social service and advocacy organization with a mission to support successful re-entry from prison and promote alternatives to incarceration. If you would like to learn more about Fortune's programs and services, you are welcome to write, to call or to just drop in and talk.

Fortune News
29-76 Northern Boulevard
Long Island City, NY 11101
Tel: (212) 691-7554
Email info@fortunesociety.org
www.fortunesociety.org

Prisoner Express appears once a year in print and online from the Durland Alternative Library at Cornell University. Designed to promote creative self-expression amongst prisoners, it publishes writing and educational projects for prisoners who sign up through their newsletter. To subscribe at no cost, contact:

Cornell University
127 Anabel Taylor Hall
Ithaca, NY 14853
Tel: (607) 255-6486
Email: alt-lib@cornell.edu
www.prisonerexpress.org

Prison Living Magazine is a magazine published four times a year for prisoners of all faiths. It offers articles that are both practical and inspirational to those in prison, as well as articles on after-release issues such as reintegration into society, finding jobs, and resources available to the ex-prisoner. Numerous articles are dedicated to entertainment, including a sports section, crossword puzzle, comics, and trivia. A subscription costs $12.00 per year. Write or call:

10645 N. Tatum Boulevard, Suite 200-661
Scottsdale, AZ 85254
(800) 419-2891
http://prisonministry.net/plmag

Prison Voices is a community outreach program, not a publication, but is listed here as another outlet where prisoners can give expression to their experiences. Originally an outgrowth of the Bay State Correctional Center (BSCC) community services program at Norfolk, MA, carefully screened prisoners meet with small groups of high-school students, college students, or other interested members of the community. The prisoners speak candidly about their lives, the events that led them to prison, and what the incarceration experience has been like for them.

Community members gain insight into the prison system and other criminal justice issues from this alternative information resource. For prisoners, it is an opportunity to serve the community while completing the remainder of their sentences.

The **Prison Voices** website features a pen-pal program to create a bridge between prisoners and people outside. For more information about the Prison Voices program contact:

Derek Estler or Jaileen Correira
Bay State Correctional Center
P. O. Box 73, Norfolk, MA 02056
(508) 668-1687, ext. 211
www.prisonvoices.com

Corrlinks/TRULINCS News Services

There are several free, electronic news services that offer weekly updates to federal prisoners via the Corrlinks.com website and TRULINCS computers. These services email prisoners articles, newsletters, and other information of interest. The following are the more established services:

Prison News Service delivers articles three times a week to federal prisoners' TRULINCS inboxes. Articles span a wide variety of topics, but focus on prison reform initiatives and breaking news of interest to federal prisoners. This is a free service of Middle Street Publishing.

Prison News Service
news@prisonlawblog.com

The Law Office of Jeremy Gordon, in partnership with their affiliated non-profit Prisology.org, sends out an exceptional weekly newsletter with the latest legal news of interest to federal prisoners. What sets this newsletter apart from all others is the extremely valuable legal analyses provided by attorneys Jeremy Gordon and Brandon Sample. This is essential reading for all jailhouse lawyers.

The Law Office of Jeremy Gordon
P.O. Box 2275
Mansfield, TX 44857
972-483-4865
info@topfederallawyer.com
www.gordondefense.com
www.prisology.org

Leading Edge Research Team delivers a weekly round-up of U.S. Supreme Court and circuit court cases, along with other legal developments of interest to federal prisoners. This service helps federal prisoners stay abreast of the latest developments in each federal circuit and at the U.S. Supreme Court.

Leading Edge Research Team
2701 Mall Drive, Suite 7-140
Florence, AL 35630
256-808-9009
www.leadingedgeresearchteam.com
info@federalcriminalparalegal.com

Legal Information Services sends out a weekly newsletter consisting of various articles and legal updates. This electronic newsletter provides a good range of articles of interest to federal prisoners. The articles focus on legal developments, along with criminal justice reform efforts by leading organizations and news about prison systems.

Legal Information Services Association
P.O. Box 636
Norwalk, OH 44857
www.lisa-legalinfo.com
newsletter@lisa-legalinfo.com

ACLU National Prison Project Publication List
From the ACLU (American Civil Liberties Union) come several publications to address areas of interest to prisoners:

Journal is a biannual newsletter featuring articles, reports, legal analysis, legislative news, and other developments in prisoners' rights. An annual subscription, normally $35, is only $2 for prisoners.

The Prisoners' Assistance Directory includes contact information and descriptions of services for over 300 national, state, local, and international organizations that provide assistance to prisoners, ex-offenders, and families of prisoners. It also includes a bibliography of informative books, reports, manuals, and newsletters of interest to prisoners and their advocates.

A sampling of ACLU's other publications include: *Breaking the Addiction to Incarceration*; *ACLU Commentary on DOJ's Proposed Standards to Prevent, Detect, and Respond to Prison Rape*; *States Aim to Make the Grade When It Comes to Shackling Pregnant Prisoners*; *Bradley Manning's Treatment Is Just the Tip of the Iceberg*; and many others.

To order any of these publications, send a check or money order to:

National Prison Project Publications
915 15th St., NW, 7th Floor
Washington, DC 20005
Tel: (212) 549-2500
http://www.aclu.org/prisoners-rights/aclu-national-prison-project-publication-list

CURE Newsletter is a national publication from Citizens United for Rehabilitation of Errants (CURE) that advocates for less incarceration and more rehabilitative opportunities for offenders. Their goal is to reduce crime through Criminal Justice Reform. To subscribe, write:

CURE
P.O. Box 2310
National Capitol Station
Washington, DC 20013
(202) 789-2126
www.curenational.org

Razor Wire Newsletter, published quarterly by the November Coalition, reports on drug war-related issues, releasing prisoners of the drug war, and restoring civil rights. A yearly subscription is $6 for prisoners and $25 for all others. Contact:

November Coalition
282 West Astor
Colville, WA 99114

Bureau of Justice Statistics Bulletin is published by the U.S. Department of Justice. It is exactly as the title suggests: 40+ pages of tables with statistics related to felony cases, providing data on demographics, criminal history, pretrial processing, adjudication, and sentencing. Not for the casual reader. But if you want it, write to:

U.S. Department of Justice
Office of Justice Programs
Bureau of Justice Statistics
Washington, DC 20531

Special-Interest Publications

As there are in the "outside" world, there are numerous publications in the prison world geared to readers with a specific area of interest.

Death-Row and Lifetime Prisoners

Compassion is a bi-monthly newsletter written by death-row prisoners. Various subscription rates are available based on personal circumstances. To subscribe, write:

Compassion
c/o St. Rose Peace and Justice
140 W. South Boundary Street
Perrysburg, OH 43551

Lifelines is the publication of the National Coalition to Abolish the Death Penalty. It is published every 4 months. For more information, contact:

Lifelines
c/o National Coalition to Abolish the Death Penalty
1750 DeSales Street, NW, Fifth Floor
Washington, DC 20036
(202) 331-4090

Lifer-Line, a monthly on-line publication available in both English and Spanish, focuses on issues of interest to life-term prisoners. It is available free for those outside of prison and mailed to prisoners as resources allow. For more information, contact:

Lifer-Line
C/O Life Support Alliance
P.O. Box 277
Rancho Cordova, CA 95741
(916) 402-3750
http://www.lifesupportalliance.org/Publications.html

Health-Related Prisoner Publications

CorrectCare is a quarterly newspaper which covers correctional health care. Prison libraries may subscribe to this publication by contacting:

CorrectCare
c/o National Commission on Correctional Health Care
1145 W. Diversey Parkway
Chicago, IL 60614
(773) 880-1460
www.ncchc.org/pubs/correctcare.html

Damien Center Newsletter is a free, bi-monthly publication focused on AIDS-related issues. For more information, contact:

Damien Center Newsletter
c/o Damien Center
26 N. Arsenal
Indianapolis, IN 46201
(317) 632-0123

Dispatch is a quarterly newsletter focused on AIDS-related issues. For more information, contact:

Dispatch
AIDS Delaware
100 W. 10th Street, #315
Wilmington, DE 19801
(302) 652-6776

Innocent and Wrongfully Convicted Prisoners

Innocence Denied offers advice and assistance to people wrongly incarcerated and their loved ones, and will support and join forces with organizations that support the freeing of innocent victims of our justice system.

Innocence Denied is also a strong advocate for education, music, art, and skills acquisition for anyone incarcerated, but especially for those who are wrongfully imprisoned.

Innocence Denied does not address prison conditions, nor complaints about various aspects of cases wherein the prisoner is not innocent. Nor does the publication provide prisoner-to-prisoner contact, as in pen-pal services. The focus is on the editorial belief that, "There should be massive protests on an innocent individual's behalf. There should be massive media coverage concerning the illegal confinement of the innocent. Judges and prosecutors who knowingly convict innocent individuals should be forced to resign [and]...prosecuted... Sadly, in reality this never happens." Subscriptions for prisoners are $6 per year; $15 for others. To subscribe, contact:

Innocence Denied
P.O. Box 18477
Pittsburgh, PA 15236
www.innocencedenied.org
innocencedenied@ymail.com

Justice Denied, a magazine focused on exposing wrongful convictions and how and why they occur. Six issues: $10 for prisoners, $20 for others. $3 for sample issue.

Justice Denied
P.O. Box 68911
Seattle, WA 98168
(202) 335-4254
www.justicedenied.org

Legal Interests

Correctional Law Reporter is a bi-monthly law publication which covers recent court decisions and legislative developments in the correctional law realm. Subscriptions are $179.95 per year. For more information, contact:

Correctional Law Reporter
C/O Civic Research Institute
P.O. Box 585
Kingston, NJ 08528
(609) 683-4450
orders@civicresearchinstitute.com
www.civicresearchinstitute.com

Justice Quarterly is a quarterly publication, published by Routledge, which contains academic articles approved by the Academy of Criminal Justice Services. Subscriptions are $75 per year and come with a membership to the Academy of Criminal Justice Services. For more information, contact:

Justice Quarterly
C/O Routledge Customer Service
325 Chestnut Street, 8th Floor
Philadelphia, PA 19106
(800) 354-1420
Email: support@tnfonline.com
www.acjs.org

Women

The Fire Inside is a bi-annual print and web newsletter providing a space where women prisoners and their supporters communicate with one another and the broader public about the issues and experiences faced specifically by women prisoners. The publication prints articles, editorials, art, and poetry, some of which are translated into Spanish. Available at no charge from:

California Coalition for Women Prisoners
1540 Market St., Suite 490
San Francisco, CA 94102
Tel: (415) 255-7036 ext. 4
Email: info@womenprisoners.org
http://www.womenprisoners.org/fire/

Juvenile

The Beat Within presents a forum for writing and artwork from juvenile prisoners across the country and editorial commentary on every published piece. Available weekly online and monthly in print, it is free to prisoners, teachers, counselors, and correctional staff. Others are asked for a donation to Pacific New Service in the name of *The Beat Within*. Write to:

275 Ninth Street
San Francisco, CA 94103
Tel: (415) 503-4170
Email: beat@pacificnews.org
www.thebeatwithin.org

RELIGIOUS

Christian

The Fishers of Men Prison Ministries Newsletter is a monthly Christian publication available in print or online. The newsletter welcomes nonfiction and fiction stories, personal essays, and poetry about God from prisoners. Free. Send subscription requests and submissions to:

5403 N. Second Street
Loves Park, IL 61111
Tel: (815) 633-7508
Email: (form available on website)
http://prisonministry.net/fompm

Inside Journal, published by Prison Fellowship, is a newspaper that reaches thousands of incarcerated men and women with the hope of the Gospel, explaining the Gospel in a way that makes sense to prisoners. **Inside Journal** includes both inspirational stories of lives transformed through Jesus Christ and practical-resource articles to help prisoners make the most of their time behind bars, whether they are close to release or incarcerated for life.

The editors believe the best way to transform our communities and make them safe is to transform the people within those communities, and that restorative change comes only through a relationship with Jesus Christ. They believe that prisoners can become productive ambassadors for Christ, both in prison and beyond. To subscribe, contact – or have your prison chaplain contact:

Prison Fellowship
44180 Riverside Parkway
Lansdowne, VA 20176
Tel: (800) 251-7411
Email: insidejournal@pfm.org
https://www.prisonfellowship.org/pf-resources/resources-officialas-chaplains

Crossroad Journal of the Arts is published by the Crossroad Bible Institute with art, articles, and poetry by prisoners for prisoners to enjoy. Subscribe or submit your work to:

Crossroad Journal of the Arts
Senior Editor: H. David Schuringa
P.O. Box 900
Grand Rapids, MI 49509

Joy Writers' Good-News Letter is sent out to encourage prisoners in their faith with poems and articles by prisoners and others. Submit your work or subscribe at:

The Joy Writers' Ministry
2001 Liberty Square Drive
Cartersville, GA 30121

Yard Out, a publication of the Prisoners for Christ Outreach Ministries, comes out three times a year with prison-related stories, articles, and poems. Write to:

Yard Out
C/O Prisoners for Christ
P.O. Box 1530
Woodinville, WA 98072
www.pfcom.org

Buddhist or Dharma

Dharma Garden, a quarterly publication, accepts submissions of articles, art-work, poetry, fiction, and reviews. To submit or subscribe, write to

Dharma Garden Newsletter
1 Fairtown Lane
Taneytown, MD 21787
Email: Dharmagardensangha@gmail.com
www.facebook.com/DharmaGardenSangha

Muslim

Prisonworld Magazine is a multi-state Muslim tabloid that presents itself as "the preferred prison entertainment magazine." Published 6 times a year with a format similar to *The National Inquirer*, the publishers also own a record company, video blog site, merchandising company, and radio network, addressing both the incarcerated and the outside world communities. All proceeds from **Prisonworld** go toward their prison outreach programs, which are unspecified in nature.

Dawah International LLC
P.O. Box 380
Powder Springs, GA 30127
(678) 233-8286
Email: dawahinternationalllc@gmail.com
www.prisonworldmagazine.com

Revolutionary Politics

4strugglemag, produced three times a year, is a joint project between political prisoner Jaan Laaman and organizers of the Toronto Anarchist Black Cross. They publish writing by political prisoners, prisoners of war, and their friends and family. Unapologetically "anti-imperialist," they support "progressive national liberation" and the struggles of the Black, Mexican, Puerto Rican, and Native American "nations" which they regard as "controlled by U.S. imperialism." **4strugglemag** advocates for their view of "justice, equality, freedom, socialism, protection of the Earth, human rights, and peace." In each issue, in addition to 3 or more main topics, they also publish poems, graphics, essays, and announcements. More information is available at:

4strugglemag
P.O. Box 97048
RPO Roncesvalles Avenue
Toronto, Ontario, M6R 3B3 Canada
Email: jaanlaaman@gmail.com
www.4strugglemag.org

Resist Newsletter is a bi-monthly publication focused on social justice issues. The suggested donation is $25 per year, but they will mail copies to prisoners for free if the prisoner doesn't have the requisite funding. For more information, contact:

Resist Newsletter
C/O Resist
259 Elm Street, Suite 201
Somerville, MA 02144
(617) 623-5110
Email: info@resistinc.org
www.resistinc.org

STATE-SPECIFIC PRISONER PUBLICATIONS

California Prisoners

Prison Focus is a biannual magazine produced by the group California Prison Focus. Issues focus on a specific theme, such as: *Survival in Prison*, *International Imprisonment*, and *Children of Prisoners*. In this magazine one finds prison-related news from newspapers and human-rights organizations. The editors print and encourage article submissions from prisoners, as well as evaluations of conditions at Pelican Bay State Prison in California. Cost for four issues: $5.00 for prisoners, $20.00 for others. Contact:

2940 16th Street #B-5
San Francisco, CA 94103
(415) 252-9211
Email: contact@prisons.org
www.prisons.org/publications.htm

California Lifer Newsletter may be found in your prison law library. If not, a year's subscription (6 issues) is $25 or 80 postage stamps. Issues provide a comprehensive (70+ pages) reporting of cases litigated and news or events of interest to California's prisoners serving indeterminate sentences. Together with attorneys and his staff, Donald ("Doc") Miller, a former physician and lifer who got his law degree while in prison, works to consult with lifers and help to provide litigation and administrative appeals.

California Lifer Newsletter
P.O. Box 277
Rancho Cordova, CA 95741
Tel: (916) 402-3750

Delaware Prisoners

Delaware Center for Justice Commentary is a free, quarterly newsletter of interest to prisoners in Delaware state prisons. For more information, contact:

Delaware Center for Justice Commentary
100 West 10th Street, #905
Wilmington, DE 19801
(302) 658-7174
www.dcjustice.org

Louisiana Prisoners

The Angolite is a magazine published bimonthly "by and for the inmates" of the Louisiana State Penitentiary. It features current events, religion, and sports sections, as well as a legal Q&A from prisoners. $20.00 for one-year subscription. Write to:

The Angolite
C/O Cashier's Office
Louisiana State Penitentiary
Angola, LA 70712
Email: support@prisontalk.com
www.corrections.state.la.us/lsp/angolite.htm

Maryland Prisoners

Maryland CURE Newsletter is the quarterly publication of Maryland CURE, covering legislative, prison system, and criminal justice news relevant to prisoners incarcerated in Maryland. Subscriptions are fulfilled through CURE membership at $2 for prisoners, $10 for individuals, and $15 for families. For more information, contact:

Maryland CURE Newsletter
C/O MD CURE
P.O. Box 23
Simpsonville, MD 21150
Email: marylandcure@comcast.net

Michigan Prisoners

Michigan CURE Newsletter is the quarterly publication of MI-CURE, covering legislative, prison system, and criminal justice news of interest to prisoners incarcerated in Michigan. For more information, contact:

Michigan CURE Newsletter
C/O MI-CURE
P.O. Box 2736
Kalamazoo, MI 49003-2736
(802) 257-1342
www.mi-cure.org

Minnesota Prisoners

The Prison Mirror is a monthly newsletter of interest to prisoners incarcerated within the Minnesota Stillwater Correctional Facility. For more information, contact:

The Prison Mirror
C/O Pat Pawlak
970 Pickett Street North
Bayport, MN 55003-1490
(651) 779-2700

Northwestern States: Oregon, Washington State, Idaho, Montana, Utah, Nevada, and Wyoming

Justice Matters is a quarterly newsletter from the Partnership for Safety and Justice that reports on criminal justice issues in northwestern states. A subscription is $7 per year for prisoners and $15 for others. Write to:

Partnership for Safety and Justice
P.O. Box 40085
Portland, OR 97240
(503) 335-8449
www.safetyandjustice.org

Ohio Prisoners
Against All Odds is a newsletter from CURE-Ohio which publishes information of interest to Ohio state prisoners. Write to:

Against All Odds
C/O CURE-Ohio
P.O. Box 4080
Columbus, OH 43214
www.cure-ohio.org

Pennsylvania Prisoners
Graterfriends is a monthly publication that provides an opportunity for prisoners incarcerated in a Pennsylvania state prison to voice their opinions and concerns about prison legislation and criminal justice issues. The newsletter strives to facilitate communication between prisoners and correctional staff and between prisoners and the outside community. Submit articles to Dee Johnson, Managing Editor, telephone extension 112.

An annual subscription is $3.00 for prisoners and $15 for others. To subscribe write:

Attention: *Graterfriends* Subscriptions
Pennsylvania Prison Society
245 North Broad Street, Suite 300
Philadelphia, PA 19107
(215) 564-6005, ext. 102
www.prisonsociety.org/pubs/gf.shtml

Virginia Prisoners

Inside Out is the quarterly newsletter of Virginia CURE which regularly covers legislative, prison, and criminal justice issues of interest to Virginia state prisoners. Subscriptions are fulfilled through CURE membership. Membership dues are $2 for prisoners (or 6 stamps), $15 for individuals, $25 for families, $50 for supporting members, and $150 for life members/ organizations, and $250 for benefactors. For more information, contact:

Inside Out
C/O Virginia CURE
P.O. Box 2310
Vienna, VA 22183
(703) 272-3624
www.vacure.org

Veterans

The Veterans Advocate is a newsletter which focuses on veterans' law, advocacy, and lifestyles. Subscriptions are $80 for 1 year or $120 for two years. To subscribe, contact:

The Veterans Advocate
C/O National Veterans Legal Services Program
P.O. Box 65762
Washington, DC 20035
(202) 265-8305
www.nvlsp.org

Unlisted or Discontinued Publications

The **Coalition for Prisoners' Rights Newsletter** had been published for 34 years, but as of June 2009 they had to stop mailing the monthly newsletter to their 9,100 subscribers due to lack of funding. The Real Cost of Prisons Project now posts the C.P.R. Newsletters online in PDF format starting with the July 2009 issue. The newsletter can be downloaded from http://www.realcostofprisons.org/coalition.html and sent to prisoners.

Prisoners can also send the "Coalition for Prisoner's Rights Newsletter" a large self-addressed, stamped envelope and they can request up to 12 issues at a time. Write to:

Coalition for Prisoners' Rights
P.O. Box 1911
Santa Fe, New Mexico 87504-1911

There are a number of other publications whose continued existence is uncertain and for which no information could be found. They include **Prison News Service**, a publication by and for prisoners in Canada and the U.S.; **Voices from Prison**, offering poetry, prose, art, and more from U.S. prisoners, **Inner Voices**, a magazine publishing literature, poetry, essays, and plays by prisoners; **Prison Poetry** by Robert R. Reldan, a prisoner at the New Jersey State Penitentiary writing to deal "with the madness of prison life;" and **Deadman Talking**, essays about life on death row written by a prisoner waiting for execution in California's San Quentin Prison.

PEN-PAL CLUBS

Cyberspace Inmates
9700 NW Louis Dr.
Cameron, MO 64429

InmateConnections.com
ConvictPenPal.com
465 NE 181st, #308
Portland, OR 97230

Inmate Scribes
P.O. Box 371303
Milwaukee, WI 53237

LoveAPrisoner.com
P.O. Box 5563
Thibodaux, LA 70302

PenACon.com
P.O. Box 533
North Dighton, MA 02764

Prison Inmates Online
8033 W. Sunset Blvd., #7000
Los Angeles, CA 90046

Prison Pen Pals
PO Box 120074
Ft. Lauderdale, FL 33312

WriteAPrisoner.com
P.O. Box 10
Edgewater, FL 32132

www.PrisonerPenPals.com
P.O. Box 19689
Houston, TX 77224

(Note: Although prisoners cannot go online, they can write this group which will then post pen pal profiles online. Online readers can send messages to prisoners via postal mail or through the service.)

Lists of Pen Pal clubs

The Pampered Prisoner can provide more information about developing pen pals. Send an email to email@thepamperedprisoner.com or write:

PO Box 141
Okotoks, AB., Canada T1S 1A4

Or

PMB #120 - 9220 SW Barbur Blvd. Suite 119
Portland, OR 97219

Appendix IV: Prisoners' Rights Organizations*

There are many prisoners' rights organizations in the United States and abroad. Some focus on local criminal justice matters while others are more global. Below is a truncated list of national organizations that advocate for criminal justice reform.

For a more comprehensive accounting, contact the ACLU National Prison Project (www.aclu.org/prisons) and obtain a copy of their *Prisoners' Assistance Directory*. This exhaustive publication can be purchased in printed form or downloaded at no cost from the ACLU website.

ACLU National Prison Project

Handles state and federal conditions of confinement claims affecting large numbers of prisoners. Publishes the *National Prison Project Journal* (available online at www.aclu.org/national-prison-project=journal-fall-2011/) and the *Prisoners' Assistance Directory*.
For more information, contact:

ACLU National Prison Project
915 15th Street, NW, 7th Floor
Washington, DC 20005
(202) 393-4930
www.aclu.org/prisons/

Amnesty International

Compiles information about prisoner torture, beatings, rape, etc. to include reports about U.S. prison conditions. They also work on death penalty issues.

* Reprinted with permission from *Prison Legal News*.

For more information, contact:

Amnesty International
5 Penn Plaza
New York, NY 10001
(212) 807-8400
www.amnestyusa.org

Center for Health Justice

Provides information related to HIV in prison. Inmates should contact them if they are not receiving proper HIV medication or are denied access to programs due to HIV status. For more information, contact:

Center for Health Justice
900 Avila Street, Suite 102
Los Angeles, CA 90012
HIV Hotline: (214) 229-0979 (allows collect calls from prisoners)
www.centerforhealthjustice.org

Critical Resistance

Seeks to build an international movement to abolish the prison-industrial complex, with offices in Florida, California, New York, Texas, and Louisiana. Publishes *The Abolitionist* newsletter.
For more information, contact:

Critical Resistance
1904 Franklin Street, #504
Oakland, CA 94612
(510) 444-0484
www.criticalresistance.org

The Exoneration Project

A non-profit organization dedicated to freeing prisoners who were wrongfully convicted. The Project represents innocent individuals in post-conviction legal proceedings; typical cases involve DNA testing, coerced confessions, police misconduct, the use of faulty evidence, junk science, faulty eyewitness testimony, and ineffective assistance of counsel. For more information, contact:

The Exoneration Project
312 North May Street, Suite 1000
Chicago, IL 60607
(312) 789-4955
www.exonerationproject.org

Family & Corrections Network

Primarily provides online resources for families of prisoners related to parenting, children of prisoners, prison visitation, mothers and fathers in prison, etc.
For more information, contact:

Family & Corrections Network
93 Old York Road, Suite 1, #570
Jenkintown, PA 19046
(212) 576-1110
www.fcnnetwork.org

FAMM (Families Against Mandatory Minimums)

Publishes the *FAMMGram* three times a year, with information about injustices resulting from mandatory minimum laws and an emphasis on federal laws. Recommended donation of $10 for a subscription.

For more information, contact:

FAMM
1612 K Street, NW, #700
Washington, DC 20006
(202) 822-6700
www.famm.org

FedCURE

FedCURE is the world's leading advocate for America's ever-growing federal inmate population. The organization focuses its efforts on the federal criminal justice system and the Federal Bureau of Prisons. Their tag line explains it all: "Working to establish a hybrid system of federal parole and increase good time allowances; and providing re-entry opportunities to federal offenders."

FedCURE
P.O. Box 15667
Plantation, FL 33318-5667
www.fedcure.com
Inmates: Corrlinks@fedcure.com

The Fortune Society

Provides post-release services and programs for prisoners in the New York City Area and occasionally publishes *Fortune News*, a free publication for prisoners that deals with criminal justice issues, primarily in New York.

For more information, contact:

The Fortune Society
29-76 Northern Boulevard
Long Island City, NY 11101
(212) 691-7554
www.fortunesociety.org

Innocence Project

Provides advocacy for wrongly convicted prisoners whose cases involve DNA evidence and are at the post-conviction appeal stage. They also maintain an online list of state-by-state innocence projects.
For more information, contact:

Innocence Project
40 Worth Street, Suite 701
New York, NY 10013
(212) 364-5340
www.innocenceproject.org

Just Detention International

Formerly "Stop Prison Rape," JDI seeks to end sexual violence against prisoners. They provide counseling resources for imprisoned and released rape survivors and have activists for almost every state.
For more information, contact:

Just Detention International
3325 Wilshire Boulevard
Los Angeles, CA 90010
(213) 384-1400
www.justdetention.org

Justice Denied

Although no longer publishing a print magazine, Justice Denied continues to provide the most comprehensive coverage of wrongful convictions and how and why they occur. Their content is available online, and includes all back issues of the *Justice Denied* magazine and a database of more than 3,000 wrongly convicted people.
For more information, contact:

Justice Denied
PO Box 68911
Seattle, WA 98168
(206) 335-4254
www.justicedenied.org

National CURE (Citizens United for Rehabilitation of Errants)

A national organization with state and special interest chapters that advocate rehabilitative opportunities for prisoners and less reliance on incarceration. Publishes the *CURE Newsletter*. Prisoners can become members for $2 per year. Contact CURE National for a listing of state and special issue chapters, many of which have their own newsletters.
For more information, contact:

CURE National
PO Box 2310
National Capitol Station
Washington, DC 20013
(202) 789-2126
www.curenational.org

November Coalition

Publishes *Razor Wire*, a biannual newsletter that reports on drug war-related issues, releasing prisoners of the drug war, and restoring civil rights. A subscription of $10 for prisoners and $30 for non-prisoners. For more information, contact:

November Coalition
282 West Astor
Coleville, WA 99114
(509) 684-1550
www.novembercoalition.org

PrisonEducation.com

The leader in prison education news and advocacy, the *Prison Education News* blog regularly publishes articles from thought leaders in the prison education realm, both incarcerated and not. Federal prisoners can sign up to receive free news alerts by adding news@prisonlawblog.com to their Corrlinks.com/TRULINCS contact list.
For more information, visit PrisonEducation.com

PrisonerResource.com

A well-researched prisoner law website with discussions about prison disciplinary proceedings, recent case law developments, prisoners' First Amendment and religious rights, and other topics of interest to prisoners, their families, and those in the legal profession. PrisonerResource.com is active on Facebook and Twitter. Federal prisoners can sign up to receive free news alerts by adding news@prisonlawblog.com to their Corrlinks.com/TRULINCS contact list.
For more information, visit PrisonerResource.com.

The Sentencing Project

A national policy research and advocacy organization that works for a fair and effective criminal justice system by promoting sentencing reforms and alternatives to incarceration. They produce reports on topics related to sentencing policy, racial disparities, drug policy, juvenile justice, and voting rights/disenfranchisement, which are available online.

For more information, contact:

The Sentencing Project
1705 DeSales Street, NW, 8th Floor
Washington, DC 20036
(202) 628-0871
www.sentencingproject.org

Appendix V: Sample Commissary List

Commissary offerings offered at each individual prison are dictated by local prison authorities. The following list will provide an idea of what sorts of items are available. This is an actual list of the commissary items and their prices at FCI Petersburg.

CANDY & NUTS

$0.65 Candy, All Star
$1.30 Candy, Dark Chocolate Bar
$0.70 Candy, Fire Balls
$0.80 Candy, Kit Kat Crispy Bar
$0.80 Candy, Jolly Ranchers
$0.60 Candy, Lemon Drops
$0.85 Candy, Milky Way
$0.80 Candy, Now & Later
$0.85 Candy, Reeses Peanut Butter Cups
$0.80 Candy, Snickers
$0.60 Candy, Starlight Mints
$0.80 Candy, 3 Musketeers
$0.80 Candy, Twix
$0.75 Candy, Sugar Free Wild Fruit
$1.95 Nuts, Almonds
$2.45 Nuts, Cashews
$1.45 Nuts, Chocolate Peanut Clusters
$2.80 Nuts, Goody Mix
$2.80 Nuts, Heavenly Trail Mix
$2.80 Nuts, Roasted Salted Peanuts
$2.80 Nuts, Unsalted Peanuts

CEREALS, CHIPS, & SNACKS

$0.55 Bagel, Cinnamon Raisin
$3.00 Cereal, Frosted Mini Wheats

$2.60 Cereal, Fruit & Nut Granola
$2.85 Cereal, Granola Vanilla Cherry
$1.30 Chips, BBQ Ruffle
$2.25 Chips, Cheetos
$1.30 Chips, Cheddar & Sour Cream
$2.60 Chips, Chili Cheese Fritos
$2.30 Chips, Nacho Cheese Tortilla
$1.30 Chips, Ripple
$2.35 Cookies, Chocolate Chip
$0.90 Cookies, Duplex Creme
$0.55 Cookies, Maria's
$1.75 Cookies, Peanut Butter Cream
$1.55 Cookies, Shortbread
$3.10 Crackers, Chex Mix Hot & Spicy
$2.25 Crackers, Graham
$2.05 Crackers, Saltines
$2.10 Crackers, Snack (like Ritz)
$0.55 Granola Bar, Oats N' Honey
$1.70 Lil Debbie, Apple Oatmeal Pies
$0.65 Lil Debbie, Iced Honey Buns
$1.85 Oatmeal, Rolled
$1.20 Olives - Pouch
$0.80 Pickle, Dill
$1.10 Popcorn, Buttered
$1.15 Popcorn, White Cheddar
$1.65 Pop-Tarts, Strawberry
$0.55 Sweet & Salty Nut Bar
$1.80 Ultra Fit Energy Bar

SOUPS & RICE

$1.95 Beans, Refried With Spices
$1.00 Mac & Cheese
$1.15 Rice, White

- $1.30 Rice, Whole Grain Brown
- $0.45 Hot & Spicy Beef Cup Soup
- $0.30 Soup, Chicken (Ramen)
- $0.30 Soup, Low Sodium Beef (Ramen)
- $0.30 Soup, Spicy Vegetable (Ramen)
- $0.30 Soup, Texas Beef (Ramen)
- $1.40 Tortilla Shells (10 Count)

FRUIT

- $2.85 Dates
- $3.10 Figs

ICE CREAM

- $2.25 Banana Pudding Pint
- $2.25 Butter Pecan Pint (No Sugar Added)
- $2.25 Strawberry Cheesecake Pint
- $0.35 Very Very Cherry Ice Pop

MEAT & FISH PRODUCTS

- $1.00 Beef Stick, Hot Beef Deli
- $1.55 Beef Stew - Pouch
- $1.55 Chili, Brushy Creek
- $1.75 Clams
- $1.60 Fish, Light Tuna in Water (3 oz.)
- $1.10 Fish, Mackerel
- $2.70 Fish, Pink Salmon (6 oz.)
- $1.00 Fish, Sardines in Oil
- $1.95 Fish, Yellowfin Tuna Steak
- $1.65 Oysters - Pouch
- $1.90 Pepperoni, Sliced
- $1.45 Sausage, Beef Summer
- $2.35 Sausage, Halal Beef Summer
- $1.65 Sausage, Honey Pepper Turkey

$1.95 Taco Mix
$1.80 Turkey Bites
$1.20 Turkey & Swiss Stick

CONDIMENTS & BEVERAGES
$1.50 Cheese, Jalapeno
$1.70 Cheese, Mozzarella Block
$1.50 Cheese, Sharp
$0.40 Cheese, Squeeze Cream
$3.30 Coffee, Columbian (3 oz.)
$3.40 Coffee, Decaf (3 oz.)
$1.60 Coffee, Cappuccino
$3.25 Coffee, Maxwell House
$1.95 Creamer, Coffeemate
$3.70 Creamer, French Vanilla
$2.75 Drink Singles, Peach Tea/Lemonade
$1.30 Hawaiian Punch BerryBlue Singles (Sugar Free)
$1.30 Hawaiian Punch Greenberry Singles (Sugar Free)
$1.30 Hawaiian Punch Juicy Red Singles (Sugar Free)
$1.30 Hawaiian Punch Lemonberry Singles (Sugar Free)
$1.30 Hawaiian Punch Orange Singles (Sugar Free)
$2.85 Honey, Pure
$1.50 Hot Cocoa Bag
$2.70 Jelly, Strawberry Jam (16 oz.)
$0.90 Juice, Lemon Squeeze
$1.20 Juice, V-8
$2.10 Mayonnaise (11.5 oz.)
$5.20 Milk, Carnation Dry
$2.70 Olive Oil
$2.45 Peanut Butter Creamy
$2.15 Peppers, Hot Giardiniera
$1.50 Salt & Pepper Shakers
$0.95 Sauce, Louisiana Hot

$1.55 Sauce, Soy
$1.80 Sauce, Sweet and Hot Asian
$2.85 Sauce, Sriracha Hot Chili
$3.75 Seasoning, Large Assorted Mix
$3.70 Seasoning, Mrs. Dash
$1.60 Seasoning, Goya Sazon
$4.85 Soft Drink, Diet Sierra Mist (12 pack)
$4.85 Soft Drink, Dr. Pepper (12 pack)
$4.40 Soft Drink, Ginger Ale (12 pack)
$4.85 Soft Drink, Mountain Dew (12 pack)
$4.85 Soft Drink, Pepsi (12 pack)
$4.85 Soft Drink, Pepsi One (12 pack)
$4.40 Soft Drink, Root Beer (12 pack)
$2.95 Splenda
$2.80 Sweet & Low (100 count)
$1.95 Tea, Bags - Keffee (48 bags)
$1.95 Vanilla Pudding
$0.40 Water, Bottled

RADIOS, BATTERIES & FANS

$2.10 AA Batteries (4 pack) Duracell
$2.10 AAA Batteries (4 pack) Duracell
$10.50 Alarm Clock
$21.50 Earbuds, JVC
$12.75 Earbuds, Sony Clip-On
$34.50 Headphones, Koss HQ1
$11.50 Headphones, Koss PTX-6
$69.20 MP3 Player, San Disk
$88.40 MP3 Player, San Disk Sport
$41.60 Radio, Sony SRF-M35
$2.50 Watch Battery, #2016
$2.50 Watch Battery, #2025
$2.50 Watch Battery, #2032

$57.50 Watch, Casio G-Shock
$15.60 Watch, Timex 1440
$7.15 Watchband, Casio G-Shock
$11.45 Watchband, Ironman
$2.10 Watchband, Velcro

HAIR & SHAVING PRODUCTS
$5.95 African Royale Hot Six Oil
$0.90 Afro, Comb
$0.80 Afro, Pick
$5.50 Bag, Shaving
$2.55 Black Doo Rag
$2.20 Brush & Comb Set, Men's Club
$2.90 Brush, Military No Handle
$1.60 Brush, Hair Vented
$3.80 Bump Stopper
$1.30 Conditioner, Balsam
$1.60 Conditioner, Coconut Oil
$3.00 Conditioner, Nexxus
$6.70 Conditioner, Panteen
$6.55 Grease, African Pride
$2.45 Grease, Murray's Pomade
$3.85 Grease, Sulfur 8 Original
$3.65 Grease, Sulfur 8 Lock Twist
$1.15 Hair Ties, Black
$2.60 Moisturizer, Pro-Line
$3.05 Protein 29 Hair Gel
$2.25 Razor, Bic Twin Blade
$12.35 Razor, Mach 3
$19.00 Razor, Mach 3 Refill
$5.00 Razor, Pro-Tection Triple Blade
$2.90 Razor, Pro-Tection Refill
$1.30 Shampoo, Basalm

$7.80 Shampoo, Head & Shoulders
$2.25 Shampoo, Aloe & Ginseng
$6.70 Shampoo, Panteen
$3.30 Shampoo, Suave 2-In-1
$2.85 Shave, Aftashave
$4.25 Shave, Magic Shave Cream Regular
$2.90 Shave, Magic Shave Gold
$2.25 Shave, Brushless Cream
$3.20 Styling Gel

HEALTH & MEDICAL
$2.50 A&D Ointment
$1.65 Acne Cream
$3.80 Antacid Tabs Variety
$1.90 Anti-diarrhea Tabs
$1.70 Artificial Tears
$0.90 Band-Aids
$2.10 Blistex
$15.75 Breath Right Nose Strips
$2.05 Calcium Tablets
$1.80 Calamine Lotion
$0.85 Chap-It Lip Balm
$2.45 Claritin (Generic)
$0.90 Clippers, Fingernail
$5.20 Corn Remover
$0.90 Cough Drops, Cherry
$0.90 Cough Drops, Honey/Lemon
$2.45 Cough Syrup
$1.90 Cream, Antifungal (Clotrimazole)
$1.70 Cream, Antifungal (Tolnaftate)
$2.20 Cream, Noxzema Skin (2.5 oz.)
$4.50 Dandrex Blue Shampoo
$3.10 Dibucane Ointment

$1.85 Earwax Drops (Carbamide)
$2.35 Eye Drops
$7.20 Fiber Laxative Konsyl
$3.45 Hand Sanitizer Foam Pump
$2.10 Hydrocortisone Cream 1%
$5.00 Kaopectate
$7.70 Lac-Dose Lactaid Captabs
$3.00 Lotion, Suave
$14.30 Lotion, Lac-Hydrin Medicated
$10.80 Lotion, Lubriderm
$2.75 Lotion, Mild Hypo-Allergenic
$5.20 Lotion, Palmer's Cocoa Butter
$2.30 Miconazole
$2.55 Milk of Magnesia (12 oz.)
$6.40 Moisturizer, Saint lve Facial
$2.50 Muscle Rub (like Ben Gay)
$6.65 Mustache Scissors
$3.50 Mylanta, Antacid Liquid
$4.40 Naproxen Anti-inflammatory
$6.65 Neutrogena T-Gel Shampoo
$2.55 Oil, Baby
$3.65 Ointment, Hemorrhoid
$20.25 Omeprazole (generic Prilosec)
$1.60 Oral Analgesic
$2.15 Powder, Bath
$4.20 Powder, Quinsana Foot
$1.90 Pumice Stone
$1.05 Q-Tips (90 count)
$8.00 Ranitidine (like Zantac)
$4.25 Scrub Pad, Stridex
$1.85 Spray, Nasal
$4.75 St. Ive's Oil Free Blemish Control
$4.75 St. Ive's Oil Free Facial Scrub

$2.05 Stick, Cocoa Butter
$3.15 Stool Softener
$3.90 Sun Block SPF30
$1.60 Tablets, Allergy
$1.65 Tablets, Aspirin
$2.55 Tablets, Ibuprofen
$2.05 Tablets, Multivitamins
$2.35 Tablets, Non-aspirin
$2.30 Tablets, Tums Sodium Free Original
$1.95 Tablets, Vitamin C
$2.55 Tablets, Vitamin E
$5.00 Theratrum Complete (like Centrum)
$2.65 Throat Lozenges
$1.20 Tissuc, Facial (100 count)
$1.15 Toe Nail Clipper
$2.50 Triple Antibiotic Ointment
$1.15 Tweezers
$1.30 Vapor Rub
$1.70 Vaseline Lip Therapy
$1.20 Vaseline, Petroleum Jelly
$6.20 Visine-A (Allergy)

DENTAL PRODUCTS

$1.70 Dental Floss
$1.45 Dental Flosser Gum Stimulator
$5.20 Effergrip Denture Adhesive
$4.65 Mouthwash, Crest Pro-Health
$0.50 Toothbrush Holder
$0.95 Toothbrush, Colgate (soft)
$1.80 Toothbrush, Denture
$2.10 Toothpaste, Aim Tarter Control
$1.90 Toothpaste, Close-Up (4 oz.)
$3.80 Toothpaste, Colgate Total

$2.90 Toothpaste, Colgate with Baking Soda
$3.50 Toothpaste, Denture Cleanser
$6.75 Toothpaste, Sensodyne (4 oz.)

RELIGIOUS ITEMS & FRAGRANCES
$6.50 Kufi
$4.50 Native American Bandana
$4.00 Prayer Oil
$4.50 Fragrance
$15.55 Rastafarian Tam
$5.40 Yalmakah

GREETING CARDS
$2.35 All Occasion Cards (5 pack)
$1.05 Birthday Card (male or female)
$1.05 Holiday Card (male or female)

ITEMS TO ORDER
$2.85 Reading Glasses (various strengths)
$12.00 - $99.00 Various Tennis Shoes, Sports Cleats, and Boots

SPORTS EQUIPMENT & CLOTHING
$5.85 Thermal Pants (LG, XL)
$6.90 Thermal Pants (2X, 3X)
$12.35 Thermal Pants (4X)
$15.75 Thermal Pants (5X, 6X)
$6.10 Thermal Shirt (LG, XL)
$6.90 Thermal Shirt (2X, 3X)
$11.85 Thermal Shirt (4X)
$16.40 Thermal Shirt (5X, 6X)
$6.50 Acrylic Scarf
$5.95 Athletic Supporter (MD, LG, XL)
$20.80 Batting Gloves (LG, XL)

$6.50 Boxer Briefs Gray, 2 Pack (SM-XL)
$8.45 Boxer Briefs Gray, 2 Pack (2X-4X)
$7.80 Briefs (SM, MD, LG, XL)
$11.05 Briefs (2X, 3X)
$15.60 Briefs (4X)
$3.95 Cap, Mesh Baseball Gray
$3.30 Cap, Knit
$11.85 Handballs
$2.10 Headband
$10.15 Knee Brace (SM, MD, LG, XL)
$9.10 Mesh Gym Bag
$18.20 Mesh Shorts With Pockets (SM-XL)
$19.50 Mesh Shorts With Pockets (2X, 3X)
$22.10 Mesh Shorts With Pockets (4X-6X)
$3.40 Mouthpiece
$5.10 Racquetballs (3 Pack)
$11.00 Socks, Gold Toe (6 Pack)
$11.00 Socks, Gold Toe Ankle (6 Pack)
$6.95 Shower Clogs (Size 8-15)
$17.55 Sweat Pants (SM-2X)
$17.55 Sweat Pants (3X, 4X)
$22.00 Sweat Pants (5X, 6X)
$15.60 Sweat Shirt (SM-2X)
$16.90 Sweat Shirt (3X, 4X)
$22.00 Sweat Shirt (5X, 6X))
$16.90 Sweat Shorts (SM-2X)
$19.50 Sweat Shorts (3X-6X)
$10.50 Tank Tops (SM, MD)
$11.45 Tank Tops (LG, XL)
$13.50 Tank Tops (2X, 3X)
$5.10 Tennis Balls
$5.60 T-Shirts, Grey (LG-3X)
$9.10 T-Shirts, Grey (4X-6X)

$12.35 T-Shirts, White (LG, XL)
$15.60 T-Shirts, White (2X, 3X)
$14.45 T-Shirts, White (4X)
$17.55 Weight Gloves (MD-XL)
$3.80 Wool Gloves
$2.20 Wrist Bands

PHOTO TICKET, COPY CARD, & STAMPS
$1.20 Global Stamp
$0.61 Sixty-one Cent Stamp
$0.49 Forever Stamp
$0.17 Seventeen-cent Stamp
$0.02 Two-cent Stamp
$1.00 Photo Ticket
$6.50 Copy Card

SUNDRY ITEMS
$1.55 Correction Tape
$22.75 Fan 12"
$19.40 Print Wheel
$7.75 Typewriter Ribbon
$0.80 Address/Phone Book
$1.10 Air Freshener, Black Ice
$12.35 Album, Photo
$6.40 Album, Photo Inserts
$12.95 Book Light, Mighty Bright
$3.65 Bottle, Serving 1 Quart
$2.30 Bowl, Plastic with Lid
$19.50 Calculator Casio FX300
$1.50 Carbon Paper (10 count)
$1.65 Cards, Pinochle
$1.65 Cards, Poker

$10.40 Chess Set
$0.55 Cup with Lid
$1.95 Cup, Insulated with Lid Clear
$11.60 Cushion, Arch Support
$1.15 Denture Cup with Lid
$3.85 Dictionary, English
$2.25 Dictionary, English/Spanish
$1.45 Document Folder, Clear
$1.80 Envelopes (Box of 50)
$0.75 Handkerchief
$2.35 Insoles, Foot Fresher
$7.75 Jug, 1/2 Gallon Clear
$5.15 Laundry Bag
$3.65 Liquid Shoe Polish, White
$6.50 Lock, Combination
$2.45 Locker Mirror
$1.10 Pad, 8.5 X 11 Ruled Writing
$1.60 Pad, Legal
$17.20 Lock, Heavy Duty
$1.10 Pen, Bic 2 Pack (Black or Blue)
$0.15 Pencils, #2
$0.80 Pencil Sharpener
$1.05 Plastic Fork & Spoon Set
$4.25 Rain Poncho
$1.95 Sewing Kit
$1.15 Shoe Laces, 54" (Black or White)
$6.45 Sunglasses
$6.05 Toilet Paper, Charmin (6 Pack)
$7.95 Towel, Large Bath
$1.95 Typing Paper (100 Count)
$2.50 Washcloth (Tan)
$1.85 Wireless Notebook

DEODORANTS & SOAPS

- $2.55 Bounce Softener
- $2.85 Deodorant, Degree
- $2.50 Deodorant, Mennen Regular
- $1.50 Deodorant, Dial Roll-On
- $2.45 Deodorant, Sure
- $6.20 Detergent, Tide
- $1.30 Dish Liquid Soap, Ajax
- $0.65 Plastic Soap Dish
- $1.85 Soap, Dove Unscented
- $2.95 Soap, Irish Spring Sport (3 Pack)
- $2.05 Soap, Ivory (3 Pack)
- $1.00 Soap, Lever 2000
- $1.70 Soap, Liquid Hand
- $1.75 Soap, Mt. Breeze Body Wash
- $3.65 Soap, Neutrogena
- $2.45 Soap, Nubian Honey Black Seed
- $3.45 Soap, Safeguard Antibacterial (4 Pack)

Appendix VI: Sample SHU Commissary List

Federal prisoners confined to the Special Housing Unit (SHU) generally have limited access to the commissary. Orders are placed once a week and delivered by commissary staff. Offerings will depend on the prison's location and the reason the prisoner is confined in the SHU.

For example, those in the SHU on administrative detention status (prisoners under investigation, in transit, or in protective custody) have access to a wider commissary selection than those in the SHU on disciplinary segregation status.

What follows is the FCI Petersburg administrative detention commissary list. The same list is used for those on both administrative detention and disciplinary segregation statuses but those on disciplinary segregation status are barred from purchasing any food, beverage, or electronic items.

FOOD ITEMS (LIMIT 1 EACH)

$2.70 Lance Variety Pack

$2.45 Creamy Peanut Butter

MEATS (LIMIT 2 EACH)

$1.10 Mackerel

$2.30 Tuna

CHIPS (LIMIT ANY 1 BAG)

$1.30 Ripple Potato Chips

$2.30 Nacho Tortilla Chips

COOKIES & CAKES (LIMIT ANY 3)

$0.55 Cinnamon Raisin Bagel

$0.90 Duplex Cream Cookies

$0.55 Maria's Cookies

CANDY (LIMIT ANY 10)
- $0.80 M&M Pretzel
- $0.80 Twix
- $0.80 Snickers
- $0.60 Starlite Mints

BEVERAGES (LIMIT ANY 3)
- $3.30 Columbian Coffee
- $3.40 Decaf Coffee

RADIO & BATTERIES (LIMIT 2 PACKS)
- $41.60 Sony Radio (SRF-M35FP)
- $12.75 Sony Earbuds (MDR-J10)
- $2.10 AA Batteries (4 pack)
- $2.10 AAA Batteries (4 pack)

POSTAGE STAMPS ($9.20 MAX)
- $1.20 Global Stamp
- $0.61 Sixty-one Cent Stamp
- $0.46 Forty-six Cent Stamp
- $0.17 Seventeen-cent Stamp
- $0.01 One-cent Stamp

HAIR PRODUCTS (LIMIT ANY 2)
- $1.30 Balsam Shampoo
- $1.30 Balsam Conditioner

HYGIENE ITEMS (LIMIT ANY 2)
- $10.80 Lubriderm Lotion
- $2.75 Next 1 Hypo-Allergenic Lotion
- $5.20 Palmer's Cocoa Butter Lotion
- $2.85 Degree Deodorant

SOAPS (LIMIT ANY 1 SOAP)

$1.85 Dove Unscented

$1.00 Lever 2000

$0.65 Soap Dish

VITAMINS (LIMIT 1 EACH)

$2.05 Multi-Vitamins

$1.95 Vitamin C

$2.05 Calcium Tablets

$2.55 Vitamin E

$5.00 Theratrum Complete Multivitamin

SHOWER CLOGS

$6.95 Sizes 8/9/10/12/13/14/15

ENVELOPES/CARDS

$1.05 Birthday Cards (Limit 2)

$1.05 Holiday Cards (Limit 2)

$0.15 Legal Envelopes (Limit 5)

OVER-THE-COUNTER MEDICATIONS (LIMIT 1 EACH)

$1.60 Allergy Tablets

$4.50 Anti-dandruff Shampoo

$1.65 Aspirin

$2.35 Non-aspirin (Acetaminophen)

$3.80 Antacid Variety Tabs

$1.90 Anti-diarrhea Tabs

$1.90 Antifungal Cream (Clotrimazole)

$1.70 Artificial Tears

$1.80 Calamine Lotion

$2.45 Claritin Tablets (Generic)

$1.65 Clearasil (Acne Medications Generic)

$5.20 Corn Remover
$0.90 Cough Drops
$0.90 Cough Drops (Honey Lemon)
$2.45 Cough Syrup
$1.85 Ear Wax Drops
$7.20 Fiber Laxative Powder (Konsyl-D)
$3.65 Hemorrhoid Ointment
$2.10 Hydrocortisone Cream
$2.55 Ibuprofen
$5.00 Kaopectate
$6.20 Lactaid Ultra Caplet
$13.30 Lamisil Antifungal Cream
$7.20 Laxative, Natural
$3.50 Mylanta/Antacid
$2.55 Milk of Magnesia
$4.40 Naproxen
$1.85 Nasal Spray
$6.65 Neutrogena T-Gel Shampoo
$20.25 Omeprazole (Generic Prilosec)
$4.20 Quinsana Foot Powder
$8.00 Ranitidine (Like Zantac)
$3.15 Stool Softener
$1.70 Tolnaftate 1% Antifungal Cream
$2.65 Sore Throat Lozenges
$6.20 Visine-A (Allergy)

Appendix VII: Sample National Menus

The Federal Bureau of Prisons produces a national menu that local federal prisons have the option to use, although they are not required to do so. If a local federal prison decides to create its own menu, they have that right as long as it conforms to nutrition and calorie standards set by national policy.

The national menus are listed here. They show what is to be served for breakfast, lunch, and dinner for a complete month. These are just examples and are subject to change by the national foodservice administrator or by the local foodservice administrator. They provide an idea of what sorts of foods are available in the cafeteria to federal prisoners.

Federal Bureau of Prisons (FBOP)
Menu Type: Mainline FY 2014
Weekly Menu Date Range: 10/6/2013 to 11/9/2013
Please note what our symbols mean:

♥ = heart healthy
= no meat or flesh entrée, and
* = pork.

Week # 1

Sunday	Monday	Tuesday	Wednesday	Thursday	Friday	Saturday
BREAKFAST Bran Flakes ♥ Breakfast Cake or Whole Wheat Bread ♥ Jelly, SF (2) ♥ Sugar, Substitute Packs. -Margarine Pat ♥ Fresh Apple ♥ Coffee ♥ Skim Milk ♥	BREAKFAST Creamed Beef Home Fried Potatoes or Boiled Potatoes ♥ Hot Oatmeal ♥ Jelly, SF (2) ♥ 2 Biscuits or Whole Wheat Bread ♥ Margarine Pat ♥ Fresh Apple ♥ Skim Milk ♥	BREAKFAST Hot Grits ♥ Breakfast Cake or Whole Wheat Bread ♥ Jelly, SF (2) ♥ Sugar, Substitute Packs Margarine Pat ♥ Fresh Apple ♥ Skim Milk ♥	BREAKFAST Bran Flakes ♥ Pancakes & Syrup or Whole Wheat Bread ♥ Jelly, SF (2) ♥ Sugar, Substitute Packs. Margarine Pat ♥ Fresh Bananas ♥ Skim Milk ♥	BREAKFAST Hot Grits ♥ Breakfast Cake or Whole Wheat Bread ♥ Jelly, SF (2) ♥ Sugar, Substitute Packs. Margarine Pat ♥ Fresh Apple ♥ Skim Milk ♥	BREAKFAST Hot Oatmeal ♥ French Toast W/Syrup or Whole Wheat Bread ♥ Jelly, SF (2) ♥ Sugar, Substitute Packs Margarine Pat ♥ Fresh Bananas ♥ Skim Milk ♥	BREAKFAST Bran Flakes ♥ Breakfast Cake or Whole Wheat Bread ♥ Jelly, SF (2) ♥ Sugar, Substitute Packs Margarine Pat ♥ Fresh Apple ♥ Coffee ♥ Skim Milk ♥
LUNCH Plain Omelet ♥ Breakfast Sausage Home Fried Potatoes or Boiled Potatoes ♥ Salsa Jelly, SF (2) ♥ Whole Wheat Bread ♥ Margarine Pat ♥ Fresh Fruit ♥ Beverage	LUNCH Chili Dogs or Vegetable Chili ♥ Potato Chips or Baked Potato ♥ Mixed Vegetables ♥ Catsup-Mustard Hot Dog Buns or Whole Wheat Bread ♥ Margarine Pat ♥ Fresh Fruit ♥ Beverage	LUNCH Chicken Tenders or Braised Chicken ♥ or Cottage Cheese # Steamed Rice ♥ Kidney Beans ♥ Carrots ♥ Whole Wheat Bread ♥ Margarine Pat ♥ Dessert or Fresh Fruit ♥ Beverage	LUNCH Hamburger or Soy Burger w/Cheese # French Fried Potatoes or Baked Potato ♥ Shredded Lettuce ♥ Catsup-Mustard-Pickles Salad Dressing Hamburger Buns or Whole Wheat Bread ♥ Margarine Pat ♥ Fresh Fruit ♥ Beverage	LUNCH Baked Chicken ♥ or Peanut Butter # Jelly, SF (2) ♥ Steamed Rice ♥ Pinto Beans ♥ Green Beans ♥ Whole Wheat Bread ♥ Margarine Pat ♥ Dessert or Fresh Fruit ♥ Beverage	LUNCH Breaded Fish or Baked Fish ♥ or Soy Burger # Salad Dressing Mac Salad ♥ Green Peas ♥ Tartar Sauce Hamburger Buns or Whole Wheat Bread ♥ Margarine Pat Whole Wheat Bread ♥ Fresh Fruit Beverage	LUNCH Kielbasa Sausage or Cottage Cheese # ♥ Potatoes Au Gratin or Baked Potato ♥ Carrots ♥ Sauerkraut-Mustard Whole Wheat Bread ♥ Margarine Pat ♥ Dessert or Fresh Fruit ♥ Beverage
DINNER Roast Beef ♥ or Cottage Cheese # Baked Potato ♥ Black Eyed Peas ♥ Green Beans ♥ Brown Gravy Whole Wheat Bread ♥ Margarine Pat ♥ Beverage	DINNER Meatloaf ♥ or Soy Burger # w/ Salad Dressing Mashed Potatoes ♥ AWK Corn ♥ V Tomato Gravy Whole Wheat Bread ♥ Margarine Pat ♥ Beverage	DINNER Vegetable Soup ♥ Chicken Salad ♥ or Peanut Butter ♥ # Jelly, SF (2) ♥ # Green Peas ♥ Lettuce-tomato-Onion- Pickles ♥ Whole Wheat Bread ♥ Margarine Pat ♥ Beverage	DINNER Pork Chops ♥ * or Hummus # Baked Sweet Potato ♥ Navy Beans ♥ Mixed Greens ♥ Whole Wheat Bread ♥ Margarine Pat ♥ Beverage	DINNER Lasagna or Beef & Noodles or Veggie Lasagna # Spinach ♥ Garden Salad ♥ Salad Dressing Garlic Bread or Whole Wheat Bread ♥ Margarine Pat ♥ Beverage	DINNER Chicken Fried Rice or Chicken & Rice ♥ or Tofu & Rice ♥ # Steamed Broccoli ♥ Whole Wheat Bread ♥ Margarine Pat ♥ Beverage	DINNER Spaghetti Meat sauce ♥ or Marinara Sauce # Spinach ♥ Garlic Bread or Whole Wheat Bread ♥ Margarine Pat ♥ Beverage

Week # 2

Sunday	Monday	Tuesday	Wednesday	Thursday	Friday	Saturday
BREAKFAST Bran Flakes ♥ Breakfast Cake or Whole Wheat Bread ♥ Jelly, SF (2) ♥ Sugar, Substitute Pks. Margarine Pat ♥ Fresh Apple ♥ Coffee Skim Milk ♥	BREAKFAST Creamed Beef Home Fried Potatoes or Boiled Potatoes ♥ Hot Oatmeal ♥ Jelly, SF (2) ♥ Biscuits (2) or Whole Wheat Bread ♥ Margarine Pat ♥ Fresh Apple ♥ Skim Milk ♥	BREAKFAST Hot Grits ♥ Breakfast Cake or Whole Wheat Bread ♥ Jelly, SF (2) ♥ Sugar, Substitute Pks. Margarine Pat ♥ Fresh Apple ♥ Skim Milk ♥	BREAKFAST Bran Flakes ♥ Pancakes & Syrup or Whole Wheat Bread ♥ Jelly, SF (2) ♥ Sugar, Substitute Pks. Margarine Pat ♥ Fresh Bananas ♥ Skim Milk ♥	BREAKFAST Hot Grits ♥ Breakfast Cake or Whole Wheat Bread ♥ Jelly, SF (2) ♥ s Sugar, Substitute Pks. Margarine Pat ♥ Fresh Apple ♥ Skim Milk ♥	BREAKFAST Hot Oatmeal ♥ French Toast & Syrup or Whole Wheat Bread ♥ Jelly, SF (2) ♥ Sugar, Substitute Pks. Margarine Pat ♥ Fresh Bananas ♥ Skim Milk ♥	BREAKFAST Bran Flakes ♥ Breakfast Cake or Whole Wheat Bread ♥ Jelly, SF (2) ♥ Sugar, Substitute Pks. Margarine Pat ♥ Fresh Apple ♥ Coffee Skim Milk ♥
LUNCH Scrambled Eggs ♥ Pancakes & Syrup or Oven Brown Potato ♥ Whole Wheat Bread ♥ Baked Turkey Ham ♥ Jelly, SF (2) ♥ Margarine Pat ♥ Fresh Fruit ♥ Beverage	LUNCH Broccoli Soup Chicken Wraps or Cheese Wrap # Salad Dressing Potato Salad ♥ Green Beans ♥ Margarine Pat ♥ Fresh Fruit ♥ Beverage	LUNCH Meat Pizza or Beef & Noodles ♥ Whole Wheat Bread ♥ or Cheese Pizza # Spinach ♥ Garden Salad ♥ Asst. Salad Dressing Margarine Pat ♥ Dessert or Fresh Fruit ♥ Beverage	LUNCH Hamburger ♥ or Soy Burger w/ Cheese # Potato Chips or Baked Potato ♥ Shredded Lettuce ♥ Catsup-Mustard- Pickles Salad Dressing Hamburger Buns or Whole Wheat Bread ♥ Margarine Pat ♥ Fresh Fruit ♥ Beverage	LUNCH Fried Chicken or Baked Chicken ♥ or Peanut Butter # Jelly, SF (2) ♥ Mashed Potatoes ♥ Carrots ♥ Chicken Gravy Whole Wheat Bread ♥ Margarine Pat ♥ Dessert or Fresh Fruit ♥ Beverage	LUNCH Fried Fish Fillet or Baked Fish ♥ or Peanut Butter # Jelly, SF (2) ♥ Macaroni and Cheese or Macaroni & Tomato ♥ Green Beans ♥ Tartar Sauce Cornbread or Whole Wheat Bread ♥ Margarine Pat ♥ Fresh Fruit ♥ Beverage	LUNCH Meatball Sub ♥ or Soy Burger # Spaghetti & Marinara ♥ Spinach ♥ Hoagie Bun or Whole Wheat Bread ♥ Margarine Pat ♥ Dessert or Fresh Fruit ♥ Beverage
DINNER Beef Stew ♥ or Soy Beef Stew # Egg Noodles ♥ Simmered Cabbage ♥ Whole Wheat Bread ♥ Margarine Pat ♥ Beverage	DINNER Pork BBQ * or Pork Roast ♥* or Hummus # Baked Sweet Potato ♥\- Black Eyed Peas ♥ Peas & Carrots ♥ Whole Wheat Bread ♥ Margarine Pat ♥ Beverage	DINNER Beef & Bean Burrito or Beef Burrito ♥ Bean & Cheese Burrito ♥ Mexican Rice or Steamed Rice ♥ Black Beans ♥ WK Corn ♥ Margarine Pat ♥ Salsa Beverage	DINNER Bean Soup ♥ # Cold Cut Hoagie or 2 Boiled Eggs # ♥ Potato Salad ♥ Lettuce Leaf ♥ Mustard Salad Dressing Hoagie Bun or Whole Wheat Bread ♥ Margarine Pat ♥ Beverage	DINNER Chili Mac ♥ or No-Meat Chili Mac # ♥ Green Beans ♥ Garden Salad ♥ Asst. Salad Dressing Corn Bread Margarine Pat ♥ Beverage	DINNER Chicken Lo Mein or Ckn & Veggies ♥ or Cottage Cheese # Spaghetti ♥ Green Peas ♥ Whole Wheat Bread ♥ Margarine Pat ♥ Beverage	DINNER Beef Tacos ♥ or Soy Tacos # Cilantro Rice ♥ Pinto Beans ♥ WK Corn ♥ Shredded Lettuce ♥ Salsa Taco Shells Margarine Pat ♥ Beverage

Week # 3

Sunday	**Monday**	**Tuesday**	**Wednesday**	**Thursday**	**Friday**	**Saturday**
BREAKFAST Bran Flakes ♥ Breakfast Cake or Whole Wheat Bread ♥ Jelly, SF (2) ♥ Sugar, Substitute Pks. Margarine Pat ♥ Fresh Apple ♥ Coffee Skim Milk ♥	BREAKFAST Creamed Beef Home Fried Potatoes or Boiled Potatoes ♥ Hot Oatmeal ♥ Jelly, SF (2) ♥ Biscuits (2) or Whole Wheat Bread ♥ Margarine Pat ♥ Fresh Apple ♥ Skim Milk ♥	BREAKFAST Hot Grits ♥ Breakfast Cake or Whole Wheat Bread ♥ Jelly, SF (2) ♥ Sugar, Substitute Pks. Margarine Pat ♥ Fresh Apple ♥ Skim Milk ♥	BREAKFAST Bran Flakes ♥ Pancakes & Syrup or Whole Wheat Bread ♥ Jelly, SF (2) ♥ Sugar, Substitute Pks. Margarine Pat ♥ Fresh Bananas ♥ Skim Milk ♥	BREAKFAST Hot Grits ♥ Breakfast Cake or Whole Wheat Bread ♥ Jelly, SF (2) ♥ Sugar, Substitute Pks. ♥ Margarine Pat ♥ Fresh Apple ♥ Skim Milk ♥	BREAKFAST Hot Oatmeal ♥ French Toast &/Syrup or Whole Wheat Bread ♥ Jelly, SF (2) ♥ Sugar, Substitute Pks. Margarine Pat ♥ Fresh Bananas ♥ Skim Milk ♥	BREAKFAST Bran Flakes ♥ Breakfast Cake or Whole Wheat Bread ♥ Jelly, SF (2) ♥ Sugar, Substitute Pks. Margarine Pat ♥ Fresh Apple ♥ Coffee Skim Milk ♥
LUNCH Cheese Omelet or Plain Omelet ♥ Home Fried Potatoes or Boiled Potatoes ♥ Breakfast Sausage Jelly, SF (2) ♥ Whole Wheat Bread ♥ Margarine Pat ♥ Fresh Fruit ♥ Beverage	LUNCH Chicken Cheese Steak or Chicken Salad ♥ or Cheese Sandwich # Salad Dressing Potato Chips or Baked Potato ♥ Carrots ♥ Hoagie Bun or Whole Wheat Bread ♥ Margarine Pat ♥ Fresh Fruit ♥ Beverage	LUNCH Tomato Rice Soup ♥ Tuna Salad ♥ or Boiled Eggs (2) ♥ Lettuce Leaf ♥ Salad Dressing Italian Pasta Salad ♥ Baked Potato ♥ Steamed Broccoli ♥ Whole Wheat Bread ♥ Margarine Pat ♥ Dessert or Fresh Fruit ♥ Beverage	LUNCH Hamburger ♥ or Soy Burger & Cheese # French Fried Potatoes or Baked Potato ♥ Shredded Lettuce ♥ Catsup- Mustard-Pickles Salad Dressing Hamburger Buns or Whole Wheat Bread ♥ Margarine Pat ♥ Fresh Fruit ♥ Beverage	LUNCH BBQ Chicken ♥ or Baked Chicken ♥ or Hummus # Potato Salad ♥ Carrots ♥ Whole Wheat Bread ♥ Margarine Pat ♥ Dessert or Fresh Fruit ♥ Beverage	LUNCH Breaded Fish Sandwich or Baked Fish ♥ or Soy Burger # Salad Dressing Steamed Rice ♥ Green Peas ♥ Coleslaw ♥ Tartar Sauce Hamburger Buns or Whole Wheat Bread ♥ Margarine Pat ♥ Fresh Fruit ♥ Beverage	LUNCH Chicken Patty Sandwich or Chicken Salad ♥ or Boiled Eggs (2) # ♥ Potato Salad ♥ Pinto Beans ♥ Lettuce/Tomato/Onion Salad Dressing Hamburger Buns or Whole Wheat Bread ♥ Margarine Pat ♥ Dessert or Fresh Fruit ♥ Beverage
DINNER Chicken Pot Pie or Chicken & Noodles ♥ or Soy Pot Pie # Navy Beans ♥ Green Beans ♥ Whole Wheat Bread ♥ Margarine Pat ♥ Beverage	DINNER Chili ♥ # Vegetable Chili ♥ Baked Potato ♥ Shredded Cheese Diced Onions & Pepper ♥ WK Corn ♥ Cornbread or Whole Wheat Bread ♥ Margarine Pat ♥ Beverage	DINNER Kielbasa Sausage ♥ Or Cottage Cheese # Oven Brown Potatoes or Baked Potato ♥ Black Eyed Peas ♥ Mixed Greens ♥ Sauerkraut-Mustard Whole Wheat Bread ♥ Margarine Pat ♥ Beverage	DINNER Minestrone Soup ♥ Beef Taco Salad ♥ or Soy Taco Salad # Salsa Steamed Rice ♥ Beverage	DINNER Roast Beef ♥ or Peanut Butter # and Jelly, SF (2) ♥ Baked Sweet Potato ♥ Simmered Cabbage ♥ Brown Gravy Whole Wheat Bread ♥ Margarine Pat ♥ Beverage	DINNER Beef Enchilada Casserole or Beef & Veggies ♥ or Soy Enchilada Casserole # ♥ Steamed Rice ♥ Mixed Vegetables ♥ Whole Wheat Bread ♥ Margarine Pat ♥ Beverage	DINNER Chicken Fajitas ♥ or Cheese Quesadilla # Mexican Rice or Steamed Rice ♥ Black Beans ♥ Mixed Vegetables ♥ Salsa Tortilla (Flour) ♥ Margarine Pat ♥ Beverage

Week # 4

Sunday	Monday	Tuesday	Wednesday	Thursday	Friday	Saturday
BREAKFAST Bran Flakes ♥ Breakfast Cake or Whole Wheat Bread ♥ Jelly, SF (2) ♥ Sugar, Substitute Pks. • Margarine Pat ♥ Fresh Apple ♥ Coffee Skim Milk ♥	BREAKFAST Creamed Beef Home Fried Potatoes or Boiled Potatoes ♥ • Hot Oatmeal ♥ Jelly, SF (2) ♥ Biscuits (2) or Whole Wheat Bread ♥ Margarine Pat ♥ Fresh Apple ♥ Skim Milk ♥	BREAKFAST Hot Grits ♥ Breakfast Cake or Whole Wheat Bread ♥ Jelly, SF (2) ♥ Sugar, Substitute Pks. • Margarine Pat ♥ Fresh Apple ♥ Skim Milk ♥	BREAKFAST Bran Flakes ♥ Pancakes & Syrup or Whole Wheat Bread ♥ Jelly, SF (2) ♥ Sugar, Substitute Pks. Margarine Pat ♥ Fresh Bananas ♥ Skim Milk ♥	BREAKFAST Hot Grits ♥ Breakfast Cake or Whole Wheat Bread ♥ Jelly, SF (2) ♥ Sugar, Substitute Pks. Margarine Pat ♥ Fresh Apple ♥ Skim Milk ♥	BREAKFAST French Toast & Syrup or Whole Wheat Bread ♥ Jelly, SF (2) ♥ Sugar, Substitute Pks. Margarine Pat ♥ Fresh Bananas ♥ Skim Milk ♥	BREAKFAST Bran Flakes ♥ Breakfast Cake or Whole Wheat Bread ♥ Jelly, SF (2) ♥ Sugar, Substitute Pks. Margarine Pat ♥ Fresh Apple ♥ Coffee Skim Milk ♥
LUNCH Scrambled Eggs ♥ Baked Turkey Ham ♥ Waffles (2) & Syrup or Oven Brown Potato ♥ Jelly, SF (2) ♥ Whole Wheat Bread ♥ Margarine Pat ♥ Fresh Fruit ♥ Beverage	LUNCH Chili Dogs ♥ Or Vegetable Chili #♥ Potato Chips or Boiled Potatoes ♥ Coleslaw ♥ Catsup-Mustard Hot Dog Buns or Whole Wheat Bread ♥ Margarine Pat ♥ Fresh Fruit ♥ Beverage	LUNCH Chicken Patty Sandwich Chicken Salad ♥ or Peanut Butter # and Jelly, SF (2) ♥ Italian Pasta Salad ♥ Lettuce Leaf -Onion & Tomato Slices ♥ Salad Dressing Hamburger Buns or Margarine Pat ♥ Dessert Beverage	LUNCH Hamburger ♥ or Soy Burger &Cheese # Potato Chips or Baked Potato ♥ Shredded Lettuce ♥ Catsup-Mustard-Pickles Salad Dressing Hamburger Buns or Whole Wheat Bread ♥ Margarine Pat ♥ Fresh Fruit ♥ Beverage	LUNCH Fried Chicken or Baked Chicken ♥ or Cottage Cheese # Mashed Potatoes ♥ Carrots ♥ Chicken Gravy Whole Wheat Bread ♥ Margarine Pat ♥ Dessert or Fresh Fruit ♥ Beverage	LUNCH Fried Fish Fillet or Baked Fish ♥ or Peanut Butter # and Jelly, SF (2) ♥ Mac Salad ♥ Green Peas ♥ Tartar Sauce Cornbread or Whole Wheat Bread ♥ Margarine Pat ♥ Fresh Fruit ♥ Beverage	LUNCH Lentil Vegetable Soup ♥ Cold Cut Hoagie or Boiled Eggs (2) #♥ Whole Wheat Bread ♥ Salad Dressing Potato Salad or Baked Potato ♥ Mixed Vegetables ♥ Margarine Pat ♥ Dessert or Fresh Fruit ♥ Beverage
DINNER Beef BBQ or Soy BBQ # Steamed Rice ♥ Green Beans ♥ Whole Wheat Bread ♥ Margarine Pat ♥ Beverage	DINNER Chicken Fried Rice or Chicken & Rice ♥ or Tofu & Rice # ♥ Black Beans ♥ WK Corn ♥ Whole Wheat Bread ♥ Margarine Pat ♥ Beverage	DINNER Pork Roast * ♥ or Hummus # Baked Sweet Potato ♥ Green Beans ♥ Whole Wheat Bread ♥ Margarine Pat ♥ Beverage	DINNER Chicken Cacciatore w/ Garlic Noodles or Chicken & Noodles ♥ or Soy Noodle Casserole # Kidney Beans ♥ Mixed Vegetables ♥ Whole Wheat Bread ♥ Margarine Pat ♥ Beverage	DINNER Scrambled Eggs ♥ Creamed Beef Home Fried Potatoes or Oven Brown Potatoes ♥ Biscuits (2) or Whole Wheat Bread ♥ Jelly, SF (2) ♥ Margarine Pat ♥ Beverage	DINNER Beef & Bean Burrito or Beef Burrito Bean & Cheese Burrito # Mexican Rice or Steamed Rice ♥ Pinto Beans ♥ WK Corn ♥ Margarine Pat ♥ Salsa Beverage	DINNER Spaghetti & Meat sauce ♥ or Marinara Sauce #♥ Steamed Broccoli ♥ Garden Salad ♥ Asst. Salad Dressing Garlic Bread or Whole Wheat Bread ♥ Margarine Pat ♥ Beverage ♥

Week # 5

Sunday	Monday	Tuesday	Wednesday	Thursday	Friday	Saturday
BREAKFAST Bran Flakes ♥ Breakfast Cake or Whole Wheat Bread ♥ Jelly, SF (2) ♥ Sugar, Substitute Pks. Margarine Pat ♥ Fresh Apple ♥ Coffee Skim Milk ♥	BREAKFAST Creamed Beef Home Fried Potatoes or Boiled Potatoes ♥ Hot Oatmeal Jelly, SF (2) ♥ Biscuits (2) or Whole Wheat Bread ♥ Margarine Pat ♥ Fresh Apple ♥ Skim Milk ♥	BREAKFAST Hot Grits ♥ Breakfast Cake or Whole Wheat Bread ♥ Jelly, SF (2) ♥ Sugar, Substitute Pks. Margarine Pat Fresh Apple ♥ Skim Milk ♥	BREAKFAST Bran Flakes Pancakes& Syrup or Whole Wheat Bread ♥ Jelly, SF (2) ♥ Sugar, Substitute Pks. Margarine Pat ♥ Fresh Bananas ♥ Skim Milk ♥	BREAKFAST Hot Grits ♥ Breakfast Cake or Whole Wheat Bread ♥ Jelly, SF (2) ♥ Sugar, Substitute Pks. Margarine Pat ♥ Fresh Apple ♥ Skim Milk ♥	BREAKFAST Hot Oatmeal ♥ French Toast & Syrup or Whole Wheat Bread ♥ Jelly, SF (2) • Sugar, Substitute Pks. ♥ Margarine Pat ♥ Fresh Bananas ♥ Skim Milk ♥	BREAKFAST Bran Flakes ♥ Breakfast Cake or ^ Whole Wheat Bread ♥ Jelly, SF (2) ♥ Sugar, Substitute Pks. • Margarine Pat ♥ Fresh Apple ♥ Coffee Skim Milk ♥
LUNCH Boiled Eggs (2) ♥ Waffles (2) & Syrup or Whole Wheat Bread ♥ Breakfast Sausage Home Fried Potatoes or Boiled Potatoes ♥ Jelly, SF (2) ♥ Margarine Pat ♥ Fresh Fruit ♥ Beverage	LUNCH Vegetarian Chili # Cheese Fries or # Vegetable Chili ♥ Baked Potato ♥ Carrots ♥ Whole Wheat Bread ♥ Margarine Pat ♥ Fresh Fruit ♥ Beverage	LUNCH Chicken Parmesan or Braised Chicken ♥ or Soy Chicken Chunks # Spaghetti & Marinara ♥ Spinach ♥ Garlic Bread or Whole Wheat Bread ♥ Margarine Pat ♥ Dessert or Fresh Fruit ♥ Beverage	LUNCH Hamburger ♥ or Soy Burger & Cheese # French Fried Potatoes or Baked Potato ♥ Shredded Lettuce ♥ Catsup-Mustard-Pickles Salad Dressing Hamburger Buns or Whole Wheat Bread ♥ Margarine Pat ♥ Fresh Fruit ♥ Beverage	LUNCH Baked Chicken ♥ or Cottage Cheese # Baked Sweet Potato ♥ Black Beans ♥ Mixed Greens ♥ Whole Wheat Bread ♥ Margarine Pat ♥ Dessert or Fresh Fruit ♥ Beverage	LUNCH Breaded Fish Sandwich or Baked Fish ♥ Or Cheese Sandwich # Salad Dressing Macaroni & Cheese or Macaroni & Tomato ♥ Spinach ♥ Coleslaw ♥ Tartar Sauce Hamburger Buns or Whole Wh. Bread ♥ Margarine Pat ♥ Fresh Fruit ♥ Beverage	LUNCH Sloppy Joe or Soy Sloppy Joe # Tater Tots or Oven Brown Potatoes ♥ Green Peas ♥ Hamburger Buns or Whole Wheat Bread ♥ Margarine Pat ♥ Dessert or Fresh Fruit ♥ Beverage
DINNER Beef Tacos ♥ or Soy Tacos # Mexican Rice or Steamed Rice ♥ Black Beans ♥ WK Corn ♥ Salsa Taco Shells Margarine Pat ♥ Beverage	DINNER Beef Stew ♥ or Soy Beef Stew # Egg Noodles ♥ Steamed Broccoli ♥ Whole Wheat Bread ♥ Margarine Pat ♥ Beverage	DINNER Pork BBQ * Or Pork Roast ♥ or Hummus # Steamed Rice ♥ Kidney Beans ♥ Mixed Vegetables ♥ Whole Wheat Bread ♥ Margarine Pat ♥ Beverage	DINNER Old Fashion Bean Soup Chef Salad • or #Tofu Chef Salad ♥ Asst. Salad Dressing Whole Wheat Bread ♥ Margarine Pat ♥ Beverage	DINNER Philly Cheese Steak or Roast Beef ♥ or Soy Burger # Salad Dressing Potato Chips or Baked Potato ♥ Green Beans ♥ Hoagie Bun or Whole Wheat Bread ♥ Beverage	DINNER Turkey Roast ♥ or Peanut Butter # and Jelly, SF (2) ♥ Mashed Potatoes ♥ Cream Gravy Mixed Vegetables ♥ Whole Wheat Bread ♥ Margarine Pat ♥ Beverage	DINNER Chicken Fajitas ♥ or Cheese Quesadilla Mexican Rice or Steamed Rice ♥ Refried Beans ♥ or Pinto Beans ♥ WK Corn ♥ • Salsa Tortilla (Flour) ♥ Margarine Pat ♥ Beverage

Appendix VIII: Free and Discounted Books for Prisoners*

This list includes free general books, free religious books, and organizations from which prisoners may order books.

We are not sure if all the companies listed are still in business. If you have updates or changes to this list, please contact the author, Christopher Zoukis at ChristopherZoukis.com.

GENERAL INTEREST BOOKS

Aleph Institute, The
9540 Collins Avenue
Surfside, FL 33154
Tel: (305) 864-5553
Website: www.alephinstitute.org

Free books for Jewish inmates and regular monthly literature, holiday offerings, and family programs.

American Correctional Association
Publications Department
8025 Laurel Lakes
Laurel, MD 20707–5075

Books to prisoners, no religion or legal. (All states except OR.)

Appalachian Prison Book Project
P. O. Box 601
Morgantown, WV 26507
aprisonbookproject.wordpress.com

Sends books to KY, MD, OH, TN, VA, WV. Cannot send to TX.

---

* *Reprinted from* College for Convicts: The Case for Higher Education in American Prisons *(McFarland & Co., 2014) with permission from the publisher.*

Arizona Read Between The Bars
C/O Daily Planet Publishing
P. O. Box 1589
Tucson, AZ 85702

Sends books only to prisoners in Arizona.

Asheville Prison Book Program
C/O Downtown Books and News
67 N. Lexington Avenue
Asheville, NC 28801
www.main.nc.us/prisonbooks/main.html

Sends free books to prisoners in NC, SC, TN, and GA. Cannot send to TX inmates.

Books 2 Prisoners
P. O. Box 791327
New Orleans, LA 70179

Louisiana prisoners only.

Books 4 Prisoners
C/O Hobo Bookstore
4040 Hamilton Avenue
Cincinnati, OH 45223

Sends books to inmates in Ohio, Indiana, and Texas prisons only.

Book' Em
P. O. Box 71357
Pittsburgh, PA 15213

Sends books to Pennsylvania and New York prisons only.

Books for Prisoners
P. O. Box 2143
Colorado Springs, CO 80901

Book Through Bars - Ithaca
C/O Autumn Leaves Bookstore
115 The Commons - 2nd Floor
Ithaca, NY 14850

Sends free reading material to inmates in ME, VT, NH, MA, RI, CT, NY, NJ, DE, MD. Does not send books to Texas inmates.

Books Through Bars - NYC
C/O Bluestockings Bookstore
172 Allen Street
New York, NY 10002
booksthroughbarsnyc.org

Sends free reading material to inmates in all states except AL, FL, LA, MA, MI, MS, NC, PA and OH, with a priority for NY. Specializes in political and history books. Also sends literary fiction and other educational books. Does not send religious literature. Donations of stamps and cash are appreciated.

Books Through Bars - Philadelphia
4722 Baltimore Avenue
Philadelphia, PA 19143
Email: info@BooksThroughBars.org
Website: www.BooksThroughBars.org

Sends free progressive political and educational materials to state and federal prisoners in PA, NJ, DE, NY, MD, VA, and WV. Does not send books to Texas inmates.

No catalog. Request books by topic and specific subject areas (for example: novels, self-help, American history, etc.).

You may request specific titles or authors, however, we may not be able to provide these. No legal books. Donations, including stamps, are greatly appreciated. Please send information regarding prison regulations for reading material being sent in.

Books to Oregon Prisoners
P. O. Box 11222
Portland, OR 97211
http://www.bookstooregonprisoners.org

Free books to Oregon prisoners only.

Books to Prisoners
C/O Left Bank Books
92 Pike Street, Box A
Seattle, WA 98104
Email Address: bookstoprisoners@cs.com
Website: www.bookstoprisoners.net

An all-volunteer, nonprofit organization that sends books to prisoners founded in the early 1970s and sponsored by Left Banks Books. BTP provides 3 books at a time and delivers to all states in the USA.

Please send a list of topics you are interested in. No legal or religious books. BTP receives over 1,000 requests for books each month. Volunteers work two evenings a week opening letters, finding books in our collection that correspond to the request, and wrapping and mailing parcels. Because of a continuing backlog of requests, prisoners sometimes wait up to six months to receive their books and have to be very patient. Friends and family writing to request books for their relatives are welcome to make a donation to help with costs.

Books to Prisoners - Vancouver
C/O Joint Effort
P.O. Box 78005
Vancouver BC V5N 5W1
CANADA

Canadian prisoners only.

Books to Prisons - D.C. Area
P.O. Box 5243
Hyattsville, MD 20782
Tel: (301) 699-0042
Email: bookstoprisoners@quixote.org
Website: http://bookstoprisons.org

Books to Prisons offers free educational as well as a wide selection of fiction and nonfiction reading material to prisoners around the United States free of charge. Please send requests for your general interests.

Boston Prison Book Program
1306 Hancock St. Suite #100
Quincy, MA 02169

Sends books to all states except CA, MI, MD, NV, TX, and Graterford, PA. Does not offer computer books, horror, romance, textbooks, true crime, or white supremacist materials. Publishes the National Prisoner Resource List free to prisoners nationwide on request.

California Coalition for Women Prisoners
1540 Market St., Suite 490
San Francisco, CA 94102
Tel: (415) 255-7036
Email: info@womenprisoners.org

SDCCWP sends books to women prisoners on various women's and political issues. Please write to request a free book list. Stamp donations are appreciated to pay for shipping.

Chicago Books To Women In Prison
C/O Beyond Media Education
4001 N. Ravenswood Ave. #204C
Chicago, IL 60613

Sends books to female prisoners in CT, FL, IL, IN, MS, and OH.

Claremont Prison Library
Project PMB 128
915-C W. Foothill Blvd.
Claremont, CA 91711

Sends books to all states. Free books on self-help, personal and spiritual growth, wellness, and metaphysical topics. No law books, technical, or GED. No catalog. Free resource guide on request.

Cleveland Books 2 Prisoners
P.O. Box 602440
Cleveland, OH 44102

Sends books only to prisoners in Ohio.

Cody's Bookstore
2454 Telegraph Avenue; Berkeley, CA 94704
510-845-7852 and
1730 Fourth Street, Berkeley; CA 94710
510-559-9500
www.codysbooks.com
US (800) 995-1180
CA (800) 479-7744

DC Books To Prisons Project
P.O. Box 34190
Washington, DC 20043-4190
www.dcbookstoprisoners.org

You can request titles, but prioritized subjects of interest preferred. List prison restrictions. Stamps appreciated. Lacks postage money to respond to all requests and puts lower priority on the following: New England, OR, WA, PA, OH, NY, NJ, WI, and IL. Please limit requests to once per 5 months.

FIRM (Furnishing Inmates Reading Material)
Attention: Don Bowman
7 West Lake Drive
St. Simmons Island, GA 31522

Sends books/materials to prison chaplains.

Gainesville Books For Prisoners
P.O. Box 12164
Gainesville, FL 32604

Sends books to prisoners throughout the United States.

The Granite Publishing Group
P.O. Box 1429
Columbus, NC 28722
Tel: (828) 894-8444
Email: info@granitepublishing.us
Website: http://granitepublishing.us

Inmates may write to receive free books on subjects that support the cultivation of planetary consciousness. The metaphysical/transformational subjects of our books range from Native American spirituality to the extraterrestrial presence. Please send postage if possible.

Inside Books Project
C/O 12th Street Books
827 West 12th Street
Austin, TX 78701
insidebooksproject.org

Sends free reading material to inmates in Texas. One request every three months. Inside Books Project also publishes the handy Resource Guide.

Internationalist Prison Books Collective
405 W. Franklin Street
Chapel Hill, NC 27516
www.prisonbooks.info

Sends free reading material to inmates in AL, MS, and LA. Does not send books to Texas inmates.

Loompanics Unlimited
P.O. Box 1197
Port Townsend, WA 98368

Legal books and prisoner issues.

Louisiana Books 2 Prisoners
1631 Elysian Fields Avenue, #117
New Orleans, LA 70117
lab2p.wordpress.com

Sends free books prisoners in the following states: AL, AR, FL, GA, KY, LA, MO, MS, NC, TN, SC, VA, and WV. Women and LA prisoners are prioritized. Does not send books to Texas inmates.

Louisiana Books to Prisoners
831 Elysian Fields #143
New Orleans, LA 70117
books2prisoners@riseup.net

Ships free books to prisoners all over the U.S., but focuses primarily on those in Louisiana.

Maoist Internationalist Ministry of Prisons
P.O. Box 40799
San Francisco CA 94140
prisoncensorship.info

Free books on Marxism, politics, history, law, dictionaries, and other reference. Free anti-imperialist newsletter and political study groups for prisoners.

Midwest Books to Prisoners
C/O Quimby's Bookstore
1321 North Milwaukee Ave. PMB #460
Chicago, IL 60622
www.freewebs.com/mwbtp

Free books to Midwest prisoners.

Midwest Pages to Prisoners Project, The
c/o Boxcar Books and Community Center
408 E. 6th St.
Bloomington, IN 47408
(812) 339-8710
www.pagestoprisoners.org

Sends free reading material to inmates in AZ, AR, FL, IN, IA, KS, KY, MN, MO, NE, ND, OH, OK, SD, TN, and WI. Does not send books to Texas inmates.

Sends up to 3 books at a time. Books can be requested every 2 months. Sends all subjects of fiction and non-fiction reading material. Priority is given to people requesting books from women's and youth facilities.

Open Books Prison Books Project
1040 N. Guillemard St.
Pensacola, FL 32501
www.openbookspcola.org

Sends free reading material to inmates in Florida. Does not send books to Texas inmates.

Pen Writing Program
588 Broadway
New York, NY 10012
(212) 334-1660

Write and request their *Prisoner Educational Catalog, Prisoner Resource List* and *Handbook for Writers.* All are free to prisoners.

Prison Book Program
C/O Parsons Bookstore
1306 Hancock St. Suite 100
Quincy, MA 02169
(617) 423-3298 (No collect calls)
Email: info@prisonbookprogram.org
Website: www.prisonbookprogram.org

Sending free books to prisoners in all states except CA, MD, MI, NV, OR, PA, or TX since 1972. You can request topics or titles: there are limited legal materials, educational, social, political, fiction, and books in Spanish. They do not offer computer books, horror, romance, textbooks, true crime, or white supremacist materials. Publishes the National Prisoner Resource List free to prisoners nationwide on request.

Prison Book Program, Redbook Store
92 Green Street
Jamaica Plain, MA 02103

Books cannot be sent to the following states: KS, NE, IA, MI, or CA.

Prison Book Project
C/O Food for Thought Books
P.O. Box 396
Amherst, MA 01004-0396
(413) 584-8975 ext. 208
prisonbookproject@riseup.net
www.prisonbooks.org

Cannot serve prisoners in Texas. Request books by topics of interest or title. No mailing list or catalogue. No hardback books.

Prison Library Project
915-C West Foothill Boulevard
Suite C 128
Claremont, CA 91711
prisonlibraryproject.org

Free books and educational material to inmates nationwide except HI, ME, MI, NE, NV, WI, PA, and VA. Book topics include self-help, personal and spiritual growth, wellness, and metaphysical books. No law books, technical, or GED. No catalogue. Free resource guide on request.

Prison Mindfulness Institute
11 South Angell St. #303
Providence, RI 02906
(401) 941-0791
www.prisonmindfulness.org
www.prisondharmanetwork.net

Sends free books on mindfulness practices, Buddhism, and other contemplative paths. Offers an online Directory of Prison Dharma Organizations, useful for prisoners seeking mentors, pen-pals, and other resources.

Prisoner Express
127 Anabel Taylor Hall
Cornell University
Ithaca, NY 14853
www.prisonerexpress.org

Free books to prisoners nationwide. Must send 8 stamps or $3.50 for postage. Specify subjects of interest.

Prisoners Literature Project
C/O Bound Together Bookstore
1369 Haight Street
San Francisco, CA 94117
Email: prisonlit@yahoo.com
Website: www.prisonersliteratureproject.com

Offers free books to prisoners; also has a prisoner resource address list free. You may request types of books – not specific titles. Topics include: Black studies, Chicano history, basic math/writing/science, books in Spanish, novels, politics, history, and more. No Christian, Islamic, horror, romance novels, or legal books. Stamps or donations are greatly appreciated but are not required. Main types of books usually requested: dictionaries, ethnic studies, basic educational books. Sorry, no Texas prisoners.

Providence Books Through Bars
c/o Paper Nautilus Books
5 Angell Street
Providence, RI 02906
info@providencebtb.org
www.providencebtb.org

Sends free reading material to inmates nationwide including targeted self-help and inspirational books upon request.

Read Between the Bars
c/o Daily Planet Publishing
P.O. Box 1589
Tucson, AZ 85702-1589
readbetweenthebars.com

Sends free reading material to inmates in AZ. Does not send to Texas inmates.

Readers Corner, The
Prison Book Program
31 Montford Ave.
Asheville, NC 28801
prisonbooks31@hotmail.com
www.main.nc.us/prisonbooks

Sends free books to prisoners in North and South Carolina, Georgia, and Tennessee only.

San Diego Books For Prisoners
C/O Groundwork Books
0323 Student Center
La Jolla, CA 92037

Sends books nationwide.

UC Books to Prisoners
P.O. Box 515
Urbana, IL 61803
www.books2prisoners.org

Sends free reading material to inmates in IL. Does not send to Texas inmates.

Urbana – Champaign Books to Prisoners Project
C/O Spineless Books
P.O. Box 515
Urbana, IL 61803
www.books2prisoners.org
ucbtp@yahoo.com

Sends all types of books to state and federal prisoners in Illinois. Has a large selection of novels, but tries to stock popular genres such as African-American history and literature, as well as dictionaries, although they're hard to maintain.

Wisconsin Books to Prisoners
c/o Rainbow Bookstore Co-operative
426 W. Gilman Street
Madison, WI 53703
(608) 262-9036
www.madisoninfoshop.org/wbtp/

Free books and reading material to prisoners in Wisconsin only.

Women's Prison Book Project
C/O Arise Bookstore
2441 Lyndale Ave. South
Minneapolis, MN 55405
www.prisonactivist.org/wpbp

Ships to all states except OR, MI, CO, and WV. Free books to women prisoners only. No county jail requests. Does not ship hardback books. Free resource guide for women and transgender prisoners. Encourages women and transgender prisoners to write articles for their newsletter. Write for more details.

FREE BIBLES and RELIGIOUS BOOKS

American Muslim Foundation
1212 New York Avenue NW Suite 525
Washington, DC 20005

Arm the Spirit
PO Box 6326 - Stn. A
Toronto, ON, M5W 1P7
Canada

Association for Research and Enlightenment
67th and Atlantic Avenue
P.O. Box 595
Virginia Beach, VA 23451

Books on spiritual growth and Edgar Cayce. Prisoners may receive 2 free books per month. Request books by topic, not titles.

American Bible Society
1865 Broadway
New York, NY 10023
Free Bible upon request.

Free Bibles, including large-print and study guides. They can be sent through a chaplain.

Bibles for America
P.O. Box 17537
Irvine, CA 92623

Bibleingo.com®
P.O. Box 19039
Spokane, WA 99219

Bible Says
P.O. Box 99
Lenoir City, TN 37771
Provides several packets of religious books.

Chapel Library
2603 West Wright Street
Pensacola, FL 32505
Provides free Christian materials and Bibles.

Coalition for Jewish Prisoners
1640 Rhode Island Avenue NW
Washington, DC 20036

Free Bible Ministry
19603 Arroyo Lane
Cordes Lakes, AZ 86333

Healing Tao Center
P.O. Box 471
Revere, MA 02151
Books on Taoist yoga methods.

Human Kindness Foundation
P.O. Box 61619
Durham, NC 27715
humankindness@humankindness.org
(919) 383-5160
Two free books, or catalogue of other hard-to-find spiritual books.

International Bible Society
P. O. Box 35700
Colorado Springs, CO 80935-3570
Free Bible upon request.

International Prison Ministry
P.O. Box 130063
Dallas, TX 75313-0063
Free Bible upon request.

Islamic Center
22551 Massachusetts Avenue NW
Washington, DC 20008
Free Koran and study guides. Can be sent through a chaplain.

Prison Fellowship
P.O. Box 2204
Ashburn, VA 20146-2204
Provides several free Christian books.

Prison & Outreach Ministries
Rev. David J. Dostiglio
World Christianship
238 Stagg Street
Stratford, CT 06615

United Prison Ministries International
P. O. Box 8
Verbena, AL 36091
Provides several free Christian books.

BOOKS DISCOUNTED FOR PRISONERS

Any bookstore, online or otherwise, will sell books to you if you send in an order and a check. However, the following are listed because they claim to be either particularly relevant to prisoner issues, or because the sell to prisoners at a discount.

ACLU
132 W 43rd Street
New York, NY 10036
ACLU Handbook on Prisoners' Rights $5.00.

A.K. Press
PO Box 40682
San Francisco, CA 94140-0682
40% discount on books to prisoners. Distributes thousands of books on all subjects. Write for a catalogue of books for sale.

F&W Publications
1507 Dana Avenue
Cincinnati, OH 45207
Write for a catalogue of books for sale.

Groundwork Books
0323 Student Center
La Jolla, CA 92037
Phone: (858)452-9625
Email: groundwork@libertad.ucsd.edu
Books are 40% off for those who can afford to pay. We will send 2 free books per person for those who cannot afford to pay.

Send your request, specifying your interests, and we will send you a detailed booklet for that area of interest. Subjects: Africa, African-American, Asia, Asian-Pacific Islander, Chicano/a, China, CIA, FBI, Police, Cultural Criticism, Ecology, Education, Feminist Theory, Labor, Latin America/Caribbean, Native American, Political Theory, Racism, U.S. History, Political Economy, Imperialism and much more, including spirituality, dictionaries, social criticism, and select novels. Stamp donations are appreciated but not required.

Oceana Publications
75 Main Street
Dobbs Ferry, NY 10522

Books on legal information for prisoners.

Prison Legal News
P.O. Box 1151
Lake Worth, FL 33460
Phone: (561) 360-2523
www.prisonlegalnews.org

Prison Legal News isn't only the premier prison law publication, they also publish and distribute a large number of books of interest to prisoners.

South End Press
7 Brookline Street #1
Cambridge, MA 02139-4146

Write for a catalogue of books for sale.

Valley Merchandisers
P.O. Box 1271
Hagerstown, MD 21741-1271

Discounted books to inmates and their families, also do out-of-print book searches. Write to us for further information.

Appendix IX: Helpful Books for Prisoners On Survival, Law, and Education

Dozens of books on prison survival and prison law are available, and perhaps another dozen cover prison education. Unfortunately, most aren't very helpful as they tend to be poorly self-published rants by former prisoners. The following list promotes high quality, responsible, and professional titles.

The author of this text highly recommends these books and has found them useful throughout the duration of his imprisonment. As such, this list of books should be considered recommended reading for anyone who is either in prison, knows someone who is, or works with prisoners.

Descriptions of each text are compiled from various online and publisher sources.

General Prison Survival Books

Behind Bars by Jeffrey Ian Ross and Stephen C. Richards. [240 pages, $14.95, Alpha (2002)]

Behind Bars is a terrific general prison survival guide. It discusses what to do if arrested, how to protect oneself from the police during interrogations and in county jail, the booking process common to many prison systems, how inmate housing works, gangs, commissary, fights, and even how to make parole and return back to normal life, among other topics. While not specific to any particular prison system, *Behind Bars* is a terrific general prison text.

Books Specific to Federal Bureau of Prisons

Down Time: A Guide to Federal Incarceration (10th edition) by David Novak. [267 pages, $45.00, David Novak Consulting, Inc. (2010)]

Down Time has been the best federal prison-specific guide to prison survival for a number of years. Covering virtually every component of federal incarceration, this text is a must-read for anyone who is in federal prison, on their way to federal prison, or knows someone (or has a client in) federal prison. The text presents easy-to-understand topical bits of information about living inside a federal prison that will help anyone unfamiliar with the experience to succeed in such a caustic environment. While not a text that delves into the micro-components of each area of federal incarceration, it is well worth a read for the general prison knowledge presented. David Novak has clearly put a lot of time and thought into his prison survival guide.

Federal Prison Guidebook (3rd revision) by Alan Ellis, Todd A. Bussert, and J. Michael Henderson. [649 pages, $79.99, James Publishing (2015)]

The *Federal Prison Guidebook* is designed to answer some of the questions that defense attorneys, prosecutors, judges, probation officers, and criminal defendants facing incarceration in a federal prison, and federal prisoners and their families might have about the Federal Bureau of Prisons. The text discusses prison programs and policies, the Residential Drug Abuse Program (RDAP), tips on how to secure a favorable prison placement and how to do time, medical care in the FBOP, along with more legal-oriented chapters about sex offenders, federal sentencing, and other matters.

In addition to these expository chapters, the main draw for this text is the prison profiles for every federal prison. These profiles provide basic information about every federal prison and their local policies and procedures. For this component, this text is the best on the market.

General Criminal Law Books

Prisoners' Self-Help Litigation Manual (4th edition) by John Boston and Daniel E. Manville. [960 pages, $45.95, Oxford University Press (2010)]

Prisoners' Self-Help Litigation Manual, in its much-anticipated current edition, is an indispensable guide for prisoner litigants and prisoner advocates seeking to understand the rights guaranteed to prisoners by law and how to protect those rights. Clear, comprehensive, practical advice provides prisoners with everything they need to know on conditions of confinement, civil liberties in prison, procedural due process, and the legal system. It is a guide on how to actually litigate, conduct effective legal research, and write legal documents.

Written by two legal and penitentiary experts with intimate knowledge of prisoner's rights and legal aid work, this book strategically focuses on federal constitutional law, providing prisoners and those wishing to assist them with the most important information concerning legal rights. It is a roadmap to winning lawsuits. Many consider it the "Bible" of prison litigation for current and aspiring jailhouse lawyers. This is the best text of its kind on the market.

Georgetown Law Journal: 44th *Annual Review of Criminal Procedure* by Georgetown University School of Law. [1138 pages, $85 list (discounts available if shipped directly to a prisoner), published by Georgetown University School of Law (2015)]

The *Georgetown Law Journal* is the "must-have" reference guide for criminal-law practitioners and especially prisoners themselves. It is a complete summary of recent decisions in federal criminal procedure (including in-prison matters), over 1,000 pages and thousands of footnoted citations. The *Annual Review of Criminal Procedure* (formerly known as the Criminal Procedure Project) is one of the most important and widely used law review publications in the U.S. It provides readers with an objective, concise, and accurate overview of criminal procedure in the United States Supreme Court and each of the twelve Federal Circuit Courts.

A Jailhouse Lawyer's Manual (9th edition) by Columbia Human Rights Law Review. [1077 pages, $100 ($30 for prisoners), Columbia Human Rights Law Review (2011)]

A Jailhouse Lawyer's Manual (JLM) is a handbook of legal rights and procedures designed for use by people in prison. Since publication of the first edition in 1978, tens of thousands of prisoners in institutions across the country have used the JLM to exercise their legal rights. Prisoners are often indigent and lack access to legal counsel while incarcerated. The JLM informs prisoners of their legal rights and instructs them about how to secure these rights through the judicial process, clearly explaining legal research techniques and how to read legal documents. Prisoners may use the JLM to address specific problems related to their treatment in prison (through a number of chapters on in-prison matters), or to deal with unfair convictions or sentences.

The Habeas Citebook: Ineffective Assistance of Counsel (2nd edition) by Brandon Sample and Alissa Hull. [224 pages, $49.95, Prison Legal News Publishing (2016)]

The Habeas Citebook is a nifty and concise self-help guide for prisoners seeking habeas relief based on claims of ineffective assistance of counsel. Navigating the complex and treacherous terrain of habeas law is never easy; claiming that your lawyer screwed up is even more difficult – especially from the confines of an ill-equipped prison law library. Brandon Sample and Alissa Hull have provided an amazing and much-needed tool for prisoners who are forced to seek relief on their own. The book is thorough but simple and readable. It provides invaluable resources, including templates and forms, that explain what, when, where, and how to file for habeas relief.

The text also provides well-organized listings of hundreds of different types of ineffective assistance of counsel, set forth in the form of citations to court rulings. The *Habeas Citebook* is an essential resource for any would-be jailhouse lawyer.

The Criminal Law Handbook: Know Your Rights, Survive the System (13th edition) by Paul Bergman and Sara J. Berman-Barrett. [680 pages, $39.99, Nolo Press (2013)]

The Criminal Law Handbook explains what happens in a criminal case from being arrested to sentencing, and what your rights are at each stage of the process. It answers your questions about every part of a criminal case from cops to crooks. It discusses arrests, booking, preliminary hearings, charges, bail, courts, arraignment, search and seizure, defenses, evidence, pleas, trials, plea bargains, sentencing, juveniles, and "crimespeak," the language commonly used in criminal statutes.

Criminal Law in a Nutshell (5th edition) by Arnold H. Loewy. [387 pages, $38.00, Thomson/West Group Publishing (2009)]

Gain an overview and develop perspective on the extensive area of criminal law with this work. Organized into eight sections for quick reference, the expert discussion explores punishment, specific crimes, specific defenses, the burden of proof, and much more. This book covers inchoate and group criminality. It also reflects the limitations of criminal law. This is a great text to help beginners understand criminal law.

Criminal Procedure: Constitutional Limitations (7th edition) by Jerold H. Israel and Wayne R. LaFave. [603 pages, $38.00, Thomson/West Group Publishing (2006)]

Intended for use by law students of criminal procedure, this is a succinct analysis of constitutional standards of major significance in the area of criminal procedure. This is not a text on criminal procedure but rather is about constitutional criminal procedure. It avoids describing the non-constitutional standards applied in each state and federally. The text provides the scope and highlights one needs to excel in understanding this field.

Advanced Criminal Procedure in a Nutshell (2nd edition) by Mark E. Cammack and Norman M. Garland. [505 pages, $38.00, Thomson/West Group Publishing (2006)]

This text is designed for supplemental reading in an advanced criminal procedure course on the post-investigation process of a criminal case. It includes a clear, concise, and thorough narrative explanation of the issues involved in the prosecution and adjudication of a criminal case, from the decision to prosecute and pre-trial release through to sentencing, appeals, and collateral attack. It is an ideal reference for students and practitioners.

Prison Education Books

College for Convicts: The Case for Higher Education in American Prisons by Christopher Zoukis. [290 pages, $35.00, McFarland & Company (2014)].

College for Convicts is one of the most important prison education texts on the market. The book explains why education for America's incarcerated class is the answer, how it is cost-effective, what is currently available, its tremendous social benefits, and how to improve it.

The United States accounts for 5 percent of the world's population, yet incarcerates about 25 percent of the world's prisoners. Examining hundreds of studies by researchers, academics, and correctional professionals together with the experience of educators and educated prisoners, this book shows that recidivism rates drop dramatically in direct correlation to the amount of education prisoners receive and the level of education attained.

Presenting a workable solution to the unmanageable costs of America's mass incarceration and high recidivism rates, this book demonstrates the great fiscal benefits enjoyed when modest sums are spent educating prisoners. Educating prisoners brings a reduction in crime, social safety, reduced spending nationally and state-wide, and a greatly improved quality of life.

Prison Education Guide by Christopher Zoukis [269 pages, $49.95, Prison Legal News Publishing (2016)].

Prison Education Guide by Christopher Zoukis is the most comprehensive guide to correspondence programs for prisoners available today. This exceptional book provides the reader with step by step instructions to find the right educational programs, enroll in courses, and complete classes to meet their academic goals. It is perfect for the incarcerated student who lacks internet access or the ability to attend education classes in person.

Prison Education Guide is the latest and best resource on the market for the incarcerated nontraditional student. It includes a detailed analysis of the quality, cost, and course offerings of all correspondence programs available to prisoners. This includes correspondence courses at the graduate, undergraduate, religious college, career, high school, personal enrichment, fee-based Bible study, and free Bible study levels. In a time when so many academic opportunities in prisons have been eliminated, this book is an invaluable reentry tool for prisoners who seek to further their education while incarcerated in order to help them prepare for life and work following their release.

Prison Disciplinary Proceedings Books

Disciplinary Self-Help Litigation Manual (2nd edition) by Daniel Manville. [368 pages, $49.95, Prison Legal News Publishing (2015)].

The *Disciplinary Self-Help Litigation Manual* by Dan Manville is designed to inform prisoners of their rights when faced with the consequences of a disciplinary hearing. This authoritative and comprehensive work educates prisoners about their rights throughout this process and helps guide them at all stages from administrative hearings through litigation.

This is an invaluable how-to guide, offering step-by-step information for both state and federal prisoners, and includes a fifty-state analysis of relevant case law. It is a specialized supplement to the *Prisoners' Self-Help Litigation Manual*, often referred to as the "Bible" for jailhouse lawyers.

However, the book proves to be just as essential for prisoners. While directed at *pro se* prisoner litigants, it is also useful for lawyers whose clients are subject to penal disciplinary proceedings. It includes an extensive case law citation index. This important new edition is undeniably a vital tool for the serious prisoner rights litigator.

Directories for Prisoners

Inmate Shopper edited by Freebird Publishers. [310 pages, $24.99, Freebird Publishers (2015)].

Inmate Shopper is an annually updated directory of companies that do business with prisoners. Each profiled listing contains the company's contact information, services rendered, reader review, and numerical rating by the publication's editors. *Inmate Shopper* helps prisoners find companies that can fulfill their needs and avoid those who have poor quality of service.

Inmate Shopper also contains articles, book reviews, ads for companies who do business with prisoners, sports schedules, and books for sale that are of interest to prisoners.

The Best Resource Directory for Prisoners edited by Mike Enemigo. [190 pages, $19.99, The Cell Block (2014)].

The Best Resource Directory for Prisoners is the main competitor to *Inmate Shopper*. Presented in a clean, professional manner without all of the fluff that advertisers seem inclined to include, this book helps prisoners quickly locate companies that can fulfill their needs. Also included is a directory of attorneys who take on *pro bono* cases, a list of free pen pal clubs, and more.

The Best 500 Nonprofit Organizations for Prisoners and Their Families (3rd edition) George Kayer, ed. [136 pages, $14.99, Freebird Publishers (2015)].

The Best 500 Nonprofit Organizations for Prisoners profiles 500 nonprofit organizations that prisoners might need to contact during their term of incarceration. Contact information, areas served, and reviews are provided for every organization listed. Also included are a number of books that are of interest to incarcerated readers.

Appendix X: Correspondence Programs of Merit*

Adams State University — Undergraduate
Extended Studies — A, B
208 Edgemont Blvd., Suite 3000
Alamosa, CO 81102
800-548-6679
www.exstudies.adams.edu
distanceadvisor@adams.edu

Accreditation:	North Central Association of Colleges and Schools, The Higher Learning Commission
Tuition:	$165 per credit hour
Payment Plan:	None
Textbooks:	Not included in tuition
Transfer:	Associate-45 credit hours; Bachelor's-90 credit hours
Time Limit:	12 months
Degrees:	Associate of Arts; Associate of Science; Associate of Science in Business Administration; Associate of Arts in Business Administration; Bachelor of Arts in Sociology (emphasis areas: Social Welfare, Criminology, Corrections, Law Enforcement); Bachelor of Arts in Business Administration; Bachelor of Science in Business Administration (emphasis areas: Management, Management Information Systems, Accounting, Small Business Management,

* Reprinted from *Prison Education Guide* (Prison Legal News Publishing, 2016) with permission from the publisher.

	Agricultural Business, General Business, Health Care Administration, Legal Studies, Marketing); Bachelor of Arts in Interdisciplinary Studies
Course Categories:	Art; Business; Criminal Justice; Economics; Education; English; Government; Health Care Administration; History; Human Performance and Physical Education; Interdivisional; Mathematics; Music; Philosophy; Psychology; Sociology; Women's Studies
Course Delivery:	Paper-based
Media Component:	N/A
Catalog:	48-page catalog (2015-2016)
Application Fee:	Waived for incarcerated students
Founded:	1921
Comments:	Great school, great program. This is my favorite correspondence program.
School Comments:	In today's competitive professional market, higher education is critical to career placement and advancement. ASU understands that you don't have time to search for educational programs and courses that meet your busy schedule. ASU's offerings are designed with you in mind and can be completed at any location and at your own pace. At Adams State University we know how important education is to all individuals, especially for those who happen to be incarcerated. Through correspondence courses, Adams State University provides

an opportunity for incarcerated students to work for college credit and towards a degree. We have helped thousands of prisoners throughout the United States to reach their education goals.

Blackstone Career Institute — Career or Vocational
P.O. Box 3717 — Dip, C
Allentown, PA 18106
610-871-0031 / 800-826-9228
www.blackstone.edu / www.blackstone.edu/inmate-information
info@blackstone.edu

Accreditation:	Middle States Commission on Secondary Schools; Distance Education and Training Council, Accrediting Commission
Tuition:	$767 per paralegal diploma program; $396 per advanced certificate program (they have occasional discounts to their tuitions)
Payment Plan:	Monthly plan available for paralegal program ($59 down/$59 month or $59 down/$30 month)
Textbooks:	Included in tuition
Transfer:	Evaluated on a case-by-case basis
Time Limit:	2 years for paralegal program; 1 year per advanced certificate program
Degrees:	Diploma of Paralegal Studies (with Distinction if grades are above 94%); Advanced Certificates: Business & Corporate Law; Civil Litigation; Criminal Law; Family Law; Personal Injury/Torts; Practical Bankruptcy Law; Real Estate Law; Wills, Trusts, and Estates

Course Categories:	Paralegal Program: Business & Corporate Law; Civil Litigation; Criminal Law; Employability Skills; Ethics Advanced Diploma Program; Family Law; Legal Research and Writing; Modern American Law; Personal Injury/ Torts; Practical Bankruptcy Law; Real Estate Law; Wills, Trusts, and Estates;
Course Delivery:	Paper-based
Media Component:	None
Catalog:	Volume 16 (2015-2016)
Application Fee:	$140 (included in the full payment and in the payment plan)
Founded:	1890
Comments:	They have a large incarcerated student base. BCI is the oldest proprietary correspondence paralegal program in the country. It usually takes 12 to 15 months to complete the paralegal program. By studying 8 to 10 hours a day I completed the paralegal program in 5 months. This school also offers several advanced certificates in specialized areas to help focus your knowledge in the areas you need most. You must either complete the basic paralegal diploma program or transfer in with a basic paralegal diploma in order to be allowed to study the advanced programs. School sends Student/Inmate Guide to Enrollment to help you get enrolled without problems. School offers interest free payments and financial aid for veterans. School has a bookstore that you can purchase law related books from. Graduates of Blackstone's paralegal program receive a 10% discount on advanced courses. By completing the paralegal program you will qualify to be a

paralegal in every state except California and North Carolina (you will need to take extra exams to practice in these states).

They use soft cover books and materials for ease of entry into most correctional facilities. Inmates from 1,200 facilities across the U.S. have already turned to Blackstone to continue their education.

School Comments: Blackstone Career Institute's goal is to educate and provide the incarcerated with the skills needed to obtain meaningful employment and economic stability and to prepare them to become providers, leaders, and examples for their families and communities. Because we understand the unique needs of incarcerated individuals and the correspondence regulations of their facilities, we have developed programs that are easily approved by education departments, processed by mailrooms and completed by students.

International Sports Sciences Association — Career or Vocational
1015 Mark Avenue — C
Carpinteria, CA 93013
805-745-8111 / 800-892-4772
www.issaonline.edu
fmiele@issaonline.edu

Accreditation: Distance Education and Training Council, Accrediting Commission

Tuition: $599 per program; $25 shipping fee per course

Payment Plan: None

Textbooks: Included in tuition

Transfer:	N/A
Time Limit:	2 years
Degrees:	Certified Fitness Trainer (CFT); Exercise Therapy Certification (SET); Personal Trainer Specialist in Fitness Nutrition (SFN); Senior Fitness Certification (SSF); Sports Nutrition Certification (SSN); Strength and Conditioning Certification (SSC); Youth Fitness Trainer (YFT)
Course Categories:	N/A
Course Delivery:	Paper-based
Media Component:	None
Catalog:	Two 14 page catalogs (2013); additional information (2013)
Application Fee:	Included in tuition
Founded:	1988
Comments:	A great place for fitness training certification courses. These degrees are certifications. You will have to supply documentation of Adult CPR/AED training in order for certification to be issued. This school does not provide this kind of training. ISSA Trainers make $25 an hour to more than $200 an hour. They are the recognized leader in fitness education in all 50 states and in more than 84 countries. ISSA has provided certification and continuing education courses to nearly 100,000 students worldwide.

Appendix XI: Sample Call-Out Sheet

In the Federal Bureau of Prisons there is a system that utilizes "call-outs" to schedule appointments for inmates who must be present in a specific department at a specific time. Each day around 2:00 p.m. to 3:00 p.m., the call-out sheet is delivered to every housing unit. This call-out sheet or call-out list contains the appointments, work detail changes, and education changes for the following day. Each day, every federal prisoner is required to review this list to see if they have any appointments scheduled.

The call-out sheet is important because this is how federal prisoners are alerted to any appointments. Federal prisoners who miss a call-out run the risk of being held accountable. This can range from merely being rescheduled to receiving an incident report for being out of bounds. As such, it is very important for every federal prisoner to review the call-out sheet each and every day.

To help readers understand the call-out process and how it works, the following is a sample call-out sheet. Call-out sheets are generally posted both in each housing unit and on the Electronic Inmate Bulletin Board System.

SAMPLE CALL-OUT SHEET:

CHANGESHEET

REGNO	NAME	FROM	TO	TIME	CATEGORY (1) QTR ASGN	CATEGORY (2) WRK ASGN
WRK DETAIL CHANGES EFFECTIVE 12-12-2015						
12345-007	ARNOLD	UNASSG	UNICOR	0001	A04-004	UNASSG
23456-058	DOE	UNICOR	UNASSG	0001	B02-052	UNICOR
34567-555	JOHNSON	IDLE	POUND AMI	0001	C01-012	IDLE
45678-056	ROGERS	BARBER ORD	DIN RM PM	0001	B03-44U	BARBER ORD
56789-018	SMITH	ORD F-N PM	ORD F-N AM	0001	F04-76L	ORD F-N PM
01234-072	SYKES	AM TRASH	PM TRASH	0001	E05-085	AM TRASH
EDUCATION CHANGES EFFECTIVE 12-12-2015						
12345-007	ARNOLD	GED1/2:00	GED1/7:30	0001	A04-004	
CALLOUTS FOR 12-12-15						
12345-007	ARNOLD	CHAPEL		0900	A04-004	UNICOR
23456-058	DOE	HEALTH SVS		1240	B02-052	UNASSG
34567-555	JOHNSON	C-SOUTH		1400	C01-012	POUND AMI
45678-056	ROGERS	PSYCHOLOGY		0740	B03-44U	DIN RM PM
56789-018	SMITH	DENTAL		0900	F04-76L	OR F-N AM
01234-072	SYKES	X-RAY		0740	E05-085	PM TRASH

About Christopher Zoukis

Christopher Zoukis, an award winning incarcerated writer, is the author of *College for Convicts: The Case for Higher Education in American Prisons* (McFarland & Co., 2014) and the *Prison Education Guide* (Prison Legal News Publishing, 2016). He regularly contributes to *The Huffington Post*, *Prison Legal News*, and the *New York Daily News*, along with a number of other print and digital media outlets.

In January 2017 he earned his Bachelor's Degree in Interdisciplinary Studies (Business/Law) from Adams State University. He is currently attending Adams State University's MBA program.

Mr. Zoukis regularly advises attorneys, prison consultants, and fellow prisoners about legal issues and federal regulations governing the Federal Bureau of Prisons operations. In 2016 his *Prison Law Blog* was named a Top 100 Blawg by the American Bar Association. Upon release he plans to attend law school and become a federal criminal defense attorney.

He can be found online at http://www.prisoneducation.com, http://www.prisonerresource.com, and http://www.christopherzoukis.com.

66752077R00286

Made in the USA
Charleston, SC
27 January 2017